To David

With kindest regards and all good wishes
for the future

Left in the Wilderness

Left in the Wilderness

The political economy of
British democratic socialism since 1979

Noel Thompson

In memoriam

Andrew Murray (1954–2001)

First published in 2002 by Acumen

Acumen Publishing Limited
15A Lewins Yard
East Street
Chesham HP5 1HQ
www.acumenpublishing.co.uk

ISBN: 1-902683-53-6 (hardcover)
ISBN: 1-902683-54-4 (paperback)

British Library Cataloguing-in-Publication Data
A catalogue record for this book is available from the British Library.

Designed and typeset by Kate Williams, Abergavenny.
Index by Indexing Specialists, Hove.
Printed and bound by Biddles Ltd., Guildford and King's Lynn.

Contents

Preface

The idea for this book was prompted by a reviewer's critical comment on a previous work, *Political Economy and the Labour Party*, that it lacked a conclusion assessing the contemporary state of British democratic socialist political economy. The point was well made. That volume was indeed innocent of an evaluative finale. In a sense, therefore, this work is the concluding chapter that the reviewer demanded: an attempt to furnish a critical and evaluative history of the political economy of *fin de siècle* British democratic socialism.

It does so by reviewing the emergence and demise of the different genres of democratic socialist political economy that have traversed the ideological firmament in the period since 1979. My trope is that of tragedy. For I argue that what we have seen in the two decades covered by the book is a desperate, frenetic and ultimately futile attempt on the part of democratic socialists to reconfigure the political economy of democratic socialism in a form that would enable it to survive and deliver in an increasingly hostile material and ideological environment – one shaped by the ideas of the New Right, the increasing globalization of economic activity, the triumph of possessive individualism and the uncritical celebration of the virtues of private as against social consumption.

The intellectual energy expended on this reconfiguration has been formid-able. But the shelf-lives of the political economies it has furnished have been short. And, as we move into the twenty-first century, none have survived in a form that significantly threatens the hegemony of neo-liberalism. Keynesian social democracy died despite the best efforts of its adherents and, by the end of the century, was of interest only to those historians of thought who made an academic living from debating the date of its demise. The Alternative Economic Strategy that was to supersede it enjoyed its own day in the sun, but was of little more than historical significance by the time Mrs Thatcher won her second election. The decentralized socialism of producer co-operatives enjoyed considerable vogue in the 1970s and 1980s and seemed to offer a political economy that could accommodate the rhetoric of individual freedom and autonomy which had given the New Right such purchase on the hearts and minds of the British populace. But, by the end of the 1980s, it had left little of practical significance and, in Britain, had existence only in the theoretical constructs of a diminishing cohort of market socialists. In the 1980s and 1990s, post-Fordist socialism bid fair to ride the historical tide of differentiated consumerism, flexible specialization and the manufacturing systems spawned by the advance of computer and information technology and so rejuvenate the democratic socialist project. But large areas of manufacturing activity stubbornly refused to assume the form that post-Fordists anticipated, and the polyvalent artisans who were to lead the socialist charge failed to emerge in the numbers required to play the historic, transformative role that they had been allotted.

By the century's close what was offered were supply-side political econo-mies of varying social democratic hues. Most obviously, the political economy of radical stakeholderism seemed to provide the basis for a centre-left econom-ics that combined the democratization and dispersal of economic power with a strategy for enhanced efficiency and competitive performance. Yet this latter was to succumb rapidly to an anodyne reconfiguration at the hands of New Labour theorists, so that by the new millennium all that remained were the vague aspirations of those Eurosocialists who hoped that if it was no longer possible to build the New Jerusalem exclusively in Britain, then it might be possible to construct it on the basis of the European Union.

The tale as told is the tragedy of British democratic socialism; a term that as used in this volume encompasses that of social democracy, except where specific reference is made to the latter's Keynesian variant. To tell it I have, however, drawn frequently on non-British socialist literature. In particular, in the chapters on producer co-operatives and labour-managed firms, I have made reference to the experience and studies of these enterprises in other countries. Again, as regards post-Fordist socialism, I have considered the works of non-British writers who have contributed to, or helped to inspire, that strain of democratic socialist political economy.

The work is dedicated to a good (democratic socialist) friend who died shortly before its completion. He would have rebuked me for letting the pessimism of my intellect corrode the optimism of my will and have reminded me that the sin of despair is as culpable in socialists as it is in those of a religious persuasion. But he would also have believed that, given time, his own intellectual optimism would have won me round to a more sanguine view of the future. I only wish that this might have been put to the test.

Noel Thompson
University of Wales, Swansea

Introduction: Left in crisis

It is tempting to pronounce British Keynesian social democracy ideologically bankrupt by the late 1970s and, certainly, by the International Monetary Fund (IMF) and US Federal Reserve, it was deemed to be literally so soon after the Labour Party came to power in 1974. In such a reading the sterling crisis of 1976, and its "cap-in-hand" denouement, assumes a pivotal significance in terms of the attitude of many on the Left who had previously given Keynesianism overt or tacit support. In this context James Callaghan merely voiced with "candour" what others had already come to believe was the futility of a demand-managed pursuit of full employment. Thus, one year before Callaghan's *mea culpa*, Harold Wilson had made clear his own view that a trade-off between inflation and unemployment was no longer an option, as the former now manifestly caused the latter.[1] It was, though, left to the Callaghan government to give practical expression to this abandonment of received social democratic wisdom. With unemployment rising in the mid-1970s, the rules of Keynesian demand management dictated a reflation of the economy. But, under the tutelage of external agencies, a Labour government pursued a restrictive

---

1. H. Wilson, *Final Term: The Labour Government, 1974–76* (London: Weidenfeld & Nicolson and Michael Joseph, 1979), pp. 267–8.

monetary and fiscal policy to tackle its precarious balance of payments position and to curb inflation. Under Keynesianism, "the proper object of dear money [was] to check an incipient boom. Woe to those whose faith [led] them to use it to aggravate a depression!"[2] Yet the Labour government did just that and the foundations of Keynesian social democracy were fundamentally shaken.

Of course, criticism of the limitations of a democratic socialism that rested on the foundation of Keynesian macroeconomics was nothing new within the Labour Party. In the immediate post-war period, G. D. H. Cole, Richard Crossman and others had warned of the dilution of socialist intent and the atrophy of socialist vision entailed by an adherence to the simplistic belief that the essential evils of capitalism could be removed by "manipulating the levers" of fiscal and monetary policy, while simultaneously implementing Beveridge.[3] Yet in the 1970s the assault upon the political economy of Keynesian social democracy assumed a qualitatively different intensity and, it must be said, theoretical sophistication. Not just in its upper echelons, but more generally within the party, there were those who, in succumbing to the siren voices of an increasingly self-confident monetarism, accepted the impotence of the macro-economics that had previously underpinned their belief in the inexorable nature of post-war social progress. Moreover, as we shall see in Chapter 1, there were those who from a different and overtly socialist perspective attacked the theoretical foundations and prescriptive corollaries of a putatively social democratic political economy that had brought a Labour government to a point where, in the interests of capital, it was prepared to threaten the material interests of its traditional social constituency.

Yet the travails of Keynesian social democracy were only part of a more general ideological and political crisis engulfing the Left in the late 1970s. It was a crisis also manifest in a fundamental reappraisal, by many democratic social-ists, of the size, composition, values, aspirations and political inclinations of what had, historically, been regarded as socialism's traditional social constitu-ency. Thus, in the late 1970s and 1980s, doubts were increasingly expressed as to whether the working class was what it had been; whether, therefore, it could be relied upon any longer as an agent of socialist progress; whether, indeed, it had ever fulfilled that role; whether it was diminishing in significance and political potency; whether and to what extent it was undergoing a process of

---

2. J. M. Keynes, "The Economic Consequences of Mr. Churchill", in *Essays in Persuasion*, in D. Moggridge (ed.), *The Collected Writings of John Maynard Keynes*, vol. IX (London: Macmillan, 1972), p. 220.
3. G. D. H. Cole, *Socialist Economics* (London: Gollancz, 1950), p. 47; for Crossman see *Labour in an Affluent Society*, Fabian Tract 325 (London: Fabian Society, 1960). For a discussion of writers in the immediate post-war period who detailed the dangers involved in the pervasive influence of Keynesianism on socialist political economy, see N. Thompson, *Political Economy and the Labour Party: The Economics of Democratic Socialism, 1884–1995* (London: UCL Press, 1996), pp. 161–8.

fragmentation; and whether other social groupings could and should be seen, and embraced, as potential agents of socialist advance. These were concerns that, again, had profound implications for the political economy which democratic socialist writers believed they should be in the business of purveying, and they intensified as successive electoral defeats of the Labour Party revealed extensive disenchantment with Keynesian social democracy, and democratic socialism in general, within the working class.

Of course, concerns of this nature had been felt and expressed before in the post-war period. In particular, in the late 1950s and early 1960s, again in the wake of a series of electoral defeats, there had been those who had suggested that Labour must continue to lose[4] if it persisted in advancing economic and social policies that failed to appreciate the embourgeoisement of significant elements of the working class and the consequent fundamental change in its composition and aspirations.[5] The debate had been given a certain focus and intensity by the publication of Anthony Crosland's *The Future of Socialism* in 1956, but erupted with an unparalleled ferocity in the aftermath of the party's 1959 electoral defeat, contention focusing in particular on an unsuccessful attempt to excise Clause IV from Labour's constitution.

In the late 1970s too, even before its 1979 defeat, a similar kind of controversy was aroused by the publication of Eric Hobsbawm's Karl Marx memorial lecture of 1978, *The Forward March of Labour Halted*. Hobsbawm's contentions were unoriginal. His argument was that "the forward march of labour and the labour movement, which Marx predicted, appears to have come to a halt in this century about twenty-five to thirty years ago".[6] This, he argued, was a consequence of the economism and increasing sectionalism of the trade union movement and a manual working class that, as a consequence of profound and accelerating structural economic changes, was shrinking rapidly.[7] For both of these reasons Labour could no longer rely on its traditional working-class constituency to support the kind of social democracy that had guided the legislative programmes of post-war Labour governments. To reconstitute a social constituency sufficient to ensure the reconquest of political power and recommence labour's forward march, a revision of democratic socialist political economy was required, one which would broaden the social basis of its support and free it from excessive reliance on what was the declining constituency of the manual working class. This could be achieved by widening the scope of the aspirations and ideals that a democratic socialist political economy encompassed and articulated.

---

4. The classic text here is M. Abrams & C. Rose, *Must Labour Lose?* (Harmondsworth: Penguin, 1960).
5. On this see too J. Goldthorpe *et al.*, *The Affluent Worker: Political Attitudes and Behaviour* (Cambridge: Cambridge University Press, 1968).
6. E. Hobsbawm, "The Forward March of Labour Halted?", in M. Jacques & F. Mulhern (eds), *The Forward March of Labour Halted?* (London: Verso, 1981), p. 1.
7. *Ibid.*, p. 14.

Whatever their originality or lack of it, history conspired to give Hobsbawm's views an apparent prescience as a New Right Conservative Party made great swathes of the skilled working class its own and acquired, in consequence, an increasingly authoritarian monopoly of political power. The electoral rout of 1983 saw a 12% and 11% loss of Labour Party support among skilled and semi-skilled workers respectively.[8] Further, as Hobsbawm himself pointed out after the 1987 election, "barely more than one skilled worker in three voted Labour, six out of ten trade unionists refused to support Labour and voted for other parties and less than half the semi-skilled and unskilled voted for the party of the working class".[9] In such circumstances, the controversy which Hobsbawm's lecture ignited inevitably gathered momentum and rumbled on into the 1980s.

In the course of this debate, analytical and prescriptive energies were focused on a range of questions related to the contemporary nature and likely social evolution of the working class. To begin with, there were those engendered by the structural changes which characterized late-twentieth-century British capitalism. As in all western industrial economies, there had been a marked post-war diminution in the relative importance of manufacturing and a growth in service industries, a development which had been particularly pronounced in Britain where, by the mid-1980s, the *private* service sector employed as many as the *private* manufacturing sector. This, it was argued by some, would, *ceteris paribus*, almost certainly precipitate a decline in support for democratic socialism. First, as Hobsbawm had emphasized, the declining relative importance of manufacturing and the attendant decline in the manual working class entailed a diminution in the size of the social constituency that had traditionally provided Labour's most solid support. Secondly, the rapid expansion in services meant the growth of a workforce which was often relatively poorly unionized[10] and with "few organisational linkages to Labour".[11] Thirdly, the service industry labour force was traditionally fragmented and mobile and, therefore, difficult to organize both industrially and politically. Fourthly, it was insecurely employed and therefore vulnerable to employer pressure to refrain from unionization. Finally, it was often poorly paid and, therefore, more likely to be interested in short-term survival than a political agenda focused on the long-term, democratic socialist transformation of the nation's economic and social life.

---

8. For a contemporary discussion of this see G. Therborn, "The Prospects of Labour and the Transformation of Advanced Capital", *New Left Review* **145** (1984), p. 31.
9. E. Hobsbawm, "Out of the Wilderness", *Marxism Today* (October 1987), p. 12.
10. "Only 16% of their 7 million workers are unionised", M. Mann, *Socialism Can Survive*, Fabian Tract 502 (London: Fabian Society, 1985), p. 4.
11. Many psephological analyses of the election defeats of 1983 and 1987 emphasized the rapid growth of the service sector as an important contributory factor. On these see, for example, G. Elliott, *Labourism and the English Genius* (London: Verso, 1993), p. 156.

If the growth of the service sector and the nature of much service employment threatened class solidarity and support for traditional democratic socialist objectives, so, it was argued, did other structural developments affecting late-twentieth-century British capitalism. Specifically, some saw the 1980s and 1990s as characterized by the growth of a peripheral relative to a core workforce. The core workforce was skilled, comparatively highly paid, had security of employment and often enjoyed a considerable measure of autonomy in the tasks it performed. The peripheral workforce was un- or semi-skilled, employed on a part-time or casual basis, suffered constant uncertainty as regards continuity of employment, had few employment rights and was generally poorly remunerated.[12] But the latter workforce was vital to meeting the need for flexibility and speed of response in a context of rapidly shifting market forces and therefore crucial to improving the efficiency, competitiveness and thence performance of the British economy. As such, it could be anticipated that its relative importance would grow.

Nor were there likely to be major obstacles to its increase. Rapidly rising unemployment, pressure on welfare entitlement and laws which circumscribed employment and trade union rights were combining, in the 1980s, to ensure that an adequate supply of such labour would be forthcoming.[13] In this regard, Thatcherite economic policy was seen as consciously aiming to "get the best of both worlds for the employing class: a diminution of the burden of maintaining the unemployed, and a malleable low-paid underclass available for intensified exploitation".[14] In the period 1981–5, it was estimated that this peripheral workforce expanded by around 16%, and by the late 1980s it was estimated that some 5 million jobs were done by part-time workers.[15] A new and rapidly expanding underclass was, therefore, a salient characteristic of the period, and its existence inevitably added to the divisions within, and the weakening of, democratic socialism's potential constituency.

The rapid growth of mass unemployment, peaking in 1983 according to official (under)estimates at over 3 million, persuaded some socialist writers that such a deepening capitalist crisis would precipitate a concomitant intensification of class conflict. Others, however, saw it as more likely to erode working-class support for the democratic socialist cause. To begin with "recession" tended to "deprive the labour movement of vital resources, morale,

---

12. For a contemporary view of this see C. Leadbeater, "In the Land of the Dispossessed", *Marxism Today* (April 1987), p. 18.
13. "The consistent thrust of legislative change . . . has been to encourage people to move off benefit and into low-paid, unskilled labour", D. Coates, *The Crisis of Labour* (London: Allan, 1989), p. 146; ". . . mass unemployment and trade union laws helped management in some industries to reorganise industrial relations towards the new model of flexible specialisation *with the workforce divided into core and periphery workers*", A. Gamble, *The Free Economy and the Strong State* (Basingstoke: Macmillan, 1994), p. 194, my emphasis.
14. Coates, *The Crisis of Labour*, p. 148.
15. Leadbeater, "In the Land of the Dispossessed", p. 19; Coates, *The Crisis of Labour*, p. 146.

market bargaining power, organisation and funds".[16] In addition, mass unemployment was fundamentally divisive, the gulf between the unemployed and those fortunate enough to secure and retain employment widening as real wages increased during the 1980s. Further, it was argued, given mass unemployment, those in work inevitably focused their energies upon retaining what they had rather than engaging in solidaristic activity in support of the unemployed. Here again, the fragmentation of the working class would be exacerbated.

Yet if structural change spelt redundancy and impoverishment for many, there was a significant improvement in real wages and living standards for the greater part of the working population in the 1980s. And, for some socialist commentators, this heralded, as it had for others in the 1950s and 1960s, the apotheosis of the affluent worker and the embourgeoisement of the skilled working class. "Labour's traditional electoral base – the blue-collar working class – was . . . being disaggregated by a process of socio-cultural embourgeoisement, undermining habitual solidarities and collective identifications."[17] To borrow from Galbraith, what was rapidly emerging in late-twentieth-century Britain was a skilled-working-class "culture of contentment"; a culture whose hallmark was the "passive acceptance of short-run comfort" at the expense of either concern for the longer term economic or environmental future or even for the more immediate fate of those who had fallen by the economic wayside.[18]

From a socialist perspective, the emergence of such attitudes of mind had profound consequences. Material contentment, by definition, entailed an erosion of those radical instincts with which actual or threatened impoverishment had imbued the working class and that had so often expressed themselves in demands for social reform. Further, the atrophy or suppression of a social conscience with regard to the poor, which seemed, to Galbraith and others, to be an inevitable concomitant of affluence, served to dampen the desire for a society from which human impoverishment had been entirely excised. As Hobsbawm wrote in 1986, there was the absence of a "hunger for a new and better kind of society": "the distance . . . between the sectors of the British people who are doing well and those who are not has grown so great that the prosperous may be reluctant to make their share of the necessary sacrifices".[19] Or, as another commentator argued, any serious attempt to mitigate material impoverishment along traditional social democratic lines was now perceived as "threatening the lifestyles and aspirations of the rest of the population"; a population that in

---

16. J. Westergaard, "The Once and Future Class", in J. Curran (ed.), *The Future of the Left* (Cambridge: Polity, 1984), p. 88.
17. Elliott, *Labourism and the English Genius*, p. 156.
18. J. K. Galbraith, *The Culture of Contentment* (London: Sinclair-Stevenson, 1992), p. 77.
19. E. Hobsbawm, "Labour's Prospects", *Marxism Today* (October 1986), p. 19.

Britain, according to a survey of attitudes to poverty carried out by the EEC in the 1970s, was displaying "an intense degree of hostility and resentment towards the poor".[20] Thus, by the 1980s, many clearly believed that the existing welfare state had done sufficient, or all that was possible, to alleviate the kind of grinding and indefensible inequalities that had preceded its existence.[21]

So democratic socialism could no longer tap into the traditional solidarities, aspirations and ethical instincts which, historically, had characterized its working-class support. A greater part of that class, particularly in the more prosperous South, now appeared to be motivated by "instrumental, pecuniary, egotistic, in short, capitalist values and attitudes", to be experiencing "a disintegration of various moral frameworks within which these had a subordinate place" and to be "fac[ing] various countervailing forms of commitment, loyalty and discipline".[22] The desire of this social segment was for home ownership rather than its collective provision; for participation in the windfalls created by privatization rather than the social ownership of those means of production which were being privatized; for the private enjoyment of material affluence rather than the social utility to be derived from collective consumption. The hour of Essex man had come and woe to any political movement that ignored his material cravings.

It was this social constituency that Thatcherite Conservatism had sought to make its own. "The government", wrote Leadbeater in 1987, was

> attempting to create a new political equilibrium based on stabilising the new economic divisions . . . At the core is a strategy to legitimise a society where roughly two thirds have done, and will continue to do, quite well, while the other third languish in unemployment or perpetual insecurity.[23]

This was an attempt which many socialists came to recognize was proving remarkably successful, as successive Conservative electoral victories testified. By contrast, the Labour Party was left to "defend the weak and marginal sections of society"[24] – marginal not just in their contribution to the economic life of the nation, but also even in terms of their significance within a diminishing and rapidly fragmenting working class.

This erosion and fragmentation of the traditional working class was also seen as being reflected in the fate of the trade union movement. Between 1969 and

---

20. C. Pond, "Rediscovering Poverty", *Marxism Today* (May 1983), p. 14.
21. On this see, for example, C. Lemke & G. Marks, "Introduction", in C. Lemke & G. Marks (eds), *The Crisis of Socialism in Europe* (North Carolina: Duke University Press, 1992), p. 12.
22. S. Lukes, "The Future of British Socialism", in B. Pimlott (ed.), *Fabian Essays in Socialist Thought* (London: Heinemann, 1984), p. 279.
23. Leadbeater, "In the Land of the Dispossessed", p. 21.
24. B. Jessop, K. Bonnett, S. Bromley & T. Long, "Authoritarian Populism: Two Nations and Thatcherism", *New Left Review* **147** (1984), p. 52.

1979, trade union membership had increased from 10.5 million to 13.3 million.[25] At the same time, there had been an intensification of militancy and a widening of aims. In contrast, union membership declined in every year of the 1980s, falling from its 1979 post-war peak to 10.2 million by the end of the decade. In addition, the percentage of the workforce unionized fell in a comparable period from 58% to 46%.[26] Further, the power of the trade union movement was weakened by a stream of legislation which, among other things, "cut back the scope of [legal] immunities and so increased the scope of common law regulation of strike activity", something which severely constrained trade union behaviour in relation to most forms of industrial action.[27]

This fall in membership and the legislative constraints on trade union activity were also paralleled by a more aggressive style of management in the private sector and an unremittingly combative approach of government to public sector unions, culminating in the miners' strike of 1984–5.[28] This resulted in the growth of a so-called "new realism" within sections of the trade union movement. This manifested itself in a number of ways, most obviously in a tendency to company, or plant, rather than national bargaining and an acceptance of "single-union"/"no-strike" agreements, in particular by unions such as the AUEW, EEPTU and UDM. So the social disintegration of the working class was mirrored by a comparable fragmentation of the trade union movement.[29] It seemed, therefore, that democratic socialists could now rely neither on a cohesive social constituency nor a strong and relatively unified trade unionism to give support and effect to their political agenda.

For those who subscribed to such a view of social change, it was clear that the political economy of democratic socialism had to be revised to accommodate these developments. It would have to take on board the loss, or attenuation, of its traditional support among the manual working class, the altered and fragmented basis of its potential social constituency and the diminution in the potency of the organizations through which that constituency had traditionally given expression and effect to its interests. The increasingly fragmented experience of its working-class support would have to be iterated in its critical analysis of capitalism and the aspirations and desires which that experience engendered reflected in its policy prescriptions. Thus Stuart Hall wrote of a

---

25. A rapid growth after "being stagnant for the previous twenty years", B. Fine *et al.*, *Class Politics: An Answer to its Critics* (London: Community Press, 1985), p. 25.
26. S. Deakin, "Labour Law and Industrial Relations", in J. Michie (ed.), *The Economic Legacy, 1979–1992* (London: Academic Press, 1992), p. 179.
27. On this see, for example, *ibid.*, p. 175.
28. ". . . the area of the negotiable has been sharply restricted; managements increasingly insist on their 'right to manage', merely offering to 'consult' with union representatives", Coates, *The Crisis of Labour*.
29. Mann wrote of a dual trade union movement – "with decentralized plant bargaining in the private sector but with maintenance, for the most part, of national bargaining in the public sphere", *Socialism Can Survive*, pp. 5–7.

new spirit of pluralism and diversity, which has become such a driving
force of the masses under advanced capitalism and which will have to be
more centrally reflected in our thinking about socialism if we are ever to
convince large numbers of people that socialism is a superior way of life.[30]

In similar vein, Ernesto Laclau averred that

> any project of a democratic and socialist transformation of society has to
> start today from wider and more heterogeneous social bases than at any
> time in the past. This heterogeneity means that the agents of historical
> change are going to be many . . . that negotiation and unstable equilib-
> rium amongst them are going to be the rule and principle of political
> life.[31]

For some, this meant embracing what were termed the new social movements: the ecology movement, the women's movement, the peace movement
and organizations supportive of ethnic minorities. If, as one commentator
wrote, socialism could be defined as striving for "the greatest possible degree of
conscious human control over the personal, social and natural environment
exercised democratically", then it "embrace[d] as socialist or as contributing to
the construction of a socialist world, a whole variety of social movements and
demands, many of which [we]re not dominated by self-conscious socialists".[32]
In its political economy socialism had, therefore, to connect with such constituencies. It had to appreciate their concerns, understand their desires and motivations and, as far as possible, accommodate and articulate their objectives. In this
vein Hall wrote of the need for the Left "to make converts to its cause, to carry
the cause to a widening set of constituencies . . . to connect with new experiences in society, to engage with its increasing complexity and in that way to
make socialism grow in relevance".[33]

Such views affected the subsequent evolution of democratic socialist
political economy in a number of ways. To begin with, some writers evinced
the need for a break with the kind of statism that had characterized Keynesian
social democracy and more fundamentalist forms of socialism. Thus there was
in much democratic socialist political economy of the 1980s and 1990s an
emphasis upon democratization and decentralization to embrace, and to allow
the expression of, the interests of a plurality of social constituencies. This is
reflected, in particular, in the political economy of municipal socialism that will

---

30. S. Hall, "The State, Socialism's Old Caretaker", *Marxism Today* (November 1984), p. 28.
31. E. Laclau, "Class War and After", *Marxism Today* (April 1987), p. 133.
32. G. Kitching, *Rethinking Socialism: A Theory for a Better Practice* (London: Methuen, 1983),
    pp. 30, 33.
33. S. Hall, "Faith, Hope or Clarity", *Marxism Today* (January 1985), p. 17.

be discussed in Chapter 2 and in the considerable interest among democratic socialist writers, in the 1970s and 1980s, in the political economy of producer co-operatives and labour-managed firms considered in Chapters 4 and 5. Such emphases on diversity, autonomy, democracy and the dispersal of power were also to be found within the political economy of market socialism (Chapter 6) and were integral too to the kind of socialist political economy which was constructed, by some, on the theoretical foundations furnished by the idea of flexible specialization and which will be considered at length in Chapter 3. One can also find a strong emphasis on the democratization of economic and political decision-making running through elements of the Alternative Economic Strategy (AES). But, as will be made clear in Chapter 1, this coexisted uneasily with a strong strain of statism and corporatism within the AES Left and its policy prescriptions.

Of course, not all on the Left were convinced that socialism's working-class constituency had fragmented in a manner that rendered fundamental ideological revision imperative. Keynesian social democracy might be bankrupt, but that was so because, of its essence, it could never hope to satisfy the material aspirations of the working class, rather than because that class and those aspirations had radically altered. Thus, as some saw it, the economy was still quintessentially capitalist, as were the social relations of production. A working class unified, or capable of being unified, by its experience of the appropriation of the surplus value that it produced remained a salient characteristic of contemporary capitalism and, therefore, central to its overthrow and any subsequent socialist transformation of society. As one writer phrased it, "the social relations of production remain tenaciously capitalist in form: offering to left-wing causes an old working class still industrially unbroken and a new and extensive working-class poor in need of non-market solutions to their poverty".[34]

As to the growth of a service sector and the decline in the numbers employed in manufacturing, in terms of class relations such developments were neither here nor there. The numbers of professional and white-collar workers had certainly grown rapidly in the post-war period. But, like the manual working class, they too experienced the exploitation and alienation which was inherent in capitalist relations of production. As such, their unions were among the most militant and "they now constitute Labour's most solid basis of support".[35] Whatever acceleration in the growth of the service sector had occurred since 1979, the fact remained that "the economy over which the Thatcherite government presides is still a capitalist one, and all the workers in it . . . must necessarily experience it as potentially radicalising".[36] As some saw it, therefore, it was "simply wrong" "to imagine that traditional working-class demands,

---

34. Coates, *The Crisis of Labour*, p. 173.
35. *Ibid.*, p. 168.
36. *Ibid.*, p. 170.

struggles and organizational forms are bound to decline with the number of industrial workers".[37]

Also, as regards the trade union movement, while membership had indeed declined since 1979, "the scale of loss, though of course very serious for the unions involved, is still modest compared with the 50% collapse in union membership figures in the inter-war depression".[38] As one commentator saw it, "in spite of government rhetoric and tough labour laws . . . it would seem that the basic institutions of workplace trade unionism remain strong; and thus far at least the impact of Thatcherism on negotiating structures has been only limited and marginal".[39]

Those who neglected all this, who looked for the reconstitution of support for socialism on a new social basis, or on the basis of a new social compromise, and who sought to reconstruct democratic socialist political economy accordingly, were simply ignoring these realities. They abstracted from the manifest centrality of class and class relations and from the relative unity and strength of the trade union and labour movement. In so doing, they were building their political economy on sand. They lacked an adequate agency for effecting the changes that they sought and, in pursuing a broad democratic alliance or conglomerate of new social movements, they ended up proposing a diversity of incremental changes more likely to dissipate the energies of the labour movement than advance the socialist cause.[40] Also, among those who saw the construction of a constituency for socialism on the basis of these new social movements, there was a tendency to ignore the fact that their social diversity resulted in a combination of socialist, non-socialist and even anti-socialist elements. This in turn made for an ideological and strategic incoherence.

On the Left, as some saw it, there had "been a shift away from, even abandonment of, the central role of class and class conflict in the analysis and formation of political strategy" and with that "a downgrading of the trade union movement"[41] – part and parcel of a tendency, particularly within the Labour Party, "to shed its trade union and class image".[42] The overwhelming desire to construct an alliance capable of winning an electoral or even social majority had, in consequence, resulted in the abandonment of fundamental elements of socialist praxis.

Consistently with this, it was also argued, in the early 1980s, that those who looked to reconfigure the social basis of socialism had neglected the obvious fact that Thatcherism had precipitated an intensification of the class struggle.

37. Therborn, "The Prospects of Labour", p. 35.
38. Coates, *The Crisis of Labour*, p. 135.
39. *Ibid.*, p. 142.
40. On this, for example, see L. Panitch, "The Impasse of Social Democratic Politics", *Socialist Register, 1994* (London: Merlin, 1994), p. 63.
41. Fine *et al.*, *Class Politics*, p. 5.
42. Gamble, *The Free Economy*, p. 185.

"We characterise the current period", wrote Fine *et al.*,

> as one of intensifying class struggle, as the weakness of the British
> economy limits the potential manoeuvres available to bourgeois social
> democracy. The Thatcher governments are an open expression of this
> situation and must be recognised as such rather than as the focus of an
> unambiguous shift to the right in British society.[43]

As these writers saw it, Thatcherism was about breaking the power of organized
labour. The deliberate intensification of depression, the legislative onslaught on
the trade union movement and the pitched battles of the steelworkers' and
miners' strikes were indicative of that. As one commentator put it, "the ruling
class had identified its objectives with great clarity" and in so doing was forcing
upon the working class a comparably lucid recognition of theirs.[44]

Further, the objective conditions were there for a decisive, socialist conflict.
Mass unemployment was engendering an intensity of discontent that created the
material basis and generated the social energies necessary for radical change.
Thatcherism was manifestly failing to deliver on its primary promises to conquer
inflation and transform the performance of the British economy. It represented,
therefore, the "despairing last throw by the ruling class to hold on to power".[45]

> The supreme irony is that, while many on the left have been busy
> announcing the death of class politics and denying the privileged position
> of the working class in the struggle for socialism, the Conservative
> government has been conducting a policy whose first – and last – premise
> is that an organised working class represents the greatest threat to
> capitalism.[46]

With the failure of the radical solutions of the New Right, the way would be
open for the pursuit of the authentic socialism of the Old Left. The political
economy of class would yet have its day, with Thatcherism speeding its advent.

So while, for many on the Left, the 1970s and 1980s were about the
fragmentation of class and traditional class allegiances, others took a radically
different view:

> Our point of departure from the newer left could not be more funda-
> mental. It is an insistence on the primacy of class in the understanding of
> movements in British society, including the new forces, and a

---

43. Fine *et al.*, *Class Politics*, p. 63.
44. A. Gamble, "Class Politics and Radical Democracy", *New Left Review*, **164** (1987), p. 119.
45. E. Wood, *The Retreat from Class* (London: Verso, 1986), p. 182.
46. *Ibid.*

corresponding commitment to, and not abandonment of, class in political intervention and strategy formation.[47]

The working class remained a coherent entity and, "in the sense of those people who are unpropertied workers and who are not involved in the supervision of collective labour", there was "a working class majority in all advanced capitalist countries".[48] It therefore remained the sole conceivable agency of profound social change.[49]

For those who adhered to such views, it was business as usual on the "class war" front. Capitalism was in crisis, class antagonism was intensifying, class unity still largely prevailed and a coherent social agent existed to effect fundamental social and economic change. However, as the 1980s progressed and, particularly, in the aftermath of the miners' strike, such an analysis, and the cries of theoretical defiance which infused it, came increasingly to sound like so much whistling in the dark. Certainly, in terms of its political economy, the Left that adhered to such an analysis could furnish little that was new or applicable to the contemporary discontents or angst of labour or to the pursuit of socialism in the 1990s. What was on offer was the traditional fare of a substantial extension of social ownership and the conscious purposive planning of economic activity, with social need not private profit in mind: old tunes that, in the 1980s, proved to be a swan song falling on increasingly unreceptive ears. Little needs to be said, therefore, about this increasingly marginal and moribund genre of socialist political economy in the present volume.

Of course, what also contributed fundamentally to the ideological crisis of the Left in this period was the popularity and electoral success of the Thatcherite New Right. And, as many saw it, this too was something which made it imperative that the Left rethought its political economy. Among other matters what such a rethink had to take on board was the extent to which the New Right, by way in particular of its anti-statism, had been able to mine a rich vein of popular disenchantment with the role played by the state in the post-war period. Here, specifically, it was recognized how easy it was to portray the state as ineffectual or worse, as regards its conduct of economic policy. Such a portrayal was, after all, consistent with the experience of macroeconomic management which had, by the 1970s, led to a combination of double-digit inflation and rising unemployment; with the experience of indicative planning that had disintegrated almost simultaneously with the publication of the first National Plan in 1965; with that of public corporations which had failed to increase efficiency, democratize economic power, respond to consumer needs

---

47. Fine *et al.*, *Class Politics*, p. 7.
48. Panitch, "The Impasse of Social Democratic Politics", pp. 94–5.
49. ". . . the possibility of realising a socialist project cannot conceivably do without working-class identity, consciousness and politics forming its mass base and organisational core", *ibid.*, p. 63.

or provide a spearhead for the rejuvenation of Britain's industrial fortunes and with the experience of a welfare state that treated its clients as supplicants not citizens. And from here, of course, it was only a short step to interpreting this unholy combination of incompetence, failure and impotence as the inevitable consequence of statist interference with the natural, benign and efficient workings of a market economy. "Thatcherism did not advance into an empty space. It invaded and seized territory from a Labourism . . . *which appeared increasingly as, simply, a less efficient or convincing manager of capitalist crisis.*"[50]

In the 1980s and 1990s, the Left sought to respond to the substance and popularity of this critique of the statism of Keynesian social democracy in a number of ways. For some, a democratic socialist political economy should assume an anti-statist form. And, as we shall see in Chapters 3 and 6, anti-statism was a powerful current in post-Fordist socialism, market socialism and the socialist political economy of producer co-operatives and labour-managed firms. Others, however, believed it was possible to formulate a socialist political economy that made the state's control, management and planning of economic activity effective, democratic and genuinely popular. That, in essence, was the objective of the AES, whose origins, historical context and trajectory will be discussed in Chapter 1. Yet there were, in the 1980s, others who believed that Keynesian social democracy could be reconfigured and rejuvenated in a manner that would allow past failings to be elided and popular faith in its efficacy restored. And the nature and fate of the attempt to do so will be discussed in Chapter 7.

Of course, the New Right also made much of the centralizing, intrusive, authoritarian and coercive character of much state economic intervention and activity. As one commentator put it, "the new Right presented itself as the only party committed to opposing the exponential growth of the state".[51] It offered to roll back its frontiers, creating space for the exercise of initiative and enterprise and giving to individuals and firms an autonomy which had been severely eroded and circumscribed in the post-war period.

This representation of an authoritarian, undemocratic state, unresponsive to popular pressure let alone individual need was, as some on the Left saw it, an essentially authentic one and democratic socialism had been tainted in consequence. The "labourism" of Keynesian social democracy had "lost its popular-democratic connections". "Social democracy ha[d] progressively assumed those postures of pragmatic and creeping authoritarianism" which had led to "a gradual suspension of many of the traditional bases of democratic representation".[52] It had effected a corporatist centralization of power barely amenable to

50. S. Hall & M. Jacques, "Introduction", in S. Hall & M. Jacques (eds), *The Politics of Thatcherism* (London: Lawrence & Wishart, 1983), p. 14, my emphasis.
51. Hall, "The State: Socialism's Old Caretaker", p. 27.
52. S. Hall, "Questions of Theory", in S. Hall, *The Hard Road to Renewal: Thatcherism and the Crisis of the Left* (London: Verso, 1988), p. 126; Hall & Jacques, "Introduction", p. 14.

democratic restraint and creating little opportunity for popular participation in policy formation. More generally, the institutions of the state, while they might retain the ideal of public service, were in fact unresponsive to those whose needs they supposedly served. Nor was there any serious attempt to render them democratically accountable to their clientele. "We know", wrote one commentator, "that it [the state] is experienced by the ordinary people, in the very moment they are benefitting from it, as an intrusive, managerial and bureaucratic force in their lives."[53] Thus the attitude of the long-term unemployed was one of "fear of the state and all its agencies", and, in general, the apparatus of the welfare state was characterized by a bureaucratic and insensitive attitude to those whom its was supposedly created to serve.[54]

The New Right's excoriation of the authoritarian and coercive character of the state and its institutions had, therefore, "exposed a weakness . . . which the Left made too little of: the deeply undemocratic character of state administered socialism".[55] Further, and damagingly, it had allowed the New Right to appropriate the language of freedom and libertarianism, to deploy it to considerable political effect, and to make it synonymous solely with the kind of autonomy which private property and an atomistic market permitted.

Much democratic socialist political economy in the 1980s and 1990s both acknowledged and sought to come to terms with these developments. The AES, despite the fact that it aimed to give the state more potent policy instruments than it had possessed under Keynesian social democracy, nonetheless stressed the democratization of both enterprise and state decision-making. Similarly, the hallmark of the political economy of local socialism, discussed in Chapter 2, was its emphasis on the need for the democratic involvement of those affected in the formulation and implementation of municipal attempts to stimulate economic activity. In addition, and in particular, the political economy of producer co-operatives and labour-managed firms and the related political economy of market socialism considered in Chapters 4, 5 and 6 had at their very core the principles of participatory democracy and the decentralization of economic power. And so, for that matter, had the political economy of post-Fordist socialism.

One final related point with respect to the New Right's anti-statism warrants notice here – namely the link it established between state involvement and the putative emergence of a culture of dependency. This, as the New Right saw it, was an inevitable concomitant of the welfarism that, in the post-war period, had been integral to Keynesian social democracy. This dependency culture had sapped initiative, polluted the springs of enterprise and encouraged a "something-for-nothing" mentality. It had, in short, undermined the basis of

---

53. Hall, "The State: Socialism's Old Caretaker", p. 221
54. Mann, *Socialism Can Survive*, p. 16.
55. Hall, "The State: Socialism's Old Caretaker", p. 27.

responsible citizenship. Again, there were those on the Left who had comparable, if differently focused, concerns. "The feeling is very deep", wrote Hall, "that the way the welfare state works makes people into passive, greedy, dependent clients much of the time, rather than people claiming rights from a state that is supposed to be their own, representing them against the logic of the market."[56] Here again, it was conceded by many democratic socialists that the anti-statist rhetoric of the New Right was consistent with contemporary experience, with the undemocratic, hierarchic, bureaucratic decision-making characteristic of the institutions of Keynesian social democracy giving popular credence to its critique of the welfare state. "Stuck at the end of the strategy of 'social democracy from above' for so long, 'the people' [were] taking a terrible revenge on Labour."[57]

What the 1980s and 1990s witnessed, by way of a socialist response, was the formulation of democratic socialist political economies that sought to address the problems and alter the popular perception of the welfare state. For some on the Left if passivity was a consequence of non-involvement, popular participation in the decision-making attendant upon social welfare delivery became a prerequisite of any effective assault on poverty. Dependency was the result of the kind of attitudes of mind that non-democratic, bureaucratic decision-making in relation to welfare issues induced; and so democratization of the welfare state was the *sine qua non* of its elimination. Greed, in relation to what could be secured from the welfare state, was a consequence of it being seen as "theirs" not "ours", with an irresponsible acquisitiveness inevitably resulting. Again, therefore, only a democratically decentralized socialism characterized by popular involvement in planning and decision-making would fundamentally alter the nature and thence the popular perception of the welfare state.

Others stressed the need for a welfare state which positively encouraged and supported the desire for individual independence: one which made it more advantageous to work than to subsist on benefit, that eliminated the high marginal rates of tax consequent upon the loss of means-tested benefits when employment was secured and which provided the incentives and information required for the exercise of the rational economic forethought necessary to prevent excessive dependence on the state as a consequence of age and illness. Such a rethinking of the nature and functions of the welfare state was one aspect of the Keynesian social democratic revisionism that was to emerge in the mid-to-late 1980s, and which will be considered in Chapter 7. It was also central to the political economy of New Labour in the 1990s that will be discussed in Chapters 8 and 9. Here, it is sufficient to emphasize, once again, that these developments in social democratic political economy may be seen as,

---

56. Hall, "The State: Socialism's Old Caretaker", in *Hard Road to Renewal*, p. 27.
57. Hall, "On the Kinnock/Hattersley Labour Party", in *Hard Road to Renewal*, pp. 208–9.

in part, a response to the popular reaction elicited by the anti-dependency dimension of the New Right's anti-statism.

Another fundamental element of this anti-statism, and one requiring separate notice, was its anti-corporatism. The New Right saw corporatism as a primary cause of that ineffectual policy-making which accounted, in large measure, for the anaemic performance of the post-war British economy. Specifically, it felt that trade union involvement at the highest level of policy formulation had done much to squeeze profitability, hinder capital accumulation, thwart enterprise, precipitate inflation and introduce an inflexibility and rigidity into the economy that precluded its speedy and effective adjustment to international market forces.

Here again, many democratic socialists recognized that this New Right critique had struck a popular and electorally advantageous chord. As regards trade unions, it was accepted that these had indeed frequently acted in a coercive, unresponsive and undemocratic manner that was guaranteed to undermine popular support, not least among their own members. Corporatism had enmeshed their leaderships in decision-making structures that rendered them largely impervious to the democratic influence of their memberships. More generally, as regards the corporatism of the 1960s and 1970s, even with a Labour government in power, decisions were taken, within and by the corporatist power bloc, with little reference to party manifestos, let alone the policies democratically determined at annual conferences. Small wonder, therefore, that the final act of the corporatist tragedy should have seen the implosion of a Social Contract that was viewed, by both trade union and party rank and file, as having been foisted on the labour movement in a bid to rescue capitalism at the expense of working-class living standards. By the late 1970s, "corporatist political structures [had become] the vehicle for engineering, legitimating . . . and administering the increase in exploitation that was necessary to sustain capitalism in crisis".[58] It was this, some argued, which explained the unpopularity of the Labour Party and the unions. It explained both the former's electoral defeats and the Conservatives' success, after 1979, in dividing the latter's membership from its leaders, something which laid the basis for a legislative assault that substantially weakened the whole labour movement.

For some, the solution was the democratization of the party and trade unions. They sought a party whose leadership was democratically elected, whose MPs were subject to reselection by their constituency parties and that was bound by conference decisions. They sought trade unions that were genuinely accountable to their members, that had real powers of decision-making at enterprise and national levels and that operated within an institutional framework which effected and supported a significant shift of power in favour of the working class. For such democratic socialists it was

---

58. L. Panitch, "Trade Unions and the Capitalist State", *New Left Review* **125** (1981), p. 38.

possible to conceive of a socialist corporatism characterized by structures which ensured, through the democratization of planning at national and enterprise levels, a decisive decision-making role for the working class and its organizations – a socialist corporatism which would, therefore, attract and retain working-class support. This was to be the position of many of those who adhered to the AES and its variants in the early 1980s.

That said, there were those within Keynesian social democratic ranks whose critique of the role of the trade union movement in post-war corporatism was very different and who condemned, in particular, the part it had played in the wrecking of the Social Contract. For them, this had represented the destruction of the last best hope of implementing the kind of incomes policy that would make possible a non-inflationary, demand-managed pursuit of full employment. Its destruction smacked of the acquisitive, sectional, self-seeking values of those who subscribed to the predatory behaviour of untrammelled market forces, rather than those of a labour movement guided by the principles of solidarity, justice and equity. The trade union movement might have been provoked into the "winter of discontent", but it was nonetheless culpable for having been unwilling to hammer out a viable and lasting incomes policy, one which could form the basis of a return to full employment and ensure wage settlements which favoured the economically disadvantaged rather than those who, through their unions, could wield near-monopsony power in the labour market. For those who subscribed to such views it was not surprising that, in the early 1980s, "union legislation, both enacted and proposed, ha[d] not attracted mass hostility from most union members. Indeed, in white-collar unions the response ha[d] been mutedly favourable when it ha[d] been tested."[59] Disillusionment with the failure to act with wider national or even working-class objectives in mind explained such acquiescence. As Hobsbawm had opined, economistic sectionalism was one of the primary reasons why the forward march of labour had been halted. Only its elimination by way of an equitable and solidaristic Social Contract, enjoying the support of the whole trade union movement, would allow that march to be resumed. As we shall see in Chapter 7, the attempt to formulate such a contract was to prove central to the attempt to revise and rejuvenate Keynesian social democracy in the 1980s.

Still others on the Left were to draw different lessons from the New Right's critique of post-war corporatism and the integral part played in it by the trade union movement. For them, it confirmed what they already believed – that corporatism was, and should remain, a dead letter. It had corrupted the trade union movement. It had enmeshed it in the machinations of those whose aim was to furnish essentially capitalist solutions to capitalist crises, and it had therefore resulted in the alienation of its working-class support. There should,

59. B. Sherman, "Trade Unions", in Pimlott, *Fabian Essays*, p. 248.

therefore, be no attempt to reconstitute corporatism even in a supposedly socialist form. Instead, the objective should be a decentralized socialism of a market socialist/producer co-operative kind, in which democratically structured enterprises would have considerable autonomy to determine their economic destiny free from the centrally determined constraints and directives that had been the hallmark of post-war social democracy. Also, and from a very different perspective, the political economists of New Labour were adamant that corporatism must be abjured. As we shall see in Chapter 9, this was particularly evident in New Labour's articulation, revision and then *de facto* abandonment of the "big idea" of stakeholderism in the 1990s

In both its rejectionist and its revisionist attitudes to corporatism we see the Left, in the 1980s and 1990s, deploying in its political economies the notion of democratization, and here some general remarks as to the multiple uses which this concept served are germane. To begin with, it was, undoubtedly, seen as an apposite and effective means by which libertarian notions could be re-appropriated from the New Right. Thatcherism had sought to make democracy synonymous with the power enjoyed by property-owning participants in a market economy. For many on the Left, it was vital to rescue the concept from this narrow and ideologically loaded definition, to extend its meaning and applicability and to infuse it with a more positive prescriptive content. It should, therefore, be applied, and be seen to be applicable, to all spheres of productive and social activity, thereby impressing on individuals the necessary connection between democracy, freedom and the opportunity to participate in the deliberations of those centres of power that materially shaped their lives. In this way the New Right's conception of democratization could be shown to be limited and lacking substance for all but those whose property conferred on them the power to make their voices heard and their wishes effective. Specifically, this broader conception of democratic rights and democratic freedom was to express itself in an emphasis, already noted within much Left political economy in the 1980s and 1990s, on democratizing economic planning at local, enterprise and national levels. For some, this was to be done through AES expedients; for others, through the multiplication of producer co-operatives and labour-managed firms. Further, the political economy of post-Fordist socialists trumpeted the possibilities of democratic empowerment opened up by the kind of enterprises emerging to satisfy the discriminating consumption of an increasingly affluent population – a view that will be considered at length in Chapter 3.

Another politically appealing corollary of New Right anti-statism, anti-collectivism and anti-corporatism was seen, by some on the Left, as its celebration of the autonomous and self-regarding activity of the individual consumer. Of course this was dangerous terrain for the Left to traverse. To endorse the possessive individualism of untrammelled consumerism threatened the abandonment of a raft of socialist principles. But it was nonetheless recognized that there were new material aspirations to be accommodated if hearts and minds were to be won or, more accurately, won back from the New Right's conscienceless consumerism. Mass unemployment might have spread wholesale impoverishment into the heartlands of Labour's traditional constituency. Yet, as one commentator using the *Family Expenditure Survey* for 1984 pointed out, in "a year in which the crisis of British and world capitalism was still very severe with 3,160,000 people officially unemployed in Britain", "there was still a considerable majority of the British labour force with a significant material stake in the system".[60] Also, despite the unprecedented post-war level of unemployment, this stake was a growing rather than a diminishing one. As Hall wrote in 1984, "if 'people's capitalism' did not liberate the people, it nevertheless 'loosed' many individuals into a life somewhat less constrained, less fundamentally regulated, less strictly imposed than it had been three or four decades before".[61] Further, as some saw it, those who experienced this loosening of material constraints were increasingly constructing their identities and rationalizing their interests not in terms of their place in the social relations of contemporary production, but rather by reference to what they consumed. So "labour, or work itself, and the sphere of production, seems to be becoming less central to the identity and consciousness of workers, while consumption . . . has become more central to the definition of their basic interests".[62]

It was true that many socialists in the 1980s and 1990s had "enormous problems coming to terms with the individualisation, the privatisation, the privatism and the consumerism of how the good life is constituted".[63] They were "out of touch with the culture of consumerism" and their policies did not embrace or even engage with "the lifestyles of the affluent and aspirant working class".[64] For this and other reasons, it was argued that many on the Left still did not "underst[and] the capacity of the market to become identified in the minds of the mass of ordinary people . . . as an expansive popular system".[65] But, for all that, much Left political economy in the 1980s and 1990s did reflect an increasing willingness to embrace the materialist and acquisitive inclinations of the self-regarding, utility-maximizing consumer. Thus there was a growing acceptance that given the increasing autonomy that growing purchasing power bestowed, many did experience participation in a market economy as something that actually conferred a sense of freedom and equality.

---

60. G. Kitching, "A Reply to Ellen Meiskins Wood", *New Left Review* **163** (1987), p. 121.
61. Hall, "The Culture Gap", in *Hard Road to Renewal*, p. 215.
62. Lukes, "The Future of British Socialism", p. 278.
63. C. Leadbeater, *The Politics of Prosperity*, Fabian Tract 523 (London: Fabian Society, 1987), p. 7.
64. *Ibid.*, p. 7.
65. Hall, "The Culture Gap", in *Hard Road to Renewal*, p. 215.

> In what Marx called "the noisy freedom of exchange" in capitalism,
> people do enjoy the "freedom" to choose, do compete, do meet the
> market as an impersonal arbiter; and they do experience all this as free
> acting individuals. People can feel free, and in large measure equal, as they
> *buy*.[66]

For some democratic socialists, this was undoubtedly the case. The New
Right's panegyrics on the freedom, autonomy and power of self-direction
which markets offered as regards the private satisfaction of needs were, in
significant ways, consistent with working-class experience, as was their complementary execration of the bureaucratic determination of what, and how, needs
should be met by social provision. To strive for the freeing of markets and
thence the widening of consumer choice, to encourage competitive pressures,
to ensure that consumers were offered what was best at the lowest price, were
objectives that, in the 1980s, were increasingly seen by many on the Left as vital
to the socialist project and its promise to materially enrich the lives of the
masses. On this point, post-Fordist socialists in particular waxed lyrical.

Yet there were also those on the Left who, while acknowledging the libertarian allure of the supposedly free market, were critical of the kinds of freedom
which it offered. First, while accepting that the choice and autonomy which
Thatcherism offered was worth having and what many craved, they argued that
the freedom and autonomy that consumer sovereignty bestowed represented
only one side of the coin. People could experience a sense of freedom as
consumers in a capitalist market economy, but "what they cannot do in
capitalism . . . is feel either so free or so equal when they *work*. Liberalism fits
well with the experience of the marketplace in capitalism but not with the
experience of the factory."[67] So fundamental questions related to the ownership
and control of the means of production remained, and until they were
addressed the freedoms which the market conferred would be partial and
evanescent. Such views inevitably directed those democratic socialists who
adhered to them back to these traditional concerns – concerns which loomed
particularly large in the AES and the political economies of producer
co-operation and market socialism.

Secondly, it was argued that the kinds of liberty and autonomy implied by
New Right notions of consumer sovereignty were, in important respects, both
circumscribed and shallow. "Thatcherism ha[d] appropriated desires for
autonomy, choice and responsibility, which should be the natural terrain of the
Left" and in that respect its challenge had to be taken seriously. But what
"Thatcherism . . . offer[ed] people [was] a very narrow, acquisitive, consumer-

---

66. Coates, *The Crisis of Labour*, p. 116, my emphasis.
67. *Ibid.*, my emphasis.

ist kind of individual responsibility."[68] The task of the Left was to take seriously the urge for individual freedom and autonomy, but to articulate it in ways that accommodated other than narrowly self-interested, acquisitive and material aspirations. Such views usually took their adherents towards the democratization of decision-making and those political economies of democratic socialism that, as already noted, had this at their core.

Thirdly, there was an acceptance by many socialist writers that the advent of a rich and variegated pattern of private consumption was indeed something to be welcomed. There should be no ascetic anathematization of the desire to indulge the consumerist urges fuelled by the onset of material abundance. What was iniquitous was the fact that, under existing economic and social arrangements, a substantial proportion of the working class could not realistically maintain or realize such aspirations. Thus

> the only tenable position for a true cultural materialist must be a deep sense of outrage that the fruits of modern, technology and know-how which social labour itself has nurtured and developed are still not available in sufficient amounts to the working people who produce them and need them . . . a labour movement that cannot identify with what is concrete and material in these popular aspirations and expropriate them from identification with the private market and private appropriation, will look increasingly as if it is trapped nostalgically in ancient cultural modes.[69]

Such sentiments did not, as such, point the political economy of democratic socialism in a particular prescriptive direction. But they were illustrative of a growing empathy with the increasingly consumerist mentality of much of socialism's traditional constituency, and they left their mark on some of the democratic socialist political economies that found expression in the 1980s and 1990s.

Fourthly, and more fertile in prescriptive terms, was the associated view that the increasing diversity, complexity and discriminating nature of popular consumption had and was continuing to produce profound changes in the structure and organization of productive activity that socialism could exploit. Specifically, it was argued that it was becoming possible for significant sections of the working population to enjoy freedom and autonomy in the sphere of production that were complementary to those that a generalized affluence had made available in the sphere of exchange. Here some on the Left linked the emergence, and market satisfaction, of increasingly differentiated consumer

---

68. C. Leadbeater, "Clearing the Decks: Round Table Discussion", *Marxism Today* (October 1988), p. 35.
69. Hall, "The Culture Gap", p. 19.

demands to the growing importance of flexible, responsive, small and medium-sized firms, characterized by their non-hierarchical, democratic and participatory nature – attributes which were, of course, particularly evident in producer co-operatives and labour-managed firms, but which were also increasingly apparent in many "capitalist" enterprises. In this context, the power of the consumer was seen as a positive transformative force that was shaping (economic) history in ways which once again favoured socialist advance. Such views will be discussed at length in Chapter 3's consideration of post-Fordist socialism but, at this juncture, it is important simply to stress that these views were another means of theorizing the complementary nature of consumer freedom and socialism, tapping into the popular resonance of the former to induce support for the latter. They were also indicative of the manner in which attempts to counter the positive response to New Right notions, particularly among the more affluent working class, materially influenced the tenor and emphasis of democratic socialist political economy in the last two decades of the twentieth century.

Fifthly, there were those who argued that the principles of consumer autonomy and choice should be embraced by the Left and applied with particular energy in the sphere of public provision. In this view of things, some of the same opportunities that were open to the private consumer to determine how and by whom needs were satisfied should be made available to those dependent upon public services. Here, too, many looked to democratization (of the bureaucracies traditionally responsible for social provision) as the way forward, but there were also those who argued for the possibility of decentralized collectivist solutions, with multiple "associations" both contracting to furnish particular (social) services and even competing with each other to do so. In a sense, therefore, it was believed that the competition and choice, and thence the kind of freedom and individual autonomy, associated with the market mechanism could be replicated in the public sphere. Leadbeater wrote,

> Labour has to establish a people's right to a minimum standard of living . . . but it also needs to adopt more flexible ways of ensuring these minimum standards are met which allow for greater *choice* within collectively financed provision. Equitable standards of provision must go along with efficiency and *choice* in their delivery . . . state provision could be complemented by other forms of provision.[70]

In the 1990s Paul Hirst and others were to develop such notions at some length in an "associationalist" political economy which, on occasion, echoed ideas on the franchising of social service provision which were being simultaneously

---

70. Leadbeater, *The Politics of Prosperity*, p. 19, my emphasis.

articulated by the New Right.[71] As we shall see in Chapter 3, here, as elsewhere, democratic socialist political economy in the 1980s and 1990s could sometimes assume an awful similarity to that which it purportedly rebutted.

Finally, there were those who were to "argue that the primary appeal of socialism to a materially prosperous working class *cannot* be its supposedly superior capacity to deliver further improvements in material living standards".[72] The advance to democratic socialism could not, and should not, be spearheaded by consumerism, however enlightened and discriminating the forms it took. Such writers accepted that material abundance was a crucial prerequisite of the good life in that it both "tend[ed] to expand the active citizenry and thus reduce the size of the passive majority". They also acknowledged that it permitted the emergence of a "citizenry of considerable skill, knowledge and intellectual sophistication", which was an essential precondition for "the construction of socialist societies and a socialist world".[73] But, for all that, like R. H. Tawney and other writers in the rich vein of British ethical socialism, these writers believed that the realization of the New Jerusalem must follow from essentially moral not material imperatives.

Until this period, a strong undercurrent of asceticism, or at least restraint, had always run through British socialist political economy. Sometimes, indeed, as with elements of early-nineteenth-century socialism, the liberating eschewal of the material was seen as being at the very core of socialist advance. Only personal asceticism would permit that prioritization of social ethics and, for that matter, social consumption, over the self-interested pursuit of the material without which a socialist society could neither be created nor sustained.[74] Only the rational circumscription of desire would free the working class to cultivate those higher intellectual faculties that were central to creative self-fulfilment and human liberation. Of course, in both the nineteenth and twentieth centuries there had been those who were critical of such ascetic predilections. For example, Crosland's *The Future of Socialism* celebrated the rising tide of post-war affluence which, as he saw it, would submerge social inequalities in a sea of material abundance.[75] In the 1980s and 1990s, however, the business of con-sumption, the concept of consumer sovereignty and the self-regarding activity of the individual consumer were given a centrality in democratic socialist political economy that they had never previously enjoyed. For post-Fordist

71. P. Hirst, *Associative Democracy: New Forms of Economic and Social Governance* (London: Polity, 1994).
72. Kitching, "A Reply", p. 126.
73. Kitching, *Rethinking Socialism*, p. 18.
74. Such was certainly the view of many early-nineteenth-century communitarian socialists. On this see N. Thompson, "Social Opulence and Private Aceticism: Ideas of Consumption in Early Socialist Thought", in M. Daunton & M. Hilton (eds), *The Politics of Consumption: Material Culture and Citizenship in Europe and America* (Oxford: Berg, 2001).
75. C. A. R. Crosland, *The Future of Socialism* (London: Jonathan Cape, 1956).

socialists in particular, socialism and mammon could certainly be reconciled; or, more accurately, socialism could embrace the rational, utility-maximizing individual as an agent of socialist change.

This more or less enthusiastic embrace by many on the Left of the virtues and socialist potential inherent in ideas of consumer sovereignty can be seen, in some measure, as part of a more general assimilation and attempted socialist reconfiguration of the notions of freedom and individual autonomy that Thatcherism had sought, and with no little success, to make its own. In this respect, it can once again be seen as part of an attempt to deny to the New Right the contemporary monopoly that it threatened to exercise over libertarian discourse. "What the Left urgently needs", wrote Hall, "is to reappropriate the concept of freedom and give it its real expression within the context of a deepening of democratic life as a whole."[76] The problem with the "Hard Left" was that it failed to see the importance of this and so had "lost the capacity to advance a convincing political vision of a more egalitarian, more open, more diverse, more libertarian, more democratic, more self-organizing kind of social-ism".[77] Thatcherism had, consequently, been able to exploit the aspirations which it ignored or deliberately eschewed.

Of course, "hard" or not, there were some who bridled at this. Miliband, Panitch and Saville, for example, attacked those "commentators on the Left" whose political economy jettisoned concepts of "'socialism', 'collectivism' etc in favour of 'individualism', the 'market' and 'popular capitalism'", commentators who "preach[ed] a 'new realism' amounting in effect to a reconciliation with capitalism and the abandonment, in practical terms, of any notion of socialist transformation".[78] Certainly, as Chapters 3 and 9 make clear, a high price was often paid by those on the Left who preached or succumbed to the new realism of discriminating affluence, market competition, anti-statism and possessive individualism. That price involved a strategic accommodation with key components of the Thatcherite agenda. In particular, it entailed an importation of notions of consumerism, consumer sovereignty, individual autonomy, freedom and choice, and the salutary nature of the market imperatives that all these unleashed, into the very core of democratic socialist political economy. And with that also went an acceptance of many of the theoretical and rhetorical parameters that had been established by the New Right in the 1980s.

However, although, in the 1980s and 1990s, many undoubtedly accepted that Thatcherism had decisively altered the political and social agenda, the language in which issues were discussed and the presuppositions of political debate, the extent of that shift was much disputed. It is also true to say that both the

---

76. Hall, "The State: Socialism's Old Caretaker", p. 27.
77. S. Hall, "Realignment", in *Hard Road to Renewal*, p. 242.
78. R. Miliband, L. Panitch & J. Saville, "Problems and Promise of Socialist Renewal", *Socialist Register, 1988* (London: Merlin, 1988) , p. 4.

willingness to admit and a preparedness to accommodate a changed agenda varied not only across the socialist spectrum but also over time. For example, it was only after privatization had gathered momentum, attracted support and achieved a measure of stability that there was a widespread willingness on the Left to abandon the notion that re-nationalization should be an important component of any democratic socialist political economy. Prior to that, most democratic socialists would, like Hobsbawm in 1987, in distinguishing "those economic changes since 1979 which ought to be reversed", have highlighted the "privatisation of what even in free market economics are 'natural monopolies'".[79] In contrast, as we shall see in Chapters 8 and 9, that was all changing rapidly by the late 1980s and early 1990s. Thus, listing the changes which more than a decade of Thatcherism had made irreversible, Gamble, in 1992, made mention of

> the sale of council houses and the spread of share ownership; the denationalisation of public sector industries; the abolition of exchange controls and the international integration of financial markets and production; the permanent contraction of manufacturing employment; and the reorganisation of work and industrial relations.[80]

By that date, for many, a grim "new realism" was indeed the order of the day – a Vichy-like acceptance of the magnitude of a defeat which might be rendered tolerable, but could not be reversed.

There were also profound institutional changes with which, it was argued, the Left had to come to terms. As many saw it,

> the state has been Thatcherized through civil service reorganisation and politically motivated promotion to key official posts; through the enhancement of Treasury control over all areas of government ... through the radical centralization of government power and the assault on local government; through a programme of denationalization and competition which would be difficult to reverse.[81]

In addition, there had been a sweeping away of corporatist structures and institutions such as the National Economic Development Council, the "little Neddies", the Price Commission and the National Enterprise Board. All of this, as we shall see, inevitably limited the Left's freedom of prescriptive manoeuvre when it came to the formulation of their political economies in the 1990s. In particular it made almost impossible the rejuvenation of Keynesian social democracy that many preached in the 1980s (see Chapter 7).

---

79. Hobsbawm, "Out of the Wilderness", p. 17.
80. Gamble, *The Free Economy*, p. 225.
81. Jessop *et al.*, "Authoritarian Populism", p. 50.

Further, it seemed to many, by the 1990s, that democratic socialist political economy had to come to terms with certain attitudes of mind and certain values that had taken popular root in the period of New Right ascendancy. For some, of course, anti-statism, anti-corporatism, possessive individualism and the desire for consumer choice might all be accommodated, or transmuted, in ways that rendered them consistent with and supportive of socialism. But there were other popular attitudes, values and presuppositions that were not so easily reconciled with socialist aspirations and socialist policy. There was, for example, the widespread belief that taxes should not be used to tackle inequality; that inflation should be curbed by a reduction in social investment and social consumption rather than by increasing personal taxation;[82] that substantial public welfare provision for the poor, disabled and disadvantaged was something that could no longer be afforded; that the lot of the poor was in many respects merited; that equality of opportunity should be preferred over equality of outcome; that consumer sovereignty provided a more efficient allocation of resources than could the democratic state.[83] As one writer phrased it, such "ways of thinking, feeling and calculating characteristic of Thatcherism have entered as a material and ideological force into the daily lives of ordinary people".[84]

Sometimes a recognition and even acceptance of these attitudinal and value changes fired the drive for ideological renewal, but it is also clear that they could precipitate, as within the Labour Party in the late 1980s and 1990s, a process of ideological degeneration and decay that ultimately rendered the social democracy which it offered little more than Thatcherism with a human face. As Coates saw it, the "quintessentially Kinnock[ite] strategy for Labour's revival", supported by Hobsbawm and others in the late 1980s, was "at worst, a tailoring of policy to existing levels of Thatcher-shaped consciousness . . . at best, counter-hegemony by stealth".[85] Similarly, Hall and Jacques wrote presciently in 1990 that "Labour's strategy lives by courtesy of Thatcherism, by what is judged to be possible in the context of the Thatcherite revolution."[86] So, for some, accommodation, renewal, revision and modernization became obfuscatory euphemisms for a more or less complete ideological capitulation. Here new realism served as a midwife to the abandonment of any attempt to formulate a distinctively democratic socialist political economy. The defensibility of such strictures will, however, be discussed at length in Chapters 8 and

---

82. For Galbraith on this see *The Culture of Contentment*, pp. 178–9.
83. As one commentator saw it, as early as 1983, "there has been no serious challenge to Thatcher's assault on the poor, no public outcry, not even a particularly effective opposition from the labour movement. As the extent of poverty has increased so, it seems, public attitudes to the poor have hardened", Pond, "Rediscovering Poverty", p. 13.
84. Hall, "Introduction", in *Hard Road to Renewal*, p. 6.
85. Coates, *The Crisis of Labour*, p. 178.
86. S. Hall & M. Jacques, "March Without Vision", *Marxism Today* (December 1990), p. 28.

9, when the nature and trajectory of the social democratic political economy advanced by New Labour in the 1990s is considered.

Finally, in assessing the forces and developments with which Left political economy had to come to terms in the two decades under consideration, we must notice briefly the increasing international economic interdependence that some have seen as the defining characteristic of the global economy in the last quarter of the twentieth century. The nature, lineaments and significance of this will be discussed more fully in Chapters 9 and 10, as will the whole question of whether the global economic developments of that period did indeed represent a distinctive watershed in international economic history. At this juncture, it can simply be noted that in Britain, and elsewhere in Western Europe, such increasing economic interdependence was seen by many as constraining and eroding national economic autonomy to a point where the notion of a unilateral democratic socialism was clearly redundant. For some of those who adhered to such a view, one possible way forward lay in the construction of a multinational socialism using, in particular, the institutions which an ever-closer integration of European Union (EU) economies was helping to construct – a position discussed in Chapter 10. However, for others, while global economic forces, and in particular those emanating from international financial capital and transnational corporations (TNCs), certainly rendered historically redundant those political economies of unilateral socialism that had guided and inspired the post-war Left, it was still possible to secure social democratic advances even within the tightly defined rules of the economic game that globalization had formulated. These writers propounded what may be termed a social democratic political economy of radical stakeholderism that aspired, for a short time in the mid-1990s, to influence the New Labour agenda. The substance and fate of that political economy will be discussed in Chapter 9.

The period covered by this volume has seen the Left in profound ideological crisis. This has been a crisis compounded of the implosion of a political economy that had enjoyed a hegemonic status for most of the post-war period; an increasingly fragmented social constituency which appeared to be falling prey to the siren call of the New Right and the acquisitive, self-seeking aspirations that it articulated and applauded; a frustration with the nature, goals, agents, institutions and achievements of post-war socialist advance; and a globalization of economic activity that has seemed to destroy the capacity of governments to pursue policies other than those consonant with the interests and imperatives of international capitalism. It is with the democratic socialist Left's attempts to respond to such an unfavourable, fin-de-siècle, historical conjuncture, through the reconfiguration of its political economies, that this volume is primarily concerned.

Chapter 1

The political economy
of the AES Left

Any explication of the political economy of the Alternative Economic Strategy (AES) must begin with its critique of Keynesian social democracy. For, in many respects, the former defined its position with reference to the latter's failings, and consciously, and for a time successfully, set out to replace it as the dominant political economy of British democratic socialism. In this regard, the AES clearly elucidated the theoretical and prescriptive deficiencies of Keynesian social democracy, traced through their consequences, provided a competing explanation of the workings of the post-war economic world and its economic history and charted the alternative available paths to a manifestly socialist future. It was, therefore, as hegemonic in its ambitions as the programme it attacked and represented an attempt, perhaps the very last, to construct a holistic British democratic socialist political economy. In so doing it established the terms of socialist economic debate in the early 1980s, and, even with its disintegration after 1983, it was to have a continuing influence on the directions in which socialist economic thinking in Britain subsequently evolved.

What Keynesian social democracy offered was an alluring vision of socially harmonious material progress free from the depression and mass unemployment which had characterized the inter-war period. It held out the prospect of steadily rising real incomes, generalized affluence and, with a trade union movement occupying a position of strength in a tight labour market, a distribution of income more favourable to the working class. In addition, the social ownership of the commanding heights would prevent the capitalist abuse of economic power, while the full and efficient utilization of productive resources would facilitate the consensual pursuit of the redistributive policies necessary for the emergence of a more just and equitable social order. It would also furnish the revenue necessary for a sustained improvement in social welfare provision. Ultimately, as a writer such as Crosland saw it, these developments and the social reforms they would permit would make for the gradualist emergence of that social equality which, he believed, should be seen as the prime, distinguishing characteristic of a socialist society.

Yet, from the early 1970s, doubts were increasingly expressed as to the efficacy of the macroeconomic instruments by which this vision of the Keynesian social democrats was to be realized. These were voiced by a number of socialist writers, but received their most effective exposition in Michael Barrett Brown's *From Labourism to Socialism* (1972) and Stuart Holland's *The Socialist Challenge* (1975).[1] Brown highlighted the essence of the problem that concerned both writers and which, in one sense or another, has engaged the theoretical energies of democratic socialist political economists ever since. Thus he wrote that "in relating the power of the new trans-national companies to that of the state, we shall have to question the assumption . . . that the nation state is a viable framework for socialism".[2] The post-war period, and in particular the 1960s and early 1970s, had seen the rapid growth of transnational corporations (TNCs) whose decisions had had a profound impact on the fortunes of national economies. In their pursuit of profit maximization, these TNCs acted in a manner that emasculated or overrode the policies of national governments. Holland made the same point with specific reference to the increasing impotence of Keynesian policy instruments, writing in *The Socialist Challenge* that

> recent acceleration in the trend to monopoly and multinational capital has eroded Keynesian economic policies and undermined the sovereignty of the capitalist nation state. The trend has resulted in a new mesoeconomic power in between conventional macroeconomics and microeconomics. In compromising Keynesian economic management, the new meso-

---

1. Prefigured in Holland's *The State as Entrepreneur* (London: Weidenfeld & Nicolson, 1972) and his various contributions to the process of Labour Party policy formation in the early 1970s. For an incisive and detailed discussion of these see M. Hatfield, *The House the Left Built: Inside Labour Policy-Making, 1970–75* (London: Gollancz, 1978). For a more encompassing account of the emergence, rise and fall of the AES in the ranks of the labour movement see M. Wickham-Jones, *Economic Strategy and the Labour Party: Politics and Policy-making, 1970–83* (London: Macmillan, 1996).
2. M. B. Brown, *From Labourism to Socialism: A Political Economy for Labour in the 1970s* (Nottingham: Spokesman Books, 1972), p. 22.

economic power has compromised the gradualism of Keynesian social democracy.[3]

These instruments had been rendered ineffectual in a number of ways. At a macroeconomic level "demand orchestration" was "ruined" when "half the orchestra" could "either play another tune or get up and leave the national stage".[4] "Multinational capital" had the power to do just that. Confronted by deflationary policies that raised interest rates, it could use international connections to finance its plans from outside the national economy or simply relocate or expand its operations elsewhere. Similarly, if it was in its interests, it could remain unresponsive to those fiscal and monetary means that Keynesian governments used to invigorate or deflate national economies. This might occur, for example, where the economic cycle, by reference to which governments pursued their demand management strategies, moved out of line with the "supply management cycle of big business".[5] Governments and TNCs would be operating in relation to different time frames and, therefore, with different priorities. Where these conflicted, companies would act to ensure that corporate decision-making was informed by their view of things and their perception of advantage.

As regards macroeconomic management, TNCs could also act *ex ante* and *ex post* to weaken the impact of devaluation on export and import prices and thereby undermine its efficacy as a means of circumventing balance of payments difficulties. In addition, the oligopoly or monopolistic power wielded by the largest corporations could thwart those efforts at price control by which Keynesians had, intermittently, through the 1960s and 1970s, sought to dampen the inflationary pressures that were imperilling the efficacy and acceptability of demand management. In relation to the conduct of fiscal policy, too, transfer pricing between transnational subsidiaries allowed the manipulation of what was declared as taxable profit, and therefore provided a means by which the revenue-raising power of government could be weakened. This had implications for the conduct of demand management and also for the level of public expenditure in general. Thus the power to inflate or deflate profits in relation to the leniency or severity of the tax regime adversely affected the capacity to fund that crucial pillar of Keynesian social democracy – the welfare state.

There were also other ways in which such corporations could ignore or subvert the economic strategy of governments. As regards regional policy, because the "giant company" played a fundamental role in determining "when and where new investment shall take place", its decisions could seriously

---

3. S. Holland, *The Socialist Challenge* (London: Quartet, 1975), p. 9.
4. *Ibid*., p. 140.
5. S. Holland, *Beyond Capitalist Planning* (Oxford: Blackwell, 1978), p. 141.

exacerbate regional disparities in incomes and economic activity.[6] Subsidies, grants and tax allowances might persuade them for a time to locate in areas requiring economic rejuvenation, but their international, footloose nature also gave them the capacity to take the money and run.

Nor, of course, could socialists, as had Crosland, rely upon competition and market forces to operate as a curb on the economic power wielded by these large corporations. The fact was that "the development of giant companies ha[d] enabled them to replace not only the market determination of prices but also the market allocation of resources".[7] Such corporations governed the market, not vice versa.

Finally, in relation to the nation's general economic performance, the growing economic significance of such companies meant that, increasingly, 'the rate of investment, employment and innovation in the pace-setting sectors of the economy would be determined by companies that owe allegiance to no particular government".[8] Thus they were no longer susceptible to the kind of exhortations, blandishments and invocation of loyalties by which governments had traditionally sought to persuade them to particular courses of action. Manifestly, new commanding heights had emerged in the economy that were neither in public ownership nor amenable to public control.[9]

For proponents of the AES, and others, the impotence of Keynesian social democratic economic management was glaringly apparent by the 1970s. What characterized that decade was the unprecedented combination of rising, double-digit (by the mid-1970s) inflation and increasing unemployment which, by the end of the decade, had topped the one million mark. At the same time, the rate of growth of the British economy had slowed, while the periodic balance of payments problems that had been experienced throughout the post-war period had become unnervingly acute. What Keynesianism had promised was that western industrial economies need no longer suffer mass unemployment. The rational, scientific manipulation of aggregate demand by an apposite combination of monetary and fiscal policy would render it an evil of merely historical interest. There might be a price to pay in terms of creeping inflation, but that was a minor aberration which could be easily accommodated. However, inflation rates of the kind experienced in the 1970s could not be dismissed as of negligible significance, while they also ran in tandem with a seemingly inexorable rise in unemployment itself. The trade-off between inflation and unemployment seemed either no longer operative, or to be one that was effective only on economically catastrophic terms.

---

6. Brown, *From Labourism to Socialism*, p. 57.
7. *Ibid*, p. 40.
8. Holland, *The Socialist Challenge*, p. 96.
9. On this see also, for example, R. Murray, *Multinational Companies and Nation States* (Nottingham: Spokesman Books, 1977).

Further, by the mid-1970s, the problem of relative economic decline had become sufficiently pressing both to engender and to exacerbate many of the difficulties which wracked the British economy. Keynesian demand management had made no claims to enhance performance directly. Its essential objective was the full utilization of resources; that secured, market forces could be relied upon to ensure that they were efficiently deployed. Yet throughout the post-war period the growth of the British economy had lagged significantly behind its major industrial and, specifically, European rivals. The effects of this were various and profound, but were most obviously apparent in a faltering improvement in living standards and increasingly acute balance of payments crises, as British industry failed to deliver a volume of exports commensurate with the population's appetite for consumer durable imports. If, then, Keynesianism was impotent as regards the attainment of its traditional objectives, it was also a political economy that had little to offer directly to the fundamental problem of Britain's economic performance.

This deficiency was something that had been highlighted by Holland and others before the debacle of 1976. In 1972 he wrote that "while Keynesian policies may be effective in re-employing unemployed resources by increasing the level of demand, they are not properly suited to overcoming deficiencies in the structure of these resources". And again, in 1975, he wrote that "what is wrong is the failure of demand management to ensure a *focused* investment response".[10] Some Keynesians had, of course, recognized the legitimacy of such strictures and consideration had been given to a fusion of Keynesianism with some form of indicative planning.[11] However, this had borne only the wizened fruit of the 1965 National Plan, the failure of which provided solid evidence for many that Keynesian social democracy lacked the mastery of the levers of power necessary to attain its objectives.[12] The growth target of 4% was missed by some considerable margin, there was no palpable improvement in Britain's economic performance and the Wilson Labour government of 1966–70 was forced to resort to the traditional expedient of deflation, before reluctantly devaluing in 1967 to alleviate a deteriorating trade position.

If, for Keynesian social democracy, 1964–70 was farce, then 1974–9 was tragedy. For the proponents of the AES, this period provided further graphic illustration of the inevitable disasters for the working class and for socialism that were attendant upon adherence to an economic philosophy that contemporary economic developments had rendered defunct. Even the critics of Keynesian social democracy accepted that the period of its ideological ascendancy had been characterized by rising living standards, increased public expenditure on

---

10. Holland, *The State as Entrepreneur*, p. 6, my emphasis.
11. See, for example, R. F. Harrod, "Are Fiscal and Monetary Policy Enough?", *Economic Journal* **74** (1964), pp. 903–15.
12. Holland, *The Socialist Challenge*, p. 377.

education, welfare and the public services, and a trade union movement sufficiently powerful to secure a reasonable share for labour of the increasing flow of goods and services which a historically high and sustained rate of economic growth made available. However, the period 1974–9 was seen by them, and even by Keynesian social democrats, as being characterized by a substantial loss of the material ground which the working class had won in the post-war period. Both before and, in particular, in the aftermath of International Monetary Fund (IMF) intervention, there were cuts in public expenditure that ensured a continued rise in unemployment that both hit Labour's working-class constituency and threatened to weaken the bargaining position of trade unions. In addition, the negotiation of a "Social Contract" with the trade union movement to control wage increases represented, for many, a deliberate attempt to pass on to labour the costs of the macroeconomic adjustments necessary to circumvent Britain's immediate economic difficulties. Certainly, it severely curbed the freedom of manoeuvre of trade unions when it came to representing and advancing the material interests of their members.

"Whither the moral basis of socialism when social democrats perspiring with fear do the capitalist work of the International Monetary Fund for it?", asked Brian Sedgmore in 1977.[13] For, as he and others saw it, the consequence of adhering to a bankrupt economic philosophy was an assault on the interests of those whom the Labour Party had been created to defend – an assault mediated by a Labour government, even if ultimately directed by those outside its ranks who had the interests of international capital more obviously at heart. Devoid of the defensible theoretical underpinning that Keynesianism had previously provided, and stripped of their belief that the tools of demand management were any longer effective as a means of pursuing the goal of full employment, the Labour government succumbed through impotence, when it did not do so through intellectual conviction, to nostra inimical to social democratic reformism. Thus, for Aaronovitch, "the main criticism . . . of the 1974–79 Labour government [was] that it accepted the logic of Britain's dominant capitalist groups"; it sought to achieve the objectives of modernization and rationalization "without any major changes in class or social relationships" and, inevitably, that ensured "the costs of adjustment had to be borne by the working class".[14]

This meant, in effect, an acceptance of rising unemployment and a willingness to constrain and weaken the power of the trade union movement, either indirectly through an erosion of the labour market power derived from full employment or directly by means of a Social Contract which set limits to

---

13. B. Sedgemore, *The How and Why of Socialism* (Nottingham: Spokesman Books, 1977), p. 82.
14. S. Aaronovitch, *The Road from Thatcherism: The Alternative Economic Strategy* (London: Lawrence & Wishart, 1981), p. 14.

wage bargaining.[15] For Francis Cripps and Frances Morrell, "high unemployment was [therefore] a foreseeable and a foreseen outcome of the policies they
[the Labour government] stood for and . . . they consciously chose to implement those policies instead of others which could have sustained full employment".[16] As to the "Social Contract", "the main thrust of Labour government
policy", this, for Aaronovitch, was aimed at "cut[ting] real wages and redistri-
but[ing] resources from labour to capital".[17] Set in this context, the defeat of the
Labour government in May 1979 was simply the funeral of an economic
ideology already demonstrably moribund. In Tony Benn's words, it ended the
pretence "that welfare capitalism was possible, successful and permanent and
could melt away the conflict of interest between labour and capital".[18]

If the overarching macroeconomic rationale of Keynesian social democracy
came in for a severe pounding from the Left, both before and during the Wilson
and Callaghan governments of 1974–9, so too did its other component parts.
Thus the public corporation, which had been the primary means of extending
social ownership, was seen as failing in a number of fundamental respects as an
instrument of socialist advance. Again these criticisms had a long pedigree, but
they acquired a new force and intensity as the whole Keynesian social democratic project began to unravel. To begin with, there was the charge that the
firms that had been nationalized were located in those sectors of industry "that
capitalism, through lack of investment, ha[d] bankrupted". In this respect,
nationalization had been a means of securing substantial compensatory
payments "for otherwise unprofitable enterprises".[19] Further, once nationalized,
"industries have been subordinated to the needs and criteria of the private
sector . . . given the policies that successive governments have obliged the state
industries to pursue, they have become not staging posts for socialism but part
of the supply lines for capitalism".[20] They were run with the commercial
interests of the private sector in mind and, where it did not conflict with these,
in a manner that prevented them becoming a burden on the public purse.
Inevitably, this severely circumscribed the objectives they could pursue and the
purposes that they could be made to serve. Thus the need to supply goods and

15. For a discussion of the conduct of economic policy in this period and the origins and fate of
   the "Social Contract" see M. Holmes, *The Labour Government, 1974–79* (London: Macmillan,
   1985), M. Artis & D. Cobham (eds), *Labour's Economic Policies, 1974–79* (Manchester:
   Manchester University Press, 1991) and A. Britton, *Macroeconomic Policy in Britain, 1974–87*
   (Cambridge: Cambridge University Press, 1991).
16. F. Cripps & F. Morrell, "The Abandonment of Full Employment", in K. Coates (ed.), *What
   Went Wrong? Explaining the Fall of the Labour Government* (Nottingham: Spokesman Books,
   1979), p. 95.
17. Aaronovitch, *The Road from Thatcherism*, p. 15.
18. T. Benn, *Arguments for Democracy* (Harmondsworth: Penguin, 1981), p. 163; see also M. Prior
   & D. Purdy, *Out of the Ghetto* (Nottingham: Spokesman Books, 1979), p. 142.
19. Hobsbawm, "The Forward March of Labour Halted?", p. 35.
20. Conference of Socialist Economists, London Working Group, *The Alternative Economic
   Strategy: a Labour Movement Response to the Economic Crisis* (London: CSE Books, 1980), p. 26.

services to the private sector at profit-enhancing prices limited the extent to which they could generate, independently, the finance necessary for their own development and expansion. Even given the requisite political will and managerial resolve, they could not therefore be used to enhance British economic performance, let alone lay the basis for a socialist transformation of society. Also, given the relative autonomy that they enjoyed, they could not easily be made an integral part of a planned restructuring of the economy in the manner of French indicative planning. Further, for many of the AES Left, it was the "pressure to make them conform to 'commercial criteria' that also dictated the pursuit of policies which alienated workers and consumers alike", thereby destroying the possibility of popular support for the idea of social ownership.[21] Workers became alienated as they were forced to respond to the same imperatives that dictated the pace and organization of productive activity and levels of remuneration in capitalist corporations, and because they had little say in how nationalized enterprises were run, the nature of the products and services they furnished and the manner in which they were produced. Consumers were alienated because they were, in many instances, confronted by public enterprises that limited choice, imposed prices and were generally unresponsive to the wishes and concerns of those whom they supplied.[22]

Crucial here, in addition to commercial imperatives, was the monolithic nature of the national corporation whose day-to-day running and, therefore, effective direction, was in the hands of professional managers answerable only to the relevant minister in government. This produced a management structure which guaranteed that "decision-making was far removed from those who worked in it or who used it as consumers". In this respect "social democracy . . . created passive clients and workers by the form of nationalisation involved".[23] For many on the Left this was the essential failing of nationalization. It had assumed an authoritarian and undemocratic character. The corporations it had created were undemocratic both in terms of their decision-making structures and in relation to the communities they purportedly served.[24] The former explained the inability of public corporations to effect a transformation of working relationships and the latter their failure to respond to social needs and so win popular support.[25] It was this potent combination of impotence,

21. Aaronovitch, *The Road from Thatcherism*, p. 16.
22. Prior & Purdy wrote of "a large state sector . . . not democratically linked to the requirements of the mass of the people as it would be under a socialist system", *Out of the Ghetto*, p. 74; also R. Murray, "New Directions in Municipal Socialism", in Pimlott (ed.), *Fabian Essays*, p. 207.
23. Aaronovitch, *The Road to Thatcherism*, p, 16; P. Corrigan, "Popular Consciousness and Social Democracy", *Marxism Today* (December 1979), p. 15.
24. Prior & Purdy, *Out of the Ghetto*, p. 143; on this see also T. Benn, "Trade Unionism in the Eighties" (1983) in T. Benn (ed.), *Fighting Back: Speaking out for Socialism in the Eighties* (London: Hutchinson, 1988), p. 183.
25. As Tony Benn saw it, writing in 1980, "the nationalised industries established by Herbert Morrison after the war have been a great disappointment . . . Huge state corporations, run on

unpopularity and workforce alienation that, it was argued, had rendered public ownership ripe for the kind of populist counter-revolution that the New Right had encapsulated in the notion of "rolling back the frontiers of the state".

Many of these deficiencies of public corporations were also seen as being replicated in the welfare state. Here again, it was argued, there was a set of institutions whose socialist potential had been attenuated, or so corrupted, that the ends they served were essentially supportive of the capitalist system. The view of the post-war welfare state operating as an instrument of social control complementary to capitalist interests had, of course, a long, if primarily Marxist, pedigree, but it was widely and vigorously articulated by socialists in the late 1970s and early 1980s. As one such commentator opined, it was "important" for socialists

> to recognise the contradictory nature of the contemporary welfare state: it signals a collective responsibility for meeting an array of social problems and needs . . . but it achieves this *through a process of centralisation in which social needs are deformed and adapted to suit the requirements of capital* and to minimise democratic control.[26]

Welfare provision had been shaped by the needs of capital rather than its recipients. It was provided by means of hierarchically organized structures, that minimized the latter's ability to determine the nature of the services they received and the manner of their delivery. Further, it guaranteed the reproduction of capitalist social relations by ensuring a labour force and reserve army of labour that was made serviceable in terms of its health, skills, subsistence and basic accommodation. As one writer put it,

> although the services which were developed in education, health and housing, and social security improved the living conditions of the working class as a whole, their fundamental purpose for the ruling class . . . was to provide, physically and ideologically, the labour power that was necessary for continuing capitalist profitability in an increasingly competitive international market.[27]

Moreover, the undemocratic manner in which welfare provision was determined and delivered denied the working class the opportunity to create a

---

the very same economic criteria as private corporations under authoritarian management have altogether failed to realise the hopes of those who campaigned for public ownership", "Granada Guildhall Lecture", *New Statesman*, 16 May 1980.

26. I. Gough, "Thatcherism and the Welfare State", *Marxism Today* (July 1980), p. 12, my emphasis.

27. P. Leonard, "Restructuring the Welfare State", *Marxism Today* (December 1979), p. 8.

welfare state whose central purpose was to satisfy *their* interests and *their* needs rather than those of capital.[28] "Health services or education or social welfare [might] be greatly expanded but their control rests firmly in the hands of a professional or bureaucratic elite."[29]

As with nationalization, so with the welfare state, for the AES Left the crucial failure of Keynesian social democracy was rooted in the absence of democracy and a concomitant lack of "active and continuous involvement of people in the way the services work and their content".[30] Only such active involvement could preclude their deformation and adaptation to suit the needs of capital; only that could prevent such services being experienced as something alien, remote, imposed and unresponsive to working-class needs and so as a welfare state which was "theirs" not "ours".[31] Without it, "the national health service" would continue to be "run by oligarchies", "social security" would remain "a maze with far too much dependence on invidious tests of means" and "even services run by local authorities [would] tend to be remote and unresponsive to grassroots pressures".[32] Further, as regards their funding, democratic pressure was central to ensuring the level of public expenditure necessary for the maintenance or improvement of social welfare provision. Only the popular pressure which democratization could engender and channel would prevent a repetition of 1976, when the crisis of British capitalism was resolved at the expense of the welfare state and those who depended upon it.

In addition, for all its achievements, the welfare state had failed to effect that substantial redistribution of resources in favour of the working class which its socialist supporters had anticipated. Crosland may have argued otherwise in *The Future of Socialism* but, by the late 1950s and 1960s, the work of Townsend, Abel-Smith, Bosanquet and others had made it clear that the major beneficiaries of the welfare state were the middle classes. It was they who had unquestionably gained from whatever cross-class redistribution had occurred. Thus, in the early 1980s, it was "calculated that the higher professional classes g[ot] up to 40% more health service expenditure than working-class men and women when they f[ell] ill"; while, as regards non-compulsory education, it was similarly estimated that the better-off received half as much again as the poor.[33] In so far as the very poor had enjoyed an improvement in living

---

28. For arguments along these lines see, for example, I. Gough, *Political Economy and the Welfare State* (London: Macmillan, 1979), N. Ginsburg, *Class, Capital and Social Policy* (London: Macmillan, 1979) and Conference of Socialist Economists, State Group, *Struggle Over the State* (London: CSE Books, 1979).
29. Prior & Purdy, *Out of the Ghetto*, p. 80.
30. Aaronovitch, *The Road from Thatcherism*, p. 100.
31. "The welfare state has not been ours. Like the old poor law it is theirs." F. Cripps *et al.*, *Manifesto: A Radical Strategy for Britain's Future* (London: Pan, 1981), p. 76.
32. *Ibid.*, pp. 75–6.
33. *Ibid.*, p. 64. On this also see, for example, J. Le Grand, *The Strategy of Equality* (London: Allen & Unwin, 1981).

standards, their benefactors had been, effectively, the tax-paying working class, and, more generally, it was apparent that the growth of public spending which had occurred in the post-war years had been paid for disproportionately by workers on average or low wages. Surveys by a team of social investigators at Nuffield College in 1972 and 1974 confirmed this. They showed that the educational and welfare reforms of the 1940s had failed to make significant inroads into the class disparities in occupational opportunity and mobility which the pioneering surveys of Townsend *et al*. had identified in the 1950s.[34] In any case, as Townsend pointed out in the early 1980s, "people's needs [were] created and therefore poverty manufactured, by the society to which people belong[ed] – by its laws and conventions, market institutions and distribution of employment, housing and social amenities".[35] So whatever countervailing force in favour of equality might be exerted by the welfare state would almost inevitably be negated by the powerful inegalitarian forces which capitalism, and in particular the capitalism of Thatcherite Britain, unleashed. As many on the Left saw it, therefore, it was small wonder that disenchantment with the welfare state and social ownership should be so widespread by the late 1970s. And, indeed, a survey published in 1981 showed that while, in 1964, 57% had favoured the nationalization of more industries, by 1979 this figure had fallen to 32%, and that the number of people supporting higher spending on social services had halved over a comparable period.[36]

For the AES Left the absence of democratic participation and accountability were the besetting sins of Keynesian social democracy. It was these that were at the root of its failure to enlist the support of the working class in defence of the welfare state and, more generally, it was the absence of democratic involvement in the whole social democratic reform programme which had allowed it to be jettisoned with negligible political repercussions in 1976. The point was neatly encapsulated by Paul Corrigan when he wrote in 1979, shortly after Labour's defeat, that

> the history of social democratic reform of the state has taught us, I believe, that by and large the centralisation of the implementation of state policy provides an arena where the working class finds it difficult to discover a full and active role . . . the specific content of reforms cannot be defended by the working class when they come under attack since those reforms are extremely distant from the lives of working people . . . all the reforms so far implemented have failed to provide any continuing democratic

---

34. On this and related matters see J. Goldthorpe *et al., Social Mobility and Class Structure in Modern Britain* (Oxford: Clarendon, 1980).
35. P. Townsend, "A Taste of Dr Owen's Medicine", *New Statesman*, 30 January 1981.
36. I. Crewe, "The Labour Party and the Electorate", in P. Kavanagh (ed.), *The Politics of the Labour Party* (London: Allen & Unwin, 1982).

experience for working people: experiences that will assist them in seeing their full role as a future ruling class.[37]

By its very nature, therefore, Keynesian social democracy had failed to create that political constituency and those social forces that might have ensured an effective defence of its achievements during a period of crisis. Rather it, and democratic socialism in general, had become identified with the authoritarian, impersonal, bureaucratic use of state power to negligible egalitarian effect but considerable economic cost.

What the AES Left provided, therefore, was a comprehensive critique of the ideological paradigm which had dominated democratic socialist political economy in the post-war period and the institutions and practices that it had spawned. The macroeconomic instruments of Keynesian social democracy were shown to be ineffectual; its extension of social ownership was portrayed as undemocratic and as failing to engender support for the socialist project or to provide the institutional means of rejuvenating the British economy; and its attempts to protect the population from the full rigours of market forces by way of the welfare state had failed on the grounds of equity and efficiency, creating institutions and a bureaucracy insensitive and unaccountable to those they putatively served. What this critique also encapsulated was an elucidation of the course of post-war British economic history that explained relative economic decline in terms of Keynesian social democracy's failure to secure and democratize those sources of economic power whose use would have pemitted a structural transformation of the British economy.[38] Here, specifically, the point was made that there had been no attempt to harness or even curb the economic power of the TNCs whose decisions had had such a profound, and often adverse, impact on the course of Britain's economic development. Nor had there been any effort, by way of the extension of industrial democracy, to engage the energies of the workforce in that fundamental transformation of the structure, operation and performance of industry that was imperative if Britain's declining economic fortunes were to be reversed.

In prescriptive terms the AES offered a very different vision of the economic road to the New Jerusalem from that of Keynesian social democracy. In truth, however, what ultimately emerged was not one but several alternative economic strategies. These ranged from a regenerated corporatist Keynesianism, to a conception of the Strategy as setting decisively in motion a fundamental, democratic socialist transformation of the state and civil society. In this regard, under the umbrella of the AES, socialists articulated a multiplicity of policies

---

37. P. Corrigan, "The Local State: The Struggle for Democracy", *Marxism Today* (July 1979), p. 209.
38. Benn, *Arguments for Democracy*, p. 216.

with a plurality of emphases. As Fine saw it, "support for the AES cover[ed] a multitude of sinners".[39] Or, as another commentator insisted, "it is helpful to treat the AES not as a programme but as a field of debate", and that was certainly an accurate categorization of its history and evolution.[40] It seemed at times like a rolling democratic socialist roadshow and seminar combined; one which, for a while, was permissively wide-ranging enough to allow the participation of a broad coalition of Left political and intellectual forces. Thus the AES was conceived, variously,

> as a cure for economic decline, as a socialist programme, as the start of a struggle for socialism, as a programme that is democratic and radical without being socialist, as a mobilizer of broad support for the socialist idea, as a way of tipping the resolution of the economic crisis in favour of the working class and against capital, as a way of establishing enclaves of socialist production and working class power in a socialist society, or as a way of generating a revolutionary socialist mass movement.[41]

This eclecticism of conception was, in part, its strength but it was, too, one of the major causes of its eventual demise. As Peter Kellner pointed out, with reference to *The New Hope for Britain*, the 1983 Labour manifesto which encapsulated many of the central elements of the AES, it provided a basis for "drawing the party's competing factions together" but was "wholly unsuited to the very different task of inviting voters to contemplate what a Labour government would actually do".[42]

However, while acknowledging the diversity of the theoretical and prescriptive currents of which the AES was composed, it must be said nonetheless that these contributions were made within what a contemporary commentator referred to as "a fairly loose *but carefully structured framework*";[43] one which distinguished it markedly from Keynesian social democracy, while still allowing it to accommodate the latter's full employment/demand management and redistributive aspirations. In that respect the AES may be said to have transcended rather than simply replaced what had been the prevailing democratic socialist paradigm.

The central stanchion of the prescriptive dimension of that "structural framework" was the democratic reconfiguration of the sources and patterns of

---

39. B. Fine, "The British Economic Disaster: Review Article", *Capital and Class* **13** (1981), p. 149; another commentator wrote of there being "several alternative economic programmes", D. Swartz, "The Eclipse of Politics: The Alternative Economic Strategy as Socialist Strategy", *Capital and Class* **13** (1981), p. 103.
40. A. Sharples, "The Politics of the Alternative Economic Strategy", *Marxism Today* (April 1981), p. 25.
41. Aaronovitch, *The Road from Thatcherism*, pp. 6–7.
42. P. Kellner, "Labour Pays the Price for Too Much Unity", *New Statesman*, 3 June 1983.
43. Sharples, "The Politics", p. 26, my emphasis.

power within the British economy. While the degree of emphasis that this received, and the manner in which it was to be accomplished, varied, this objective nonetheless permeated all aspects of the political economy of the AES Left. For Meacher, it was the "regular use of power by the dominant established class in Britain, in favour of its own class interest, that constitute[d] the central impediment that ha[d] brought about and prevent[ed] escape from Britain's persisting economic decline". "The idea", therefore, "that we can get sustained economic growth in the interests of the people and under their control without changes in their social and property relations" was, for an AES supporter such as Aaronovitch, "an illusion."[44] "In the last analysis", wrote Meacher, "Britain's economic strategy is not a matter of economic theory, of whether one model is right and another wrong, but a class question and a power question."[45] For what bound Britain "to the current economic orthodoxy is obviously not the clear and demonstrable success of those policies but the fact that they reflect the interests, in both ideological and power terms, of the dominant economic elite."[46]

What was needed, therefore, in the often quoted words of the Labour Party's *Programme, 1973*, was a "fundamental and irreversible shift in the balance of power and wealth in favour of working people and their families".[47] Some protagonists of the AES considered that this might be effected in a Fabian spirit which did not provoke a vigorous and obstructive response from those whose power would be attenuated. But, for others, there was a recognition of, and indeed an enthusiasm for, the social conflict which would be provoked. Thus the London Group of the Conference of Socialist Economists (CSE) stressed that "the central demands of the AES . . . would necessarily conflict with the interests of big capital" and that the response of AES supporters must necessarily be "aggressive, attacking the power of big capital domestically and through its foreign connections" with a view to "further and more decisive struggles until the power of private capital had been destroyed".[48] For Rowthorn, too, "the AES [was] just part of a much wider attack on the power and privileges of the upper classes", though he recognized that this fact was "often neglected" by many "supporters of the AES who usually present it in purely economic terms, and fail to point out how it links up with the wider movement for social reform".[49]

Yet whether the possibility of conflict was trumpeted or muted, the fact remained that the AES aimed, primarily, to effect a fundamental socialization

---

44. M. Meacher, *Socialism with a Human Face: The Political Economy of Britain in the 1980s* (London: Allen & Unwin, 1982), p. 36; Aaronovitch, *The Road from Thatcherism*, p. 47.
45. Meacher, *Socialism with a Human Face*, p. 196.
46. *Ibid.*, p. 223.
47. Reiterated in Labour Party, *Labour's Programme, 1982* (London: Labour Party, 1982), p. 4.
48. Quoted in D. Webster, *Labour and the New Left*, Fabian Tract 477 (London: Fabian Society, 1981), p. 14.
49. B. Rowthorn, "The Politics of the Alternative Economic Strategy", *Marxism Today* (January 1981), p. 5.

and democratization of economic decision-making, the former being seen as a necessary but not a sufficient condition for the latter. This extension of social ownership was viewed by the AES Left as a primary means of giving to a democratically elected Labour government the power to implement that transformative strategy which the British economy so signally required. Such power had been manifestly absent after 1965, when Labour's National Plan showed clearly that without it the road to failure was paved with the frustrated expectations of those who believed you could substitute good intentions for effective policy instruments. A substantial extension of public ownership and social control of economic activity was seen as a fundamental means of rectifying this. "Our social and economic objectives can be achieved only through an expansion of common ownership substantial enough to give the community decisive power over the commanding heights of the economy."[50] Opinion might vary as to what constituted the commanding heights and, therefore, the necessary extent of public ownership, but the general objective was one to which all AES supporters adhered.[51] Also, while opinion might vary, from the mid-1970s onwards many pressed for the nationalization of between 20 and 25 major companies in sectors, such as electronics, pharmaceuticals and health equipment, which were profitable, rapidly growing and at the technological cutting edge.[52] Ownership of these would reside in a National Enterprise Board (NEB) that would, in addition, use public funds "to create new companies and new science-based industries . . . using new public enterprise to lead the way".[53] What was envisaged, in effect, was the creation of highly competitive public companies that would in themselves improve economic performance but would also, in an oligopolistic context, spur the private sector to follow suit. In addition, the NEB would take an equity stake in key private sector firms whose strategic position and, therefore, performance, were seen as important. In this way, it would secure the requisite leverage to ensure that such firms acted in a manner consistent with the economic objectives of a rolling, five-year plan formulated by a National Planning Council (NPC). The NEB would, in effect, perform the role of a holding company similar to the Istituto per la Recostruzione Italiano (IRI), which writers like Holland saw as having played a crucial part in transforming the performance of the Italian economy.[54] Further, this holding company would be able to pool the expertise of those enterprises

---

50. Labour Party, *Labour's Programme 1982*, p. 9.
51. On the evolution of thinking on public ownership within the Labour Party in the 1970s see Hatfield, *The House the Left Built*, pp. 79ff.
52. This number was seen as ensuring a state presence in all the Standard Industrial Classification categories.
53. Labour Party, *The New Hope for Britain: Labour's Manifesto* (London: Labour Party, 1983), p. 1.
54. As with so many of the ideas which the AES embodied, this again had its origins in the late 1960s and early 1970s, with figures such as Richard Pryke, Michael Posner and Stuart Holland and the Labour Party's Public Sector Group, formed in 1971, making a substantial contribution to Left thinking.

over which it enjoyed control and, therefore, offer a general range of supportive services to increase efficiency and instil best practice. In this respect it would also enhance the performance of those enterprises that remained wholly in the private sector.

As regards the financial sector there were, again, degrees of radicalism. Some argued in favour of the extension of public ownership to insurance companies, pension funds and the merchant banks, and even for a significant incursion into the clearing bank sector.[55] There were many variations on this AES theme, with other proposals, such as those coming from the Trades Union Congress (TUC) and from within the Labour Party, being less radical and giving less emphasis to the extension of public ownership and more to the hardy perennial of a National Investment Bank (NIB), which would, among other sources of funds, tap into a proportion of insurance company and pension fund deposits.[56] The AES was also envisaged as exercising control over bank lending to ensure a greater commitment to long-term investment in British manufacturing; something historically absent from the City's relationship with indigenous industry. Thus "a [contemporary] survey of the early seventies showed that 73% of borrowing by non-financial enterprises [in Britain] was short-term. In France, Italy and Germany the proportions were 49%, 47% and 30% respectively."[57]

"Hitherto the mixed economy ha[d] been unbalanced by the restriction of the public sector to basic utilities and often declining industries dependent for their growth on private manufacturing demand and further hamstrung by the discriminatory pricing policies imposed against them."[58] Henceforward, social ownership would cease to be simply an institutional means of rationalizing, at public expense, failed areas of the private sector. It would no longer be limited to those industries that required rejuvenation or lacked the capacity to determine the economic shape of things to come. It would be associated with growth not decay and become a means of securing the power to make decisions in those sectors whose economic significance was expanding. In the words of the Labour Party's 1982 *Programme*, "the public sector should be substantially extended to include profitable firms in key sectors of industry and finance".[59] The balance of power was to be shifted decisively in favour of public ownership: "Our social and economic objectives can be achieved only through an expansion of common

---

55. See, for example, R. Minns, *Taking Over the City: The Case for Public Ownership of Financial Institutions* (London: Pluto, 1982); "an attack upon the position of the banks and insurance companies should be central to the policies of the future Labour government", R. Minns, "Challenging the Bankers", *New Statesman*, 21 August 1981; see also the views of the Conference of Socialist Economists as expressed in *The Alternative Economic Strategy*.
56. Again there were different views aired by AES supporters over the extent of the NIB's powers and the sources from which it would secure its funding. The idea of the state establishing a public bank was also mooted by the Labour Party.
57. Minns, "Challenging the Bankers".
58. Meacher, *Socialism with a Human Face*, p. 177.
59. Labour Party, *Labour's Programme 1982*, p. 48.

ownership substantial enough to give the community decisive power over the commanding heights of the economy". The *Programme* went on to quote Aneurin Bevan's view that while "the victory of socialism need not be universal to be decisive . . . it is a requisite of social stability that one type of property ownership should dominate. In the society of the future it should be public property." The "longer term goal" must be "to replace the bulk of private ownership by these diverse forms of common ownership". For only that would "provid[e] the essential foundations for a democratic socialist Britain".[60]

Whatever else can be said about the proponents of the AES, they were serious about the business of power – getting it, keeping it, using it. Theirs was a political economy which was conscious of the causes and past consequences of policy impotence. While Keynesian social democrats believed that the existing structures of economic authority could be left intact, their coercive powers mitigated by redistributive measures, selective public ownership and the maintenance of full employment, the AES Left saw those very structures as the cause of increasing mass unemployment, growing disparities of wealth and income, intensifying social antagonism and a relative economic decline which would exacerbate all of these trends. Crosland predicated social transformation upon the rising material prosperity which Keynesian social democracy guaranteed; in contrast, the supporters of the AES saw a socialist transformation of the bases and use of power as the fundamental prerequisite of a generalized and egalitarian affluence. Only once the economic sources of class power had been eroded, circumscribed or altogether removed could economic decline be arrested and the material well-being of the working class be prioritized and secured.

As to reversing decline, the economic power which a substantial extension of public ownership in the industrial and financial sectors would bring would at last create the capacity for effective planning.[61] Outright nationalization, equity stakes and the promotion of new public enterprises would provide ownership of productive capacity on a scale and of a nature sufficient to give the NEB potency as a planning instrument. By the same token the NIB, even in its less radical versions, through its control over the scale and direction of financial flows into British industry, would also be able to act as an effective mediator of the planning decisions emanating from the NPC.

Of course, this left a considerable range of economic activity and formidable centres of economic power whose decision-making could not be easily rendered consistent with planning objectives in this overtly directive manner. Here, the concept of the "planning agreement" was to have a critical role. This idea was variously conceived by the AES Left, but received what was in many

---

60. *Ibid.*, p. 9.
61. The link was clearly made in *ibid.*, p. 9.

respects its definitive expression in a Department of Trade paper drafted by Tony Benn in 1974:

> The basic objective of the planning agreements system is to secure the conformity of leading companies with national economic priorities, in return for supporting requested industrial developments, giving financial assistance etc. The basis for such agreements will therefore include such criteria as price control, the level of home and overseas sales, the regional distribution of employment, domestic investment levels, industrial relations practices and product development. These agreements will need to be on a tripartite basis with the unions involved at the outset. Once corporate policies in these areas have been agreed on an annual and rolled-forward five-year basis, the government would be in a position to grant selective financial assistance for at least the minimum period necessary to meet the demands of medium-term corporate planning . . . The information from them will then be available to the government in planning its own strategy . . . this new conditional system . . . will form an important instrument in securing the compliance of large multinational corporations with the government's own economic objectives.[62]

The National Plan of 1965 was seen to have failed for many reasons but, in particular, because it lacked teeth. It had been genuinely and narrowly *indicative* in a way that, for example, French "indicative" planning had never been. It had indicated what would need to happen and what would be the consequences of an historically, for Britain, unparalleled 4% rate of growth, but it had no means of ensuring that private enterprise acted in a manner consistent with this central objective or, for that matter, any others which it established. Planning agreements, in combination with a much expanded public sector, would furnish such means.

As applied to 100 major companies, operating in what remained of the private sector, they were to do so in a number of ways.[63] First, and fundamentally, such agreements would provide a flow of the kind of economic information needed to ensure the pursuit of corporate objectives consistent with the National Plan and to identify what changes in corporate behaviour had to occur if planning goals were to be attained. There was here a recognition that, for planners, knowledge was power, and the kind of information flow which planning agreements would provide was the *sine qua non* of effective economic policy-making.

---

62. Quoted in Aaronovitch, *The Road from Thatcherism*, p. 63.
63. "We propose to bring large companies within the planning system by requiring them to negotiate with government Agreed Development Plans covering key issues in the development of the economy", Labour Party, *Labour's Programme 1982*, p. 40.

Secondly, planning agreements provided a framework within which incentives and coercion could be applied to firms to make certain that they acted in a manner consistent with national planning objectives: to ensure that they adhered to price controls, embarked on job-creating investment, located productive capacity in particular areas, tailored output to enhance export performance, invested in technological innovation or engaged in the production of the import-substituting goods necessary to staunch a haemorrhage of purchasing power from the domestic economy. Compliance would attract financial rewards and recalcitrance the removal of government support or, if necessary, the appointment of an "official trustee" to the board of the offending company or, *in extremis*, its outright nationalization. "Agreed development plans with all leading companies" were a way of ensuring that they "play[ed] a constructive role in supporting the national plan and our plans for individual regions and sectors".[64]

Thirdly, the idea of planning agreements embodied the notion of a radical extension of industrial democracy both as an end in itself and as a potent means of ensuring that private capital acted in a manner which facilitated the pursuit of planning goals. If the AES was about power, it was also, for the AES Left, about its democratization. As Benn made clear, planning agreements were to be the product of tripartite negotiations "with unions involved at the outset". They would, therefore, establish a means by which workforces could, with the information statutorily available to them, play an important part in enterprise decision-making. Further, from the point of view of compliance, this democratization was seen as a means by which trade unions could ensure that private enterprise did not subvert the planning process and thence the policies of a democratically elected Labour government.

There was also, particularly in Labour Party policy documents, a macro conception of the "democratization" of planning. Specifically, there was to be trade union involvement in a National Economic Assessment that would consider, in broad terms, what distribution of income was consistent with macroeconomic planning objectives. In the words of the Labour Party's 1982 *Programme,* this Assessment was seen as "com[ing] to embrace such issues as the share of the national income going to profits, to earnings from employment, to interest, to social benefits and to other incomes" and would "also . . . take a view on the movement of costs and prices which will support and sustain expansion and will be compatible with our economic and social objectives".[65] And all this, it was accepted, could only be done with trade union involvement. Only the participation and support of the trade union movement would make possible

---

64. Labour Party, *The New Hope for Britain*, p. 11. At this juncture the term "agreed development plans" was preferred to "planning agreements".
65. Labour Party, *Labour's Programme 1982*, p. 24.

non-inflationary full employment and, over time, rising living standards and better-funded public services. In discussion of these measures, some were prepared here to use the term "incomes policy" or "conditional incomes policy". Others preferred to talk of "the planned growth of incomes". But whatever the favoured epithet, the trade union movement was clearly envisaged as having a fundamental role to play.[66]

Of course, for some on the AES Left there seemed, in these schemes, to be a very real danger of a rejuvenated or reconstituted corporatism. It might be a corporatism that gave greater power to the trade union movement, but, none-theless, it would still involve merely the more effective management of capitalism. As such, it would still preclude, or make highly problematic, the business of socialist transformation, it would obstruct the growth of a socialist consciousness among the working class and deny workers direct access to the real levers of economic power. Yet, once again, planning agreements were seen as providing a potential antidote to a trade-union-hierarchy-mediated incorporation of the working class into the corrupting business of capitalist macroeconomic management. This was so because they allowed workers, at a grassroots level, to make significant inroads into the privileges and prerogatives of management and thence into the very heart of capitalist power, something that would impinge upon and shape the planning process.

Thus Hodgson saw trade unions being "involved in setting up planning agreements and . . . using the provisions of the legislation to enforce certain investment and production proposals on management. An extended planning agreements system could help to increase productivity, whilst widening workers' participation in production."[67] Again, for Meacher,

> the relevance of planning agreements for the workforce is that it extends joint decision-making into areas traditionally beyond the scope of collective bargaining . . . since planning agreements can only work effectively if they have won trade union and workers' co-operation, they represent a highly significant extension of the industrial franchise.[68]

In effect, they would establish the basis for "joint control at company and plant level between local management and trade union/worker representatives over

---

66. Cripps *et al.*, *Manifesto*, p. 146; G. Hodgson, *Labour at the Crossroads: The Political and Economic Challenge to the Labour Party into the 1980s* (London: Martin Robertson, 1981), p. 212. See also Prior & Purdy, *Out of the Ghetto*, p. 129 and D. Purdy, "The Social Contract and Social Policy", in M. Prior (ed.), *The Popular and the Political* (London: Routledge, 1981), pp. 110–11, on the manner in which the idea of a "Social Contract" could be articulated to embrace the democratization of decision-making at micro- and macroeconomic levels. For similar ideas on this to those of Purdy see G. Hodgson, *Socialist Economic Strategy*, Labour Party Discussion Series, No. 2 (Leeds: ILP, 1979), p. 36.
67. Hodgson, *Labour at the Crossroads*, p. 202.
68. Meacher, *Socialism with a Human Face*, pp. 179, 180.

all those industrial decisions now unilaterally determined by management outside the current scope of collective bargaining".[69] The same point was made in the 1983 Labour Party manifesto, *New Hope for Britain*, which saw "agreements" as "link[ing] planning at all levels firmly to a radical extension of industrial democracy".[70] Planning agreements would confer new rights of information, consultation, representation and decision-making on the workforces in private companies, making those companies accountable to those whom they employed as well as to the community as a whole in the guise of the NPC.

There was, of course, a crucial tension here in the AES strategy, which critics were quick to highlight, between its centralizing and decentralizing aspects. On the one hand there were the NEB, the NIB and the NPC; the first, for example, owning a substantial proportion of the nation's productive capacity and also acting as the "nerve-centre of a national network of planning agreements", embracing all those large companies which were not already in public ownership.[71] On the other hand there was a trade union movement and individual workforces which, it was anticipated, would increasingly erode managerial prerogatives, exercising decision-making power with respect to investment, development, marketing, mergers, the organization of the productive process and the allocation of resources within enterprises. Workplace organizations were to wield considerable authority as regards the formulation and implementation of planning agreements, and, therefore, their decisions would inevitably impinge upon, as well as help to give effect to, those of national planning institutions. Of course, the theory was that trade unions and workplace organizations would act as mediators of the information necessary for planning, as the guarantors of its accuracy and as the initiators and monitors of plan implementation. But with the best fraternal will in the world, the scope for conflict between the ideal of dispersing power, and rendering its use accountable to the workforce, and the centralization of power to give a potency and effectiveness to policy-making that it had manifestly lacked during the ascendancy of Keynesian social democracy, was, to say the least, considerable.

For many supporters of the AES, too, the involvement of the workforce in every area of decision-making within a company or industry was to be merely the prelude to an extensive and decisive move in the direction of full workers' control. To "make a reality of democracy in industry" it was vital to move "towards worker control of private companies". Such democratization would also entail "thoroughly socialising the existing nationalised industries", giving to the workforce in public corporations the same participative and decision-

---

69. M. Meacher, "Models not Rhetoric", *New Statesman*, 14 August 1981.
70. Labour Party, *The New Hope for Britain*, p. 11.
71. R. Jenkins, *Tony Benn: A Political Portrait* (London: Writers and Readers Publishing Co-operative, 1980), p. 169.

making powers as those which they would possess when workers' control had transformed the private sector.[72] Such developments were also seen as imperative if the re-emergence of a reconstituted corporatism was to be obviated.[73]

Yet, whatever the disparate aspirations with which they were infused, planning agreements, in the context of the AES, were clearly to play a key role in the process of democratizing economic planning and thence effecting a transference of power to the working class. Herein, for many, indeed one might argue for most of its supporters, lay the essence and fundamental radicalism of the AES. In the Fabian tradition of a technocratically informed spirit of social service, Keynesian social democrats had been in favour of taking and using certain macroeconomic powers for social ends. What many AES supporters sought was something more profoundly transformative. They took the notion of democracy seriously: first, by way of dispersing economic power so that all might participate in the decisions that shaped their lives and those of the society in which they lived;[74] secondly, by opening up national planning and its institutions to the influence and inputs of the labour movement; and thirdly, by giving a democratically elected Labour government a popular authority, with respect to economic policy-making, which it had signally lacked in the 1960s and 1970s. So, in adhering to the central elements of this strategy, the Labour Party, for the first and perhaps the only time in its post-war history, gave pre-eminence, at least *in abstracto*, to the business of transferring the levers of economic power from the hands of private capital into those of Labour's social constituency and its political representatives.

For many AES supporters, this democratization of economic life was also seen as vital to that planned restructuring of the British economy which would play a crucial part in levering Britain out of the economic crisis and reversing the continuing relative decline which Keynesian social democracy had failed to arrest.[75] Here there were two notions. To begin with there was the view that participation of the workforce in the process of planning by way of "agreements" would provide a flow of information and innovative ideas that would both expedite the process of planning and, equally importantly, allow workers

72. Labour Co-ordinating Committee, *There is an Alternative: Policies for Prosperity in the Eighties* (London, n.d.), p. 12.
73. See here, for example, the Conference of Socialist Economists, *The Alternative Economic Strategy*, p. 20.
74. As Tony Benn saw it, the AES was about "the diffusion of power through greater democracy", *Arguments for Democracy*, p. 223.
75. One formulation of this view is apparent in TUC policy documents produced during the late 1970s and early 1980s; see, for example, TUC, *Plan for Growth* (London: TUC, 1981). Thus P. Wintour wrote of "TUC papers . . . propos[ing] a . . . technocratic justification" of industrial democracy, which centred on "enabling Britain to compete more effectively in world markets", "Driving Under the Influence", *New Statesman*, 31 July 1981.

to internalize planning objectives. In this respect, the democratization of decision-making would create the popular identification with planning goals that was vital for their attainment. In addition, it was believed that the heightened commitment to their productive tasks of a workforce participating in enterprise and, through their trade unions, national decision-making would help engender that marked increase in productivity needed to accelerate economic growth and transform Britain's competitive position in world markets. The AES therefore embodied a "recognition of the importance of the team at work and of collective and interactive effort";[76] labour efficiency being viewed here as, in considerable measure, a function of worker involvement in the production process and the *esprit de firm* which that created.[77]

So, like the New Right, and in contrast to Keynesian social democrats, the AES Left accepted that Britain's economic difficulties were largely a consequence of supply-side failures. They were a function of the deficient quality and commitment of labour. They were a consequence of inadequate and misdirected capital investment. They were a product of structural deficiencies and the political impotence and entrepreneurial failings that had allowed these to persist. As Hodgson put it in 1980, in consequence of the ascendancy of the AES "the emphasis of the economic strategy of the Labour Party" had come to rest "on the 'supply side' of the economy. In other words it aims at a transformation of the social relations of production both to humanise and democratise work *and to increase output and productivity*."[78] "Simple, short-term demand management [was] inadequate for dealing with structural problems of industry. The Tories [were] right in recognising the need to act on the 'supply side'."[79] However, while the Conservatives' policies took the form of tax cuts and untrammelled markets, those of the AES would involve the substantial extension of social ownership, the democratization of power wielded both by enterprises and policy-makers, the purposive planning of economic activity and substantial public control over the investment activity of financial intermediaries. Only thus could a supply-side revolution be effected and a higher rate of growth in labour productivity be sustained.

The AES was therefore, at one level, most definitely concerned with the economic rejuvenation of Britain. Yet while in no sense discounting the purely material advantages to be derived from the effective democratization of economic and social life, some of its advocates saw the ultimate goal as the creation of an economic system organized on a different basis and with reference to different economic principles than those which prevailed under

---

76. Hodgson, *Labour at the Crossroads*, p. 199.
77. Meacher, *Socialism with a Human Face*, p. 158.
78. Hodgson, *Labour at the Crossroads*, p. 209, my emphasis.
79. Conference of Socialist Economists, *The Alternative Economic Strategy*, p. 136.

capitalism – one which would, therefore, call conventional capitalist conceptions of prosperity into question. For such proponents of the AES, democratization would, they believed, allow decisions to be made by reference to non-market criteria using information other than that which market activity generated. Thus "through . . . the democratic planning process" it should be possible to "develop a new idea of what prosperity is and what economic growth is for".[80] "The point of democracy", wrote Francis Cripps, "is to change the criteria and pressures under which decisions are made." What this meant was that the role of profit as the sole or primary guide to the allocation of resources and productive activity would be diminished.[81] Correspondingly that of social need, as expressed through the channels that the democratization of economic life created, would grow in significance. As it was phrased in *New Hope for Britain*, "the profit test would have to make way for the human test".[82] This would necessitate the evolution of "a strategy to define the kind of employment which ought to exist in a socialist society. There must be wide-spread . . . debate about how we can create more jobs *of the kind which everyone recognises to be socially useful, productive and satisfactory to the people who undertake them.*"[83]

Examples of such strategies already existed at a microeconomic level. A number of workers' organizations had formulated production plans that sought to link productive capacity more directly to social requirements, rather than the maximization of profit. In the early 1980s, the most often cited of these was that produced by the workers at Lucas Aerospace whose combine committee of 13 unions covering 17 sites had, in the context of the threat of major restructuring and redundancies, drafted an alternative plan for the company.[84] This technically detailed, economically sophisticated, comprehensive corporate plan suggested a reorientation of Lucas' manufacturing capacity from the production of armaments-related products, for which it was believed there was a diminishing demand, to the production of equipment which satisfied manifest social needs – in particular, those related to public health. Lucas provided evidence, therefore, of how the democratization of corporate decision-making might operate in practice, with worker-controlled firms making decisions, allocating resources

---

80. Labour Co-ordinating Committee, *There is an Alternative*, p. 9.
81. Cripps *et al.*, *Manifesto*, p. 127; see also Conference of Socialist Economists, *The Alternative Economic Strategy*, p. 44.
82. Labour Party, *The New Hope for Britain*, p. 5.
83. Cripps *et al.*, *Manifesto*, p. 181, my emphasis.
84. Lucas Aerospace Confederation Trade Union Committee, *Lucas Aerospace: Turning Industrial Decline into Expansion – A Trade Union Initiative* (London, LACTUC, 1979); Lucas Aerospace Shop Stewards' Combine Committee, *Lucas: An Alternative Plan* (Nottingham: Spokesman Pamphlet, 1978). On this see also H. Wainwright & D. Elliott, *The Lucas Plan: A New Trade Unionism in the Making* (London: Allison & Busby, 1982), D. Elliott, *The Lucas Aerospace Workers' Campaign* (London: Young Fabian Pamphlet, 1977) and M. Cooley & H. Wainwright, "The Lucas Plan: Its Lessons for Labour", *New Socialist* **2** (1981), pp. 13–16.

and organizing production by reference to criteria other than that, solely, of profitability. Furthermore, while the Lucas Plan was particularly impressive, it was only one of a number of examples of such alternative corporate planning in the late 1970s and early 1980s.[85]

It was in the general context of such thinking that alternative non-market measures of the efficient use of resources, such as the social audit, were mooted by AES supporters. For, it was argued, only through the application of social-cost–benefit analyses would it be possible to "get beyond the criteria of private profitability while retaining some kind of social efficiency in the allocation of resources".[86] For example, it was believed that with the notion of a social rather than a market audit of efficiency in play, the way was open for modes of economic calculation which would ensure that "the full, finite resource and environmental costs of all goods and services would be reflected in their prices".[87]

Also, for many on the AES Left, democratization was about more than the pursuit of narrowly economic objectives. It was at root about socialist trans-formation. Democratization might improve economic performance; it might enhance economic prosperity and prospects; it might make for a more rational and ordered economy with goals and means more clearly articulated and more generally understood; but it was also seen as calling into question existing social relations. It called into doubt the necessity for the existing distribution of power, the competence of those in whose hands that power resided and the effectiveness and manner in which they used it. In short, it called into question, and through the deliberate erosion of managerial prerogatives it challenged, the existing class basis of economic authority.[88]

The democratization of economic life which the AES Left sought was also seen as the key to inculcating that sense of working-class empowerment and self-confidence which was a fundamental prerequisite for any transfiguration of existing economic and social relations. It would instil a popular conviction that socialism could be brought into being by the working class itself. Thus Meacher wrote of it "converting the experience of alienation and the feel of exploitation into a clearly formulated idea of a non-exploitative free society".[89] In this view of things, democratization was a *sine qua non* for the making of socialists. For only when the working population, through its participation in the process of economic decision-making, had acquired a sense of a truly free

---

85. Published examples include the Institute for Workers' Control Motor Group, *A Workers' Inquiry into the Motor Industry* (London: CSE Books, 1979), Speke Joint Shop Stewards' Committee, *Dunlop, Jobs for Merseyside: A Trade Union Report*, S.1.: The Committee, 1979 and H. Beynon & H. Wainwright, *The Workers' Report on Vickers* (London: Pluto, 1979).
86. Conference of Socialist Economists, *The Alternative Economic Strategy*, p. 70.
87. Meacher, *Socialism with a Human Face*, p. 186.
88. Hodgson, *Labour at the Crossroads*, pp. 200, 201.
89. Meacher, *Socialism with a Human Face*, p. 205.

and democratic socialist society could it be made a reality, and, certainly, only then would such a society be likely to endure the counterattacks which its construction would inevitably provoke. Socialism and socialist consciousness had to emerge in the course of a struggle for the democratization of economic power. It was not something that could be bestowed or engendered by a socialist elite. As one proponent of the AES put it, "it is in the process of people changing the actual structures within which they live their lives that consciousness itself most effectively changes".[90]

In the shorter term, though, the AES was about escaping the impotence of Keynesian social democracy. The substantial extension of public ownership, economic planning and the democratization of economic decision-making were all means to that end. They would go some considerable way to destroy, or corral, those unaccountable and malign sources of economic authority which had thwarted and distorted the economic policies of governments, particularly Labour governments, since 1945. Yet, as the proponents of the AES were only too aware, there would remain profound constraints on policy-making emanating from outside the British polity. Of significance here, as already noted, was the power of the transnational corporations. For these entities could behave in ways which both precipitated and exacerbated those balance of payments and exchange rate crises which had been such a characteristic feature of the British economy in the post-war period. In addition, their significance to the economy, in terms of output, employment and, in particular, exports, made it difficult for governments to pursue an economic strategy which ran contrary to either their domestic or their international interests.[91]

Of course, the AES proposals for public ownership and planning agreements underpinned by financial incentives and penalties would, it was believed, go some way to bring such corporations to heel and prevent their further subversion of national policy autonomy. Yet it was recognized that their capacity to undermine or limit the effectiveness of policy by expedients which affected the current and capital account of Britain's balance of payments – such as transfer pricing, the transfer of funds and foreign exchange dealings – would remain significant. In addition, the general external constraints imposed by a precarious balance of payments position and capital movements, actual and threatened, still represented severe limitations on national economic sovereignty. So too did the existence and growing importance of international economic institutions such as the European Economic Community (EEC), the IMF and the General Agreement on Tariffs and Trade (GATT), all of which imposed pressures on their members to conform in policy-making to the logic and imperatives of free market capitalism. Thus, for Tony Benn, the Treaty of Rome

---

90. P. Devine, "The Labour Party – Why the Decline?", *Marxism Today* (January 1980), p. 16.
91. Conference of Socialist Economists, *The Alternative Economic Strategy*, p. 27.

was "the only written constitution in world history that entrench[ed] the principles of capitalism and bureaucracy in the very centre of its provisions".[92] Adherence to it meant that, in effect, "the UK no longer has full control of commercial policy and this means that many major decisions about trade in steel, shipbuilding and textiles, for instance, are in the hands of the EEC".[93] Tariffs and other import controls were impermissible under the articles of the Treaty of Rome and of the GATT. In consequence, governments had, in large measure, to accept that the structural reshaping of the British economy would proceed according to market forces and, therefore, in the interests of transnational capital, rather than under the control of democratically elected governments and in the interests of the British people. This had already resulted in the "disintegrat[ion] of major industries and regions in the Community, and threaten[ed] to realise an inner and outer Europe of rich and poor countries".[94] In such a context, there was a real danger that "Britain's future within the EEC" would become that of "an impoverished and de-industrialised region on the periphery of an industrial heartland stretching from the Ruhr to the Seine and lying south of the English channel".[95]

In addition, projected developments within the EEC threatened to curtail policy-making autonomy still further. As Stuart Holland pointed out in 1980, "the principles for EMU [European Monetary Union] as recommended by progressive stages" point to the eventual emergence of "a common monetary unit; a centralised credit policy; a common external monetary policy; a unified policy on capital markets; [and] common decision-making on the volume, scale, mode of finance and use of public budgets and budgetary policy".[96] So, among many other things, future membership would eliminate the possibility of the kind of state-led industrial rejuvenation that was at the core of the AES. Many proponents of the AES would, therefore, have agreed wholeheartedly with Hodgson's view of the EEC as "a bureaucratic and undemocratic institution committed to reinforcing the power of capital in Europe and blocking any move towards socialism in any member country".[97]

As regards the IMF, the experience of 1976 had shown clearly, if evidence was needed, that it operated in a manner which insisted upon adherence to fiscal prudence as a condition of support when a crisis of capitalist confidence in sterling occurred. Thus crises would always be resolved under IMF auspices in a manner consistent with the interests of international and domestic capital. Alternative policies, such as those involving controls over capital movements,

---

92. Benn, *Arguments for Democracy*, p. 150.
93. Aaronovitch, *The Road from Thatcherism*, p. 92.
94. S. Holland, *Uncommon Market: Capital, Class and Power in the European Community* (London: Macmillan, 1980), p. 8.
95. Hodgson, *Labour at the Crossroads*, p. 220.
96. Holland, *Uncommon Market*, p. 41.
97. Hodgson, *Labour at the Crossroads*, p. 220.

would fall foul of IMF rules and so would evoke its hostility and preclude its support.

Further, the abolition of exchange control by the Conservative government in 1979 made

> the external constraints upon domestic economic policy sharper and more powerful . . . Increase[d] freedom for capital to move between countries, enhance[d] the international capitalist discipline on conditions of production and conditions of work and pay, and further limit[ed] the autonomy of national economic policy or strategy.[98]

International bankers, speculators and TNCs could now move funds even more easily across national frontiers and "impose policies upon nation states by creating crises of confidence that were miraculously ended when capital had its way".[99]

Given these constraints, what could be done to restore national sovereignty as regards the conduct of policy? Or, in the terms of the AES, how could the powers lost to TNCs, international financial institutions, financial intermediaries and the EEC be restored to democratically accountable governments? How could the democratic accountability of economic power be reasserted?

As many AES supporters saw it, "the Alternative Economic Strategy [sought] to counterpose national self-government against the anarchic pressures of a global market system".[100] This was to be effected, in large measure, by "planned" or "managed" trade; it was "the planning of our trade" which would "prevent the undermining of all our efforts by the working of the international market and international companies".[101] Certainly, it would only be by the planning of trade that the latitude to pursue reflationary policies could be created, let alone that freedom of manoeuvre which would be required to embark on a strategy involving the extension of social ownership, industrial democracy and the planning-agreement control of the commanding heights of the private sector.

Here there were differences over exactly what planned trade entailed. All were agreed, however, that at the very least it necessitated import control. The conceptual framework behind this aspect of the AES flowed from many sources, although a particularly important contribution came from the Cambridge Economic Policy Group, which made a general tariff on manufactured goods a key element in their proposals for macroeconomic expansion.[102] In this context,

---

98. Conference of Socialist Economists, *The Alternative Economic Strategy*, pp. 110–11.
99. Benn, "Granada Guildhall Lecture".
100. F. Cripps, "The British Crisis – Can the Left Win?", *New Left Review* **129** (1981), p. 93.
101. Labour Co-ordinating Committee, *There is an Alternative*, p. 4.
102. See, for example, F. Cripps & W. Godley, "Control of Imports as a Means of Full Employment and the Expansion of World Trade: The UK Case", *Cambridge Journal of Economics* **2** (1978), pp. 327–34. For a fuller discussion of this see N. Thompson, "Economic Policy and the Development of Economic Opinion in the 1970s", in R. Coopey & N. W. C.

however, the TUC also proposed the fixing of import-penetration ceilings by the government to protect what it saw as core industries,[103] and the Labour Party, in line with this, committed itself to "set import ceilings on an industry-by-industry basis across a broad range of sectors".[104]

A number of policy instruments were suggested to implement such a protective strategy. Tariffs were one, but other measures "include[d] . . . negotiation of voluntary export restraints, imposition of quotas and use of public purchasing agreements". In addition, "selective financial assistance could be used to encourage the purchase of UK equipment . . . [while] agreements could be negotiated with multi-nationals on matters such as plant location, intra-firm trade and UK-produced component content".[105] With such a panoply of controls and instruments, an AES-inspired government could set about the business of expanding domestic demand free from the fear that balance of payments constraints would, as they had in the past, emasculate attempts at reflation. Imports would only be allowed to expand *pari passu* with exports, and the planning of trade would become an integral and fundamental part of that more general democratic planning which would effect a structural transformation of the British economy. It would become, as some saw it, a "necessary and permanent feature of an economy subject to democratic planning".[106] This in turn, of course, implied an abandonment of the EEC or at least a fundamental revision of Britain's terms of membership.[107]

Left- and right-wing critics of the AES attacked such proposals on the grounds that they were imbued with a xenophobic and self-interested nationalism which sought to export the unemployment resulting from import penetration to other countries. But AES supporters argued that what was crucial was the increase in productive activity which a measure of protection would allow. Over time, as they saw it, this would promote a more rapid expansion of British imports than would be the case if periodic balance of payments crises condemned the economy to a "stop/go" trajectory. "Other countries would not lose, in fact would gain, because they would increase their exports to Britain compared with what they can hope to achieve while the government's present highly deflationary policies remain in force."[108] "A planned limitation in the rate of growth of imports into Britain" was actually "in the interest of working people in other countries as

---

Woodward (eds), *The Troubled Economy: Britain in the 1970s* (London: University College of London Press, 1996), pp. 55–80.
103. See TUC, *Economic Review* (London: TUC, 1976).
104. Labour Party, *Labour's Programme 1982*, p. 21.
105. Conference of Socialist Economists, *The Alternative Economic Strategy*, p. 97.
106. *Ibid.*, p. 98.
107. As Tony Benn put it, "we should have to deal with the Treaty of Rome. We could not solve any of the problems under a constitution which makes it illegal to interfere with market forces", T. Benn, "The Unemployment Tragedy" (1983), in *Fighting Back*, p. 176.
108. Meacher, *Socialism with a Human Face*, p. 170.

much as it is in our own interest." The Labour Party's 1983 manifesto, looking as it did to protection as a means of creating a "framework" for "an orderly *expansion of trade*", was adamant that it did not, therefore, renege on the principles of socialist internationalism.[109] "The objective of the AES [was] not autarky but autonomy", an autonomy which would be used to reflate and also to effect a planned restructuring of British industry involving the state and the trade union movement, rather than one dictated by the untrammelled operation of international market forces.[110]

However, to give policy-makers the autonomy to reflate, plan and restructure it was necessary not just to manage trade, but also to secure control over those international capital movements which affected the British economy. If deficits on the current account of the balance of payments could derail economic policy and circumscribe a government's freedom of manoeuvre, those on the capital account could equally destabilize sterling and also reduce the availability of funds for that investment, in both the public and private sectors, necessary to generate employment and transform economic performance. Further, such deficit-creating flows of funds were to be expected in the aftermath of the election of a Labour government committed to the raft of radical policies which the AES encapsulated. In the event of such electoral success there would almost certainly be a flight of capital in search of locations more favourable to post-tax profitability. Capital flight, actual or threatened, was, after all, one of the principal means by which the international financial community policed the economic policies of nations to ensure their conformity with the canons of contemporary capitalism. So

> the first step which must be undertaken . . . from the moment any future Labour government comes into office, is to impose emergency controls on the City and the banking system to block movements of funds out of sterling and fix the exchange rate, to regulate interest rates and to ensure the supply of funds to the government for investment in the public spending increases we need.[111]

Some looked, indeed, to an even more radical strategy, with a Left government taking over sections of the City, including foreign-owned assets located in this country, and paying compensation from a fund provided by British-owned assets abroad. Here, as with so many other aspects of the AES, there was a desire to establish a continuum between short-term, radical measures and funda-

---

109. Labour Party, *The New Hope for Britain*, p. 10, my emphasis.
110. London CSE Group, "Crisis: The Labour Movement and the Alternative Economic Strategy", *Capital and Class* **8** (1979), p. 76; *ibid.*, pp. 76, 85. On this see also T. Benn *et al., A Ten Year Industrial Strategy for Britain* (Nottingham: IWC, 1975).
111. Labour Co-ordinating Committee, *There is an Alternative*, p. 21.

mental longer-term objectives which, when attained, would lay the basis of a socialist economy.

Such a continuum was also apparent in conceptions of the planning of trade. For it was clear that some of the AES Left believed that, in the longer term, it must mean more than the manipulation of tariffs and quotas to ensure a parallel expansion of imports and exports. For these writers, planned trade was, potentially, a means of breaking free from that pattern of trade, capital movements and international financial connections which, as they saw it, had disadvantaged the British economy and which were a major cause of the nation's relative economic decline. "The mechanisms of free trade and multinational business are destroying Britain's economy. Our present international relationships lock us into destructive patterns of trade and investment in many other countries and commit us to supporting an anarchic free world"; "the ways in which Britain is tied into the system [of international trading] is an important cause of the weakness of British industrial capitalism. The AES must therefore seek ways of restructuring this international dependence."[112] In this context, "import controls would provide a powerful weapon against the multinationals and would allow a left-wing government to alter the geographical pattern and character of Britain's manufacturing imports".[113] This was the logical concomitant of a planned restructuring of the British economy. Such planning could not succeed in a context where the expansion and decay of industries within the domestic economy were the unplanned outcomes of the forces unleashed by an anarchic system of international "free" trade. It could not succeed where the economy was constantly exposed to the major dislocations and disturbances which, since 1972, had afflicted the global economy. On the contrary, national economic planning required an "alternate international order . . . within which self-governing countries" could consciously "determine their own futures in agreement with others"[114] – an order based on stable bilateral agreements and one too where, it was hoped, trade might be consciously conducted in a manner more favourable to Third World countries, the particular victims of the existing international economic order.[115] The planning of trade was, therefore, economically imperative, potentially liberating and decidedly virtuous.

As regards the substance of the AES, one final aspect is worthy of note, and that is its conception of agency. Here, while there was, again, a diversity of emphases among the Strategy's proponents, there existed also a significant measure of agreement. In contrast to much of the democratic socialist political

---

112. Cripps *et al.*, *Manifesto*, pp. 20–1; Conference of Socialist Economists, *The Alternative Economic Strategy*, p. 103.
113. B. Rowthorn, "Britain and Western Europe", *Marxism Today* (May 1982), p. 27.
114. Cripps *et al.*, *Manifesto*, p. 10.
115. On this see, for example, Meacher, *Socialism with a Human Face*, p. 183.

economy of the 1980s and 1990s, the advocates of the AES shared a definite clarity of vision. To begin with, trade unions were to play a fundamental role at the micro- and macroeconomic levels. In the period 1969–79, the percentage of the workforce who were unionized had risen from 46% to 55%. That period had seen an unprecedented post-war level of industrial unrest that had encompassed the destruction of both the Heath and Callaghan governments. The 1970s also witnessed the emergence of left-wing trade union leaders such as Hugh Scanlon of the AUEW and Jack Jones of the TGWU who had a marked enthusiasm for industrial democracy and workers' control. In addition, events at Upper Clyde Shipbuilders and Fisher Bendix showed that this was a movement which had the potential to assume responsibility for the management of industry and, as the alternative corporate plans forthcoming from Lucas Aerospace, Vickers and the workers of other companies indicated, the capacity to conceive of ways in which productive activity could be reoriented to serve more obviously social and socialist ends. In the 1970s and early 1980s, trade unions were, understandably, seen as a key agency by means of which crucial elements of the AES, most obviously the democratization of economic power, could be put in place.

In addition there was the state. The AES Left was only too aware that the state was not a politically neutral mechanism which could be unproblematically used to implement the transformative policies which they advanced. This was another reason why the democratization of power was seen as such an integral element of what they proposed. As has been indicated, such a democratization would not simply occur at the level of the firm; rather, it would inform the planning process at all levels through to the national.[116] Given that, it would then prove possible to counter or neutralize a conservative, capitalist-serving state bureaucracy. Here the input of the trade union movement into strategic economic decisions at both a micro and a macro level would also furnish a vital extra-parliamentary source of support, strengthening the hand of an AES-implementing government and holding it to its commitments. This was particularly important in view of the opposition that could certainly be expected from those whose power would be attenuated and whose interests would be adversely affected. Further, public power would be significantly strengthened by the extension of social ownership, the application of planning agreements, the use of import and capital controls, the abandonment of the EEC and the expansion of public expenditure. By these means, national economic sovereignty could, in considerable measure, be restored and the nation state once again possess the means of effectual economic policy-making.

---

116. Labour Party, *Labour's Programme 1982*, p. 42, looked to "The trade union movement" being "able to make a systematic and detailed input into national planning as part of the process of extending industrial democracy."

Finally, it was believed that as a consequence of the extra-parliamentary pressure in favour of a radical economic strategy and, crucially, the Labour Party's own democratization, a Labour government could be transformed into a suitable instrument for initiating and sustaining a socialist transformation of Britain. Such a government had proved a broken reed in the past, most obviously when the Wilson/Callaghan governments elected on an AES-shaped manifesto proceeded to dilute or ignore key elements of the Strategy, resorting initially to an insipid Keynesianism and then, *faute de mieux*, to an other-directed monetarism. However, the AES Left came to believe that with constitutional reforms within the Labour Party ensuring that party policy was formulated by the NEC in the light of conference decisions, with the Labour leader directly elected by the party as a whole and with Labour MPs subject to periodic reselection, a Labour government would be bound to pursue, energetically, the effective implementation of a rank-and-file-supported, conference-endorsed, AES.[117] With a democratized Labour Party, the Left would have a political instrument and agency for the wholehearted and undaunted pursuit of the socialist economic policies that the AES embodied.

Yet despite its considerable critical and prescriptive strengths and the significant impact that it initially had within Labour Party ranks, the AES was characterized by fundamental weaknesses, tensions and deficiencies which made it unlikely that it would see the light of political day or, if it did, that it would emerge as anything other than a parody of the intentions of its progenitors.

To begin with, in terms of both its critical analysis and its policy prescriptions, it was an unstable amalgam of disparate and sometimes conflicting elements. It sought to accommodate those Keynesian social democrats who saw in its expansionary dimension the quintessential remedy for rapidly rising unemployment;[118] those Left Keynesians who linked that expansion to the protectionist planning of international trade; the Clause IV Left, for whom it held out the prospect of a substantial step towards the realization of their statist socialist vision of the New Jerusalem; and the New Left, who saw it as concerned with the democratization of economic and political life and as effecting a decisive transference of decision-making power to the working class.[119]

---

117. For the battle to effect such a democratization of the Labour Party see P. Seyd, *The Rise and Fall of the Labour Left* (London: Macmillan, 1987).
118. "In the hands of the TUC . . . and according to the Right and Centre Labour MPs, the alternative is presented as a plan for growth, a way of ending the stagnation and dwindling competitiveness of British manufacturing industry", D. Coates, "Labourism and the Transition to Socialism", *New Left Review* **129** (1981), p. 5.
119. Geoff Hodgson was one among many, in the early 1980s, who, though believing that "the Alternative Economic Strategy [was] . . . a major achievement of socialist thought", also recognized that it was "open to varying sometimes conflicting interpretations", "On the Political Economy of the Socialist Transformation", *New Left Review* **133** (1982), p. 62.

Strains within this broad church manifested themselves in a number of ways. Tensions between the corporatist Keynesians and those who took seriously the strategy's declared transformative intent were apparent in their conflicting perceptions of the role and potentialities of such entities as the NEB and the National Economic Assessment (NEA). Thus the NEB was conceived of, by the former, as something approximating to the Industrial Reorganisation Corporation of the 1960s,[120] while the latter saw it as the means of effecting a substantial transference of economic power from private enterprise to the state. Similarly, corporatist Keynesians saw the NEA as encapsulating the notion of a Social Contract and creating the institutional basis and procedural mechanisms for a *de facto* incomes policy. Others saw it as a crucial instrument of socialist planning and as a means of democratizing the planning process.

As to the tensions between the statist and democratizing Left, between those who saw the AES as a means of centralizing and those who saw it as an opportunity to disperse economic power, these were manifested in their different perceptions of the degree of autonomy that they believed should be granted to enterprises. Thus while the former conceived of the AES as a national strategy, involving national economic planning and the central guidance and direction of economic activity, the latter stressed the enterprise autonomy involved in the formulation of the kind of worker plans produced at Lucas, Vickers and elsewhere.

There was also clearly a tension between the extra-parliamentary, democratizing elements of the Left who sought to mobilize the working class and the more "statist and parliamentary preoccupations" of others.[121] Thus, as one of its supporters saw it, the AES was "packaged as reformist but it contains implicit and unspelt revolutionary implications".[122] And clearly there were adherents of the AES who saw it as providing a basis, and indeed the necessity, for a mass mobilization that would counter opposition by means of extra-parliamentary agitation and struggle. Hodgson wrote that "the effect of a push for its implementation would be the mass mobilisation of the working class in a direction which would lead to the total transformation of society", while others looked to the creation of "organs of direct democracy . . . to counterbalance the inevitable reaction of monopoly enterprises and state institutions".[123] So there was a manifest tension between those who saw the AES as consistent with an essentially parliamentary road to socialism and those who saw it as part of a strategy of working-class mobilization and direct action. It was a tension that mirrored that between those who favoured the substantial extension of social ownership and those who placed a greater faith in planning

---

120. Wickham-Jones, *Economic Strategy and the Labour Party*, p. 94.
121. Coates, "Labourism and the Transition", p. 15.
122. Hodgson, *Socialist Economic Strategy*, p. 27.
123. *Ibid.*; London CSE Group, "Crisis", p. 89.

agreements as the best means of ensuring that major industrial corporations acted in a manner consistent with AES objectives. Thus, in support of the former position, one commentator argued that such agreements were merely "putting off today" that nationalization which would be necessary, and more difficult, tomorrow – necessary both to "weaken the strength of MNC [multinational corporation] capital abroad" and to stimulate "similar developments in other countries".[124]

Further, as regards protectionism, there were not only essentially technical disputes over the form this should take, but also fundamental disagreements over the purposes which it was to serve.[125] Thus there were those who saw it as a means of planning international trade in a manner which prioritized ethical considerations, but there were also those who saw it in narrowly Keynesian terms as a necessary insulatory adjunct to any expansionary strategy. Again, this reflected an underlying struggle between those who looked to an AES which would secure the traditional economic objectives of Keynesian social democracy – full employment, balance of payments equilibrium, stable prices and steady growth – and those who saw it as a means of transforming the nature of existing social, commercial and international relationships.

In political terms, these disparate theoretical and prescriptive stances showed themselves, throughout the 1970s and early 1980s, in the visceral hostility of most of the leadership and Right of the Labour Party to all but corporatist-Keynesian readings of the AES; a hostility which manifested itself in the 1970s in a strategy of subversion/dilution and, in the early 1980s, in a half-hearted support for what appeared in the party's policy documents and manifesto.[126] Indeed, throughout the period, a constant critical fire from this quarter was directed against key components of the AES: such criticism being levelled, among other things, at the extensive powers proposed for the NEB, the scale of the proposed extension of social ownership, the efficacy of the strategy as regards the problem of inflation, the powers and role of the Official Trustee, and the extent and nature of the compensation to be given when firms were taken into public ownership.[127]

Even within the wider labour movement vigorous and unqualified support was not always forthcoming. And certainly it is true to say that "the alternative economic strategy was never endorsed throughout the party".[128] Moreover, while the TUC "passed motions supporting aspects of the Left's policies, they were not presented in detail as an economic package", and although the ideas

124. B. Fine, *Multinational Corporations, the British and the Alternative Economic Strategy* (London: Birckbeck, 1981), p. 36, *ibid.*, p. 38; see also B. Fine & L. O'Donnell, "The Nationalised Industries", in D. Currie & R. Smith (eds), *Socialist Economic Review* (London: Merlin, 1981).
125. On this see Wickham-Jones, *Economic Strategy and the Labour Party*, p. 187.
126. See *ibid.*, pp. 114–15.
127. *Ibid.*, p. 90.
128. *Ibid.*, p. 115.

underpinning the economic proposals which it outlined in its *Economic Review* were similar to those informing the AES, it has been argued that it "did little to popularise or explain" them.[129] In this context, too, according to Tony Benn, there was really "no top-level union support for the [AES] industrial policy at the crucial moment when it was reversed."[130] After 1983, given the scale of unemployment and the onslaught of Thatcherism, it was also the case that the TUC embraced a "new realism" which was inherently inimical to the ideas of social transformation which the AES had embodied.

So the coalition that, for a time, could be induced to support, or say it supported, the AES was inherently fragile and unstable. Of its very nature it was unlikely to survive either victory or defeat. The late 1970s provided a clear indication of the tensions that would emerge, and the dilution or subversion of AES policies that would occur, in the case of electoral success, while the rapid demise of the AES after Labour's 1983 defeat illustrates how rapidly it was to be jettisoned in the aftermath of political failure.

Also, as regards the political preconditions for the successful implementation of the AES, the democratization of the Labour Party was clearly central. Without that, many recognized it would be impossible to ensure that the leadership and the parliamentary party acted on the mandate for fundamental change that any electoral endorsement of the AES gave them.[131] Further, only democratization would ensure the requisite mass movement necessary to face down the political and other opposition that the pursuit of an unadulterated AES would certainly provoke.[132] Once, therefore, the process of democratizing the party lost momentum, as it certainly did after, if not before, the defeat of Tony Benn for the deputy leadership then, for many, the crucial *modus operandi* of the whole strategy was lost.

Yet coalitions, fragmented political support and the absence of political preconditions aside, there were also the lacunae, theoretical deficiencies and inconsistencies in the strategy itself.

There was, for example, the presupposition that national power could still be used to secure socialist objectives. Holland *et al.* had quite rightly highlighted the power of the TNCs to erode national economic autonomy and frustrate the intentions of policymakers. But such concerns were as germane to the pursuit

---

129. *Ibid.*, p. 135; L. Panitch & C. Leys, *The End of Parliamentary Socialism: From New Left to New Labour* (London: Verso, 1997), p. 122.
130. Wickham-Jones, *Economic Strategy and the Labour Party*, p. 155.
131. For a contemporary view of the centrality of the democratizing component of the AES see J. Eaton, M. Barratt Brown & K. Coates, *An Alternative Economic Strategy for the Labour Movement* (Nottingham: Spokesman Books, 1975).
132. Some hard Left critics stressed that proponents of the AES underestimated the scale of this; see, for example, A. Glyn, *Capitalist Crisis: Tribune's Alternative Economic Strategy or Socialist Plan* (London: Militant, 1978), pp. 45, 65 and Coates, "Labourism and the Transition", p. 10. Of course, Glyn's alternative of "a clear call to the rest of the working class on a world scale to support the expropriation of British capital and follow suit with the expropriation of their own bourgeoisie" made the AES look, by comparison, the epitome of hard-nosed realism. *Ibid.*, p. 75.

of the AES as they were to the emasculation of Keynesian social democracy. In addition, as one commentator saw it, "in circumstances in which a Left government [is] coming into and exercising power, there seems little doubt that MNCs [multinational corporations] would organise politically and collectively to destabilise society and to halt Left advance". It was also the case that given the dependence of "UK MNCs' production on overseas operations", "left advance" in Britain was particularly "vulnerable to the collective action of this section of capital".[133]

Moreover, as the 1980s progressed, there was too an increasing recognition on the Left that such insulatory AES adjuncts as exchange control and tariffs had ceased to be within the realm of practical politics. This development was a consequence both of the practical and ideological triumph of global neo-liberalism and of the increasing integration of Britain's economic fortunes with the EU and its liberalizing philosophy and dynamic.[134] This was something which Holland himself recognized in the early 1980s when he argued for the necessity of a multilateral pursuit of the AES by the European Left.[135] Erstwhile proponents of import controls, such as the Cambridge Economic Policy Group, came to a similar view, with a diminishing faith in the efficacy of protectionist measures proceeding *pari passu* with an increasing advocacy of the need for European-wide reflation and devaluation.[136]

Many of those tensions and deficiencies which characterized the AES were also to be highlighted in the early 1980s by events in France. There the socialists took power in 1981 on the basis of the Left's *Common Programme* – a raft of economic and social policies with marked similarities to what the AES offered. At its core was a reflationary strategy that included a substantial increase in public investment, primarily in the nationalized industries, and a significant redistributive element designed to boost the purchasing power of less-affluent households.[137] To facilitate the expansion of investment, and as a prerequisite for what was seen as a necessary rationalization and restructuring of parts of French industry, there was also a substantial extension of social ownership with the nationalization of 36 private banks, two finance companies and 11 industrial conglomerates,[138] the latter including firms which played a key role in France's

---

133. B. Fine, *Multinational Corporations*, pp. 31–2.
134. For a fuller discussion of economic globalization and its implications for democratic socialist political economy see in particular Chapters 8 and 9.
135. See Chapter 10.
136. Wickham-Jones, *Economic Strategy and the Labour Party*, p. 187.
137. On the nature of the relation between the components of the strategy see, for example, P. Hall, "The Evolution of Economic Policy under Mitterrand", in G. Ross *et al.* (eds), *The Mitterrand Experiment: Continuity and Change in Modern France* (Oxford: Polity, 1987), pp. 54–5 and G. Ross, "From One Left to Another", in *ibid.*, p. 201.
138. J. McCormick, "Apprenticeship for Governing: An Assessment of French Socialism in Power", in H. Machin & V. Wright (eds), *Economic Policy and Policy-making under the Mitterrand Presidency, 1981–84* (London: Pinter, 1985), p. 46.

export performance and which were at the cutting edge of its technological development.[139] In addition, there were measures inspired by the notion of *autogestion*, which aimed to foster a decentralization of power both inside and outside the workplace. Thus the Auroux Laws were introduced to strengthen the position of unions at enterprise level.[140] This was the stuff the AES Left's dreams were made of.

The general objectives of the *Common Programme* were first, to effect a substantial reduction in the level of unemployment and, through the stimulus which public investment expenditure would give to private investment expenditure, to touch off a cumulative expansion of the French economy. Secondly, through public investment and the restructuring and rationalization that an extension of social ownership would permit, to effect a substantial improvement in the overall performance of the French economy. Thirdly, through the revenue-raising consequences of reflation, to finance a substantial increase in social welfare expenditure.[141] Fourthly, to effect a redistribution of income and wealth. And, fifthly, through the implementation of measures giving expression to *autogestion*, to effect the democratization of enterprise decision-making. The parallels with the AES are striking, even as regards the manifest tension between the Programme's statist/dirigiste and decentralizing/democratizing elements. Remarkable too is the fact that the disintegrative trajectory of the strategy was almost exactly replicated, at a theoretical level, by that of Left political economy within the Labour Party in the 1990s.

The pathology of that disintegration has been exhaustively detailed by a number of commentators. 1981–2 saw the implementation of much of what the French socialists had promised. The programme of nationalization was carried through, tax revenues were channelled into major investment projects in the nationalized industries and the minimum wage was increased by 10%, pensions by 62% and family allowances by 40%.[142] However, this massive increase in purchasing power produced a substantial inflow of imports, and consequent pressure on the foreign exchanges precipitated three devaluations of the franc between 1981 and 1983. The period 1982–4 witnessed a radical policy U-turn with cuts in public expenditure, the introduction of an incomes policy, increases in taxation and the implementation of price and exchange controls. Thus a short period of expansion was followed by austerity and defla-

---

139. On this see, for example, D. McShane, *French Lessons for Labour*, Fabian Tract 512 (London: Fabian Society, 1986), p. 2.
140. H. Machin & V. Wright, "Introduction", in Machin & Wright (eds), *Economic Policy and Policy-Making under the Mitterrand Presidency*, pp. 1–2.
141. "In year 1, the year of radical optimism, it [the socialist government] actually expanded Welfare State benefits and enacted almost all of the social policy commitments which Francois Mitterrand had made in his election manifesto", Ross, "From One Left to Another", in G. Ross *et al.* (eds), *The Mitterrand Experiment*, p. 201.
142. Hall, "The Evolution of Economic Policy", p. 55.

tion and, in tandem with this, there was a marked reversal of the redistributive measures of 1981–2 in favour of the corporate sector. As one commentator put it, "the government deliberately manipulated the costs of austerity in 1982–84 so that they would be imposed upon the workers and consumers".[143]

Also, at an ideological level, the emphasis was no longer on the redistribution of income, wealth and power but on efficiency, performance and economic modernization. As one contemporary commentator phrased it, "austerity, efficiency, modernisation and competitiveness have become the catch-phrases of a government which came into power three years ago promising to put imagination into power".[144] Or, in the words of another writer, "emphasis was being placed on individual initiative, effort and enterprise, on competition, on profit".[145] The theoretical constructs, language and aspirations of the socialist government assumed the form of a supply-side economics with a socialist patina and strong neo-liberal inflections. Some might argue that the socialists had "helped to build a more competitive French economy with a human face . . . This is their major accomplishment."[146] But by the mid-1980s, what was on offer was no longer recognizably socialist and indeed involved the abandonment of previous commitments to reducing unemployment, raising the living standards of the poor and eroding concentrations of economic power.[147] The language of supply-side political economy now ushered in a different set of priorities. Efforts might be made to square efficiency with equity but, as the post-1982 austerity programme made clear, where tensions between the two principles emerged they were resolved in favour of the former. The new language of priorities also meant that different voices from those to which the French socialists had traditionally listened now carried greater weight. For, on efficiency and competitiveness, the poor had little and the rich had much to say.

As we shall see in Chapter 9, social democratic political economy in Britain was to take a similar ideological course, even if the absence of access to political power was, in some respects, to slow the process of ideological adulteration and obscure its practical implications for some little time. At this point, though, it is important to consider what lessons contemporaries drew from the failed Mitterrand experiment, for its failure had profound implications for democratic socialist political economy in France and elsewhere and not least for the AES Left in Britain.

The conclusion most decidedly and often drawn was that the failure of the Mitterrand experiment highlighted the limited freedom of policy manoeuvre

---

143. *Ibid.*, p. 57.
144. K. Dixon & D. Perraud, "Le Fin: France Abandons Socialism", *Marxism Today* (January 1985), p. 27; see also McShane, *French Lessons*, p. 5.
145. Machin & Wright, "Introduction", p. 3. This was particularly the case when Laurent Fabius became prime minister in 1984.
146. McCormick, "Apprenticeship for Governing", p. 62.
147. Ross, "From One Left to Another", p. 204.

possessed by "intermediate" economies in an open international economy.[148] No economy of the size of France could buck international economic trends which, in the early 1980s, were those making for global recession in the wake of the strongly deflationary policies being pursued by the major economic powers. As one writer put it, "the redistributive Keynesianism of 1981–2 ultimately foundered on France's vulnerability to developments in the international economy".[149] Of course, the lessons which might be drawn from this were by no means unambiguous. It was argued, for example, that in more favourable economic circumstances what had been attempted might well have proved successful. But then it was equally suggested that had the international economy been buoyant there would have been little need for the pursuit of the strongly reflationary strategy that lay at the core of the *Common Programme*. Either way, the utility of economic policies involving Keynesian expansionism was called into question as success became contingent on the state of the international economy rather than the nature of national policy initiatives.

It was also argued that what had been required for the success of the Common Programme was sufficient insulation to protect it from the massive inflow of foreign imports which expansion precipitated. In this reading the strategy was doomed to fail because "Mitterand opted for deflation and *continuing openness in the international economy*."[150] "French attempts at reflating inside an *open trading economy* at a time when its major trading partners were deflating [necessarily] turned out to be a disaster."[151] Yet the alternative was substantial import and foreign exchange controls of a kind which would inevitably have called into question France's membership of the EEC and the European Monetary System (EMS), something of which the Left were "constantly reminded".[152] This was the price that would have to be paid for a redistributive, expansionary Keynesianism that seriously aimed to tackle the problems of unemployment and inequalities of income and wealth. And, on the French and British Left, there was, in the 1980s, an increasing recognition of just how high a price that would be. There was, too, a complementary realization that if the cost of a neo-autarkic strategy was indeed too high then it had also to be accepted that "state power" was indeed decidedly "constrained by the rules of international competition" and that therefore "socialists" must, henceforward, "be less sanguine about the virtues of unrestricted Keynesianism" as part of any future Left economic strategy.[153] As the French socialist

148. Machin & Wright, "Introduction", p. 4.
149. Hall, "The Evolution of Economic Policy", p. 56.
150. *Ibid.*, my emphasis.
151. McShane, *French Lessons*, p. 4, my emphasis.
152. *Ibid.*, 5.
153. J-P. Fitoussi, "Comment", in Machin & Wright (eds), *Economic Policy and Policy-Making under the Mitterrand Presidency*, p. 66; Hall, "The Evolution of Economic Policy", p. 70.

Prime Minister Laurent Fabius put it in 1985, "l'état a rencontré ses limites: ils ne doit pas les dépasser."[154]

Other conclusions were drawn from the French experience which also had a bearing on the perceived viability of the AES and, for that matter, Keynesian social democracy. Specifically, the failure of the private sector to respond to "pump-priming investment" in a much-expanded public sector cast doubt on the extent of the dirigiste potential of the latter.[155] If such a strategy failed in France, where the public sector accounted for 32% of industrial activity, 24% of the labour force, 90% of bank deposits and 85% of all bank loans,[156] it was even more likely to do so in Britain where the economic significance of the public sector was less and would remain so even under the AES.

For different reasons, therefore, the failure of the Mitterrand experiment had, by the mid-1980s, made apparent to many on the Left the essential deficiencies of the AES and its reflationary Keynesian component. However, this practical illustration of its political and economic weaknesses played only a part, if an important one, in precipitating that rapid atrophy of support for the AES that was apparent by the early 1980s. For in large part, too, the demise of the AES was a result of the electoral defeats suffered by a Labour Party which had ingested, if not digested, a substantial part of it into its policy documents. Of course, opinion within the Labour Party had already begun to shift against the AES Left even before the debacle of 1983, but in many respects it is true to say that the AES finally died at the hands of the British electorate in that year.

So, with the AES dead or dying, and with Keynesian social democracy in a similar state for some of the same and for many other reasons, the problem in the 1980s became that of finding or formulating a political economy on the basis of which the forward march of labour could be resumed. What alternative socialist political economies were available to provide theoretical underpinning for the democratic socialist project? How could the ideological triumphs of the New Right be reversed? How was the post-Mitterrand-experiment Left to cope with the manifest threat posed to *any* national democratic socialism by increasingly untrammelled and powerful global economic forces? In view of the experience of the early 1980s, what kind of democratic socialist political economy could the Left in Britain put forward to retrieve the political support it had manifestly lost? It is with their attempts to furnish answers to these questions that the remainder of this volume will be concerned.

---

154. Quoted from Machin & Wright, "Introduction", 3.
155. On this see, for example, *ibid.*, p. 17.
156. McCormick, "Apprenticeship for Governing", p. 46.

Chapter 2

The political economy of new municipal socialism, 1981–6

Despite its defeat in the 1979 general election the Labour Party continued to make advances in the local elections of 1980 and 1981, most notably securing control of the Greater London Council (GLC). The Labour Party having being denied access to the levers of national power, such gains appeared to offer it the opportunity to pursue a socialist agenda on a local or regional basis. Further, as a consequence of the reorganization of local government in 1974, there now existed local authorities, particularly in metropolitan areas, which had the resources to employ staff to research, formulate and pursue policies on an extensive scale.[1] Of significance, too, as regards the promotion and implementation of such policies, was the political progress made in local government by the Labour Left in the late 1970s and early 1980s,[2] which resulted in their control not only of the GLC, but also the West Midlands

---

1. J. Mawson & J. Miller, "Interventionist Approaches in Local Employment and Economic Development: The Experience of Labour Local Authorities", in V. Hausner (ed.), *Critical Issues in Urban Economic Development*, vol. 1 (Oxford: Clarendon Press, 1986), p. 149.
2. For some of the reasons for the increasing influence of the Left within local government in the 1970s see, for example, A. Cochrane, "Local Economic Policies: Trying to Drain the Ocean with a Teaspoon', in J. Anderson *et al.*, *Redundant Space in Cities and Regions* (London: Academic Press, 1983), p. 285.

County Council, Sheffield City Council and a number of London boroughs.[3] This rise of a new municipal socialism replicated at local level the more general resurgence of the Left within the party in the late 1970s[4] and it had comparable consequences in terms of support for "alternative (local) economic strategies", similar to those which the party was offering the national electorate.[5]

Given the straitened economic circumstances that many councils confronted in the early 1980s, there seemed a particularly pressing need for a radical departure from existing canons of local economic policy. From the late 1970s, the West Midlands economy had seen a rapid decline of its diverse, metal-based manufacturing industries that precipitated a rise in unemployment from 6% in 1979 to around 16% by 1986.[6] In Sheffield, there were the adverse local employment consequences of the national difficulties of the steel industry in the early 1980s.[7] In London, it has been estimated, some 800,000 manufacturing jobs were lost between 1961 and 1981 – a decline of approximately 60% in its manufacturing population. In consequence, by the early 1980s, London had "the highest absolute concentration of unemployed workers not only in the UK, but in all advanced industrial nations".[8] Just as relative economic decline, rising unemployment and public expenditure curbs signalled the bankruptcy of the macroeconomic dimension of Keynesian social democracy, so inner city decay, the deindustrialization of previously prosperous regions and the widening of regional disparities in income, employment and economic activity appeared to highlight its failure at a micro and regional level.

Local authorities had been actively involved in the promotion of economic activity in the post-war period, and increasingly so from the late 1970s. However, their activity had been essentially "property-led, business and

---

3. M. Boddy & C. Fudge, "Local Socialism? Local Councils and New Left Alternatives', in M. Boddy & C. Fudge (eds), *Local Socialism? Labour Councils and New Left Alternatives* (London: Macmillan, 1984), p. 8.
4. "In many cities the New Left progressively displaced in branches, districts and on councils, a traditional hierarchy dominated by right-wing trade union officials and by long-established councillors often dispensing patronage", G. Green, "The New Municipal Socialism', in M. Loney *et al.* (eds), *Politics or Welfare? The State of the Market in Contemporary Britain* (London: Sage, 1991), p. 276.
5. For a discussion of the more purely political consequences of the Left's advance at local level see K. Bassett, "Labour, Socialism and Local Democracy", in Boddy & Fudge (eds), *Local Socialism*.
6. For a brief discussion of the local economic backdrop against which the West Midlands County Council pursued its strategy see D. Elliott & M. Marshall, "Sector Strategy in the West Midlands", in P. Hirst & J. Zeitlin (eds), *Reversing Industrial Decline? Industrial Structure in Britain and Her Competitors* (Oxford: Berg, 1989)
7. See, for example, Sheffield City Council, Department of Employment and Economic Development, *Steel Crisis* (Sheffield: Sheffield City Council, 1986).
8. A. Eisenschitz & D. North, "The London Industrial Strategy: Social Transformation and Modernising Capital", *International Journal of Urban and Regional Resources* **10** (1986), p. 419. On the magnitude of London's employment problem at this juncture see also P. Nolan & L. O'Donnell, "Taming the Market Economy: A Critical Assessment of the GLC's Experiment in Restructuring Labour", *Cambridge Journal of Economics* **11** (1987), p. 252.

market-oriented and competitive",[9] being primarily concerned to publicize the economic virtues of local areas, while providing advice, land, premises, subsidies and loans for enterprises. These regenerative expedients were increasingly seen by the Left as involving a "zero-sum" game played with other local authorities that precluded any significant inroad into the problems of unemployment and deindustrialization. It was argued that the policies adopted by local authorities did nothing to challenge capitalist relations of production or to effect a shift in the balance of power in favour of working people and their families. Even where municipal labourism did manage to do the right things *for* people, it rarely discussed what it did *with* people. There was no attempt on the part of local authorities to engage the energies of the local population in the business of economic rejuvenation. There was no effort to ensure democratic participation in the formulation and implementation of local economic policy. There was no desire to empower labour with respect to local economic decision-making and no recognition of the advantages such empowerment might bring in terms of support for a radical policy of economic rejuvenation. This rejection of such capitalist-oriented, paternalistic, "beggar-my-local-neighbour" policies, and the condemnation of their negligible effect on the economic problems localities suffered, formed the prolegomenon to the new municipal Left's determination "to formulate an alternative form of local economic planning which would not only improve working conditions and job prospects, but also shift the relations of production in favour of workers themselves".[10]

As at a national level within the Labour Party, so within a number of local authorities in the late 1970s and early 1980s, the ascendant Left possessed the power, the political conviction, the determination and the intellectual self-confidence necessary to reformulate the principles of political economy that had previously informed and guided party thinking and policy-making. There existed, as one commentator has put it, "a desire to explore the possibility of what seemed, amidst the ravages of Thatcherism and the bankruptcy of Labour's postwar legacy, to be one area that offered a glimmer of hope for the development of radical alternatives".[11]

These alternatives drew practical, ideological and theoretical sustenance from a variety of sources. On a practical level, the Home-Office-funded National Community Development Programme (NCDP), introduced in the 1970s, established research teams and fostered the pursuit of development projects predicated upon a more interventionist role for the local state and stressing the need for greater accountability on the part of industry to the local

9. M. Boddy, "Local Economic Strategies", in Boddy & Fudge (eds), *Local Socialism?*, pp. 163–4.
10. Eisenschitz & North, "The London Industrial Strategy", p. 421.
11. M. Boddy & C. Fudge, "Introduction", in Boddy and Fudge (eds), *Local Socialism?*, p. vii.

community. These projects were, as one commentator has put it, "a key influence on the growing acceptance of the need for intervention in production by the 'new urban left'".[12] In this sense it is correct to view the new "municipal socialism in the 1980s [as growing] out of local socialism in the 1970s".[13] For example, as early as the mid-1970s, in the London borough of Wandsworth, this kind of approach was being adopted in an attempt to alter the nature and structure of production,[14] with ideas being generated that were also to "feed into the policies later introduced at the Greater London Council".[15]

In addition, as already noted in the previous chapter, the 1970s saw the emergence of a trade unionism that reacted to demands for restructuring and redundancy proactively rather than defensively. As noted, shop stewards and trade union combines at Lucas Aerospace, Vickers, Fisher Bendix and other companies responded by formulating alternative economic plans for their companies, schemes that aimed not only to guarantee employment, but also to alter the nature of production, prioritizing the social utility of what was manufactured and creating a more human-centred labour process. Such microeconomic initiatives were clearly of a character and on a scale that suggested a possible positive future role for local authorities run on radical lines.

On a practical level, too, there was legislation which opened up the possibility of a more active developmental role for at least some local authorities. Section 137 of the 1972 Local Government Act gave local authorities the power to levy a rate of up to 2p in order to provide the means of taking action which it was considered would be in the interests of the inhabitants of the area, but which was not otherwise authorized.[16] In the case of the GLC, with its substantial ratepayer base, this provided a substantial sum (c.£30m p.a.) to finance initiatives. In addition, there was the 1978 Urban Programme and the Inner Urban Areas Act that gave "designated authorities additional development powers" and "acted as an important stimulant to the development of local authority and employment initiatives".[17]

The ideological underpinning for what was attempted derived, as we shall see, from a number of sources. At this point it is sufficient to say that, in many respects, the political economy of the kind of local socialism that was in the ascendant in the early 1980s represented a microeconomic rendition of the AES

---

12. Eisenschitz & North, "The London Industrial Strategy", p. 420; on this see also M. Rustin, "Lessons of the London Industrial Strategy", *New Left Review* **155** (1986), p. 76.
13. Green, "The New Municipal Socialism", p. 274.
14. On this see A. Eisenschitz & J. Gough, *The Politics of Local Economic Policy* (London: Macmillan, 1993), p. 75.
15. A. Clarke & A. Cochrane, "Investing in the Private Sector: The Enterprise Board Experience", in A. Cochrane (ed.), *Developing Local Economic Strategies: Some Issues and Ideas* (Milton Keynes: Open University Press, 1987), p. 5.
16. On this see M. Lyons, "The 2p Rate and Powers for Economic Development', *The Planner* **69**(5) (1983), pp. 163–4.
17. Mawson & Miller, "Interventionist Approaches", p. 150.

– a strategy for socialism in one borough or one metropolitan county when, after 1979, the implementation of a national AES was no longer on offer. Theoretically, prescriptively and conceptually much of what the new municipal socialism proposed was derived from, or paralleled, the AES.[18] It was the case too that some of those who made a significant contribution to the AES were also involved in the formulation of this political economy of new municipal socialism. Specifically, as regards the GLC, the Conference of Socialist Economists (CSE) played an influential role, in particular providing members of the Economic Policy Group, the GLC's main economic policy-making body.[19] It was also the case that the influence of the CSE on local economic policy initiatives extended beyond the capital,[20] while in the West Midlands the Conference of Socialist Planners, together with working parties spawned by the West Midlands Labour Party, were an important influence on the development of local policy.[21]

Yet, as the 1980s progressed, one can detect influences other than those emanating from the AES in the output of the theoreticians and proponents of local socialism. Specifically, volumes such as the GLC's *London Industrial Strategy* (1985) were infused with a rhetoric and analysis that derived inspiration from a political economy of flexible specialization and post-Fordism which had its roots in the work of writers such as Michael Piore and Charles Sabel;[22] a political economy which was to be embraced by a number of British socialists in the 1980s with all the uncritical enthusiasm of the newly converted.[23] The nature of this input to analysis and policy will be discussed below, but these ideas will also be considered at much greater length in Chapter 4, because they were to have a more general influence on the evolution of democratic socialist

---

18. Parallels with the AES were noted by a number of commentators and some saw the policies pursued by local authorities as furnishing both a testbed and the microeconomic foundations for a future national strategy. On this see, for example, Cochrane, "Local Economic Policies", pp. 278, 303; Clarke & Cochrane, "Investing in the Private Sector", p. 8.
19. ". . . a left-wing think tank, it brought together a range of academics, shop stewards and political activists", Nolan & O'Donnell, "Taming the Market Economy", p. 354.
20. "The Conference of Socialist Economists . . . has been a further influence upon new local economic initiatives, challenging Keynesian assumptions about demand management and the economy, focussing theoretical attention upon the sphere of production, and contributing important insights about the international restructuring of the manufacturing sector, changes in the labour process and the role of the state", J. Benington, "Local Economic Strategies: Paradigms for a Planned Economy", *Local Economy* 1 (1986), p. 11.
21. Elliott & Marshall, "Sector Strategy", p. 230; Benington, "Local Economic Strategies", p. 11.
22. Of particular importance here were C. Sabel, *Work and Politics* (Cambridge: Cambridge University Press, 1982) and C. Sabel & M. Piore, *The Second Industrial Divide* (New York: Basic Books, 1984). For the application of these ideas to local economic development by other British writers in the 1980s see, for example, contributions to Hirst & Zeitlin (eds), *Reversing the Economic Decline?*
23. Most notably there was Robin Murray, chief economic adviser of the GLC. On this see Nolan & O'Donnell, "Taming the Market Economy", p. 254, who also suggested that the GLC's analysis of contemporary capitalism drew "selectively" on the theoretical approach of the French Regulationist School of Palloix, Aglietta, Boyer and Liepitz.

political economy in the 1980s and 1990s. Here it is sufficient to say that the ideas and policy prescriptions this post-Fordist socialism inspired did not always, even at a local level, mesh easily with those generated by the AES.

Like the AES, a primary objective of new municipal socialism was the defence and creation of jobs in response to the employment-destroying consequences of contemporary cuts in public expenditure[24] and the catastrophic industrial restructuring precipitated by a government intent on adhering to deflationary monetary and fiscal policies whatever the employment costs. Given the magnitude of this task, it was believed by many on the Left that there was a need for decisive intervention in the productive base of the local economy, on a scale and of a kind radically different from any previous post-war attempts by local government to engender prosperity. To effect this, some local authorities[25] considered it imperative to create arm's-length organizations in the form of local enterprise boards.[26] These boards would permit intervention that might otherwise have been deemed *ultra vires* and open to legal challenge. Once such organizations had been created, as in the case of the Greater London Enterprise Board (GLEB), such intervention could and did take the form of the outright public ownership of companies, equity stakes, part ownership with workers' trusts and the creation of producer co-operatives.[27]

Yet the objective of such intervention was not just to save jobs or create employment. It was also designed to effect the restructuring of sectors of the local economy necessary to put them on a more stable and efficient economic footing. As one commentator wrote with respect to the West Midlands Enterprise Board (WMEB), "the overall aim was to upgrade industry as a whole from a low-wage, low-investment and low-productivity sector to one where higher levels of investment and productivity could support improved wages and working conditions".[28] There was, therefore, an overtly productivist or supply-side dimension to this new municipal socialism that aimed to raise output and employment through a combination of policies: an increase in investment; the utilization of efficient technology; an improvement in the quality of management; and strategic sectoral planning. Securing these objectives would modernize the local economy, raise productivity, increase the level of high-quality employment, improve working-class living standards and enhance the quality of working life.

---

24. For figures on the rate support grant reduction for the years 1978–86 and a discussion of its consequences see D. Blunkett & K. Jackson, *Democracy in Crisis: The Town Halls Respond* (London: Hogarth, 1987), pp. 143–65.
25. Other local authorities such as Sheffield pursued their strategy through existing institutional machinery. In Sheffield's case a Department of Employment and Development.
26. For example, the Greater London Enterprise Board, the West Midlands Enterprise Board, Lancashire Enterprise Ltd and the Merseyside Enterprise Board.
27. See T. Hayter, "Industrial Democracy: The GLEB Experience", in M. Mackintosh & H. Wainwright (eds), *A Taste of Power: The Politics of Local Economics* (London: Verso, 1987), p. 143.
28. Elliott & Marshall, "Sector Strategy", pp. 234–5.

However, for an organization such as the GLEB, while restructuring was certainly about the rejuvenation of the local economy, it was also concerned to promote what it termed a "restructuring *for* labour" that would, over time, effect a radical transformation of the relations between capital and labour in those firms receiving GLEB support. As Robin Murray, chief economic adviser of the GLC, put it, "one of the main functions of a public body concerned with industrial intervention is to ensure that any restructuring that does take place is undertaken in the interests of labour and not at its expense".[29] Restructuring for labour meant a concern with "strengthen[ing] the position of workers" and this involved, at the most basic level, ensuring their right to join a union, the compliance of employers with existing employment legislation, and wages and conditions at least comparable to those generally prevailing in the sector.[30] Yet while guaranteeing basic union rights and improving a workforce's terms and conditions of service were considered important, they were only two aspects of what was to be achieved under this heading. For, by means of "enterprise planning", restructuring for labour was also to involve the participation of labour, management and the enterprise board in strategic decision-making at both firm and sectoral levels. Such planning would encompass the humaniz-ation of the production process, the upgrading through training and appropriate technology of the quality and skills of labour,[31] a wider, non-discriminatory extension of employment opportunities, a more equitable distribution of income and the more deliberate organization of employment to satisfy social needs.

The strategy of restructuring for labour also had clear and conscious parallels with the AES. As with the *National* Enterprise Board, so with their local equiv-alents, objectives were to be achieved, in part, through the extension of social ownership. Further, a crucial means of attaining the goals of the enterprise boards was by way of democratized enterprise decision-making through "enterprise planning agreements"; although here it should be noted that the "GLEB's enterprise planning was intended to be far more extensive than the planning agreements of the other enterprise boards and to involve a much wider involvement by the workforce in ongoing decision-making."[32] Also, as with their AES equivalents, enterprise planning agreements were to be the product of tripartite negotiation between trade unions, management and, in

---

29. Murray, "New Directions in Municipal Socialism", p. 220.
30. P. Totterdill, "Local Economic Strategies as Industrial Policy: A Critical Review of British Economic Developments in the 1980s", *Economy and Society* **18** (1989), p. 500.
31. "From the beginning GLEB's aim was to create 'high-quality, long-term' jobs in which workers, through their trade unions, would be given far-reaching rights to help determine key decisions through a system of industrial democracy known as enterprise planning", J. Palmer, "Municipal Enterprise and Popular Planning", *New Left Review* **159** (1986), p. 118.
32. A. Cochrane, "In and Against the Market: The Development of Socialist Economic Strategies in Britain", *Policy and Politics* **16** (1988), p. 161.

effect, representatives of the local state; and when in place the agreements would, in theory, perform a range of functions comparable to those which had been envisaged for their national counterpart. As the authors of the *London Industrial Strategy* saw it,

> the enterprise plans are to be agreed by the unions, the management and by GLEB and will normally cover the following: product and market strategy; future investment and technical change; location; pricing policy; employment levels and conditions; skill levels and training; and equal opportunities. Their aim is to achieve a quite new extension of the scope of collective bargaining.[33]

Further, advocates of new municipal socialism believed that if participative democracy was to be extended into the private sector by enterprise planning and other means, then it should also be at the heart of the service and product provision in which local authorities were *directly* engaged. Here the AES critique of the Keynesian social democratic state as bureaucratic, technocratic and paternalistic, where it was not downright authoritarian, was transposed to the local state.[34] There was, in this view of things, a need to make that state amenable to popular pressure and to facilitate a popular input to policy-making and resource allocation.[35] In the case of the GLC, this took the form of "using state resources to strengthen the organisations of working-class people and develop the capacity of these organisations to put pressure on the state".[36] As Hilary Wainwright put it in a tribute to the GLC after its abolition in 1986, "instead of trying to do it for people, they provided support for people to do it for themselves".[37] The objective was to bridge the gulf between policy-makers and people. In this workers were also seen as a well-spring of ideas which, with the requisite democratic structures, could be fed into the running of industrial concerns. So, with sufficient resources, education and channels of communication, the populace could initiaite and actively share local government initiatives. In the words of one commentator, such popular planning involved "the spreading of economic information and analysis beyond elite policy-makers; bringing voluntary groups and local communities into the economic debate; enabling workers to contribute

---

33. Greater London Council, *London Industrial Strategy* (London: GLC, 1985), p. 56.
34. On this see, for example, Cochrane, "Local Economic Policies", p. 298.
35. On the infrastructure seen as necessary to sustain such "popular" policy-making see J. Chandler & P. Lawless, *Local Authorities and the Creation of Employment* (Aldershot: Gower, 1985), p. 257.
36. M. Mackintosh & H. Wainwright, "Introduction", in Mackintosh & Wainwright (eds), *A Taste of Power*, p. 18. London saw the creation of a Popular Planning Assembly in this period; see G. Blazyca, *Planning is Good for You: The Case for Popular Control* (London: Pluto, 1983), p. 86 and the formulation of a People's Plan for the Docklands, see Blunkett & Jackson, *Democracy in Crisis*, p. 140.
37. H. Wainwright, "Bye Bye GLC", *New Statesman*, 21 March 1986.

imaginatively to the development of their industry and services".[38] These actions would eliminate the remoteness and insensitivity of local bureaucracy and qualitatively improve service provision in a local context.

Like the planning agreements of the AES, the concept of "enterprise planning" was invested with portentous significance. It carried a formidable burden of aspirations and aims, not all of which were easily reconcilable. It was to involve the workforce in a range of decision-making previously the prerogative of management. In that respect, it was clearly seen as a vehicle for encroaching control,[39] laying the basis for a socialist economy in which worker ownership and management were the norm, and instilling the requisite managerial skills and self-confidence in the workforce to permit such a transformation of the social relations of production. However, such agreements were also regarded in more narrowly instrumental terms as the necessary basis for effective planning at enterprise and at a sectoral level. They were, in particular, to be a means of gathering the requisite information for informed decision-making on the part of the GLEB and also on the part of enterprises themselves. Through worker participation they would ensure both that the workforce was clear as to the objectives to be pursued and that it was committed to their pursuit. Enterprise planning was also to be a crucial means of plan enforcement. It would formally link objectives, and the decision-making their attainment required, to whatever support was offered, whether in the form of equity stakes or loans. It was a way, in short, of making firms publicly accountable for the financial assistance which the enterprise board provided; a recognition that, as Robin Murray phrased it, "in a single plant, the best enforcers of an enterprise plan are . . . the workforce themselves".[40]

As regards the democratization of enterprises, it should be pointed out that many municipal socialists also emphasized the role of the local authorities in supporting and creating the right conditions for producer co-operatives to flourish. Emphasis had been placed on this in the London Labour Party's *Manifesto for the GLC* (1981), "because we regard the creation of new jobs under the control of working people as a distinct advance".[41] But, in addition, the point was made that local authority support for workers' co-operatives was cost-effective because they had a better survival rate than most small firms. And certainly, in the early 1980s, there was a proliferation of co-operatives in Britain, with 337 being registered in 1982 alone.[42]

---

38. Blunkett & Jackson, *Democracy in Crisis*, p. 141.
39. "GLEB's intention – not always adhered to – [was] that the unions, generally through their elected shop stewards, should progressively gain greater control over management decisions", Hayter, "Industrial Democracy", p. 194.
40. Murray, "New Directions in Municipal Socialism", p. 225.
41. Labour Party, *Manifesto for the GLC* (London: Labour Party, 1981), p. 15.
42. Clarke & Cochrane, "Investing in the Private Sector", p. 21; Chandler & Lawless, *Local Authorities*, p. 116 and D. Ghilespy *et al.*, *Socialist Enterprise: Reclaiming the Economy* (Nottingham: Spokesman Books, 1986), p. 52.

Enterprise agreements were also seen as an important means of committing firms to certain terms and conditions of service for their workforce. As noted, the aim was not simply to provide jobs but to provide high-quality, well-remunerated and, where possible, skilled employment and to "persuade" firms away from the notion that economic survival lay in the cutting of wage costs and the "sweating" of labour. As regards the quality of occupations, this was conceived of in terms of their skill content, the conditions under which they were performed and also, fundamentally, the products or the service which they furnished. With respect to the latter, great emphasis was placed, in particular by the GLC and GLEB, on planned production for social use.[43]

For new municipal socialists this notion had a number of dimensions. As regards the nature of the products themselves, the 1981 *Manifesto for the GLC* had defined "socially useful products" as "products which . . . assisted human beings rather than maimed them; products which were produced in ways which conserved energy and raw materials rather than wasted them; and products whose manufacture, repair and recycling were carried out by non-alienated labour".[44] Thus socially useful production was conceived of by many very much in terms of *what* was produced and *how* it was produced. Here the pole star was the Lucas Plan;[45] a plan with a morally unambiguous and economically defensible objective. The production of weapons of mass destruction for which there was a faltering demand would be replaced by products of comparable technological sophistication which clearly mitigated human suffering, signally added to the quality of human life and manifestly satisfied a definite social need. Such plans set the business of economic calculation on a different basis and, in so doing, challenged the logic of the competitive market that, in periods of depression, pointed remorselessly in the direction of plant closure and redundancies.[46]

Considerable efforts were made by the GLC to foster and facilitate such socially useful production. The council established a Popular Planning and Industrial Development Unit that resourced and worked with community organizations, trade unionists and user groups to formulate "alternative" production plans.[47] In addition, there was the creation of five technology networks, "intended to service the needs of groups of workers seeking to emulate

---

43. "The GLEB puts an emphasis on what it calls socially useful products", Greater London Council, *London Industrial Strategy*, p. 42.
44. Quoted in Hayter, "Industrial Democracy", p. 197.
45. "In the GLC the Lucas Plan was an important model to both politicians and officers", Mackintosh & Wainwright, "Introduction", p. 6.
46. On this see, for example, J. Palmer & H. Wainwright, "Plans, Co-operatives and the Struggle for Socialism", *Socialist Review* (October 1983), p. 16.
47. On this see Murray, "New Directions in Municipal Socialism", p. 224 and Mackintosh & Wainwright, "Introduction", p. 8.

the Lucas example".[48] These networks were also seen as playing a part in improving the quality of occupations through the creation and dissemination of human-centred technology, ensuring that technical advance harnessed and enhanced rather than eliminated productive skills. As such, they represented an experiment in community-based technology transfer.

However, the idea of socially useful production was to be laden with even heavier aspirational and conceptual baggage. Estimations of social utility were clearly seen by some as a possible alternative, non-market determinant of resource allocation; all too necessary as "profit [was] no longer an accurate guide to the way out of the economic crisis. It is like a compass that has lost its bearings and points in the opposite direction to the way in which we need to go. What is required is a new economic guide."[49] For some this new guide necessitated computation in terms of social utility rather than market price. For others it meant an evaluation of the social costs and benefits of production to form an estimate of the "social rate of return" on any public or private investment; an estimate that would take account of data additional to that generated by the market. So, in the political economy of the new municipal socialists, there surfaced once again the notion of a social/socialist cost–benefit analysis that, if used to determine "profit" and "loss" and rates of return, would, it was believed, profoundly affect the subsequent allocation of public and private resources.[50]

Yet if, consistently with this, the *London Industrial Strategy* argued for policies that operated "in and against the market", it clearly failed to furnish guidelines as to when the imperatives of the latter should be set aside in favour of the directives of the GLEB and the GLC. A distinction was indeed made between the economic "boundaries" set by the market and "the goals of investment" established by GLEB. And where the latter came into conflict with the former then the GLEB was "directed to follow the non-market goals within the limits set down".[51] But what those limits were, when they were deemed to be transgressed, and when market limitations were to be considered insuperable, were not made apparent in either the 600-page *Strategy* or other GLC publications of the period. The theoretical avenue of socially useful production explored by proponents of the AES at a national level was, therefore, also traversed at local level by some of the new municipal socialists – in both cases to little theoretical or practical effect.

48. G. Hackett *et al.*, "Socially Useful Production", in Mackintosh & Wainwright, *A Taste of Power*, p. 203.
49. Statement of GLC Economic Policy Group, quoted in Cochrane, "In and Against the Market", p. 161.
50. On this see, for example, Ghilespy *et al.*, *Socialist Enterprise*, p. 74 and K. Jefferis & M. Robinson, "Social Investment in Production", in Clarke & Cochrane (eds), *Developing Local Economic Strategies*, pp. 67–8.
51. Greater London Council, *London Industrial Strategy*, p. 45.

In terms of establishing the directions in which socially useful production might proceed, much, again, was expected from the alternative enterprise plans that, it was believed, the encouragement of industrial democracy would foster. "The process of matching needs with resources [would] have to be done 'from below' through workers and community-based organisations drawing up their own plans, meeting their needs as consumers and producers."[52] Of course, this still left unresolved the question as to whether popular planning meant: (i) planning on the basis of essentially non-market criteria; (ii) planning that, in some measure, simply took some non-market criteria into account; or (iii) planning that merely involved an enhanced informational flow to decision-makers, regardless of the criteria by reference to which their decisions were made.[53]

Theoretical weaknesses and tensions aside, this new municipal socialism of the early 1980s also clearly operated under severe constraints. Some of these were apparent at the outset, while others became apparent as policies were implemented. These constraints not only jeopardized the success of the economic strategies that were pursued, they also raised important questions and major doubts about the efficacy and general utility of seeking to formulate and implement a political economy of local socialism at all.

The policies of the GLC and GLEB proceeded under the slogan of "in and against the market", "restructuring *for* labour" and "socially useful production". Yet, increasingly, it was necessary to accommodate market criteria of success/ failure and take on board capitalist objectives in the process of restructuring. What rapidly became apparent to commentators was that in seeking to rejuvenate a local economy in the context of hostile market forces, the extent to which local authorities could act in a manner contrary to the market and its imperatives was narrowly circumscribed. Thus, as regards the firms that were assisted or restructured, local enterprise boards had to accept that profitability remained the bottom line and this was often to pose the choice of social progress *or* economic survival.[54] In fact, by 1986, "the commitment to social criteria for investment [had] largely been dropped" in favour of a concern to secure those market solutions to enterprise difficulties most favourable to labour.[55] Even enterprise boards such as GLEB had, by the mid-to-late 1980s, come to acknowledge that enterprise planning had "achieved neither the

---

52. Coventry Trades' Council and the Lucas Aerospace Shop Stewards Combine Committee, *Popular Planning for Social Need*, 1981, quoted from J. Gyford, *The Politics of Local Socialism* (London: Allen & Unwin, 1985), p. 80.
53. Certainly, for some, "the workforce and the community were . . . seen as a major untapped source of product ideas", Hackett *et al.*, "Socially Useful Production", p. 204.
54. On this see I. Newman, "Greater London Enterprise Board: Vision and Reality", *Local Economy* **2** (1986), p. 66; M. Geddes, "The Capitalist State and the Local Economy: 'Restructuring for Labour' and Beyond", *Capital and Class* **35** (1988), p. 97.
55. Cochrane, "In and Against the Market", p. 163.

restructuring for labour initially hoped for nor any major achievements on equal opportunities".[56] Increasingly, too, the essential criterion of success of enterprise board activity became not the extent to which labour had become empowered in the course of restructuring, but whether value for money was secured in terms of job creation and the stimulation of private investment. In fact, in these respects, Left local authorities did achieve considerable success: success that became an increasingly prominent part of the case they made for their continued existence.[57]

In addition, as we have seen, the notion of socially useful production was variously interpreted, often in a manner which made only a passing obeisance to non-market estimations of worth. As an operational construct it was therefore necessarily problematic, particularly when ideas of restructuring to upgrade product quality and capture niche markets assumed prominence. This process of upgrading usually necessitated movement "up market" to higher-value-added products, and that meant a focus on luxury or near-luxury demand. To say in this context, as some did, that this process involved the restructuring and reorienting of productive capacity to meet the more diverse, discriminating and discerning expression of the *social* needs which were emerging in the 1980s was, quite simply, as one commentator remarked, "to devalue the term socially useful production", to the point where it was emptied of all meaning.[58]

Moreover, as regards the role of the Technology Networks, while they certainly played a part in skill-creating and human-centred technology transfer, a report on their activities in the mid-1980s concluded that most of what they produced, whatever its other qualities, could not be defined as socially useful: "since 1986, the Networks have been increasingly geared to commercial product innovation and consultancy, similar to mainstream innovations centres".[59] As with other elements of the new municipal socialist political economy, market pressures would therefore seem to have materially altered the nature and purpose of these networks, so that they increasingly internalized market criteria of viability and success.

Yet, although the evolution of new municipal socialism may be seen as the slow corruption of ideals exposed to the exigencies of capitalist economic reality, it has to be said that, almost from the outset, it involved a strategy that was necessarily more *in* than *against* the market. Despite the rhetoric of enterprise planning and sectoral strategies, local enterprise boards were operating, in the early 1980s in particular, in a cold and hostile economic climate, with

56. A. Cochrane, "The Future of Local Economic Strategies", in A. Cochrane (ed.), *Developing Local Economic Strategies*, (Milton Keynes: Open University Press, 1987), p. 137.
57. Cochrane, "In and Against the Market", p. 166. On this see too Chandler & Lawless, *Local Authorities*, p. 232.
58. Newman, "Greater London Enterprise Board", p. 63.
59. Eisenschitz & Gough, *The Politics of Local Economic Policy*, p. 204.

unemployment rising rapidly, bankruptcies multiplying and local communities economically eviscerated. In such circumstances, it was almost inevitable that they would have to operate more as a rescue than a strategic planning directorate. In order to square this circle, the GLC established an early warning unit so that crises could be anticipated in sufficient time to permit a strategic rather than a reflex response. But in fact, as the *London Industrial Strategy* admitted, the urgency of market pressures meant that "early warning" was very "rarely . . . about anticipating crises. More usually, it has been about bringing together the power of the GLC and GLEB with that of the trade unions to save something out of the crisis."[60] So the GLC, from the outset, was frequently "trapped" into "small scale rescues and even smaller scale initiatives with co-operatives". In consequence, "between 1984 and 1986 most of its activity was oriented towards rescuing previous investments from collapse".[61]

Furthermore, from their inception the GLEB, the WMEB and other enterprise boards acted, in greater or lesser measure, to repair the deficiencies of the market and supplement the services and support which small and medium-sized enterprises could expect and secure in a market context. Specifically, enterprise boards often filled gaps in the capital market that precluded firms borrowing or that made it prohibitively expensive for them to do so. In addition, they provided advice on marketing, technological possibilities, restructuring, reorganization and market trends. In that respect, they performed an important supportive function in furnishing a range of services and information that no single enterprise could conceivably afford. The danger here, however, was that in addition to abandoning any emphasis on social investment, "the enterprise board simply ends up . . . contributing to the better management of capitalist enterprise", or, as another commentator put it, "becoming radical management consultants". Added to this were the dangers inherent in developing that close relationship with private firms necessary if infrastructural and financial support were to be suitably tailored to enterprise requirements.[62] Either way, municipal socialism was transmuted into municipal capitalism, with policy reverting to what the new municipal socialists themselves had previously condemned in the post-war economic development activity of local authorities.

In this context, with market pressures subverting what were seen as socialist goals, and with enterprise problems demanding immediate solutions, strategic coherence was necessarily eroded. Publications such as the GLC's *London Industrial Strategy*, *London Financial Strategy* and *London Labour Plan* might suggest otherwise but, in fact, what existed by the mid-1980s was a range of disparate

60. Greater London Council, *London Industrial Strategy*, p. 53.
61. Cochrane, "In and Against the Market", p. 162.
62. Boddy, "Local Economic Strategies", p. 181.

initiatives reflecting the calculated ad hocery that, by that date, had become the distinguishing characteristic of the GLEB.[63] These documents, analytically and prescriptively impressive in many respects, were nonetheless a retrospective construction of order from what had rapidly become a reactive chaos;[64] a veritable owl of Minerva taking aspirational flight from County Hall in the dusk of imminent GLC abolition.

The new municipal socialist "advocates of local economic planning" were also sometimes "described as 'hobbit socialists'" because of the microcosmic nature of their economic strategies.[65] Criticism of this kind took a number of forms. To begin with, some highlighted the irony that at a time when the impact of multinational capital in a global context was growing and when, increasingly, its impact on local economies could be transformative or devastating, the political economy of "hobbit socialism" should place emphasis on economic regeneration through indigenously rooted small and medium-sized enterprises in circumscribed locales. The problems of London and the West Midlands in particular were, in large measure, the result of decisions made in head offices far removed from both areas and clearly not amenable to any influence emanating from local enterprise boards.[66] As Nolan and O'Donnell argued,

> the London economy is dominated by the decisions and activities of some of the world's largest multinational companies. Making sense of their strategies and the wider role of the state, in the context of the reorganisation of economic relations within and without the advanced capitalist countries, should be a first priority for analysis. Yet it is precisely these considerations which are absent from the GLC's account.[67]

The GLC and GLEB were, in effect, seeking to destroy the power of Mordor from the confines of the Shire.

Even in the case of *national* corporations, such was their centralized and hierarchical structure that they too were likely to be impervious to the blandishments or threats of local authorities. Also, given the limited scale upon

---

63. Totterdill wrote of "a record of ad hoc and opportunistic investment" characterized "by the relative scarcity of clear decision rules informed by detailed analyses of local industries". Totterdill "Local Economic Strategies as Industrial Policy", p. 496.
64. One commentator wrote of the GLEB that in "attempt[ing] to be a bank, management consultancy, rescue and turnaround agency, technology and transfer institution", it lacked "conceptual focus" and, in truth, this list of problematically incompatible functions could well be lengthened. M. Best, "Sector Strategies and Industrial Policy: The Furniture Industry and the Greater London Enterprise Board", in Hirst & Zeitlin, *Reversing Industrial Decline*, p. 219.
65. A statement by SERA's Local Socialism Working Group, quoted in Gyford, *The Politics of Local Socialism*, p. 106.
66. N. Harris, "What to Do With London? The Strategies of the GLC, 1981–86", *International Socialism* **2** (1986), p. 120.
67. Nolan & O'Donnell, "Taming the Market Economy", p. 257.

which enterprise boards could act, the greater part of the local economy would certainly remain in private hands uninfluenced and unaffected by municipal socialism.[68] For some, localism equated with prescriptive impotence, an impotence that could be remedied, and then only partially, by national policies of industrial regeneration.[69] Local economic policy could make a significant difference to the prospects of industry and the position of labour only if it was an integral part of a wider economic strategy. Enterprise boards, for all their efforts, could "achieve their full potential as agents of restructuring [only] within the context of a broader industrial policy framework based on the implementation of sector strategies".[70]

If socialists were serious about the business of rejuvenating British industry, and in a manner favourable to the interests of labour, there was no alternative to a national industrial policy involving the extension of social ownership and the introduction of economic planning.[71] In that regard, new municipal socialism was often seen as a distraction from the crucial debate that should focus on the manner and means of gaining social control over multinational and indigenous capital and the uses to which that control could be put. Though deriving a measure of its intellectual provenance from the AES, municipal socialism was therefore regarded by some on the Left as an obfuscatory sideshow, strong on gesture and short on substance. It was political theatre rather than something concerned with the realities of political power. There was no substitute for a socialist macroeconomics and that meant, of course, that there was no alternative to formulating an electorally appealing national economic strategy which would allow political power to be wrested back from the Tories. All else was sound and fury signifying nothing.

On the purely practical grounds of job creation this was seen by many to be clearly the case. The GLC estimated that "by the end of December 1984, GLEB had allocated nearly £14.5m to 100 projects, saving or creating 2322 jobs, due to rise to 3529 within two years".[72] As regards the WMEB, estimates suggested that by March 1986 it "had approved investments totalling £14.2m in 39 companies with a combined workforce of around 5000".[73] Sheffield could and did make similar claims. Clearly, such figures represented only a marginal impact on the problem of unemployment. Also, leaving aside the fact that these numbers were less than had been anticipated, it was also the case that they represented gross not net figures, obfuscating the fact that, as some forcefully argued, the policies of local enterprise boards tended simply to "redistribute jobs between

---

68. See Eisenschitz & Gough, *The Politics of Local Economic Policy*, p. 120.
69. Eisenschitz & North, "The London Industrial Strategy", p. 429.
70. Totterdill, "Local Economic Strategies as Industrial Policy", p. 496.
71. A. Cochrane, "What's in a Strategy? The London Industrial Strategy and Municipal Socialism", *Capital and Class* **28** (1986), p. 187.
72. Greater London Council, *London Industrial Strategy*, p. 45.
73. Elliott & Marshall, "Sector Strategy", p. 231.

geographical areas and social groups rather than lead to net job creation".[74] Here the theoretical argument was that an overall increase in employment was dependent upon a rise in aggregate demand. Where that was absent local authorities simply participated in a "zero-sum" game as regards employment, unless, of course, they raised the competitiveness of the national economy *in toto*, expanding employment through an increase in export demand. However, given the marginal nature of their expenditure and capital inputs, this could be considered unlikely. A significant increase in net employment was therefore dependent upon the pursuit of an apposite macroeconomic strategy. "Even a small change in macroeconomic policy [was] likely to cause a bigger dent in Britain's unemployment figures than the combined efforts of a few radical councils."[75] Also, by implication, whatever employment-creating good municipal socialism accomplished could easily be negated by sectoral problems or secular trends in the national labour market.

Those involved in the policy-making of Left local authorities, and the enterprise boards that aimed to give their policies practical expression, were therefore only too aware of the severe limitations under which they operated. The *London Industrial Strategy* explicitly stated that "in almost every private sector we have studied, the extension of social control for the purpose of restructuring requires intervention at national level" and went on to declare the need for a "national public investment body . . . with the powers, the staff and the funds to control the commanding heights of the main sectors of the economy".[76] In addition, it stressed the importance of establishing a national production board which "would co-ordinate sectoral policy and [its] implementation, linking with unions, local councils and a co-ordinated public sector".[77] Similarly, John Benington, of the WMEB, recognized a definite limit to what could be achieved by "building from below while the overall structure of society is controlled otherwise".[78]

Each of these commentators clearly accepted that the new municipal socialism had only a marginal impact on job creation which would be, and was being, overwhelmed by general economic trends and the decisions of a few major economic players.[79] Rather than seeking to eliminate the problem of local unemployment and effecting an immediate regeneration of local economies, they therefore frequently argued that the rationale and objectives of the new municipal socialism were primarily exemplary and prefigurative. For example, Benington

---

74. Eisenschitz & North, "The London Industrial Strategy", p. 434.
75. M. Goodwin & S. Duncan, "The Local State and Local Economic Policy: Political Mobilisation or Economic Regeneration", *Capital and Class* **27** (1986), p. 34; on this see also Totterdill, "Local Economic Strategies as Industrial Policy", p. 490.
76. Greater London Council, *London Industrial Strategy*, p. 61.
77. *Ibid.*
78. Quoted in Gyford, *The Politics of Local Socialism*, pp. 106–7.
79. Mawson & Miller, "Interventionist Approaches", p. 145.

saw the pursuit of initiatives in a West Midlands context as "a crucial opportunity to forge and test the components for a *national alternative economic strategy*", and other commentators similarly took the line that new municipal socialism was about "practical exploration and experiment", "show[ing] that there is a socialist economics of common sense", "illustrating principles" and developing functional socialist alternatives that, in the final analysis, could "not spring fully grown from the seedbed of theory".[80] Municipal socialism would not "solve unemployment or provide for a major redistribution of resources", but it was "the means for setting the agenda for what should be done and how it can be achieved".[81] And, in this prefigurative regard, there were many who considered it decidedly worthwhile.[82]

Those who adhered to such a prefigurative reading of the political economy of municipal socialism saw certain kinds of criticism as misplaced. For them, the new municipal socialism was not, as one Tawney-inspired commentator implied, an attempt to skin the tiger claw by claw. Nor did it suggest a "retreat" to "villages" of social control in which questions of ownership could be "evaded".[83] Nor were its proponents guilty of "wishful thinking" or involved in "seek[ing] to implement a socialist plan at local level without devising effective means to neutralise" the "forces" which multinational capital could set in motion.[84] Nor could they be accused of "using the state against capital rather than struggling to transform the state itself".[85] On the contrary, as regards this last criticism, the GLC and the GLEB sought, through worker participation in economic planning and user involvement in public service and product provision, to democratize the local state in ways which would prefigure what might ultimately be achieved on a national basis.

Yet even if judged by prefigurative criteria, the policies of new municipal socialism should still have been expected to display a measure of ideological resilience and practical viability to be deemed successful. Specifically, they should have shown a capacity to resist the corrosion of capitalist pressures and capitalist values. They should have provided some indication that, with the requisite support, they could furnish a radical alternative to capitalist practice, whether in terms of provision for collective consumption, the regeneration of industry, or a more environmentally and ethically defensible allocation and utilization of resources. Yet, in the many and varied ways already noted, the new municipal socialism was decidedly deficient in these respects. Socially useful production proved a conceptual millstone, where it was not emptied of

---

80. Benington, "Local Economic Strategies", p. 9; Blazyca, *Planning is Good For You*, p. 97; Boddy, "Local Economic Strategies", p. 176.
81. Blunkett & Jackson, *Democracy in Crisis*, p. 5.
82. On the achievements of the West Midland Enterprise Board see, for example, Elliott and Marshall, "Sector Strategy", p. 246.
83. N. Harris, "What to do with London?", pp. 130, 134.
84. Nolan & O'Donnell, "Taming the Market Economy", p. 261.
85. Geddes, "The Capitalist State", p. 85.

meaning or effectively ignored. Market criteria of success and failure were increasingly adhered to. Enterprise planning, and the extension of industrial democracy which that notion entailed, rarely resulted in anything of lasting practical significance. To the extent, then, that it was claimed to be prefigurative, the nature of the micro failure of the new municipal socialism furnished grounds for profound scepticism as regards the utility and practical efficacy of many of those principles and policies which the AES, at a macro level, had suggested might furnish the basis for socialist progress. In that regard, its history could be taken as prefigurative of the AES's likely fate.

As to the fate of the new municipal socialism itself, the tendency to succumb to market pressures and capitalist values, while clearly evident even before the demise of the metropolitan authorities in 1986 and the stringent rate-capping which preceded it, became even more apparent from the mid-1980s onwards.[86] The loss of the 1987 election was also to accelerate this trend as, for many, it finally buried the hope that a Labour government would emerge to give the kind of support that would allow radical initiatives to survive, flourish and furnish the exemplars for national economic policy-making. From the mid-1980s local enterprise boards operated more obviously with reference to commercial criteria, as did institutions such as Technology Networks. As regards the formulation of local economic policy, "the types of local economic initiatives which have been developed in the mid-1980s are largely character-ized by attempts to assist indigenous business activities to survive and grow or assist new firm development".[87] From the mid-1980s, therefore, "modified market approaches [became] the dominant form of local economic strategy".[88]

Furthermore, the idea of "local jobs plans", which became increasingly prominent in Labour Party literature after 1987, marked a clear move back towards the integration of local economic policy with something approximating to a revamped Keynesian corporatism.[89] Thus the Labour Party's *New Jobs for Britain* envisaged local authorities furnishing the detailed local plans for infrastructural development and increased service provision which, when aggregated, would furnish a detailed basis for an employment-creating increase in public expenditure generating over a million jobs. However, what was

---

86. Totterdill, "Local Economic Strategies as Industrial Policy", p. 516, remarked that "the boards largely abandoned their social role as instruments of restructuring for labour, even before the abolition of parent authorities". On this see also A. Clarke & A. Cochrane, "Investing in the Private Sector", and M. Best, "Strategic Planning and Industrial Policy", *Local Economy* **1** (1986), pp. 65–77.
87. J. Sellgren, "Local Economic Development and Local Issues in the Mid-1980s", *Local Government Studies* **13** (1987), p. 65.
88. Cochrane, "The Future of Local Economic Strategies", p. 136.
89. Though "even before the 1987 general election campaign . . . Some authorities sought to move the political focus towards more traditional Keynesianism in the form of 'Local Jobs Plans'", Totterdill, "Local Economic Strategies", p. 513. On this see also Centre for Local Economic Strategies, *Economic Sense: Local Jobs Plans, a National Perspective* (London: CLES, 1987).

manifestly absent from that document was "the group of ideas around 'Produc-tion for need', 'Socially Useful Production', 'Useful Work' and 'Restructuring for labour', which have been important amongst many authorities".[90] Absent too was any idea of a local industrial policy built upon the democratization implicit in enterprise planning. Rather, the proposed strategy was usually justified in essentially Keynesian terms, although its defenders sometimes deployed a kind of subfusc monetarist patois which emphasized that the proposals would not engender inflationary pressures in local labour markets, would not result in the crowding out of local enterprise and could be expected to "push the actual employment rate closer to the natural rate" while, ultimately, reducing the latter.[91] Such concerns showed only too clearly the distance that had been travelled from the ethos and ideology of new municipal socialism.

As to the corporatist aspect of *New Jobs*, local authorities were to be given the opportunity to participate in a National Economic Assessment and in the NEDC. In effect, this would replicate at national level the local corporatism implicit in such ideas (increasingly popular within the Labour Party in the late 1980s) as local public/private partnerships.[92] Thus one commentator in this period identified the emergence of a "locally based or at least locally negotiated form of corporatism, in which major interests are involved in discussing and influencing future patterns of urban development", with discussion focused on "the identification of local possibilities for investment and development, the provision of land and infrastructure and the local provision of relevant training".[93] Here, as elsewhere in the late 1980s, there was a return to the local economic development philosophy of the 1960s and 1970s.

Finally, as local authority economic development strategies evolved away from the principles (and most of the objectives) that had fired the new municipal socialism, and as, in particular, the emphasis shifted to public/private partnerships and a determination to ensure an attractive local economic climate for existing and prospective enterprise, so, inevitably, the notion of rivalry and competition once again came to the fore.

> Under conditions not of their own choosing, left-wing local socialists are being forced to make history through styles of parochial rivalry, competi-tion and conflict which make ordinary competition between firms seem positively co-operative . . . THE ECONOMY, as seen from up here, IS THE

---

90. A. Batkin, "The Impact of Local Authorities on Labour Party Economic Policy", *Local Economy* **2** (1987), p. 22.
91. M. Campbell, "The Economics of Local Jobs Plans", *Local Economy* **2** (1987), p. 86.
92. As to these, Sheffield City Council was, significantly, one of the first out of the starting blocks.
93. Cochrane, "The Future of Local Economic Strategies", pp. 137, 140.

OLYMPIC GAMES. It's there: it moves: it takes place regularly: and it spends money. Our job is to FIX IT – IN ONE SPOT. Our spot.[94]

So whereas restructuring for the municipal socialists of the early 1980s was about resolving not only the economic problems of particular locales, but also the struggle between labour and capital in favour of the former, restructuring in the late 1980s was, increasingly, about a struggle between localities to maximize inward investment and minimize its opposite.[95] "There is little optimism now", wrote one commentator in 1988, "merely the hawking voice of the political sales-man, marking up his meagre offerings by marking down those of his comrades. We are all, now, Municipal Capitalists. Our Comrades are Not Our Friends."[96] Even allowing for a *soupçon* of irony, such a view was not far from the truth.

So the distinctive "against the market" elements of the political economy of the new municipal socialism had no lasting significance as regards the conduct of local economic policy. As late as 1987 Murray was to write of "decentralised, democratic planning" as "an idea whose time has come".[97] But the fact is that those elements of municipal socialism which did survive the early 1980s, and which proved influential in the rest of the decade, were those which emphasized the need to rejuvenate local economies by putting in place the support structures necessary to allow local enterprise to anticipate, respond to and competitively profit from the *market trends* generated by contemporary *market forces*. And it was this market-focused localism, integrated into a political economy of post-Fordist socialism, that burgeoned in the 1980s and proved particularly influential within the Left in the latter part of that decade. That political economy will be discussed at length in the next chapter. Here, though, the point that must be stressed is that it was ideas as to how local enterprise might perform more effectively *in the market* that enjoyed prescriptive influence and longevity. As something prefigurative of a distinctive and viable political economy of democratic socialism, the new municipal socialism had given up the ghost by the time publications such as the *London Industrial Strategy* were, ironically, both celebrating its achievements and giving it its fullest and most coherent exposition.

94. J. Davies, "From Municipal Socialism to . . . Municipal Socialism", *Local Government Studies* **14** (1988), pp. 19, 21.
95. Totterdill, "Local Economic Strategies as Industrial Policy", p. 516.
96. Davies, "From Municipal Socialism", p. 22.
97. R. Murray, *Breaking with Bureaucracy: Ownership, Control and Nationalisation* (London: CLES, 1987), p. 34.

Chapter 3

The political economy of post-Fordist socialism

In the long dark days of Thatcherism, in the days when Keynesian social democracy had been buried in the ideological avalanche set in motion by the New Right, when the local socialism of the GLC had been abolished by Thatcherite fiat, and when the Left political economy of the AES had been abandoned by all but its most purblind adherents, there were those who sought to understand the nature and source of the power wielded by the forces of darkness and, in the light of that understanding, set democratic socialist political economy upon new theoretical and prescriptive foundations. The most intellectually sophisticated and ambitious of such attempts was that which has sometimes been referred to as post-Fordist and sometimes as "flec spec" socialism, and which was articulated with a particular conviction and energy in the 1980s and early 1990s.[1]

---

1. Post-Fordism and flexible specialization have been distinguished by Wood on the basis that the former is a more supply-side driven response to product innovation and differentiation while the latter is more demand-driven and is characterized by an acute sensitivity to market imperatives, S. Wood, "Introduction", in S. Wood (ed.), *The Transformation of Work* (London: Unwin Hyman, 1989). I have no wish to challenge such distinctions. But, as I am seeking to identify the superstructure of socialist ideology and expectations that have been built upon the contemporary sociological, organizational and technological developments which have been associated with both labels, I will be less exercised by taxonomic precision than those, like

Central to it was a new periodization of the history of capitalism into pre-Fordist, Fordist and post-Fordist epochs. The pre-Fordist regime need not detain us. As to the *differentiae specificae* of Fordism, these were, first, the organization of production to permit long runs of standard products aimed at a mass market. This involved the application of the principles of Taylorist scientific management to an extended subdivision of labour, together with the utilization of a dedicated technology requiring an uninterrupted output of basic products for its efficient and profitable application. This organization of labour was also one that entailed a strict division between the conception and execution of tasks, necessitating, in consequence, rigidly hierarchical command structures.

Secondly, the Fordist organization of production, predicated as it was on an expanding mass market, was seen as intimately connected with those political economies that stressed the need to engender and maintain a buoyant aggregate demand. This, it was argued, was at the heart of the $5-a-day, high-wage strategy which Henry Ford himself adopted and explained the symbiotic relationship between Keynesianism and Fordist mass production that ushered in the golden age of post-war capitalist prosperity. Thus, for some, it was the integration of the regulatory policies and institutions of Keynesianism with a Fordist mode of production that created that stable regime of accumulation which transformed the material basis of life for the bulk of the population of western industrialist nations in the 1950s and 1960s.

Thirdly, integral to both the stabilization of aggregate demand and to a general, social acceptance of the productive methods characteristic of Fordism was an assumption by the state of responsibility for wide-ranging social welfare provision. This, and the policies that it led to, both bolstered working-class purchasing power, particularly in periods of economic downturn, and compensated, in some measure, for the ennui, alienation and attenuation of creative energies that resulted when the obsessive pursuit of productivity gains necessitated a relentless subdivision of labour. In the words of one commentator,

> the hegemony of visions of efficiency based on mass production, and the spread internationally of mass consumer markets, was complemented by the social democratic and labour post-war projects of managing the economy with Keynesian fiscal and monetary tools, and the construction of a welfare state that went beyond poverty relief to become a system of genuine income support and maintenance.[2]

Wood, who have sought to introduce a measure of definitional clarity into a confused debate between post- and neo-Fordists over the developmental trajectory of contemporary capitalism. For my purposes, therefore, flexible specialization will be seen as an integral element of post-Fordism; those who wish may, however, keep Wood's distinction in mind.

2. J. Mathews, *Age of Democracy: The Politics of Post-Fordism and Social Form* (Melbourne: Oxford University Press, 1989), p. xi.

Yet, if the quarter century after the Second World War witnessed the apotheosis of Fordism, the next two decades were to see it descend into crisis. For those who embraced and deployed the notion of Fordism in their periodization of history, the causes of its tribulations were manifold. Indeed, they tended to iterate an explanation of the dynamics of its crisis that was decidedly overdetermined. To begin with, such commentators insisted on the exhaustion, in the 1970s and 1980s, of the productivity gains that had hitherto been derived from the implementation of Taylorist principles. As Adam Smith had made clear in the Wealth of Nations, the progressive subdivision of labour, and its attendant intensification, occasioned certain social and psychological diseconomies that could offset the productivity gains otherwise derived from it. Intellectual atrophy, and the attenuation of initiative and creativity which that produced, inevitably had deleterious consequences for labour productivity.[3] In suppressing labour's creative instincts, Taylorism thereby created a workforce incapable of effecting those incremental improvements in the productive process that Smith, for one, had seen as a major source of productivity gains. Furthermore, it was a labour force that was ill-adapted to the innovation and change which technological development increasingly demanded. In addition, deskilling, monotony and hierarchic decision-making structures instilled an oppositional mentality in the workforce that bore fruit in official and unofficial, overt and covert, industrial action. Also, "when labour [was] too weak to protest openly and collectively, rising rates of health-related absenteeism, early retirement, and increases in chronic illness disrupt[ed] production" and increasingly "strain[ed] social welfare systems that provide[d] for the sick and the disabled".[4]

Two other aspects of the position of labour under Fordism were seen as significant in precipitating its crisis. Firstly, the commitment of national governments to the maintenance of full employment made for a strong and confident trade union movement. In addition, the dominance of mass production methods and the concomitant organization of labour made for "a homogenisation and levelling of the working class which both facilitate[d] organisation and, given the intensive interconnections of Fordist mass production, increase[d] the propensity of capitalism to succumb to industrial action".[5] Thus a powerful and united trade union movement was well-placed to reap the greater part of whatever productivity gains Fordism was still able to generate. Inevitably, this had adverse consequences for profitability, investment levels and thence the long-run dynamism of economies built substantially on Fordist foundations.

---

3. On this see *ibid.*, p. 71.
4. C. Sabel, *Work and Politics* (Cambridge: Cambridge University Press, 1982), p. 199.
5. J. Hirsch, W. Bonefield & J. Holloway, *Post-Fordism and Social Form* (London: Macmillan, 1991), p. 20.

Secondly, as noted, as part of that Fordist compromise with the working class that involved adherence to the principle of raising and maintaining working-class demand, the post-war period saw, in most western industrial nations, the construction or extension of a welfare state. This had two consequences. On the one hand, it was argued, it required the collective use of a significant part of the economic surplus that Fordist production generated, while on the other hand it introduced rigidities into the labour market that made it increasingly difficult to restore profits by the traditional, Fordist means of reducing labour costs when flagging productivity squeezed profitability. In this reading, therefore, "the network of welfare state regulations and apparatuses impli[ed] a form of institutionalisation and legalisation of social demands and services which block[ed] a smooth reduction of the standard of material reproduction".[6] In this regard, post-Fordist socialists were at one with both the Marxist Left and the New Right in seeing the economic crises of the 1970s and 1980s as a function of a profitability squeezed by trade union power and the growth of collective consumption.[7]

It was in terms of the realized and rising material aspirations of the working class that post-Fordist socialists also explained the accelerating inflation of the 1970s and the continuing problem of rapidly rising prices in the 1980s. Fordism, it was argued, embraced the notion of a high-wage economy. It instilled an instinctual consumerism into the working class, creating a consumerist culture in which affluence was seen as the unproblematic and ultimate goal of all human striving.[8] Only with a working population infused with such materialist goals and values could producers be assured of a mass market for their standardized products. Only thus could Fordism continue to work. But such demands, made limitless by mass advertising and made real by the level of wage increases secured in a full employment context, sowed the seeds of inflation. In so doing they helped undermine the kind of macroeconomic stability which, in the 1950s and 1960s, had made certain the continued profitability of Fordist mass production methods. So, by rapidly increasing supply-side costs, "the proximate cause of Fordism's downfall, according to these theorists, was the same as what had been at the root of its earlier success: an economy geared to high wages, high employment, high consumption, and high welfare spending".[9]

---

6. *Ibid.*, p. 19.
7. See, for example, A. Glyn & R. Sutcliffe, *British Capitalism, Workers and the Profits Squeeze* (Harmondsworth: Penguin, 1972) and G. Pilling, *The Crisis of Keynesian Economics: A Marxist View* (Beckenham: Croom Helm, 1986).
8. "the social democratic compromise has only permitted social measures within an extremely hedonistic, individualistic, late capitalist culture, and the latter always threatens to corrupt the former", M. Harrington, *The Next Left: The History of a Future* (New York: Holt, 1986), p. 57.
9. J. Foster, "The Fetish of Fordism", *Monthly Review* **39** (1988), p. 29.

However, while such an explanation of the inflationary crisis confronted by western capitalism in the 1970s and 1980s was fine, if unoriginal, it sat uneasily beside another post-Fordist argument: that the crisis of Fordism was really one of market saturation. As expressed by one commentator, for example, it was "the saturation of domestic markets" that

> radically undermined the Fordist logic. Despite the frantic efforts of mass producers of consumer goods, who have resorted to such methods as aggressive marketing, advertising, building in obsolescence, and creating or stimulating new desires, there are only so many cars . . . that people can absorb.[10]

In part, it was argued, this saturation was a result of the massive expansion in the output of standard goods that Taylorist management and Fordist organization made possible; in part, too, it was seen as a consequence of the global proliferation of Fordist methods of production, with newly industrializing nations adding substantially to output at considerably lower labour cost than western industrial producers. As Sabel and Piore saw it, "the spread of mass-production technology beyond its original homelands has . . . exacerbated the problems stemming from the saturation of markets – markets whose growth defined the post-war boom".[11] Further, while technological advance might, for a time, allow western Fordist producers to stay ahead of the game, the standard nature of the mass-produced product constrained its sophistication and the extent to which it could be innovatively developed and so made it relatively easy for low-labour-cost producers to imitate. "The more standardized the product and routinized the productive process, the easier it is for unsophisticated managers, engineers, and workers to copy."[12] Moreover, this process of imitation and adaptation was seen as likely to accelerate as low-cost producers acquired a technological sophistication and skill base which approximated more closely to that of their western rivals. Thus "as imitators go about their business, they begin to catch up faster. Each round of imitation facilitates the next one by creating skills, institutions, and infrastructures . . . which are at the disposal of later industrialists."[13]

Yet if market saturation was frequently understood as absolute, it was also, crucially, theorized in terms of consumer palates jaded by the kind of products which Fordist production methods furnished. Not only, it was argued, had existing demand for standardized products been satisfied, but, with the growth

10. J. Mathews, *Tools of Change: New Technology and the Democratization of Work* (Sydney: Pluto, 1989), p. 30.
11. Sabel & Piore, *The Second Industrial Divide*, p. 189.
12. *Ibid.*, p. 195.
13. *Ibid.*, p. 196.

of affluence, the nature and structure of demand was changing radically in the last quarter of the twentieth century. In place of the standardized, consumers began to desire the customized.[14] In place of a mass demand for consumer goods, there grew up one which was highly differentiated, and in place of large and uniform markets there emerged fragmented, multiple, volatile and often evanescent niche markets, generating demands to which it was profoundly difficult for inherently inflexible Fordist producers to respond.[15]

For some, this growth of a highly differentiated demand for customized products was seen as a reflexive consequence of rising affluence. For others, such as Sabel, it was precipitated by Fordist producers themselves as they desperately sought to circumvent the saturated markets which they confronted. Thus

> once mass markets began to stagnate and competition intensified . . . a contrasting circle of causality emerged. Firms tried to woo customers by differentiating their products and re-educating the public to appreciate them; the more successful they were, the more they could invest in flexible technologies to increase their efficiency, and the faster the mass markets contracted.[16]

Those who saw the late-twentieth-century travails of industrial producers in terms of a crisis of Fordism, therefore, seem to have explained them, on the one hand, as a consequence of the supply-side, profit-squeezing, cost consequences of an inflationary excess of public and private demand and, on the other, as a consequence of an oversupply of standardized products, aggravated by the rapid Fordist industrialization of new economic powers and the growth of a differentiated demand for non-standard goods. To put it kindly, there was a fundamental explanatory tension here which those who deployed the notion of Fordism for analytical purposes did little to resolve.

Other factors making for Fordist crisis were added to this explicative mélange. Thus it was argued that the separation between the conception and execution of productive tasks, one of the Taylorist hallmarks of Fordism, left producers ill-equipped to exploit the spate of technological innovation which characterized the last quarter of the twentieth century. Specifically, the computerization of productive processes increasingly demanded labour that could conceive and execute, and that could grasp the productive opportunities provided by computerized technology, reacting creatively to its potentialities

---

14. As early as 1977 Fred Hirsch, in *The Social Limits to Growth* (London: Routledge, 1977), remarked on the growth in demand for positional goods.
15. ". . . demand is being expressed in specialised market niches. Quality rather than quantity is increasingly the road to profitability", Mathews, *Tools of Change*, p. 1.
16. Sabel & Piore, *The Second Industrial Divide*, p. 191.

and the problems which its utilization posed. Taylorism looked to program-mable human capital unthinkingly and reliably reproducing a standard set of actions; the computerization of production increasingly demanded a worker with the autonomy and creative intellectual skills necessary to control sophisti-cated, programmable, fixed capital equipment in ways that exploited its flexibility and adaptive potential. A Fordist/Taylorist workforce, therefore, made for productive units that could neither exploit nor survive the technological revolution of the late twentieth century. Economic history was passing them by.

Finally, the crisis of Fordism was also considered as partly a by-product and partly a cause of the ecological crisis induced by the rapid and global industrialization of the post-war period. Such environmental degradation had two aspects that pertained to Fordism's particular difficulties.[17] First, mass production entailed a mass and growing demand for specific inputs, precipitat-ing an "apparently imminent exhaustion of world supplies of the raw materials used in manufacturing"[18] – an exhaustion that had already significantly raised input costs. Secondly, nations had responded to environmental damage with a variety of controls and standards that militated against the standardization of products upon which Fordism had relied for its success. Indeed, this variety of legally enforceable, environmental measures militated in favour of producers geared to that differentiation and customization of output already remarked on in relation to increasing consumer affluence. Both developments, it was sug-gested, exacerbated the difficulties faced by Fordist producers.

For the future, therefore, any viable regime of production and accumulation in western industrial nations would have to come to terms with those contemporary developments that threatened the demise of Fordism. It would have to regain, by non-Taylorist methods, the momentum of labour productiv-ity gains that had characterized "golden-age capitalism". It would need to be distinguished by production processes that dispelled the labour alienation that was, under Fordism, sapping workforce commitment to productivity growth and quality output. It would have to meet, in some manner, the challenge of low-cost, Third-World, mass producers. It would have to cope with the increas-ing volatility of domestic and international markets and display the flexibility and responsiveness necessary to engage with increasingly differentiated, sophisticated and rapidly changing consumer tastes. Finally, it would have to respond to the challenges and opportunities generated by a formidable and accelerating pace of technological change – particularly that emanating from advances in information technology.

---

17. "Consumers, workers, even nature itself all reacted to the tremendous increase in the production of standardized goods in ways that threaten the stability of mass markets", Sabel, *Work and Politics*, p. 198.
18. Sabel and Piore, *The Second Industrial Divide*, p. 191.

However, it was the very crisis of Fordism and the nature of the problems it presented which, for some commentators, created the space for steering industrial and, more generally, economic policy, in a socialist direction; and the banner under which such advances were to be made was that of flexible specialization. This is not to suggest that all who marched under it were socialists or possessed socialist sympathies, or that the notion of flexible specialization pointed unproblematically in a socialist direction. Yet it did, for all that, embody elements, and imply developments, the socialist potentialities of which were seized upon, highlighted and exploited by a number of writers in Britain and elsewhere to produce what some have termed a "flec spec" or post-Fordist socialism.

Flexible specialization was defined as

> a strategy of permanent innovation: accommodation to ceaseless change, rather than an effort to control it. This strategy is based on flexible, multi-use equipment, skilled workers and the creation, through politics, of an industrial community that restricts the forms of competition to those favouring innovation. For these reasons the spread of flexible specialization amounts to a revival of craft forms of production.[19]

It was also a system of production characterized by the manufacture of

> small or medium rather than large volumes of each part or product; frequent changes in the basics of product design and/or production methods; a product portfolio of several models for the same plant, rather than exclusive concentration on one or a few goods; reliance upon the greater task versatility, skills and decision-making abilities of production workers because of the frequency of model changes and the irrelevance of detailed Tayloristic controls.[20]

Flexible specialization pointed, therefore, to the elimination of any division between the conception and execution of tasks and facilitated the introduction of team working, involving task rotation.[21] It was these salient characteristics that imparted, or would impart, to industries and firms organized according to flexible specialization principles, the resilience and adaptability necessary to

---

19. *Ibid.*, p. 17.
20. B. Jones, "Flexible Automation and Factory Politics: The United Kingdom in Comparative Perspective", in Hirst & Zeitlin (eds), *Reversing Industrial Decline?*, p. 99; on this see also P. Hirst & J. Zeitlin, "Flexible Specialisation vs Post-Fordism: Theory, Evidence and Policy Implications", *Economy and Society* **20** (1991), p. 2.
21. For example, in the car industry in the 1970s, see H. Katz & C. Sabel, "Industrial Relations and Industrial Adjustment in the Car Industry", *Industrial Relations* **24** (1985), pp. 295–315.

circumvent or meet the challenges which were undermining Fordism. They would, at the same time, open up avenues for the pursuit of recognizably socialist objectives.

Central to the socialist potentialities of flexible specialization was the nature of the labour that it demanded. The swift adaptation of output to rapidly changing niche markets was the *sine qua non* of survival and success in a post-Fordist world. Short production runs, the constant reconfiguration of the productive process and the use of technologically complex, multi-purpose machines to accommodate such ceaseless change all demanded a radically different kind and organization of labour from that which had characterized Fordist production. Flexible specialization put labour at the centre of the production process or, as one commentator put it, "post-Fordism sees labour as the key asset of modern production".[22]

To begin with, and of particular importance, labour operating techno-logically sophisticated capital equipment, in constantly reconfigured industrial processes, required the necessary polyvalent skills to adapt and be productive. Where Fordism had looked to deskilled automata, flexible specialization required a highly skilled labour force subject to constant retraining and skill enhancement.[23] For some, this rejuvenated the notion of the skilled craftsman playing a creative and interactive role in the production process, constantly deploying cognitive skills and thereby eroding the "boundary between intellectual and manual work".[24] Thus it was argued that flexible specialization had an inherent tendency to eliminate hierarchical divisions between conception and execution and, more generally, that it moved away from the fragmentation of tasks that had been integral to Fordist mass production.[25] Sabel categorized this as "high technology cottage industry: the unity of conception and execution, the abstract and the concrete".[26] It seemed to some,

---

22. R. Murray, "Fordism and Post-Fordism", in S. Hall & M. Jacques (eds), *New Times: The Changing Face of Politics in the 1990s* (London: Lawrence & Wishart, 1990), p. 49.
23. See, for example, R. Hyman, "Flexible Specialisation: Miracle or Myth?", in R. Hyman & W. Streeck (eds), *New Technology and Industrial Relations* (Oxford: Blackwell, 1988), p. 49; also Foster, "The Fetish of Fordism", p. 29. Some in the 1980s argued that this was already affecting the structure of the workforce: "the proportion of intermediate and low-skilled jobs is constantly diminishing with the introduction of such systems as FMS", K. Ebel, "Social and Labour Implications of Flexible Manufacturing Systems", *International Labour Review* **124** (1985), p. 144.
24. Sabel, *Work and Politics*, p. 224; see also on this M. Harrington, *Socialism: Past and Future* (London: Pluto, 1993), p. 116.
25. In their classic study of the West German car industry, H. Kern & M. Schumann wrote of "new production concepts . . . that are no longer based on fragmentation of tasks, divorce of conception from execution and subject to supervision and surveillance", *The End of the Division of Labour?*, quoted from Mathews, *Tools of Change*, p. 35; on this see also G. Thompson, "Flexible Specialisation, Industrial Districts, Regional Economies: Strategies for Socialists?", *Economy and Society* **18** (1988): 527–45, p. 533. For a discussion of the fusion of conception and design in the French engineering industry see W. Cavestro, "Automation, New Technology and Work Content", in Wood (ed.), *The Transformation of Work*, pp. 233–4.
26. Sabel, *Work and Politics*, p. 220.

therefore, that "post Fordism finally [made] it possible to realise the social democratic dream of reconciling the interests of capital in securing high rates of productivity with the interests of the working class in . . . *fulfilment at work*".[27]

Imbued with a diversified range of skills, in a production process where it once again played a pivotal role, labour would, inevitably, secure a degree of autonomy manifestly absent from Fordism, but of a kind that had characterized the nineteenth-century industrial craftsman. Sabel looked, for example, to the emergence of a stratum of "broadly skilled craftsmen who install, maintain and supervise the operation of capital equipment" and were able to assert their "workplace autonomy".[28] Another commentator wrote of "workers" being "less tied to machines and more independent of their rhythm" and of this "open[ing] the door . . . for the utilization of alternative forms of work organisation such as autonomous groups".[29] Others wrote of the proliferation of "semi-autonomous units", as employers abandoned attempts to subject those whose adaptable skills were crucial to the smooth operation of production "to the punitive surveillance and supervision that prevailed under Taylorism".[30] It was argued that only such autonomy, group or individual, would furnish the flexibility necessary for the constant changes in the productive process required by the small- and medium-batch production that differentiated demand required.

Such autonomy and independence would in turn demand a consensual, co-operative and, many suggested, a more democratic approach to the conduct of industrial relations. Skilled labour was coming to occupy a position of considerable power, because its skills were crucial to economic success. That power had to be accommodated before it could be utilized. Workers had, therefore, to be managed "in ways which [would] stimulate their active commitment to efficient and high quality production".[31] In this context, commentators wrote of the need for "a web of trust and co-operation among workers and management"; of "a comprehensive switch to flexible specialis-ation . . . push[ing] managements to 'high trust' relations with their work-forces" and of "social partners need[ing] to co-operate".[32] Inevitably, it was believed, such co-operation had to recognize the *de facto* decision-making autonomy of skilled workers and work groups and this meant a preparedness to

27. S. Clarke, "New Utopias for Old: Fordist Dreams and Post-Fordist Fantasies", *Capital and Class* **42** (1990), p. 131, my emphasis; "the 'right to work' is a radical dogma in the midst of capitalist recession: the right to creative work goes even further", G. Kelly, "Useful Work and Useless Toil", *Marxism Today* (August 1982), p. 17.
28. Sabel, *Work and Politics*, pp. 48, 187.
29. Ebel, "Social and Labour Implications", pp. 140–1.
30. Mathews, *Age of Democracy*, p. 71.
31. Hyman, "Flexible Specialisation", p. 49.
32. M. Piore, "The Decline of Mass Production and the Challenge to Union Survival", *Industrial Relations Journal* **19** (1986), p. 211. On this see J. Tomaney, "The Reality of Workplace Flexibility", *Capital and Class* **40** (1990), p. 38.

share real, decision-making authority over the organization, pace, direction, conditions and remuneration of production. Thus labour would be able to take advantage of "the less authoritarian, more participative democratic workplace which [was] emerging".[33] Firms organized on flexible specialization principles would be characterized by flatter command hierarchies,[34] limited surveillance and supervision and the kind of democratization of decision-making which would not only instil commitment to organization goals, but would also allow enterprises to reap the benefits of expertise freely and creatively given – to reap, in effect, what Lester Thurow categorized as the "soft productivity gains" of a co-operative and harmonious working environment.[35] The goals of workplace democratization and the economic rejuvenation of a moribund Fordist economy were, after all, one and the same.[36]

Moreover, given this autonomy and given, therefore, the need for labour's commitment to a productive enterprise to be freely bestowed, it was clearly imperative that it should be actively and meaningfully engaged in decision-making. An extension of industrial democracy was therefore seen as inevitable; it was to be the *quid pro quo* for the commitment required of skilled and autonomous labour. As one commentator phrased it, post-Fordists "harnesse[d] aspirations towards workers' direct involvement in production decisions, or direct industrial democracy, to the commercial success of firms deploying the strategy".[37] A historic moment had arisen when even short-run economic expediency seemed to be consistent with the application of socialist principles to enterprise management: "The participative and democratic workplace" was becoming "the most efficient and productive workplace".[38]

So an economy characterized by flexible specialization embodied potentialities for the realization of distinctively socialist aspirations. In place of the social, psychological and intellectual diseconomies attendant on the progressive subdivision of increasingly unskilled tasks, it held out the possibility of work demanding a functional versatility on the part of a labour force distinguished by the multiplicity and sophistication of the skills which it possessed and deployed.

33. Mathews, *Tools of Change*, p. 2.
34. "The social relations of these new systems of production and distribution are different from those of mass production . . . Where there is rapid change and uncertainty, flatter hierarchies and greater lateral communication are more functional", M. Rustin, "The Trouble with 'New Times'", in Hall & Jacques (eds), *New Times*, p. 304.
35. For a discussion of these gains from a socialist perspective see Harrington, *Socialism: Past and Future*, p. 147.
36. Discussion of this was particularly extensive in US organizational theory literature of the 1980s; see, for example, L. Hirschorn, *Beyond Mechanization: Work and Technology in a Post-Industrial Age* (Boston: MIT Press, 1984) and T. Kochan *et al.*, *The Transformation of American Industrial Relations* (New York: Basic Books, 1986).
37. P. Garrahan & P. Stewart, "Management Control and a New Regime of Subordination: Post-Fordism and the Local Economy", in R. Burrows *et al.* (eds), *Fordism and Flexibility* (London: Macmillan, 1992), p. 117.
38. Mathews, *Tools of Change*, p. 34.

The ideal of labour, involving a many-sided craftsmanship that fused manual dexterity and cognitive power, to be found in the Marx of the *Philosophical Manuscripts*, the Morris of *News from Nowhere* and in much of the writing of the guild socialists, was often latent, and sometimes overtly enunciated, in the work of post-Fordist socialists. Certainly, there were strong Morrisian inflections in Sabel's hope that labour might become "joyful, self-creative association".[39] And, in this context, it is interesting to note too how often the terms "craft" and "craftsmanship" were used by those who saw in flexible specialization opportunities to effect a profound transformation in the nature of labour.

Other contemporary developments were also seen as significant in relation to the socialist potentialities of flexible specialization. In particular, there were the late-twentieth-century mutations in the structure of many enterprises and industries which flexible specialization was seen as producing. For, as many saw it, in an economic world where flexibility was at a premium, small became not only beautiful but also supremely efficient. This was evident in the economic success of a number of what, borrowing from Alfred Marshall, were termed "industrial districts". These were to be found in the so-called "Third Italy", "stretching from the Venetian provinces in the North through Bologna and Florence to Ancona in the South", in Jutland, in Baden-Württemberg and in the Sukaki district of Japan,[40] and were characterized by a multiplicity of interdependent, small and medium-sized enterprises, using relatively inexpensive but flexible technologies and, for the most part, highly skilled and polyvalent labour. In the context of these industrial districts, firms possessed the flexibility advantages of relative smallness of size, while securing the economies of scale that close and stable interdependence offered.

And given their size, such firms opened up the possibility of, indeed they necessitated the development of, more democratic and less authoritarian forms of governance than had distinguished capitalist enterprise in the Fordist period. As Hirst viewed it,

> it should be evident that changes in industrial structure have breathed life into the idea of a democratic economy based on a plurality of sizes of firms and styles of governance. Small and medium-sized firms have grown in relative importance and also in their autonomy from larger ones.[41]

Where size, through the economies of scale it permitted, had been the key factor in economic success, decision-making, as regards the greater part of the labour force, was likely to be remote and non-participative. But where size was no longer

---

39. Sabel, *Work and Politics*, p. 220.
40. On these see, for example, C. Sabel, "Flexible Specialisation and the Re-emergence of Regional Economies", in Hirst & Zeitlin (eds), *Reversing Industrial Decline?*, p. 22.
41. Hirst, *Associative Democracy*, p. 142.

crucial – when, for example, small and medium-sized firms could, at reasonable cost, acquire cutting-edge, flexible technology;[42] when quality rather than low-cost quantity was of the essence; when economies of flexibility or scope were greater than economies of scale; and when, in any case, many economies of scale could be secured through the close interdependence that industrial districts facilitated – firms of a size in which democratic decision-making became not just feasible, but also vital for economic success emerged and prospered.[43]

Also, where small was proving successful and where the democratization of decision-making carried with it significant productivity gains, the opportunities for the creation and success of producer co-operatives and labour-managed firms were considerably enhanced. Historically, as we shall see in Chapters 5 and 6, such enterprises had tended to be small. They relied for their success on the highly differentiated skills that their labour force could offer, and they drew heavily on its freely given commitment. For many "flec spec" socialists, such enterprises therefore clearly possessed many of the vital requisites for enterprise success in a post-Fordist economic world.[44] Here again, the increasing importance of flexible specialization was creating economic circumstances that militated in favour of an economically decentralized democratic socialism.

One other aspect of the democratization associated with flexible specializ-ation should be noticed and that relates to what some commentators saw as the dispersal or decentralization of economic power which it seemed to precipitate. This had a number of aspects. To begin with, there was the dispersal of power within enterprises consequent upon the greater autonomy of decision-making enjoyed by sub-groups and individual "craftsmen". Further, there was an increasing tendency on the part of large companies to decentralize decision-making to units of production. This was a process that enhanced the flexibility and adaptability of corporations; it was facilitated by advances in information technology that allowed individual productive units to make use of centrally provided services, information and finance without the need for a comparable centralization of decision-making power.[45] Thus many commentators argued that computer-automated manufacturing would allow "vertically integrated operations to uncouple their production processes – leading to the emergence of many small, single product or single function companies".[46]

---

42. For a discussion of this see S. Brusco, "The Emilian Model: Productive Decentralisation and Social Integration", *Cambridge Journal of Economics* **6** (1982), p. 172.
43. In fact, in the 1980s, many contemporary commentators were stressing the *diseconomies* of scale. See, for example, R. Hayes & S. Wheelwright, *Restoring our Competitive Edge: Competing Through Manufacturing* (New York: Wiley, 1984) and W. Abernathy, K. Clark & A. Kantrow, *Industrial Renaissance: Producing a Competitive Edge for America* (New York: Basic Books, 1983).
44. "German socialists have . . . argued that there may well be an entirely new future for co-operative enterprise in the advanced economies", Hirst, *Associative Democracy*, p. 147.
45. On this see, for example, Hyman, "Flexible Specialisation", p. 50.
46. C. Gill, *Work, Unemployment and the New Technology* (Cambridge: Polity, 1985), p. 72.

Further, the emergence of economically dynamic industrial districts resulted in a decentralization of economic power within the nation state to regions and localities. Their success, as relatively autonomous economic entities, had resulted in "the re-emergence of regions as meaningful economic units".[47] At the same time their emergence was seen as contrasting with the impotence of macro-economic management at a national level. Given, then, that "the national level ha[d] lost its economic primacy" (as evidenced by the inefficacy of Keynesian demand management) and that "many of the most pressing problems in economic management turn[ed] on the relative decline of the nation state", some other more effective geographical unit of decision-making had to be found and the industrial region or district seemed to provide it.[48] In this way, post-Fordist notions were used both to explain the *de facto* decentralization of economic authority and to press for the conscious development and acceleration of this trend. Economic power was being, could be and should be, brought closer to those affected by it and, in that sense, rendered amenable to more informed and precise democratic control.

In other ways too the gospel of flexible specialization represented good news for those who wished to highlight the compatibility of a democratic socialist political economy with current economic trends. As noted, industrial districts tended to be distinguished not only by the proliferation of relatively small enterprises, but also by the extent of co-operation and interdependence that grew up between such firms. Indeed, the collaborative and co-operative nature of the economic relationships that developed within industrial districts was seen as crucial to the success of the size of firms which flexible specialization engendered. So, while accepting the benefits to be secured from competition, post-Fordist socialists were adamant in rejecting the free market model of the New Right, "precisely because [they] emphasize[d] the importance of social relationships that secure[d] crucial inputs and vital collective services for firms" – inputs which could "not be guaranteed by the model of sovereign enterprises purchasing the factors of production in open markets".[49] Economic success depended "not on cut-throat competition among atomistic entrepreneurs but rather on a complex set of subcontracting relationships based on co-operation and mutual trust".[50] Such relations between producers and their suppliers, and even with their "competitors", allowed firms to cope with the volatility of demand, to minimize supplier transaction costs, to spread the expense of responsive innovation and its risks[51] and to reap economies of scale by means of

47. P. Hirst & J. Zeitlin, "Introduction", in Hirst & Zeitlin (eds), *Reversing Industrial Decline?*, p. 46.
48. Hirst, *Associative Democracy*, pp. 7, 74–5; see also Thompson, "Flexible Specialisation", p. 539 and S. Wood, "Introduction", in Wood (ed.), *The Transformation of Work*, p. 13.
49. Hirst & Zeitlin, "Flexible Specialisation", p. 42.
50. J. Zeitlin, "Local Economic Strategies: An Introduction", *Economy and Society* **18** (1989), p. 369.
51. On these points see *ibid*., pp. 368–9, Sabel, *Work and Politics*, p. 226 and Sabel, "Flexible Specialisation", p. 35.

co-operative institutions which pooled "the costs of supporting developed networks of collective services for marketing, consultancy, technological information, financial services and the purchasing of inputs".[52]

So the principles of solidarity, mutuality and even communitarianism informed, and would increasingly inform, the relationships which prevailed within industrial districts.[53] It was the acceptance and application of these principles that gave firms their adaptability, their resilience, their innovative dynamism and, thence, their competitive edge.[54] Flexible specialization was seen as succeeding, therefore, in an oxymoronic context of co-operative competition. Solidaristic institutions, it was argued, would give practical expression to such principles. The notion of collectively servicing the needs of firms has already been noted, but provision of the requisite institutional infrastructure was also seen as having wider political implications. In this context, local politics and political institutions were regarded as having a crucial role to play in "reinforcing local interdependencies, strengthening the local socialisation of production, and sharpening the specialisation of the local economy",[55] all of which would further foster local/regional solidarities. Thus, in an article on the industrial district of Modena, Brusco and Righi pointed to the initiatives of local government that established "industrial parks" to foster "orderly development", "the loan guarantee consortium" which "aimed to secure special financing for small firms; and the creation of 'real service centres' . . . directed towards supplying information on technology and markets to industrial districts specializing in particular sectors".[56] Here the political economy of "flec spec" socialism was consonant with, and supportive of, the new municipal and regional socialism discussed in the previous chapter.[57]

The oxymoronic strategy of co-operative competition might embody profound tensions, tensions that would be all too apparent when it was invested with prescriptive substance. But it did, nevertheless, strike a chord with many democratic socialists who warmed to ideas of a non-statist, pluralist, decentralized collectivism in which producer co-operatives and labour-managed firms infused with a spirit of mutuality played a central role. If flexible specialization breathed new life into nineteenth-century notions of the polyvalent craftsman,

---

52. Hirst & Zeitlin, "Flexible Specialisation", 46.
53. Sabel & Piore, *The Second Industrial Divide*, p. 278.
54. "Crucial to the renewal of the industrial district in the late 20th century . . . are strong institutions and infrastructure: relations of trust based on face-to-face contact, a 'productive community' historically rooted in a particular place, a strong sense of local pride and allegiance." K. Robins, "Global Times", *Marxism Today* (December 1989), p. 20.
55. Eisenschitz & Gough, *The Politics of Local Economic Policy*, p. 123; see also Zeitlin, "Local Economic Strategies", p. 369.
56. S. Brusco & E. Righi, "Industrial Policy and Social Consensus: The Case of Modena", *Economy and Society* **18** (1989), p. 405.
57. L. Weiss, "The Italian State and Small Businesses", *Archive of European Sociology* **25** (1984), pp. 214–41.

it also reinvigorated the political economies of communitarian and municipal socialism that had been out of favour, within the mainstream Left, for the greater part of the twentieth century. In these respects, and others, it seemed therefore to offer a radical, democratic socialist alternative untainted by the failures associated with Keynesian social democracy.

Just as postmodernism was declaring meta-history, and, in particular, Marxian meta-history, redundant, post-Fordist socialism was constructing a grand explanatory framework resting on unashamedly materialist foundations. And if this post-Fordist socialism had, at its core, the notion of the uncertainty of the economic world confronted by contemporary producers, it nonetheless offered to socialists an alternative, overarching certainty derived from an understanding of the motive forces of historical change, their materialization in things past and their likely shaping of things to come. It furnished a new and optimistic meta-history to replace a Marxist rival tarnished by explanatory and predictive failure and adhered to by only a small and dwindling fraction of the British Left. It provided a new periodization of nineteenth- and twentieth-century western economic history with, seemingly, considerable explanatory power. It embodied an explanation of the contemporary crisis that transposed Marxian notions of a falling rate of profit and underconsumption/market saturation into a new explanatory framework. It accommodated the notion of the changing contemporary structure (and not just the aggregate level) of demand, and it considered investment not simply in relation to its organic composition, but also with respect to its technological character and the nature of its impact upon the productive process. Of course, there was the danger that in assuming a "prophetic style" it "unleashed a method of policy dissemination, where the prescriptive message is carried in the assertion of a trend".[58] But, that said, it was a message with a micro- and a mesoeconomic import that addressed, or attempted to address, the nature of capitalist change at the level of enterprises and districts, as well as at that of the macroeconomy. Therein lay part, at least, of its appeal to many socialists.

Post-Fordist socialism could offer anew the hope that the present was pregnant with a socialist future. It was not crudely determinist. It did speak in terms of potentialities. But it nonetheless made clear the manifold possibilities for socialist advance that contemporary capitalism was generating. Not since inter-war Marxism had there been a political economy which gave such strong cause to believe that the God of history was playing on the side of the angels. Some interpreted this as "merely an expression of hope that the tendencies of capitalist development will prove to be the salvation of social democracy".[59] But where hope was at a premium, with an authoritarian neo-liberalism in the

---

58. A. Pollert, "Dismantling Flexibility", *Capital and Class* **34** (1988), p. 67.
59. Clarke, "New Utopias for Old", p. 133.

ascendant, and the New Right having seemingly secured the freehold of No. 10, those economic philosophies that purveyed it pedalled their wares in a sellers' market. If, then, as some contemporary critics suggested, there was a slippage of critical standards by those on the Left who embraced such a political economy with enthusiasm, it was a slippage born of the desire to descry pattern and hope in a world turned upside down.[60] As one writer put it, "the post-Fordist hypothesis . . . [was] the nearest thing we have to a paradigm which can link widespread changes in forms of production to changes in class relations, state forms and individual identities".[61]

But, explanatory and predictive power aside, more potent still was the vision which post-Fordist socialism encapsulated: a vision in large measure untainted by past failures. Like the AES, it sought a redistribution and democratization of power but, avowedly, of a more radical kind and using means uncompromised by central planning institutions such as the NEB and NIB. It was about the decentralization of economic policy-making to regions to provide the social and industrial infrastructure of economic success. It was about the diffusion of economic power to workforces through the new potency of a labour force both skilled and autonomous. It involved the decentralization of power away from the central offices of national unions to the workplace, where labour could bargain more effectively and across a wider range of issues than traditional trade unionism. It was about the decentralization of decision-making power away from the head offices of large corporations to the units of production of which they were comprised. The post-Fordist vision therefore embodied an aspiration for a fundamental shift in the balance of economic power and its democratization, without the kind of corporatist collectivism that had played a part in vitiating the appeal of the AES.

Moreover, at the heart of the post-Fordist vision was something that had been lost for the greater part of the twentieth century, but that had had a profound and visceral appeal for many on the British Left – the vision of the polyvalent labourer: the rounded, independent artisan, no longer wielding just the power of the lathe or the slide rule but the computer, no longer just a figment of utopian nostalgia but in the very vanguard of history, the dream of the whole man made flesh. For post-Fordist socialists, these new artisans were truly the shock troops of the revolution, or at least its IT variant. Each workplace could become a Kelmscott: a locus of joyful and creative labour. It would produce customized products for discriminating consumers in a democratized and decentralized polity of skilled artisans imbued with civic virtue. This was a vision that, it was believed, could win back just that social constituency that was abandoning the Left in droves to embrace the popular capitalism of the New Right in the 1980s.

---

60. K. Williams *et al.*, "The End of Mass Production?", *Economy and Society* **16** (1987), p. 404.
61. Rustin, "The Trouble with 'New Times'", p. 303.

For many socialists, the great attraction of post-Fordism was that it did indeed offer fertile conceptual and rhetorical terrain upon which to do battle with the New Right. For it contested concepts which Keynesian socialism, or even AES socialism, either left unchallenged or upon which they had little critical purchase. Post-Fordist socialists talked the New Right talk, without walking the New Right walk. They embraced the notions of flexible labour, consumer sovereignty, the consumerist aspirations of labour, receptivity to market imperatives (and, in particular, those stemming from competition), together with an acceptance of the need for radical industrial restructuring and a fundamental, supply-side revolution. And, in doing so, they bid fair to rescue such concepts and discourse from the pernicious uses to which they had been put by the New Right.

Thus labour flexibility was to be derived from the existence of well-remunerated, skilled and reskilled, polyvalent artisans, not from a low-paid, unskilled and intermittently employed workforce. Responding to consumer sovereignty meant a response to the differentiated demand for customized, high-quality products that demanded skill and creativity in their manufacture, not the production of the cheap and nasty for an undiscriminating mass market. The willingness to accommodate market imperatives and react to competitive pressures meant a determination to compete on quality and by way of innovation, not simply the honing of one's competitive edge by reducing labour costs to regain market share. Flexible producers would move up market in the direction of a high-wage economy, not down market to compete with newly industrializing mass producers, utilizing subsistence wage labour. Industrial restructuring would involve the decline of the mass-producing, staple industries but, at the same time, the rapid growth of medium and small-scale, high-quality manufacturing enterprises. It would not entail, as with the New Right, the burgeoning of a low-wage, low-status, "McJobs" service sector where heritage and theme parks substituted for coal mines and shipyards.

As regards the need for a supply-side revolution, post-Fordism and the New Right were at one in their belief that this was what held the key to the rejuvenation of industrial economies, particularly that of Britain. "Flexible specialization in its policy implications [was] a radical supply-side policy."[62] In that respect, its proponents believed it differed from what the Left had previously offered. The AES, for example, had said "almost nothing about the problems of design, production, organisation and marketing which were at the

---

62. Hirst & Zeitlin, "Flexible Specialisation", p. 43; "The social democratic Left's supply side strategy has also attempted to increase flexibility and competitiveness but in this case by stimulating the introduction of flexible automation . . . and by developing highly skilled workers through modernised training schemes", G. Albo, "Competitive Austerity and the Impasse of Capitalist Employment Policy", *Socialist Register, 1994* (London: Merlin, 1994), pp. 146–8.

root of the UK's industrial failure".[63] Rather it was a strategy that "strengthened the worker's capacities to resist technical change". Likewise, Keynesian social democracy, among its other failings, offered "no direct purchase on the major economic issue of our time, which is the restructuring of production".[64] However, where the New Right looked to heighten market incentives and intensify market pressures to increase labour effort and thence productivity, post-Fordist socialism stressed the complexity of the institutional, political and attitudinal preconditions which would have to be met before enhanced productivity could be expected to transform national economic performance. They looked to the creation of a "progressive competitiveness",[65] a supply-side revolution to which solidaristic social attitudes, policies and behaviour were integral.

Then, to truly steal the New Right's thunder, there was "flec spec" socialism's apotheosis of the discriminating consumer. In a period when consumption came to be seen as a, if not the, quintessential expression of identity, when self was, for many, coming to be defined in the purchase of designer labels, when the realm of freedom was entered via the checkout and the proliferation of plastic gave many the illusion of consumer sovereignty, a socialism based on the doctrines of flexible specialization seemed in harmony with the mood of the age. Post-Fordist socialists could offer the discriminating consumer of customized, high-quality products as the archetype of a new revolutionary vanguard, effecting a transformation in the position of labour by demanding goods produced by non-alienated, multiskilled artisans, in small computer-resourced workshops, characterized by co-operative and democratized decision-making. For them, it was the discriminating consumer, not the hardy-handed son of toil, who could be relied upon to precipitate those revolutionary changes in the organization of production that would lay the basis for a liberated proletariat within a socialist economy and polity. Not only could rich consumers enter the New Jerusalem, but their activity in the shopping malls of England's green and pleasant land would prove instrumental in its construction. A Benetton Britain would be a socialist Britain and, of course, given the relative attractions of Benetton and socialism in the 1980s, this seemed to some to have salutary implications as regards political support. Nowhere was the spirit of this new consumer socialism more fervently embraced than in the pages of *Marxism Today*, which entered into the spirit of what it termed, with unnerving originality, "New Times" by launching its own credit card and range of designer products, giving the impression, as one writer

---

63. P. Hirst, "The Politics of Industrial Policy", in Hirst and Zeitlin (eds), *Reversing Industrial Decline?*, p. 285.
64. R. Murray, "Benetton Britain: The New Economic Order", in S. Hall & M. Jacques (eds), *The Politics of Thatcherism* (London: Lawrence & Wishart, 1983), p. 56.
65. *Ibid.*, p. 155.

put it at the time, that where you stood on consumption had become the "litmus test of the whole issue of socialist renewal".[66] The workers of the world need no longer unite, they could go shopping instead, and the revolution would follow swiftly in the wake of their purchases.

Joyful labour and customized abundance: who could ask for anything more? Small wonder that confronted by such an all-encompassing socialist vision – one which tapped into potent traditions of socialist thought, which accommodated the aspirations of those who had succumbed to the siren call of an aggressively acquisitive materialism, which addressed and explained the current crisis and which identified historical trends and how to exploit them – some on the Left should, indeed, have let their critical standards slip.[67]

So did post-Fordist ideas furnish the basis of a coherent, defensible and recognizably democratic socialist political economy applicable to the problems of contemporary British capitalism? Let us begin here with a contemporary critical rebuttal that was made of key post-Fordist claims before looking at each of its elements in more detail. Thus,

> for many radical and Marxist critics the attendant ethos of flexibility is part of a more general recipe for more insecurity of employment, techno-logical deskilling, segmentation of workforces, effort intensification and the erosion of union checks upon managerial authority. From this pers-pective flexible manufacture is frequently labelled neo-Fordism; a more sophisticated system of exploiting labour and production technology than was possible under conventional, Fordist, mass production methods.[68]

As regards the central issue of skilling/deskilling, post-Fordist socialists stressed, in particular, the skills necessitated by the fusion of conception and execution which computer technology increasingly demanded. In fact, the skilled programming of machines and programming adjustments were, as studies of US experience showed, often restricted to "management strata".[69] In addition, far from fusing conception and execution, many commentators saw "increasing internationalisation, computerisation and telecommunications" as "removing conception even further from the shop floor".[70] It was also pointed out, again with reference to the United States, that CNC technology, requiring considerable off-line programming, removed that programming from the

---

66. J. Saville, "*Marxism Today:* An Anatomy", *Socialist Register, 1990* (London: Merlin, 1990), p. 36.
67. As one commentator pointed out, in Britain, it was with "the idea of 'associational socialism', as developed by Paul Hirst ... that the notion of flexible specialisation has the closest contemporary affinities. Though others saw it as a contemporary articulation of a Proudhonist conception of co-operative socialism", Thompson, "Flexible Specialisation", p. 535.
68. Jones, "Flexible Automation", p. 95.
69. *Ibid.*, p. 104.
70. Wood, "Introduction", p. 30.

operator, once again severing the link between the conception and execution of tasks.[71] Many commentators were adamant, therefore, that "there [was] no generalisable trend toward the technologically driven, flexible, craft work suggested by the flexible specialisation theorists". The fact was that contemporary technology could be as easily, and was as often, used to deskill as otherwise, and there was "no clear development towards an upgraded craft revival".[72]

It was true that many firms in the 1980s and 1990s were characterized by a greater functional flexibility of their workforce than had previously been the case. But the fact that workers now undertook a range of tasks "d[id] not usually involve qualitatively increased skilling, since the constituent tasks [were] already so deskilled".[73] Often such flexibility entailed no more than multiple machine minding with attendant maintenance tasks. In consequence, it had more to do with the intensification of labour than the emergence of a polyvalent labour force imbued with a greater sense of its own worth and dignity. As one commentator put it, "employees who can perform a variety of routine functions will doubtless be of greater value to the employer; but their own sense of meaning, dignity and control in work may reveal no significant improvement".[74] In fact, as some surveys made apparent, in pressing for functional flexibility the intention of employers was not multiskilling, but the erosion of those demarcations that previously hindered the smooth flow of the production process and engendered internecine union disputes.[75]

If, then, the proliferation of autonomous, or semi-autonomous, flexibly skilled artisans was a problematic notion, what of the tendency to industrial democracy which, in part, were seen as resulting from their newly acquired and technologically anchored status? Certainly, in the 1980s and 1990s, it was the case that, in some industries and sectors of industry, individuals and work groups were given greater responsibility for the organization, pace and scheduling of production than they had had before. The organization of teamwork production by Volvo at Kalmar and Tørslanda was one, but only one, example of this. However, it has been contended that such delegation, and with it powers of job reform, did not necessarily "negate the overall directive control of management; a control which could be applied coercively if self-discipline fails to yield the

---

71. On this, with respect to the US car industry, see H. Shaiken, *Work Transformed: Automation and Labor in the Computer Age* (New York: Holt, Rinehart and Winston, 1984).
72. Tomaney, "The Reality of Workplace Flexibility", p. 50; on this see also J. Gough, "Industrial Policy and Socialist Strategy: Restructuring and the Unity of the Working Class", *Capital and Class* **29** (1986), p. 65 and Pollert, "Dismantling Flexibility", p. 62. H. Shaiken, S. Herzenberg & S. Kuhn, "The Work Process under More Flexible Production", *Industrial Relations* **25** (1986), p. 182, pointed to computer numerically controlled (CNC) and flexible manufacturing systems (FMS) technology as frequently encompassing the demise of "the all-round machinist".
73. Eisenschitz & Gough, *The Politics of Local Economic Policy*, p. 135.
74. Hyman, "Flexible Specialisation", pp. 54–5.
75. Tomaney, "The Reality of Workplace Flexibility", p. 46.

required outcomes".[76] Similarly, experiments in group work in Volkswagen in the 1970s were seen by employers as "a means of using groups to undercut trade union influence within the plant".[77] As one writer put it, such developments and other forms of participation in decision-making have very often proved "soft on power", doing little in terms of democratizing strategic decision-making or even making it more transparent.[78] Even those who stressed the positive opportunities for greater industrial democracy opened up by flexible specialization admitted here the very real dangers of "a manipulated communitarianism in which power relations remain as they were but are voluntarily, even happily, accepted . . . as managerial strategy turns towards the feigning of human relations in production".[79] Thus flexible working arrangements, the delegation of power over the organisation of production and the semi-autonomy of groups and individuals could become a means of manufacturing consent – a way of identifying the labour force with company objectives that were, in effect, still determined by a distinct managerial stratum. A study of team working at the Nissan car plant in the north-east of England came to just such a view, seeing these developments as "essential to the manufacturing of consent for subordination in production. Whatever else these new social and organisational arrangements create at the level of new, flexible working arrangements, we can interpret them as constituting essential mechanisms for a new regime of subordination."[80] So seemingly greater autonomy gave workers the shadow not the substance of power within enterprises. They might play a more significant part than previously in determining the means by which capitalist objectives were pursued but not in the determination of the objectives themselves.

Here, too, as with the skilling/deskilling of labour, technological innovation was seen as having an ambivalent role. On the one hand, by opening up the possibility of linking the conception and execution of tasks it made, in theory, many of the old hierarchical command structures unnecessary. On the other, studies demonstrated "the use of new technology to wrest control from production workers and further centralise management control" and also its role in re-emphasizing "hierarchical organisational principles".[81] In addition, new technology in the 1980s and 1990s clearly provided the means of reinforcing control from a "distant centre", with "the introduction of relatively

---

76. Hyman, "Flexible Specialisation", p. 54.
77. Gill, *Work, Unemployment and the New Technology*, p. 68.
78. *Ibid.*
79. Harrington, *Socialism: Past and Future*, p. 192.
80. Garrahan & Stewart, "Management Control", p. 116.
81. Quoted from Pollert, "Dismantling Flexibility", p. 61; Jones, "Flexible Automation', p. 103. For a perceptive discussion of these tensions see, in particular, S. Zuboff, *In the Age of the Smart Machine: The Future of Work and Power* (New York: Basic Books, 1988). A US survey of managers in the metallurgical industry suggested that they saw FMS as a means of "wrest[ing] some of the control away from labour . . . put[ting] it back in the hands of management where it belongs", Gill, *Work, Unemployment and the New Technology*, p. 83.

inexpensive microelectronic systems" allowing "the work system and productive process [to] be subject to a higher degree of management regulation". So, for some managements, machine monitoring systems were clearly seen as particularly useful in identifying "idle buggers".[82] Technology could be and was being used, therefore, as a way of reinforcing traditional, centralized, hierarchical command structures in industry.[83]

In addition, leaving aside whether small and medium-sized firms really did play a more significant part in the manufacturing sector in this period,[84] their proliferation did not in any case necessarily make for a greater democratization of industrial decision-making. Thus, where the pursuit of flexibility led to the decentralization of tasks and the consequent emergence of a multiplicity of small firms and outworkers, as in the "Third Italy", this often occurred *pari passu* with increasing opportunities for larger corporations to establish exploitative, rather than simply collaborative, relationships with client firms and suppliers. Where that occurred, there was often little scope within smaller firms for any significant democratization of decision-making. In such circumstances, it was almost inevitably the large corporations that made the crucial enterprise decisions.

Also, with respect to small firms in the Emilia Romagna, one commentator wrote that

> internally, task specialisation and a more conventionally hierarchical division of labour may develop as small firms acquire more sophisticated computer-controlled machines and computerised design and inspection systems, either because the owner-artisans themselves begin to monopolise this more strategic work, or because they hire specialist programmers and the like.[85]

So even in small firms, traditional hierarchies and exploitative, or at least dominant/subordinate, relationships that were initially absent could re-emerge over time as a consequence of technological and economic imperatives.

It was true that where a strong trade union movement existed it might be able "to ensure that flexibility [was] based on collective, democratic structures". Thus one writer highlighted the example of the UTOPIA project of the Swedish

---

82. Tomaney, "The Reality of Workplace Flexibility", p. 49. On this see also J. Child, "New Technology and Developments in Managerial Organisation", *Omerga* **12** (1984), p. 21.

83. Shaiken *et al.*, "The Work Process", pp. 168, 175. On perception of flexibility as "essentially an employers' offensive" see, for example, C. Crouch, "United Kingdom: The Rejection of Compromise", in C. Crouch & G. Baglioni (eds), *European Industrial Relations: The Challenge of Flexibility* (London: Sage, 1990), p. 336.

84. For some doubts as to the growing relative importance of small firms in industrial economies see G. Thompson, "The American Industrial Policy Debate: Any Lessons for Britain?", *Economy and Society* **16** (1987), p. 62.

85. Jones, "Flexible Automation", p. 111.

print unions, which aimed to ensure reference to skill-enhancing criteria for the design of new computerized technology.[86] But it was also the case that the kind of industrial organization associated with flexible specialization was one that, in many instances, proved inimical to the growth of the kind of trade union power necessary to seize the opportunities for democratization which new technology presented. Thus Brusco noted in the industrial districts of the Emilia Romagna the existence of a "secondary" sector of small firms, firms able to "hire and fire as the volume of orders changes both because legislation against unfair dismissal does not apply to firms with less than 15 employees *and because of their scanty unionisation*".[87] And, in fact, a major impetus to the growth of the industrial districts of the "Third Italy" was the determination on the part of employers, in the 1970s, to escape what they saw as the restrictive practices and excessive demands of overly strong trade unions by setting up in areas where their writ did not run. In these districts, it was estimated that around half of the industrial labour force was non-unionized. Thus Benetton, one of the archetypes of flexible specialization, employed, in the 1980s, some 1,500 workers directly "in small plants of 50–60 employees, where the union is absent or impeded". Similarly, Murray's study of the "cottage industry segment" of the Bolognese engineering industry "suggest[ed] that in the early 1980s there was a scarce to non-existent union presence".[88]

For many, indeed, an industrial structure characterized by numerous small and medium-sized producers clearly militated against the organization of the working class in trade unions. The inevitable disparities of conditions of work, remuneration and job security, the geographical scattering of workers in an industry, the specialist fragmentation of industries themselves, and the nature of the social relations prevailing in small units of production, all made difficult the effective unionization of workforces and solidaristic bargaining over pay and conditions, let alone any democratic erosion of the prerogatives of management. In addition, where the autonomous, highly skilled and multiskilled artisan existed in the workforce, "the craftsman's assertion of workplace autonomy" could lead "to a defence of privileges against other work groups' claims to equality".[89] In other words, all the problems for labour solidarity of the existence of a privileged labour aristocracy could once again come to the fore.

The relationship noted above between large firms and their suppliers or clients also had a bearing not just on the scope for industrial democracy, but also, fundamentally, on the whole question of the decentralization of

---

86. Mathews, *Age of Democracy*, p. 108.
87. Brusco, "The Emilian Model", p. 174, my emphasis.
88. F. Murray, "The Decentralisation of Production – The Decline of the Mass Production Worker?", *Capital and Class* **19** (1993), pp. 91, 89, my emphasis. Nor did Benetton conform to the flexible specialization ideal as regards its structure and organization. Wood, "Introduction", p. 24.
89. Sabel, *Work and Politics*, p. 187.

production and decision-making power. For post-Fordist socialists, such decentralization was a function of fragmenting markets. Large corporations gave greater autonomy to particular plants and divisions in order to allow them to respond more flexibly to a shifting and diversifying demand. Furthermore, to increase flexibility and reduce the overheads that they generated, large firms availed themselves of a network of subcontractors who could respond rapidly and reliably as demand fluctuated. However, as such systems developed in Japan, for example, this decentralization of production rarely if ever involved a decentralization of power, as large corporations continued to exercise close control over quality, work schedules and product development. Also, with respect to the Emilia Romagna, as one commentator noted, "through decentralisation corporations continued to exert strict control over production, while letting the small firm pay the costs and face the risks of production, thereby using decentralisation as a means of reducing and shifting the corporation's risks and losses".[90] Such action implied subordination, not the decentralization of real decision-making.

Of course, the fragmentation of markets also permitted the multiplication of independent or semi-independent specialist producers engaged in small batch production and so, it was argued, an increase in the number of independent decision-makers. Such was certainly the case in a number of the industrial districts mentioned above. But even here, while specialization might "divide a previous pattern of ownership", it nonetheless "tend[ed] to increase concentration of ownership within larger specialist areas. Thus corporate concentration continue[d]".[91] Again the implications of this run contrary to the notion that flexible specialization was precipitating a significant dispersion of economic control.

But what of working conditions and the remuneration of labour where regimes of flexible specialization were in the ascendant? To begin with, it is worth noting that small firms in the Emilia Romagna did not always react to recession and a diminution in demand in the way that post-Fordist socialists anticipated. In theory, the response should have been to seek out new niche and quality markets, competing innovatively and qualitatively rather than in the traditional fashion of seeking to lower costs and prices. In fact, many reacted in a manner more consistent with neo-classical than post-Fordist economics, intensifying the exploitation of their workers and often jettisoning the defining characteristics of flexible specialization, that is, co-operative and polyvalent methods of working. But even in more buoyant periods there existed many small firms engaged in subcontract work that had all the characteristics of the sweatshop, however flexible or artisanal their work methods. Sometimes the

---

90. Murray, "The Decentralisation of Production", p. 81.
91. Eisenschitz & Gough, *The Politics of Local Economic Policy*, p. 174.

sweating took the form of self-exploitation and sometimes it resulted from the paternalistic despotism of the small entrepreneur. Either way, an intensification of labour and a lowering of remuneration were the order of the day.[92] Even those who have reported favourably on the economic achievements and performance of the "Third Italy" admitted

> a clear connection between the proliferation of small enterprises and the use of black labour . . . situations where social welfare contributions are evaded . . . where labour is paid lower wages than the minimum set by national agreement, works in substandard conditions, or does not achieve agreed levels of supplementary bonuses and holiday pay.[93]

Further, as a number of commentators stressed, the teamworking, flexibility and job rotation which flexible specialization and associated technology permitted were often seen not as an opportunity for job enrichment but as a means, primarily, of eliminating waste and intensifying pressures on management and workers. Thus in Japanese enterprises committed to the JIT (just in time) system, with its emphasis on low inventory levels and the elimination of wasted production time, it was suggested that flexibility and semi-autonomous group work were actually "the very tools of work intensification".[94] Certainly, the eradication of labour alienation was not a primary consideration in their introduction.

The fact was that under capitalist relations of production the primary objective continued to be the extraction of surplus value. If this could be done through skill enhancement, job enrichment, increased work and group autonomy and the greater democratization of decision-making, well and good. But these things were always a means to an end, and where they failed to deliver, they were jettisoned or circumscribed. If demand faltered, if profitability could be enhanced by subcontractor sweating or the intensification of labour, if squeezed profitability could be countered by abandoning national agreements, accepting substandard working conditions or pressing for subsistence wages, then capitalist imperatives would ensure that such expedients were adopted. In periods of recession in particular, flexibility could assume coercive forms that were clearly designed to tip the balance of power in favour of capitalist employers. Unless, therefore, the existence of a golden mean of prosperity was assumed, whatever gains were secured under the auspices of flexible specialization had to be deemed provisional.

That said, it was argued that trade unions could ensure that, once made, such gains would not be easily relinquished, and that some kind of ratchet effect

---

92. Murray, "The Decentralisation of Production", p. 82.
93. Brusco, "The Emilian Model", p. 170.
94. Tomaney, "The Reality of Workplace Flexibility", pp. 35–7.

would be operative. Such an argument was, of course, used during the golden age of Keynesian social democracy with reference to the advances secured by the labour movement during that period, and that in itself should have given those who deployed it pause for thought. But, in addition, as we have seen, there was also evidence of an inverse correlation between trade union strength and the kind of industrial structures and organization that characterized a post-Fordist world. There were substantial grounds for believing, therefore, that in such an economic environment unions would not wield the power necessary to ensure that gains once made were retained.

It was also argued by post-Fordist socialists that in periods of economic recession it was an economy based on the principles of flexible specialization that would most effectively weather the storm. For flexible specialization was all about adaptability in an increasingly volatile economic world; it had the capacity to ensure that as one niche snapped shut, another was prised open; and, of its essence, it was about shifting resources to the production of goods that were wanted, from those the demand for which was diminishing. The problem was that this view of things tended to assume away the possibility of a *general* deficiency in demand. Indeed, there was much in the political economy of flexible specialization which presumed the essential validity of Say's Law, any mismatches between supply and demand being seen as partial not general.

It was also argued by critics of post-Fordist socialism that economic downturns, and what they set in motion, would be likely to exacerbate another unfortunate characteristic of flexible specialization – namely a tendency for the emergence of a dual labour force distinguished by a skilled, well-paid and securely employed core and an ill-remunerated, unskilled or semi-skilled, intermittently employed periphery. If it was the polyvalent core that was used to give the system functional flexibility, then the danger was that it would be the unskilled periphery that would be used to give it the necessary numerical flexibility in the event of fluctuating demand, particularly in the service sector.[95] In the case of the "Third Italy" that meant, "for the vast majority of workers who do not possess the market powers of an elite of male machinists, technicians and designers, a shift towards a fragmented, informal and casual cottage industry [which] spells a return to the worst excesses of industrial capitalism".[96] So, for example, the responsiveness of Benetton to rapidly changing fashion trends was "rooted in the vulnerability of the most insecure

---

95. Gill wrote of a "dark vision: the creation of a pyramid of skills that concentrates a few creative and meaningful occupations at the top, while the rest wind up with fewer skills and subject to new forms of monitoring and electronic control", *Work, Unemployment and the New Technology*, p. 87.
96. F. Murray, "Flexible Specialisation in the Third Italy", *Capital and Class* **33** (1987), p. 92. On this see also S. Negrelli & E. Santi, "Industrial Relations in Italy", in Crouch & Baglioni, *European Industrial Relations*, p. 194.

and disadvantaged sections of the workforce"; something which both mirrored and confirmed other social divisions.[97]

Moreover, not only could a core and periphery exist within a firm, they could also emerge from the kind of relationship that grew up between dominant firms such as Benetton and their many subcontractors and franchisees. And, in the latter instance too, the labour force of the peripheral firms would possess few of those characteristics and little of that autonomy which "flec spec" socialists held so dear. On the contrary, as one commentator tellingly wrote, in the context of such a relationship "franchisees and sub-contractors often become prisoners of their own property".[98]

The discussion of post-Fordism and flexible specialization has focused so far on whether, as some believed, it created or was likely to create opportunities that could be seized upon to make progress towards attaining certain socialist objectives. What has not been considered is the post-Fordist meta-history which informed so much of what flec spec socialists had to offer: whether the difficulties of western industrial capitalism in the past three decades could indeed be interpreted as the result of a crisis of a mass-production or Fordist economy and, crucially, whether there was evidence to suggest that flexible specialization was likely to emerge as the dominant economic paradigm for developed industrial economies in the twenty-first century.

Here, what is apparent from much of the literature is that, throughout the 1980s and 1990s, mass production continued to possess a remarkable capacity to furnish a variety of products for a rapidly changing and differentiated demand. Indeed, mass producers of consumer durables were frequently the progenitors of a differentiated demand that they then subsequently serviced. To take just one example, the Nissan factory in the north-east of England produced, in the 1980s, almost 200 variants of its Bluebird. More generally, as a number of commentators remarked, Japanese competitive success from the 1960s onwards was built, in part at least, on the capacity to use assembly-line factories flexibly to achieve both greater efficiency as regards production and greater variety as regards output. Also, in the late-twentieth century, modular production expanded the demand for standardized products while, at the same time, increasing variety through the multiple ways in which modules were combined.[99] As Sayer stressed, "we should be wary of (1) assuming mass production to be synonymous with inflexibility . . . and (2) assuming that mass

---

97. Hyman, "Flexible Specialisation", p. 56.
98. R. Murray, "Ownership, Control and the Market", *New Left Review* **164** (1987), p. 90.
99. M. Elam, "Puzzling out the Fordist Debate: Technology, Markets and Institutions", *Economic and Industrial Democracy* **11** (1990), p. 21; Williams *et al.*, "The End of Mass Production?", p. 42; for a discussion of increasingly flexible production in the car industry see S. Wood, "Between Fordism and Flexibility? The US Car Industry", in Hyman and Streeck (eds), *New Technology and Industrial Relations*, p. 119.

production and flexible production are alternatives".[100] Of course, as he also pointed out, if such assumptions were challenged then the binary opposition that informed the Fordist/post-Fordist reading of contemporary history would begin to disintegrate.

Other evidence also cast doubt on the demise of what has been categorized as Fordism and the increasing dominance of what has been denominated post-Fordism. Fordist enterprises were supposedly characterized by a large, relatively stable, high-wage, core workforce. The emergence of post-Fordism was, in contrast, distinguished by the growth of flexible and peripheral labour forces. However, a 1987 British survey indicated little change in the use of temporary work in the 1980s. There had been an aggregate increase in part-time employment during this period but, significantly, such employment had declined as a percentage of the manufacturing workforce and, as one contemporary commentator wrote, "if peripheral work is taken to mean non-standard contractual status, deviating from a full-time norm, there is little evidence that there has been a recent increase".[101] Further, a study published in 1986 concluded that

> myths about the advance in flexible working practices have misled many people into thinking that fundamental changes have taken place on a very wide scale. On the contrary, the fundamental changes are extremely narrowly concentrated in particular corners or, very occasionally, particular sectors of industry. And even when these changes have been taking place, they can be incomplete, halting or superficial.[102]

So, in the Britain of the 1980s, there was little evidence of the contractual flexibility that a belief in the inexorable advance of flexible specialization would have led one to expect.

There were, then, major problems of empirical evidence and conceptual clarity facing those who wished to establish their socialism on the growing significance and manifest virtues of flexible specialization. Hirst and Zeitlin wrote that their "preferred form of evidentialization for flexible specialisation is . . . the analytical case-study conducted at the micro-level of particular firms, regional economies or industrial sectors".[103] But even if a substantial volume of

100. A. Sayer, "Post-Fordism in Question", *International Journal of Urban and Regional Research* **13** (1989), p. 672.
101. See Pollert, "Dismantling Flexibility", pp. 51–3; on the decline of the importance of part-time working in manufacturing in the 1980s see also R. Penn, "Flexibility in Britain During the 1980s: Recent Empirical Evidence", in Burrows *et al.* (eds), *Fordism and Flexibility*, p. 83.
102. Quoted in Tomaney, "The Reality of Workplace Flexibility", p. 46.
103. Hirst & Zeitlin, "Flexible Specialisation", p. 34. In this context Murray, "Flexible Specialisation", p. 87, pointed out that Sabel's *Work and Politics* highlights only "one sector of the Bologna engineering industry at the expense of more Fordist ones", while Tomaney,

such supportive evidence had been forthcoming, that still left post-Fordism struggling to substantiate the more general claim that "tendencies can be observed towards the displacement of mass production by *flexible specialization as the dominant technological paradigm of the late twentieth century*".[104] Such substantiation would, after all, have required evidence not simply of a micro- but also of a macro- or mesoeconomic kind and, ideally, with a comparative historical and international dimension. In fact, there was a paucity of evidence indicating, for example, just what percentage of productive activity in each Standard Industrial Classification was flexibly specialized or whether, crucially, that percentage had changed over time. Furthermore, until post-Fordists could iterate unambiguous criteria for determining where flexible mass production ended and flexible production began,[105] where fragmented markets for customized goods began and specialized mass markets ended and, in addition, "state[d] criteria of dominance which would allow us to determine whether and when one form of production comes to dominate a particular area", such evidentialization of paradigmatic shifts would remain problematic.[106] An absence of conceptual clarity therefore also weakened the case of those who sought to argue that flexible specialization was en route to becoming the "dominant technological paradigm of the late twentieth century". And, in general, there was much truth in Sayer's remark, with respect to binary periodizations of the industrial/post-industrial, modernist/postmodernist, Fordist/post-Fordist, organized/disorganized capitalism kind, that they risked "ending up with overly burdened dualisms and *overly elastic concepts*".[107]

If shakily grounded in conceptual and empirical terms, the concept of flexible specialization, and the democratic socialist political economy conjured from it, must also be faulted for its analytical lacunae. Some of these have already been touched upon; in particular, its failure to construct a satisfactory macroeconomics and its neo-classical tendency to assume, by default, that flexibility was a sufficient condition for full employment. In addition, despite a recognition of the constraints that it imposed upon national economic policy-makers, post-Fordist socialists had little to say about the increasing freedom of international capital movements that characterized the 1980s and 1990s and the damaging volatility which these imparted to the global economic system. Presumably, it was believed that the more flexible the specialization the more easily such volatility could be costlessly accommodated. Similarly, because no

"The Reality of Workplace Flexibility", p. 34, has claimed that Piore & Sabel's views on Japan were distorted by a reliance solely on management sources – especially those emanating from US management consultants.
104. Hirst & Zeitlin, "Flexible Specialisation", p. 36, my emphasis.
105. For a contemporary discussion of the impossibility of this task see Williams *et al.*, "The End of Mass Production?", p. 417.
106. *Ibid.*, p. 415.
107. Sayer, "Post-Fordism in Question", p. 666, my emphasis.

doubt of their belief that the future would be small and flexible, post-Fordist socialists had precious little to say about the continually expanding power of transnational corporations; a power which grew throughout the 1980s and even more rapidly in the following decade with the rash of mergers which, particularly in the financial sector, punctuated its close.[108] The question of what space these huge mergers left for diversity and devolution was rarely addressed, although it is interesting to note that even in the 1980s the larger Emilian firms frequently established close alliances with multinational capital, something which both attests to the power of the latter and, as regards the Emilia Romagna, "casts doubt on the extent of market diversification and the independence of small capital" in this region.[109]

In so far as the position of transnational corporations was discussed at all by post-Fordist socialists, it was with a view to suggesting that such corporations had also recognized the advantages of decentralizing economic power, thereby rendering production more flexible and making work groups and skilled labourers more autonomous. The post-Fordist argument was that in terms of their structures of corporate decision-making and their organization of production, transnational corporations were converging on the trail blazed by firms that had embraced the principles of flexible specialization. Yet little evidence of such corporate behaviour was evinced to substantiate such a view. And, whatever devolution of decision-making occurred within these corporations, it almost invariably left considerable concentrations of power, and the capacity to formulate global strategy, at the centre – something that, in 2000–01, those employed by BMW at Longbridge, Ford at Dagenham, Vauxhall (General Motors) at Luton and Motorola at Bathgate found to their cost.

Furthermore, these corporations remained entities which, as those involved in microeconomic policy-making in the GLC and elsewhere clearly recognized, were unlikely to be influenced or constrained much by the local or regional state in which post-Fordist socialists made such a considerable aspirational investment. Post-Fordism, as we have seen, did feed into the predilection for decentralized socialism and, in particular, for socialism in one municipality, which was current in Britain in the early 1980s. Yet post-Fordist socialists seem to have been slow to learn the lessons of its failures and to appreciate the severe constraints on those who sought to give prescriptive effect to a local or even regional socialism. They failed to recognize the ineluctable apotheosis of the authoritarian transnational corporation and that the "new times" of which they wrote were, in that regard and others, global not local.

---

108. As early as 1989 we have commentators writing of "a huge burst of activity centred around mergers, acquisitions, joint ventures, alliances, inter-firm agreements and collaboration activities of various kinds", Robins, "Global Times", p. 23.
109. Murray, "Flexible Specialisation", p. 87.

What was also problematic in post-Fordist socialism was its concept of agency. Just how and by whom was the project to be realized? Here the national and local states were seen as having an essentially permissive role. They could put in place institutions that facilitated the emergence of the virtuous and beneficial aspects of flexible specialization, but they were not seen as the *primus mobilae*. Clearly, too, trade unions were viewed as a means of seizing the positive potentialities which flexible specialization generated, but, as we have seen, trade unionism or, certainly, traditional trade unionism, fitted uneasily into the post-Fordist scheme of things. There were also, as we have seen, forces at work in those local economies where flexible specialization was of particular importance that threatened to undermine the negotiating power of trade unions on both traditional matters and that wide range of issues with which post-Fordist socialists anticipated trade unionists would become engaged. Fragmentation, flexibility and ideas of social pluralism, the hallmarks of the post-Fordist vision, also seemed to militate against the notion of a working class sufficiently homogeneous to use either the political or industrial organs of the labour movement to implement a programme conducive to the emergence of a decentralized socialist economy.

Of course, it can be argued that, for post-Fordist socialists, the local and national state, the social democratic party and the trade union geared to fragmented plant-level bargaining, were seen as having an essentially subsidiary role in the realization of their vision. For, in the final analysis, what drove the forces of progress was the market. The hero/agent of the socialist project was no longer the producer, or the social democratic politician, or the shop steward, still less a homogeneous working class, but the discriminating consumer. It was his/her actions, mediated by the market, that actively created the possibility of social and industrial progress. Here, and elsewhere, there was a resonance with the New Right, born in part of a desire to deny it the political mileage to be derived from an exclusive embrace of that most potent of contemporary entities, the sovereign consumer. Thus, in stressing the value and virtues of possessive individualism, customized demand and the liberating possibilities of interactive technology, there was a sense in which post-Fordist socialists sought to reclaim what they saw as the prevailing *Zeitgeist* for socialist ends. But, the danger was that in supping with the devil they would forget about the length of the spoon and succumb to what one commentator defined as a "tacit accommodation to the values of resurgent capitalism". And certainly there is much to be said for the view that the post-Fordist socialist aim "of redefining the socialist project in individualist terms, for tactical or rhetorical reasons, seem[ed] doomed to concede more to the ethos of the Thatcherite age than it c[ould] ever hope to win back from it".[110]

---

110. Rustin "The Trouble with 'New Times'", pp. 313, 314.

Chapter 4

Towards a decentralized socialism? The political economy of producer co-operatives and labour-managed firms

The 1960s and 1970s in Britain saw a marked increase of interest in the idea of workers' control and worker ownership that manifested itself in a number of ways.[1] It was apparent in the political economy of writers such as Stuart Holland and Michael Barrett Brown, and through their work, and that of others, it became a significant current of economic thinking within the AES. It drew inspiration from the New Left libertarianism of these decades and from that anti-statism and support for the democratization of economic decision-making that has been touched on in earlier chapters. It was fuelled by the work of the Institute for Workers' Control, established in 1964, that produced a stream of publications in the 1960s and 1970s to inform the work of trade unionists who were active and interested in formulating plans for the worker control of the firms in which they were employed. The idea was also taken up by trade union leaders such as Jack Jones, general secretary of the TGWU, and Hugh Scanlon, of the AEUW, and it helped to inspire work-ins and sit-ins such as those at Upper Clyde Shipbuilders and Fisher Bendix in the early 1970s. These developments provided a fertile soil in which a Left political economy, that had at its heart the

---

1. For a fuller discussion of these see N. Thompson, *Political Economy and the Labour Party: The Economics of Democratic Socialism, 1884–1995* (London: UCL Press 1996), pp. 206–12.

idea of the transformative capacities of producer co-operatives, could take root and flourish. The next two chapters will consider this political economy as it was articulated in Britain and elsewhere. It will examine its coherence, its rebuttal of critics, the theoretical debates that it engendered, the general fortunes of the enterprises whose formation it helped to inspire in the 1970s and 1980s and the future appeal and practicability of such a Left political economy.

Producer co-operatives may be differentiated into those that are essentially labour-managed firms (hereafter LMFs) and which are owned by non-members – the state perhaps or a holding company or a financial institution – and those owned by their members, worker-owned firms (hereafter WOFs). Of course, many producer co-operatives are in fact hybrids, part-owned by their members and part-owned by outsiders. Where necessary, a distinction will be made between LMFs and WOFs, but where this is deemed unnecessary, where what is said relates to LMFs, WOFs and hybrids, the term producer co-operatives (hereafter PCs) will be used.

It was Benjamin Ward's article, "The Firm in Illyria: Market Syndicalism", published in 1958 in the *American Economic Review*, that set the agenda and established the ground rules for much of the critique and defence of PCs which followed over the next three decades.[2] In Ward's model, "the means of production [were] nationalized and the factories turned over to the general management of elected committees of workers who . . . set prices and output policy in their own material self-interest". Ward then proceeded to consider the likely behaviour of these units and the implications it had for a socialism constructed on the basis of what he termed a "market syndicalism".[3] This was essentially an LMF economy in which ownership still resided with the state. But what he had to say as regards behaviour with respect to pricing and output was also applicable to WOFs.

Ward's piece was quintessentially neo-classical in its methodology, applying the notion of constrained maximization to determining the rationality and efficiency of microeconomic behaviour by LMFs. Firms in a competitive capitalist economy sought to maximize profits and in so doing produced up to a point where the allocation and utilization of resources was optimized. For Ward, however, the LMFs, unlike private firms, sought to maximize not profits but net revenue per worker. Constructing a simple model of such a firm with some fixed costs, a single variable labour input and one product, Ward was able to show that an LMF would both hire too few labourers and operate with a perverse supply curve where output would be reduced when prices rose and vice versa. The reason for this was that the objective of maximizing income would be arrived at when the increment to firm income produced by its marginal member equalled average member income. Any price increase would

---

2. B. Ward, "The Firm in Illyria: Market Syndicalism", *American Economic Review* **48** (1958), pp. 566–89.
3. *Ibid.*, p. 566.

result in an equivalent rise in the value of labour's marginal product. However, as average member income would rise to a greater extent because of the existence of fixed costs, a majority of members could now secure an increase in income by laying off colleagues and thence reducing output. And, as the good, rational revenue-maximizers which neo-classical theory presupposed they were, it could be assumed that that was exactly what they would do.

Much of the literature that followed represented an attempt to relax Ward's simplistic assumptions and so extend the model to situations of imperfect competition, monopoly and firms with multiple inputs and outputs, as well as situations of uncertainty and incomplete information. Commentators also sought to consider the theoretical consequences of pursuing a wider range of objectives than simply maximizing net revenue[4] and to explicate and develop the model's macroeconomic implications.

As regards monopoly and imperfect competition, the literature seemed to confirm the pessimistic and critical conclusions of the competitive case. Thus, it was contended that in these contexts PCs would tend to operate at a lower level of output and charge a higher price and use a more socially inefficient combination of resources than their capitalist counterparts.[5] The introduction of multiple inputs and outputs resulted in a less perverse supply curve, but one that was still less elastic than that of a PC's capitalist equivalent. In addition, in these circumstances, PC employment would be lower than that furnished by capitalist enterprises.[6]

These unpropitious conclusions were replicated at a macroeconomic level. A perverse supply curve implied that any attempt to tackle unemployment in a PC economy through the expansion of aggregate demand would actually exacerbate the problem. And, even assuming a positively sloping supply curve, the relative inelasticity of this could render a PC or PC-dominated economy less amenable than its capitalist counterpart to a full-employment strategy delivered by demand management. So, with output proving less responsive to demand stimuli than in a capitalist economy, recourse to a Keynesian employment strategy would be much more likely to precipitate inflation than employment growth;[7] this was a telling criticism given the rate of inflation in western industrial economies in the 1970s.

---

4. See, for example, A. Bergson, "Market Socialism Revisited", *Journal of Political Economy* **75** (1967), pp. 655–73 and M. Berman, "Short-Run Efficiency in the Labour-Managed Firm", *Journal of Comparative Economics* **1** (1977), pp. 309–14.
5. See, for example, J. Meade, "The Theory of Labour-Managed Firms and Profit Sharing", *Economic Journal* **82** (1972), pp. 402–28; J. Meade, "Labour-Managed Firms in Conditions of Imperfect Competition", *Economic Journal* **84** (1974), pp. 817–24; J. Vanek, *The General Theory of Labor-Managed Market Economics* (Ithaca: Cornell University Press, 1970).
6. E. Domar, "The Soviet Collective Farm as a Producer Co-operative", *American Economic Review* **56** (1966), pp. 734–58.
7. On this see, for example, D. Milenkovitch, "Is Market Socialism Efficient?", in A. Zimbalist (ed.), *Comparative Economic Systems* (Boston: Kluwer, 1984), pp. 87–8.

However, these conclusions, strongly critical of the efficiency and viability of PCs and, by extension, a PC economy, provoked a vigorous response in the 1970s and 1980s. In part, this came from those thinking within an essentially neo-classical framework but also, more fundamentally, from those who questioned that framework's methodological and epistemological foundations. As to those working within the neo-classical tradition, some suggested that if PCs were free to hire labour, then it would be possible for their members to benefit from expanding output in response to an increase in price up to the point at which the marginal revenue product of hired labour was equal to its marginal cost. In such circumstances PCs would theoretically become as efficient as their capitalist counterparts. On similar lines, if the expedient of hiring labour was eschewed and, instead, new members were recruited who, initially, received a relatively low income, the elasticity of the firm's supply curve could be increased.[8]

A non-perverse output response to increased demand might also be secured, in the short run, if members were free to vary their working time and effort, assuming individual workers had a positively sloped supply curve of labour.[9] Likewise, it was argued that if employment opportunities were available outside PCs, this would allow the possibility of their members moving into and out of these alternative occupations and, where the revenue secured by such employment was pooled with that generated by the PCs themselves, behaviour consistent with a non-perverse, short-run supply function was more likely to result.[10] It was also suggested that if PCs were governed by some central authority, so that the quasi-rent resulting from a rise in product price did not accrue to the PC, then the inefficiencies resulting from that output-restricting behaviour, which sought to maximize it and share it among as few members as possible, would be eliminated. Moreover, and most importantly, if the formation and dissolution of PCs were relatively easy then a rise in, or contraction of, demand, could be accommodated in this way without the exaction of quasi-rents and resultant inefficiency.[11]

It was also argued, for example by Vanek, that the relevant comparison was *not* that between capitalist firms and PCs in competitive, imperfectly competitive and monopoly situations, but that between enterprises operating in an economic environment which embodied powerful, in-built imperatives to

---

8. See, for example, J. Meade, P. Pelikan & R. Kocanda, "The Socialist Enterprise as a Participant in the Market", *Czechoslovak Economic Papers* **9** (1967), pp. 49–64.
9. N. Mygind, "From the Illyrian Firm to the Reality of Self-Management", in S. Jansson & A. Hellmark (eds), *Labor-Owned Firms and Workers' Co-operatives* (Aldershot: Gower, 1986), p. 81.
10. On this see, for example, J. Bonin & L. Putterman, *The Economics of Cooperation and the Labor-Managed Economy* (London: Academic Press, 1987), pp. 34–5.
11. On this see, for example, S. Estrin, "Workers' Co-operatives: Their Merits and their Limitations", in J. Le Grand & S. Estrin (eds), *Market Socialism* (Oxford: Clarendon, 1989), pp. 178–9. For an early theoretical elaboration of this see Vanek's *The General Theory of Labor-Managed Market Economics*.

compete (the situation as he saw it in a PC economy) and capitalist firms functioning in economic circumstances where there were strong, inherent pressures making for the emergence of oligopoly and monopoly. Thus Vanek argued that "it can be expected that, all other things being equal, the point of maximum efficiency, which also is the point of long-run equilibrium for a labor-managed firm, will be reached for a lower level of output than for a firm operating with a hired labor factor". As he saw it, this meant that there would "be room for more firms in a given industry". Therefore, "on grounds of several arguments, labor management can be expected . . . to yield market structures more competitive than any other free economy".[12]

For these and other reasons it was believed that even without departing from neo-classical conceptions of economic rationality, and even allowing for the Illyrian version of constrained maximization, PCs might attain at least as efficient a utilization of labour resources and as optimum a level of output as an economy dominated by capitalist, profit-maximizing enterprises. Put another way, even if members retained the individualistic and self-seeking instincts which characterized competitive capitalism, the economic behaviour of PCs could be expected to conform fairly closely to the accepted canons of economic rationality, at least when it came to the short-run determination of output and the employment of labour.

That said, it was noted that such expedients as hiring labour to meet an increase in demand, and the intervention by a central authority to appropriate the quasi-rents that rising prices generated, would precipitate a significant departure from a strict interpretation of PC principles. As to the former, it would involve the employment of those who had no membership (and, in the case of WOFs, no ownership) stake in the firm and who would not, therefore, share in the economic residual which the collective effort of its workforce created; something, it was argued, that could entail a reversion to essentially capitalist practices and social relations of production. As to the latter expedient, it involved a subversion of the ideals of PC autonomy and the decentralization of economic power.

However, theoretical rebuttals of the Illyrian critique were also strengthened by reference to the contemporary behaviour of PCs. Rather than such enterprises being quick to lay off labour to maximize the net revenue and quasi-rents accruing to their memberships, the job security they offered was, clearly, often superior to that provided by their capitalist counterparts. Evidence from France for the period 1970–5 certainly pointed to such employment-retaining behaviour: for example, construction co-operatives increasing employment by

---

12. J. Vanek, "Decentralization under Workers' Management: A Theoretical Appraisal", in J. Vanek, *Self-Management: The Economic Liberation of Man* (Harmondsworth: Penguin, 1975), p. 355.

5% as against a 12% fall for industry as a whole.[13] For Italian PCs job security was manifestly a primary objective, even when it was "at odds with maximizing per-worker income of existing members".[14] In Denmark, in the 1970s and early 1980s, PCs were "expansive compared to their typical capitalist twins . . . in regard to employment", with "no sign of an inelastic or even backward-sloping supply curve for the self-managed firms".[15] Evidence on US PCs, while sparse, nonetheless suggested that their workforces enjoyed stability and regularity of employment.[16] While for Mondragon, in the Basque region, "it [was] claimed that there has not in fact been a single case of involuntary redundancy during the group's history".[17] The fact was, of course, that the PC ethos meant that the ideal of self-sacrifice for the collective good was what usually dominated decision-making and not narrowly self-interested maximizing behaviour, whatever the maximand. This is a point to which we will return because a number of commentators were to insist that this represented a substantial rock upon which much of the neo-classical critique of PCs foundered.

But the perversity of employment practice and short-run output behaviour comprised only some of the criticisms that were made of PCs. Considering the longer-term behaviour of WOFs, it was also suggested that such enterprises had an inherent tendency to underinvest. This argument was developed in a variety of ways and at different levels of theoretical sophistication and abstraction. Writers such as Jensen and Meckling contended that where such firms were constituted on the basis of collective rather than individual ownership rights, then members would tend to favour the distribution of any surplus created in payments to workers, rather than its investment in a capital stock whose value could not be individually realized.[18] Any attempt to institute a policy of "high compulsory profit retention in a collective account" would therefore be "liable to be self-defeating; the collective account may retain its large share of profits but it will be a large share of a declining total", as the workforce exerted pressure to take gains in the form of wages.[19] Further, in relation to a collectively

---

13. E. Batstone, "Organization and Orientation: A Life-Cycle Model of French Co-operatives", *Economic and Industrial Democracy* **4** (1983), p. 147.
14. A. Zevi, "The Performance of Italian Producer Co-operatives", in D. Jones & J. Svenjar (eds), *Participatory and Self-Managed Firms* (Lexington: Lexington Books, 1982), p. 250.
15. Mygind, "From the Illyrian Firm", p. 97.
16. D. Jones, "The United States of America: A Survey of Producer Co-operative Performance", in F. Stephen (ed.), *The Performance of Labour-Managed Firms* (London: Macmillan, 1982), p. 67. On this see too C. Gunn, *Workers' Self-Management in the United States* (Ithaca: Cornell University Press, 1984).
17. R. Oakeshott, *The Case for Workers' Co-operatives* (London: Routledge, 1978), p. 195.
18. See, for example, E. Furbotn & S. Pejovich, *The Economics of Property Rights* (Cambridge, Mass.: Ballinger, 1974) and M. Jensen & W. Meckling, "Rights and Production Functions: An Application to Labor-Managed Firms and Co-determination", *Journal of Business* **52** (1979), pp. 469–506. On the willingness of workers to save and invest where the assets of PCs are owned by them, see also L. Sirc, "Workers' Management under Public and Private Ownership", in B. Chiplin *et al.* (eds), *Can Workers Manage?* (London: IEA, 1977), pp. 51–86.
19. Oakeshott, *The Case for Workers' Co-operatives*, p. 83.

owned and financed enterprise asset structure, Vanek suggested the existence of a tendency to underinvestment. Thus those whose capital was sunk irrevocably in the firm's assets would seek to recoup their individual investment by way of a return higher than that required by the private capitalist. The more quickly the individual sought to amortise his/her investment, the higher would be the expected yield and the greater the differential between desired return on investment in WOFs and that in comparable capitalist enterprises. In these circumstances the former could be expected, over time, to invest considerably less than the latter and, indeed, there would exist a pronounced tendency to eat into the firm's net worth.[20]

Yet even when the assumptions of Vanek were relaxed, and the possibilities of share ownership by non-PC members or borrowing from financial intermediaries were admitted, formidable obstacles to securing the funding necessary for an optimum level of investment could still be adduced. To begin with, there were the acknowledged difficulties that PCs in general had in acquiring outside finance, even when that was ideologically acceptable to the membership. PC workers, it was argued, usually had limited collateral to offer by way of security to potential lenders. In addition, because of the relative paucity of PCs in all western industrialized economies, potential lenders viewed them as ventures whose track record was less predictable and, therefore, as being relatively risky. Inevitably, it was argued, this would affect both the supply and the price of investment capital.[21] It was also stressed that PCs had what were termed agency problems in raising finance outside the firm. As Cornforth *et al*. put it, "there is a contradiction between co-operative principles which subordinate capital to members' interests, and the 'rights' and returns capital is able to demand in the open market".[22] Thus PCs looked for finance without relinquishing control, but, conventionally, investors looked to have at least some decision-making power as regards the enterprise in which they invested. Some suggested, therefore, that "a rational banker would only lend to a co-operative if s/he could put conditions on the loan such that the co-operative was forced to behave in a way analogous to a capitalist firm".[23] But even when this was seen as overly pessimistic, it was still conceded that such "rational bankers", to the extent that worker management denied them control, might be expected to look for a premium over and above the rate at which they would normally be prepared to lend. Here again, therefore, there was reason

---

20. For a concise and lucid exposition of this argument see D. Miller, "Market Neutrality and the Failure of Co-operatives", *British Journal of Political Science* **11** (1981), p. 321.
21. A. Ben-ner, "Producer Co-operatives: Why do They Exist in Capitalist Economies?", in W. Powell (ed.), *The Nonprofit Sector: A Research Handbook* (New Haven: Yale University Press, 1987), p. 436n. See also on this S. Bowles & H. Gintis, "An Economic and Political Case for the Democratic Firm", in D. Copp, J. Hampton & J. Roemer (eds), *The Idea of Democracy* (Cambridge: Cambridge University Press, 1992), p. 378.
22. C. Cornforth *et al.*, *Developing Successful Workers' Co-operatives* (London: Sage, 1988), p. 218.
23. Miller, "Market Neutrality", p. 320.

to suppose that PCs would borrow on less favourable terms than their capitalist competitors, and some commentators saw this as another cause of their tendency to underinvest and thence their relative rarity in capitalist economies. As regards WOFs, there was also evidence indicating that they were "unhappy about accepting 'excessive' external financing because of the consequential loss of control over the future of the firm".[24] That said, most British PCs did have to have recourse to external loans, so borrowing on less competitive terms was not simply a purely theoretical disadvantage.

As to raising funds by recourse to issuing equity, this was recognized by commentators as being inconsistent with a strict interpretation of WOF ideals. But even as regards LMFs, such shares would have to be non-voting. This would raise the potential risk of workers, who could leave the co-operative at any juncture, deciding on generous remuneration during their time with the company and, in effect, leaving the shareholders to foot the bill.[25] This was deemed to be all the more probable given the existence of a limited secondary market in which such shares could be offloaded, in part because of this incipient predilection for asset-stripping behaviour on the part of the workforce.[26]

It was also contended that WOFs were inherently risk-averse and that this would also make for a sub-optimal level of investment. In particular, the fact that workers in such firms could not detach their employment from their investment risks meant both that they were unwilling to commit that part of the surplus which accrued to them to further investment in the enterprise and/or that they would require a higher rate of return before investing in their WOF in the first place. Either way, it was argued, such firms would experience constraints on investment funding.[27] Indeed, it was suggested that the desire for risk diversification on the part of workers militated against the formation of WOFs in the first place and was one reason why they were so few in number. Thus "unless workers highly value control rights, it is rational for them to diversify their financial portfolios and to let the enterprises in which they work be financed by various other individuals to whom control rights will be granted where expedient".[28] It was also argued that those who might seek to establish a WOF

---

24. I. Forbes (ed.), *Market Socialism: Whose Choice?*, Fabian Tract 516 (London: Fabian Society, 1986), p. 7.
25. On this see Meade, "The Theory of Labour-Managed Firms".
26. ". . . the LMF membership market involves lumpy assets that are traded infrequently", G. Dow, "Democracy Versus Appropriability: Can Labour Managed Firms Flourish in a Capitalist World?", in S. Bowles, H. Gintis & B. Gustaffson (eds), *Markets and Democracy: Participation, Accountability and Efficiency* (Cambridge: Cambridge University Press, 1993), p. 193.
27. For an elucidation of such problems see, for example, A. Ben-ner, "Comparative Empirical Observations on Worker-Owned and Capitalist Firms", *International Journal of Industrial Organization* 6 (1988), p. 21; also S. Bowles, H. Gintis & B. Gustaffson, "Introduction", in Bowles *et al.* (eds), *Markets and Democracy*, pp. xvii–xviii.
28. L. Putterman, "After the Employment Relation: Problems on the Road to Enterprise Democracy", in Bowles *et al.* (eds), *Markets and Democracy*, p. 29. On this point see also J. Elster "From Here to There: Or, if Co-operative Ownership is Desirable, Why are There so Few

would often have little wealth to begin with, certainly less than conventional capitalist entrepreneurs, and that this would make them loath to risk the little they possessed in establishing such a company. However, there will be more discussion of the reasons advanced for the low incidence of PCs in due course.

So, in the last three decades of the twentieth century, a formidable case was made suggesting that PCs, and in particular WOFs, would underinvest and, for that reason, could be expected to operate only on a small scale in non-capital-intensive sectors. Unable to compete with their capitalist rivals because of the cost and paucity of finance available, they were seen as condemned to the inter-stices of the capitalist economy. Here, even those sympathetic to the formation of PCs admitted that, in the absence of radical institutional change, such enter-prises were indeed likely to remain "inappropriate for the production of goods which require capital intensive techniques" and "inappropriate" too for "high risk industries and . . . industries subject to rapid technological change". To have the best chance of survival, it was further argued, they should be concen-trated in industries where small-scale production was efficient, where change was slow and where capital/labour ratios were low.[29]

Available empirical evidence would certainly appear to substantiate this view of things. In western industrial economies, PCs were indeed generally small. As regards the Italian PC sector, of the 15,000 PCs that comprised the *Lega natzionale delle co-operative e mutue* (the largest PC consortium) in the 1980s, it was estimated that only some 5–6% of the firms did 50% of the business. This meant, in effect, that "the League [was] made up both of a small number of larger concerns, often well managed and able to compete on equal terms with private and public sector firms, and of a vast number of small and sometimes struggling concerns".[30] It was in effect a co-operative sector *a due velocita*, with the additional problem that the bigger co-operatives seemed increasingly focused on efficiency and competitiveness and to be moving away from co-operative principles and ideals. Thus they were "reluctant to support promotional activities for the movement, seeing them as an added cost, as a dissipation of their energies, and even as a risk in that they may increase competition from inside the movement".[31] This, of course, seemed to lead to the unfortunate conclusion that where PCs were successful and grew, they would leave behind or dilute their inspirational ideals, and that it was only when they remained small that co-operative principles would continue to be embraced.

Co-operatives?", *Social Philosophy and Policy* **6** (1989), p. 94. On this theme see too L. Putterman, "On Some Recent Explanations of Why Capital Hires Labour", *Economic Inquiry* **22** (1984), pp. 171–87.

29. Forbes, *Market Socialism*, pp. 7–8; Miller, "Market Neutrality", p. 320.
30. J. Earle, *The Italian Co-operative Movement: A Portrait of the Lega natzionale delle co-operative e mutue* (London: Allen & Unwin, 1986), p. 204.
31. *Ibid.*

In Britain, there was only one co-operative with a workforce of over 500 in the 1980s and, in 1982, the average size of worker-owned firms was 15 members.[32] In 1988 Cornforth *et al.* stated that British "co-operatives in general are very small, with mean size about 7 . . . and a median of only 4"; while "the average size of new starts is small and is possibly getting even smaller".[33] In the United States too the size of PCs was small and, as in the case of the UK, they were concentrated in skilled-labour crafts and trades. In France, in the early 1980s, the fact that the *Société des co-operatives ouvrières de production* (SCOP) was made up of over 600 co-operatives employing some 30,000 people also highlighted the small average size of its members.[34] In many ways, therefore, it was hard not to accept the view that, in the 1970s and 1980s, "intellectual and socio-political interest in the concept of workers' self-management outstrip[ped] the empirical prominence of these forms".[35]

In addition, this evidence suggested, as the theoretical speculation noted above would lead one to expect, that PCs were concentrated in a relatively small number of sectors. Principally, they were clustered where skilled-labour input, rather than capital, was the decisive factor of production, where technological change was relatively slow and where economies of scale were relatively unimportant. Thus there were, and are, few PCs in any heavy industry sector.[36] The one exception to this was the steel co-operative ULGOR, in Mondragon. This is an interesting example because it was the location of the one strike in Mondragon's history, suggesting that some at least of the advantages which distinguished PCs were a function of their small size rather than their corporate character.

In Italy, PCs in the 1980s and 1990s were concentrated in construction and a number of specialized manufacturing sectors such as ceramics, glass, china, machine tools and textiles, although there was also significant expansion in the retailing and professional services sectors.[37] In Mondragon, too, there was a measure of output diversity. Thus the group included housing co-operatives, chain stores, co-operative farming enterprises and a significant range of high-technology operations, drawing upon the local supply of trained engineers graduating from Mondragon's educational facilities. But, as in so many other ways, Mondragon, in terms of its diversity and high-technology focus was, and is, exceptional.[38] In France, the majority of PCs were located in the construction, printing and mechanical engineering industries.[39] In Britain, there were PCs in textiles, leather and clothing, while in the United States most were, again, craft-

---

32. Ben-ner, "Comparative Empirical Observations", p. 11.
33. Cornforth *et al.*, *Developing Successful Workers' Co-operatives*, p. 25.
34. E. Batstone, "France", in Stephen (ed.), *The Performance of Labour-Managed Firms*, p. 99.
35. Bonin & Putterman, *The Economics of Co-operation*, p. 5.
36. Estrin, "Workers' Co-operatives", p. 183.
37. Earle, *The Italian Co-operative Movement*, pp. 205–6.
38. Oakeshott, *The Case for Workers' Co-operatives*, p. 165ff.
39. J. Defourney, S. Estrin & D. Jones, "The Effects of Worker Participation on Enterprise Performance: Empirical Evidence from French Co-operatives", *International Journal of Industrial Organization* **3** (1985), p. 200; Batstone, "France", p. 99.

based and concentrated in such activities as plywood manufacture and foundry work.[40] PCs could "advance beyond their artisanal enclave", but such advances would be limited and on a narrow front, and there were few indications in the 1980s and 1990s that this would change significantly in the future.[41]

Yet those supportive of the idea of PCs suggested ways in which the factors making for underinvestment, and all that followed from it, could be countered. To circumvent the deleterious investment consequences of collective owner-ship, Vanek, for example, suggested full external financing by outside, non-voting equity capital.[42] In such circumstances, investment would no longer be constrained by the desire for an unrealistically high return and the temptation to make inroads into the net worth of capital would be avoided. The pristine ideal of a WOF would be abandoned in favour of an LMF that would pay the market rate of interest and therefore have a vested interest in maintaining the capacity of assets to meet such financial obligations. In this context, Vanek sought to stress that control was the essence of the socialist ideal of self-management and should be distinguished from ownership. As he saw it, private asset ownership (and therefore access to finance on market terms) and worker self-management (that is, LMFs) were entirely compatible, so long as ownership rights were distinguished from decision-making and control rights and the former did not impinge upon the exercise of the latter.[43]

Clearly Vanek's solution to underinvestment represented an eschewal of the economic philosophy underpinning and inspiring most WOFs, which deemed that membership and ownership rights should coalesce in the workforce. For such reasons, many socialists and WOF supporters considered it to be an unacceptable solution to the problem of finance. Also, on a practical level, as Vanek himself admitted,

> to have full external financing . . . and thereby obtain the benefits noted, one can never rely on the conventional private banking system. Conventional banks, whether in Victorian England or the modern United States, would hardly lend much to a producer co-operative, and the co-operatives themselves might shun such funding. It must take an act of political will, or a philanthropic . . . group of men to provide the necessary characteristics of the capital market which would support the smooth and efficient operation of a participatory economy or a participatory sector.[44]

---

40. Jones, "The United States of America", p. 55.
41. Estrin, "Workers' Co-operatives", p. 183.
42. See, for example, J. Vanek, "Some Fundamental Considerations on Financing and the Form of Ownership under Labour Management", in H. Bos (ed.), *Economic Structure and Development* (Amsterdam: North-Holland, 1973).
43. On this see, for example, Putterman, "After the Employment Relation", p. 137.
44. J. Vanek, "The Basic Theory of Financing", in J. Vanek, *Self-management, the Economic Liberation of Man* (Harmondsworth: Penguin, 1975), p. 455.

To which it might be added that while, historically, PCs in Britain have occasionally owed a debt to acts of private philanthropy,[45] even where such philanthropy was unproblematic, it was never, nor could it be expected to be, on a sufficient scale to mitigate significantly the problem of deficient PC finance.

Of course, this left the act of political will – a Pandora's box of a notion which a number of writers sympathetic to the formation of PCs sought to unpack. Thus, leaving aside the idea of private external finance, it was suggested by a number of commentators that publicly owned co-operative banks, or corporations, or holding companies might fulfil the role of external financiers of PCs. Miller, for example, suggested the possibility of "a plurality of agencies, with firms having the choice [of] which agency to approach for capital. One obvious possibility would be to have several national investment banks and many smaller banks based in different regions competing with each other to lend to enterprises."[46] These financial intermediaries would furnish public investment funds. Their plurality and the choice they gave would limit the extent to which their control of finance could be used coercively to interfere with enterprise decision-making. In addition, they could be envisaged as having a proactive role in the formation of PCs and as furnishing a crucial part of a more general support structure for them. Others argued more simply for a single co-operative bank along the lines of the *Caja Laboral Popular*, which did play a crucial and successful role with respect to the Mondragon complex of PCs.

The idea of holding companies was also mooted, with Estrin, for example, again making the distinction between ownership and control. The former, he opined, should be vested in "competing holding companies . . . Collectively, these holding companies would own all the productive equipment in the economy, and lend it to producer co-operatives at the market rate of interest."[47] Once more, the problem of limited and expensive finance, and thence underinvestment, could be circumvented. Also, as with Miller, this expedient involved the decentralization of economic power, although a decentralization in which the possibility of choice loomed less large. Here too, though, the point can be made that, like Vanek, what Estrin had in mind were LMFs rather than WOFs.

Finally, though with no pretence to do exhaustive justice to the institutionally imaginative contributions of those who have written on the financing of PCs, there was the notion of a "supporting corporation . . . [to] accumulate

---

45. As was the case, for example, with Scott Bader. An account of this firm can be found in J. Thornley, *Workers' Co-operatives: Jobs and Dreams* (London: Heinemann, 1981).
46. Miller, "Market Neutrality", p. 310.
47. Estrin, "Workers' Co-operatives", p. 188.

a capital base for the self-managed community, to acquire investment capital from the external capital market, to use this capital to provide financing for self-managed corporations and to ensure that self-managed firms operate according to the basic principles of self-management".[48] However, such a solution to the problem of finance, to the extent that it involved the utilization of private funds, once again raised, and in acute form, the potential tension between ownership and control. Also, as with the other expedients detailed, the reduction in the residual, resulting from debt-servicing, could be portrayed as diminishing worker identification with enterprise success and thence adversely affecting productive effort.

As noted, banks, corporations and holding companies of the kind discussed all tended to violate, to a greater or lesser extent, the notion of worker ownership. They were largely expedients for the financing of LMFs rather than WOFs, strictly defined; although for those democratic socialists who saw the social control of capital rather than its social ownership as crucial to the emergence of a socialist economy, this was no great cause for concern.[49] Yet also implicit in these institutional expedients was an erosion, or threatened erosion, of the extent of labour management enjoyed by those enterprises that resorted to them, although, as Mondragon made apparent, it *was* possible to combine external finance with individual and collective worker stakes in firms characterized by labour management and considerable enterprise autonomy. And, indeed, a number of proposals along Mondragon lines were made by democratic socialist writers.

In this regard, there was, for example, the idea of members' capital accounts. These were accounts that were to be credited with a proportion of any surplus which an enterprise generated. They would serve a multiplicity of functions: providing a source of investment finance; maintaining the principle of worker ownership; and identifying the interests of the workers more closely with the success of the firm than would be likely with purely external financing. Of course, such equity stakes raised again the spectre of concentrated risk and, in addition, the vulnerability of the enterprise to mass exit. However, that said, such individual capital accounts did work extremely well in conjunction with collectively owned capital and external co-operative bank finance in the context of Mondragon.[50]

So the argument that PCs must necessarily underinvest, like the case for supply perversity and underemployment, was, in some measure, countered by

---

48. R. O'Connor & P. Kelly, *A Study of Industrial Workers' Co-operatives* (Dublin: ESRI, 1980), p. 31.
49. See, for example, P. Bardhan & J. Roemer, "Market Socialism: A Case for Rejuvenation", *Journal of Economic Perspectives* **6** (1992), pp. 101–16 and Estrin, "Workers' Co-operatives", p. 185.
50. On this aspect of the Mondragon co-operatives see Oakeshott, *The Case for Workers' Co-operatives*, H. Thomas & C. Logan, *Mondragon: An Economic Analysis* (London: Allen & Unwin, 1982) and W. Whyte & K. Whyte, *Making Mondragon: The Growth and Dynamics of the Worker Co-operative Complex* (Ithaca: Cornell University Press, 1988).

their proponents. The view that a dynamic, growth-oriented, high-investment, decentralized socialist economy might be based primarily on PC foundations was shaken but not, it could be argued, irreparably by the *theoretical* criticism it sustained in the closing decades of the twentieth century.

That said, in *practice*, PCs did clearly suffer from the circumscribed sources of finance upon which they could draw. Their size and sectoral limitations made that all too evident. Moreover, as Vanek intimated, however imaginative the institutional solutions, it was the case that what was required to bring them to fruition was political will. And, for the most part, with the exception of the Basque region and parts of Italy, the political will and initiative were largely absent. Mondragon and the "Third Italy" apart,[51] there was no substantial institutional support oriented to solving the problem of financing PCs in western industrialized economies in the 1970s and 1980s. In Britain, legal restrictions on deposit-taking institutions and banks made it difficult for a financial intermediary, which could service, let alone induce, the rapid expansion of a PC sector, to emerge.[52] We have noted the role played by local enterprise boards in a previous chapter but, even in the early 1980s, their contribution to the expansion of the PC sector in Britain must be considered marginal. In the case of France there were, again, legal problems with mobilizing local savings for PC development.[53] The PC sector in the United States has also suffered from the absence of an appropriate financial infrastructure. In Italy, there was talk in the 1980s of "forging instruments to attract private savings"[54] to be utilized by PCs, and PC consortia certainly played a significant role in providing funds and eliciting private and state funding. But even here, in the 1980s and 1990s, there remained substantial financial constraints upon the expansion of such enterprises.

To summarize briefly, then, despite the theoretical defence of PCs against the charge of underinvestment and despite the imaginative practical solutions which were put forward to tackle the actuality of investment constraints, the major financial obstacles in the way of a much expanded role for such enterprises were all too apparent by the last decades of the century and were clearly manifested in the size, sectoral concentration and, as we shall see below, in the numbers of PCs. On these counts, therefore, those who wished to build a socialist economy on such "market syndicalist" foundations had little cause for optimism and much for concern as the century drew to its close.

One other prerequisite of economic dynamism that must be noted here in relation to the critique of PCs is that of innovation. For it was argued that the constitution and ethos of such enterprises rendered them less able to innovate

---

51. ". . . the only successful and democratically structured workers' bank in history", Oakeshott, *The Case for Workers' Co-operatives*, p. 165.
52. Cornforth *et al.*, *Developing Successful Workers' Co-operatives*, p. 217.
53. Oakeshott, *The Case for Workers' Co-operatives*, p. 143.
54. Earle, *The Italian Co-operative Movement*, p. 214.

and to cope with structural and market change than their capitalist counter-parts. Once again, the concentration of employment and investment risk in PCs was adduced as something making for such conservatism and inertia. In addition, it was posited that only the prospect of superprofits could induce the kind of entrepreneurial flair essential to any firm's capacity to innovate. It was also suggested that the kind of participative and democratic structures which characterized PCs must entail a cumbersome and turbid mode of decision-making that precluded the kind of innovative and responsive attitude to change necessary to survive and prosper in a competitive economy.

Looking at each of these reasons for expecting innovative failure, it can be said that, as regards risk, even those supportive of PCs accepted that "the concentration of assets implied both by worker ownership and by the fact that workers are unable to diversify their labor-related assets will tend to render the democratic firm unduly conservative".[55] Even so, there is considerable evidence, particularly from PCs in Italy and from the Mondragon complex, that they have, with the requisite support, proved just as willing to indulge in informed risk-taking – in relation, for example, to product innovation – as their capitalist rivals.

It could also be argued that the notion of capitalist entrepreneurs innovatively inspired by the prospect of superprofits, while consistent with neo-classical economic mythology, had little basis in the reality of corporate capitalism, where innovative progress was clearly the product of routinized research and development. Financial constraints and size might prevent PCs from replicating such efforts but that, and not the inability of the innovative entrepreneur to appropriate the residual, was manifestly the major obstacle to technological and product development. Where the requisite finance was available then, as Mondragon and Italian enterprises showed, PCs could operate at the innovative cutting edge.

Finally, there was the argument that the sluggishness of democratic decision-making must have an adverse impact on the business of innovation itself. This was an argument with a long pedigree. It can be found in the work of J. S. Mill and Alfred Marshall and, among nineteenth-century socialist writers, in that of the Webbs, the latter seeing expertise rather than participation as the *sine qua non* of efficient, responsive and innovative decision-making. Rebutting this argument, proponents of PCs made a number of points. Estrin and Svejnar, for example, suggested that "one might expect the better communication implicit in such organisations to facilitate the free flow and use of information about ways to improve productivity . . . and to reduce workers' suspicions of new work methods and practices".[56] Also, it was argued, the democratic and

---

55. Bowles & Gintis, "A Political and Economic Case", p. 389.
56. S. Estrin & J. Svejnar, "The Productivity Effects of Worker Participation: Producer Co-operatives in Western Economies", *Journal of Comparative Economics* **11**, 1987, p. 43.

participatory nature of PCs would permit workforce goals to be more closely aligned with those of the enterprise. So a more sustained effort to improve and innovate could be expected than from a capitalist workforce where decision-making occurred within hierarchical and authoritarian structures. In addition, a number of PC proponents suggested the need to take *some* account of the flexible specialization literature which, as we have seen in Chapter 3, stressed that late-twentieth-century innovation was increasingly a function of the kind of enhanced, intra-firm communication and exchange of ideas that partici-pative, democratic decision-making encouraged.[57] If there was substance to this aspect of post-Fordist socialism, then, as regards innovation, PCs had a head-start over their rivals. Moreover, it was argued by defenders of PCs that the very orientation of *small* firms to niche marketing made PCs particularly receptive to servicing rapidly changing market demand. Far from encouraging inertia and conservatism, the nature of PC decision-making structures and the attitude of mind which characterized their members were seen, therefore, as consistent with an innovative ethos.

Nor, it was argued, need participatory decision-making preclude hierarchical structures where these were required for swift and innovative responses to changing circumstances. Also, where a measure of managerial autonomy was crucial to the innovative process, it was considered possible for a PC workforce to concede this and yet ensure the crucial goal of democratic accountability without a complex, time-consuming system of participatory decision-making.

This argument that participatory and democratic enterprise structures were inimical to the business of innovation was, of course, part of a more general view of the constitution of PCs as being incompatible with effective manage-ment *per se*. Specifically, it was contended that the incentive structures which characterized such enterprises were not such as to elicit the requisite managerial effort, in terms of either the monitoring of the workforce or the informed and calculated decision-making integral to competitive success and survival. Such abilities were unlikely to be deployed, it was argued, where they went unrewarded by ownership of the residual or performance-related remunera-tion. But in PCs the residual either accrued to the enterprise or was distributed in a relatively egalitarian fashion among enterprise members. In the absence of a significant disparity of reward, therefore, the differential effort involved in

---

57. "A second argument for democratic governance is that it produces better decisions by exploiting . . . the superior information structures . . . made possible by involving those directly affected in making decisions", Bowles & Gintis, "A Political and Economic Case", pp. 386–7; also Estrin & Svejnar, "The Productivity Effects of Worker Participation", p. 43. Though, of course, the informational advantages of democratic decision-making and the spur to innovation that they give need to be predicated on worker ownership or worker control. On the advantages and limitations of the "informationally participative" firm see, for example, M. Aoki, "The Motivational Role of an External Agent in the Informationally-Participative Firm", in S. Bowles & H. Gintis (eds), *Democracy and Capitalism: Property, Community and the Contradictions of Modern Social Thought* (New York: Basic Books, 1986).

successful industrial leadership would not be forthcoming. Such a view can be found in Mill's *Principles of Political Economy* (1848), and, more recently, in the 1970s and 1980s, in the work of Alchian, Demsetz, Jensen and Meckling, who argued that in the absence of a residual income derived from property rights, managers would have no incentive to supervise their workforce efficiently.[58]

These problems were also seen as compounded by a lack of discipline and motivation on the part of the PC workforce itself. In part, this was viewed as a consequence of the workplace culture and attitudes of mind inculcated by the process of participatory and democratic decision-making. Where managerial decisions ceased to be the prerogative of a few and became the concern of the many and/or where all were equally empowered in terms of property rights, then the sanctions and authority necessary to implement decisions were weakened or absent and indiscipline, disorganization and inefficiency were the inevitable concomitants.[59] In part, too, lack of workforce motivation was seen as a consequence of an egalitarian corporate ethos that inevitably sapped initiative and effort, in the same way that the absence of a private-property-derived residual income, or significant income differentials, enfeebled the entrepreneurial spirit. There was, it was suggested, a "free rider problem", with the "income-sharing nature of producers' co-operatives" "dilut[ing] work incentives and . . . generat[ing] strictly sub-optimal effort criteria".[60]

It was also asserted that the solidaristic behaviour and collectivist mentality engendered by, and characteristic of, PCs, inevitably militated against the kind of ruthless but necessary decisions that were often required for enterprise survival. Specifically, the charge was made that such firms tended to delay redundancies, even if these were vital for their continued existence.[61] More generally, it was suggested that collectivist instincts, attitudes and structures were inimical to an entrepreneurialism whose essence was informed and rapid choice based on particular kinds of expertise. Such expertise, it was contended, was vital to making successful commercial decisions and "consequently attempts to initiate democratic worker control of production [were] ill-conceived". In this regard, too, it was argued that entrepreneurship was an essentially individualistic aptitude and activity and that, paradoxically, the

---

58. J. S. Mill, *The Principles of Political Economy* (London, 1848), pp. 792–3; A. Alchian & H. Demsetz, "Production Information Costs and Economic Organization", *American Economic Review* **62** (1972), pp. 77–95; Jensen & Meckling, "Rights and Production Functions".
59. This "control problem" is discussed by S. Webb & B. Webb in "Co-operative Production and Profitsharing", *New Statesman*, special supplement, February 1914, pp. 1–31 and more recently by P. Wiles in *Economic Institutions Compared* (Oxford: Blackwell, 1977) and Jensen & Meckling, "Rights and Production Functions", pp. 488–9. J.S. Mill also remarked upon the constraints on managers of producer co-operatives as regards the pursuit of an independent course of action, *Principles*, pp. 792–3.
60. A rendition of the argument is given, if rejected, by Bonin & Putterman in *The Economics of Co-operation*, p. 38.
61. See, for example, O'Connor & Kelly, *A Study of Industrial Workers' Co-operatives*, p. 37.

emergence of PCs was often dependent on the very qualities which their collectivist character would ultimately constrain and erode.[62]

In this regard, it had also long been contended that a major problem with PCs was the deficiency of entrepreneurial talent among those workers who came together to establish them. Such an argument was advanced by Alfred Marshall in *Industry and Trade* (1920),[63] and more recent commentators have similarly noted a "bias against the formation of PCs in capitalist economies stem[ming] from the scarcity of individuals possessing [the requisite] entrepreneurial skills".[64] In this context, the point was also made that the kind of executive skills which were created and developed in a capitalist economy were not of the kind best suited to the management of PCs. There was, it was argued, a self-reinforcing problem here. Thus because of the scarcity of the entrepreneurial talent appropriate to their management, fewer PCs were formed, and because the PC sector, in consequence, continued to be small, the flow of appropriate entrepreneurial talent would necessarily remain a trickle.[65] Further, where the sector remained small, the market for such managerial ability would be limited, with consequent deleterious implications for the career advancement of those who did combine entrepreneurial flair and a sympathy for democratic management – a strong disincentive in itself to the effort involved in acquiring that combination of skills in the first place.[66]

As regards the deficient skills of worker managers, it was also suggested that "the high salience of wages and working conditions to workers may make them myopic in their role as owners".[67] Thus employment in capitalist enterprises created a certain caste of mind and a particular agenda. It focused the attention of the workforce on those aspects of a firm's operation which impinged most immediately and directly upon its material well-being. It did so because the cash nexus encompassed the essence of the worker's relationship to the firm and it did so too because these were the only aspects of labour's existence that were amenable, through bargaining, to a measure of amelioration and control. With the formation of a PC, a different caste of mind was required, one which encompassed the strategic and the long term. However, it was likely that such

---

62. D. O'Mahoney, "Labour Management and the Market Economy", *Irish Journal of Business and Administrative Research* **1** (1979), p. 31.
63. A. Marshall, *Industry and Trade* (London, 1920), p. 26.
64. Ben-ner, "Producer Co-operatives", p. 436; "most workers are not likely to possess entrepreneurial abilities", Ben-ner, "Comparative Empirical Observations", p. 21.
65. Many commentators have noted "the lack of a pool of workers experienced in democratic management" and the associated problem of "both developing and recruiting staff with specialist managerial skills", Bowles & Gintis, "A Political and Economic Case", p. 392; see also Cornforth *et al.*, *Developing Successful Workers' Co-operatives*, p. 210.
66. On this see, for example, C. Fanning & T. McCarthy, "A Survey of Economic Hypotheses Concerning the Non-Viability of Labor-Directed Firms in Capitalist Economies", in Jansson & Hellmark (eds), *Labor-Owned Firms*, p. 33.
67. H. Hansman, "The Viability of Worker Ownership", in M. Aoki, B. Gustaffson & O. Williamson (eds), *The Firm as a Nexus of New Treaties* (New York: Sage, 1990), p. 168.

a mindset would emerge only slowly and, in the interim, short-run, pecuniary gain would be likely to be pursued at the expense of long-run, stragtegic progress.

Finally, as regards the managerial deficiencies of PCs, it was argued that in the absence of marketable equity, and thence the market's judgement of success or failure expressed in a rise or fall of share price, there would be considerable problems in monitoring and assessing the performance of management – even should the determination and the skill be there to do so.[68]

Some of the criticisms made and reservations expressed about the likely and actual quality and effectiveness of management could be easily rebutted, but others undoubtedly posed more substantial problems for the proponents of PCs. To begin with, there was the view that democratic and participatory structures precluded, or made difficult, effective managerial decision-making; or, phrased differently, that "the process costs of collective choice mechanisms can . . . be high", involving the investment of "considerable time and effort in knowledge about the firm and other workers' preferences, and in the meetings and other activities necessary to reach and implement effective collective decisions".[69] However, where productive units were small, the proponents of PCs contended that participatory decision-making would not prove problematic and where they were larger it was, in theory, "possible to develop complex collective structures which combined features of representative democracy and direct democracy and which were both efficient and allowed considerable scope for workers to influence the management of their organisation".[70] There was, of course, the potential pitfall that "representative forms of democracy may attenuate the worker's participation in control to the point where worker ownership loses some of its important potential advantages", in particular, the effort gains which came from close identification with the objectives of the firm.[71] In practice, though, as evidence from larger enterprises in Mondragon showed, it was possible to implement effectively just such a combination of representative and direct democracy without such a loss.[72]

The response of PC supporters to the argument that democratic and participatory forms of organization prevented a rapid response to change has already been dealt with in relation to the charge of innovative failure. Nor did they give much credence to the view that equity valuation was required to assess managerial performance. Indeed, the point was made that such a view

---

68. Jensen & Meckling, "Rights and Production Functions", p. 499.
69. Hansman, "The Viability of Worker Ownership", p. 168.
70. Cornforth *et al.*, *Developing Successful Workers' Co-operatives*, p. 154.
71. Hansman, "The Viability of Worker Ownership", p. 172.
72. L. Putterman, "Some Behavioural Perspectives on the Dominance of Hierarchical over Democratic Forms of Enterprise", *Journal of Economic Behaviour and Organization* **3**, 1982, p. 140; although even at Mondragon size clearly created managerial problems, with the only strike ever having occurred in the largest steel plant.

was at the root of that short-termism which was such a characteristic feature *and failing* of much of British industry in the post-war period. There were, it was suggested, other and better indicators of managerial performance and there was little to interfere with their application to PCs.

Equally insubstantial, it was believed, was the charge that management in such enterprises would face particular and intransigent problems resulting from an intractable, "free-riding" labour force, denied the incentives and liberated from the coercion necessary to ensure sustained productive effort. Both theory and empirical evidence suggested the opposite was the case. Thus it was contended that because individual remuneration was more directly and integrally related to corporate success than in capitalist firms, PCs would facilitate the kind of mutual monitoring which precluded "free riding" or, at least, rendered it negligible.[73] Further, for a number of reasons, this "horizontal reinforcement" of effort could be effected at considerably less cost than in capitalist enterprises.[74] First, because it *was* horizontal and not hierarchical, the degree and therefore the costs of overt coercion were diminished. Secondly, "workers frequently have virtually costless access to information concerning work activities of fellow workers", the very information that was necessary to ensure effective monitoring.[75] Thirdly, a situation where the remuneration of all was dependent on the size of the surplus created an expectational culture among the workforce as regards effort which, in effect, represented a costless monitoring of their own behaviour.[76] Such monitoring meant fewer supervisors, less need for sophisticated control systems and a reduction in the capital investment required to institute technical forms of control.[77] All this, it was pointed out, was consistent with studies that had been done of enterprises characterized by participatory management structures and decision-making.[78]

In assessing the costs of management and in considering associated issues of labour productivity in relation to remuneration and monitoring, supporters of PCs also emphasized that it was needful to remember with what one was comparing the performance of such enterprises. As they pointed out, the neoclassical model abstracted from class relations and the notion of class conflict and

---

73. Among many other commentators on this see, for example, Bowles & Gintis, "A Political and Economic Case", p. 377, Ben-ner, "Producer Co-operatives", p. 437 and Milenkovitch, "Is Market Socialism Efficient?", p. 93.
74. A. Gelb & K. Bradley, "The Mondragon Co-operatives: Guidelines for a Co-operative Economy?", in Jones & Svenjar, *Participatory and Self-Managed Firms*, pp. 155–6.
75. Bowles & Gintis, "A Political and Economic Case", pp. 377, 391.
76. M. Meurs, "Agency Problems and Comparative Systems Theory", in Bowles *et al.* (eds), *Markets and Democracy*, p. 122.
77. On this see Putterman, "After the Employment Relation", p. 129 and Batstone, "Organization and Orientation", p. 148.
78. On this point see Putterman, "After the Employment Relation", p. 129; also Gelb & Bradley, "The Mondragon Co-operatives", p. 155 and the other studies of Mondragon mentioned above.

had done so since its origins, with, for example, W. S. Jevons insisting that the fundamental conflict in economic life was no longer that between capital and labour, but that between producer and consumer. Predicated upon such a view of things was a set of harmonious production relations within which "claims are enforceable at zero cost to the exchanging parties".[79] Missing from this was the systemic antagonism between capital and labour which had typified industry since the emergence of capitalist relations of production. As one writer put it, the "effects of conflicts of interest between workers and employers, or between management and owners, are largely neglected".[80] The reality, of course, as the proponents of PCs were quick to insist, was a perpetual, sometimes covert sometimes overt, struggle, characterized by shirking, Luddism, St Mondays, calculated absenteeism, working to rule, passive resistance to managerial directives and, when the veneer of harmony was finally shattered, strikes and lockouts. In these circumstances, Pareto optima were, necessarily, difficult to come by and the costs of monitoring to ensure the requisite approximation of pay and product were likely to be complex and costly. "There will be no stable equilibrium in this economy. The two classes prefer different equilibria. In this economy of conflict resources will be wasted."[81] Of course, as Prais and others insisted, industrial conflict was correlated in significant measure with plant size.[82] But the fact remained that "for any given sized firm the [producer] co-operative has a better chance of industrial peace than private or state enterprises".[83]

As to the PC workforces' myopic perception of their management role, this is something that has already been discussed in relation to the problem of underinvestment. That discussion intimated that, as PC proponents saw it, given the apposite combination of collective and individual property rights, there was no reason why the labour force of such enterprises should not take a broad, long-term, strategic perspective, as opposed to one focused narrowly on the immediate gratification to be derived from improvements in wages and conditions. In addition, they believed that whatever disadvantages might result from the concentration of employment and equity risks, a short-term perspective was unlikely to be among them. Indeed, they contended, an overriding concern with the maintenance of employment would be more likely to result in an unshakeable determination to forgo short-term gain in order, at all costs, to ensure longer-term enterprise survival. And, in fact, as we have seen, empirical evidence on the employment record of PCs did reinforce such a view, while other data in the 1970s and 1980s actually pointed to a strong tendency to

79. Bowles & Gintis, "A Political and Economic Case", p. 382.
80. J. Elster & K. Moene, "Introduction", in J. Elster & K. Moene (eds), *Alternatives to Capitalism* (Cambridge: Cambridge University Press, 1989), p. 3.
81. Mygind, "From the Illyrian Firm", p. 76.
82. See, for example, S. Prais, *The Evolution of Giant Firms in Britain* (Cambridge: Cambridge University Press, 1976).
83. O'Connor & Kelly, *A Study of Workers' Co-operatives*, p. 17.

self-exploitation, where such action was seen by members as necessary for the continued existence of their firms. Of course, from another angle, this could be seen as one of the signal deficiencies of such enterprises.

So far so good as regards the case for the defence, but a major problem or associated group of problems remained and these related to the availability and retention of quality management. Here, as we have seen, even proponents and supporters of PCs admitted that there were major difficulties. As numerous studies pointed out, there was often a lack of financial, organizational and entrepreneurial skills both within and available to such firms.[84] Further, there was frequently a problem in persuading co-operators of the necessity of expertise and, on occasion, of the imperative need to seek and heed professional advice. Even where the need for such expertise was recognized, there were also the cost difficulties which small co-operative enterprises had in tapping it. Proponents of PCs also conceded, as noted above, that there was a limited supply of, and market for, those who could furnish the requisite combination of competitive, individualistic and social skills necessary to enable a co-operative enterprise to survive in a hostile competitive environment.

Clearly, then, there was a set of interconnected problems which militated strongly against the formation and survival of PCs. Of course, it was argued, these weaknesses could, in some measure, be mitigated. There was the possibility of "buying in" management expertise on a temporary basis, of utilizing the services of management consultants and of creating common marketing and financial services to furnish collectively the expertise to inform managerial decision-making that no single co-operative could afford. Further, Estrin, for example, gave to the co-operative holding companies whose creation he suggested, "the entrepreneurial function of spotting new profitable openings, and transferring resources from low to high productivity uses – the formation of profitable new firms and the closure of loss-making ones". "In this way", he argued, "the entrepreneurial deficiencies of co-operatives can be filled by alternative, market-oriented institutions."[85] And there were other imaginative suggestions of this kind. It should be noted, though, that Estrin's proposal was predicated upon the prior existence of a substantial co-operative sector and thence the solution of the problem it purported to solve.

In practice, the *Caja Laboral* of Mondragon did provide advice and guidance to PCs, particularly at the time of their formation, thereby facilitating the business of management. And it was also envisaged that co-operative banks in other countries would fulfil a similar role.[86] Co-operative consortia, such as the *Lega* in

---

84. For one example see N. Ireland & P. Law, *The Economics of Labour-Managed Enterprises* (London: Croom Helm, 1982).
85. Estrin, "Workers' Co-operatives", p. 187.
86. For such suggestions see Defourney *et al.*, "The Effect of Worker Participation", p. 215.

Italy, provided assistance and guidance to the management of co-operatives,[87] while in France the SCOP offered similar aid and advice. In Britain, in the post-war period, there existed a number of organizations which aimed to provide supportive expertise and guidance to PCs. But the problem of the paucity of management and entrepreneurial skills remained and was another important and self-reinforcing constraint on the development of the co-operative sector.[88]

The absence of managerial talent and the restricted sources of internal and external finance available to PCs were, however, just two of the elements of what may be seen as the generally inhospitable economic environment in which these entities sought to exist. It was not just that they "ha[d] to survive in a world which [wa]s not of their own making",[89] though that certainly imperilled their existence. It was the fact that it was an actively hostile, capitalist world driven by values and imperatives which were fundamentally inimical to the moral philosophy and economic ethos of PCs.[90] The next chapter will therefore consider the nature and lineaments of that inhospitable capitalist economic environment. It will discuss the difficulties which it created, and must continue to create, for PCs, and will assess what impact these and other problems noted in this chapter had on their numbers, behaviour and performance. Finally, it will consider what theoretical and practical basis exists, after several decades of debate, for the optimism evinced by socialist writers in the 1970s and 1980s as to the pivotal position of PCs in the construction of a future decentralized socialist economy.

---

87. On this and the other functions performed by the *Lega* see Earle, *The Italian Co-operative Movement*. For a brief discussion of the role of the *Lega* and other Italian co-operative consortia see, for example, J. Thornley, "Workers' Co-operatives and Trade Unions: The Italian Experience", *Economic and Industrial Democracy* **4** (1983), pp. 321–44.
88. On the need for a supportive financial, management training and management consultancy infrastructure see, for example, E. Comisso, *Yugoslav Worker Self-Management Under Plan and Market* (New Haven: Yale University Press, 1980) and U. Leviatan & M. Rosner, *Work and Organization in Kibbutz Industry* (Philadelphia: Norwood, 1980).
89. A. Rainnie, "Small Firms, Big Problems: The Political Economy of Small Business", *Capital and Class* **25** (1985), p. 163.
90. Bowles & Gintis, "A Political and Economic Case", p. 393.

Chapter 5

"In a world which is not of their making": The political economy of producer co-operatives and labour-managed firms

A fundamental aspect of the antagonistic environment that PCs confronted, and which was discussed in the literature of the 1970s and 1980s, was the general caste of mind created by their relative rarity. For that produced a strong tendency to see only capitalist enterprises as offering stability and security and to view PCs as precarious experiments born of visionary ideals.[1] And, as we shall see, it was often the case that only *in extremis*, when "conventional" capitalist alternatives had been exhausted and the dole queue beckoned, that workers were prepared to risk the expedient of co-operatives. This in turn meant that PCs not only entered a hostile capitalist world, but were also frequently constructed from the wreckage of enterprises which capitalist competition had already destroyed and stigmatized as bankrupt. It is true that some such "phoenix co-operatives" did survive,[2] but, at the very least, their inauspicious birth militated against a flying competitive start in the economic race and, in Britain, most met the fate of the short-lived Meriden, KME and *Scottish Daily News* PCs of the 1970s.[3]

---

1. On this see, for example, D. Miller, *Market, State and Community: Theoretical Foundations of Market Socialism* (Oxford: Clarendon, 1989), p. 326.
2. Particularly in the "Third Italy".
3. For a good account of the life and death of these see, for example, Jenkins, *Tony Benn: A Political Portrait*, Oakeshott, *The Case for Workers' Co-operatives* and also K. Coates (ed.), *The New Worker Co-operatives* (Nottingham: Spokesman Books, 1976).

Also seen as inimical to the formation of PCs were the prevailing values and associated aspirations of a capitalist society. Where ruthless competition, acquisitiveness, material success and self-realization through consumption were seen as moral and behavioural norms, then it was likely to be difficult for PCs to secure workforces whose behaviour would be informed by the radically different value systems which distinguished such enterprises. As Elster wrote, "if workers' preferences are shaped by what they observe to be the actual economic arrangements, the values of self-realization, participation, and community will be down-graded, making the formation of co-operatives even more unlikely".[4] Put another way, it was recognized that in an economy dominated by capitalist enterprise and values the endogenous preference formation of the workforce would operate strongly against PC formation.

Similarly, where hierarchical principles of control were a salient characteristic of the manner in which decision-making was generally effected, this, it was argued, would be likely to have adverse repercussions on both the determination and the capacity of workers to establish enterprises such as PCs in which radically different organizational tenets prevailed. This was not simply a function of inertia, although commentators did not discount the force and significance of that factor. It was also the case that those whose attitudes and capacities had been moulded by hierarchical organizations were likely to lack the mindset and inclinations required to participate fully in decision-making, given the responsibilities which that entailed. Thus, for Putterman, "co-operative experiments in capitalist societies . . . begin in an environment in which hierarchical principles of control have tended to minimise decision-making capacities of most workers, and to have concentrated such abilities in a comparatively small class of managerial personnel".[5]

The inhospitability of the economic environment confronted by PCs was, however, seen as taking many other forms. To begin with, it was clear that the institutional structures that had emerged in the economic sphere over the previous two centuries were ones which had been constructed to service capitalist enterprises. On numerous counts this disadvantaged PCs, in particular, as noted above, in terms of availability of finance. But, more generally, it was also appreciated that there was a problem of accessing the information that was necessary for economic survival and success. As Arrow pointed out, the informational channels, structures and institutions which informed the decision-making of capitalist enterprises were neither geared nor suited to the provision of what PCs were likely to require. In his words, "creating a different entity such as the labour-directed firm requires a differential investment in new information channels".[6] But, as has been noted above, investment for these enterprises was a

---

4. Elster, "From Here to There", p. 110.
5. Putterman, "Some Behavioural Perspectives", pp. 150–1.
6. K. Arrow, *The Limits of Organization* (New York: Norton, 1974), p. 2.

particularly scarce resource and, in any case, the problem was not one that could really be tackled by an *individual* PC. It was a systemic one and required a solution of that nature. A number of proponents of PCs did believe that such a solution was possible and their ideas will be considered below. But it can be said here that this absence of informational channels, structures and institutions to service their requirements, was recognized as a formidable obstacle to PC success.

Existing economic and social arrangements also disadvantaged PCs in other ways. Legal and fiscal systems discriminated against them while "isolated co-operatives [could] be disadvantaged . . . by negative externalities created by capitalist firms".[7] Further, the price mechanism often prevented them internalizing the positive externalities which they themselves created. As regards this last point, it was contended that PCs generated certain obvious public goods for which, in a capitalist context, they received no recompense. For example, as J. S. Mill pointed out, and as others have subsequently stressed, democratic social relations and participative decision-making inculcated the habits of mind and capacities necessary for active and responsible citizenship. Or, as a writer on the democratic and participative relations of production characterizing Pacific northwest plywood PCs put it, "participation is . . . the process by which society itself comes to enjoy a citizenry endowed with the civic virtues, one that is public-spirited, informed, responsible, capable and competent in self-rule".[8] But this contribution to the creation of civic virtue and the positive social externalities it generated went unrewarded in a capitalist context.

The labour movement also made its contribution to the hostile world that PCs confronted. Thus, in Britain in particular, organizations that sought to advance enterprise democratization had, historically, enjoyed little support and considerable opposition and criticism from that quarter. The guild socialists in the early part of the twentieth century, elements within the ILP in the inter-war period, some within the Labour Party and elements within the trade union movement from the late 1960s onwards, did give the idea of PCs their support.[9] Yet, until that later period, at least in Britain, one must agree with Oakeshott that "compared with the vast artillery batteries and massed infantry battalions of the organized working class and the opposing forces of organized capitalism, it is clear that they [the supporters of PCs] [we]re but 'dwarfish' skirmishing forces on the flanks of the great class battlefield".[10]

The Left's own theoretical critique of such enterprises has a long and substantial history. In Britain it can be traced back at least as far as the Chartist

---

7. A. Clayre, "Introduction", in A. Clayre (ed.), *The Political Economy of Co-operation and Participation* (Oxford: Oxford University Press, 1980), p. 20.
8. E. Greenberg, "Industrial Democracy and the Democratic Citizen", *Journal of Politics* **43** (1981), pp. 966–7; for a more extended study of these co-operatives, see E. Greenberg, *Workplace Democracy: The Political Effects of Participation* (Ithaca: Cornell University Press, 1986).
9. See above.
10. Oakeshott, *The Case for Workers' Co-operatives*, p. 51.

socialist Ernest Jones's attack upon the views of the co-operator E. V. Neale in 1851. In his *Notes to the People*, Jones's critical appraisal of PCs encapsulated salient aspects of the theoretical assault which many on the Left were to mount later in the nineteenth and on into the twentieth century.[11] Jones firmly believed that such enterprises had little chance of survival. As he saw it,

> it rested in the power of the great moneyed class to prevent and to destroy the associative movement wherever they choose *unless co-operation were backed by political power*. I argue that they would do this, partly by restrictive and injurious laws and partly by means of competition. For the co-operator would have to compete with the great capitalist, and the latter, as possessed of the larger capital, and, of consequence, enabled to buy and to manufacture cheaper than the co-operator, would be also enabled to undersell, and thus to destroy him.[12]

So Jones acknowledged what even proponents of PCs were to recognize a century later, namely that without the requisite legal and institutional support structures that in turn depended on the acquisition of political power and the will to use it, PCs were constantly vulnerable to capitalist competition and legislative onslaught. Further, where they did survive for any length of time, it could only be in consequence of a self-exploitative reduction of remuneration that left their workforces no better off than those of their capitalist rivals. For co-operatives "have got to compete with the capitalist who lowers his prices in competing with the co-operative manufacturer. The capitalist compels all his wages slaves to work for less and the co-operative manufacturer is obliged to lower his profits in order to compete with the monopolist, who lowers his wages."[13]

Later in the century such views were to be reiterated and supplemented by the Fabian and Marxist Left. Both Fabians and Marxists thought in terms of a degenerative life cycle for PCs that would start as alternatives to the capitalist system and gradually succumb to capitalist imperatives and temptations in ways which would be manifested in both their organization and their market behaviour. Democratic practices would be circumvented or diluted, while ownership and control would increasingly pass into the hands of a small number of members or into those of outsiders who, if the PC was successful, would wish to invest in it.[14] For Beatrice Potter, this is certainly what had

---

11. On this see, for example, N. Thompson, *The Real Rights of Man: Political Economies for the Working Class, 1775–1850* (London: Pluto, 1998), pp. 115–16.
12. E. Jones, "The Co-operative Movement", in *Notes to the People*, vol. 1, 1851, p. 473, my emphasis.
13. E. Jones, "Discussion at Halifax", *ibid.*, vol. 2, p. 797.
14. See here S. Webb & B. Webb, "Co-operative Production and Profit-sharing" and *A Constitution for the Socialist Commonwealth of Great Britain* (London: Fabian Society, 1920), pp. 27–58.

occurred and was occurring in Britain in the late nineteenth and early twentieth centuries.

> The ideal . . . of a self-governing co-operative workshop . . . vanishes into an indescribable industrial phantom . . . in all cases, without a single exception, outside shareholders hold the balance of power. Nor is this all; the minority of working shareholders are practically disenfranchised by the disqualification to act on the committee of management . . . So called associations of workers are constantly resolving themselves into associations of small masters.[15]

As the Webbs were later to put it in *A Constitution for the Socialist Commonwealth of Great Britain* (1920), "in the relatively few instances in which such enterprises have not succumbed as business concerns, they have ceased to be democracies of producers managing their own work, and have become associations of capitalists . . . making profits for themselves by the employment for wages of workers outside their association".[16] One could not eat of the fruit of the tree of capitalist knowledge and remain uncorrupted; but neither could one eschew the temptation of capitalist practice and survive.

Similarly, while Marx himself saw in PCs a means by which labour acquired a consciousness of both its class interests and its capacity to manage the means of production, he was adamant that they could neither subvert nor circumvent capitalist relations of production and were therefore destined to conform to their imperatives or fold – a view which was shared by subsequent generations of Marxists. They might also, it was feared, divert workers from an appreciation of their true interests, which lay in the destruction of the capitalist system, not in its attempted subversion by the competitive practice of co-operatives.[17]

This notion of a necessarily degenerative life cycle for PCs, which finds expression throughout the history of socialist political economy, was to be reiterated and developed in the work of late-twentieth-century commentators. Again, the underlying idea which informed their thinking was the corruption of capitalist ideals by PC immersion in an inhospitable, if not actively hostile, capitalist environment. The cause, nature and *differentiae specificae* of these cycles varied according to the writer. Some saw them, for example, as being essentially a function of the cyclical character of capitalist economies. Thus "WOFs are frequently formed during the downswings of the economy when the rate of

---

15. B. Potter, *The Co-operative Movement in Great Britain* (London: Allen & Unwin, 1891), pp. 147–8.
16. Webb & Webb, *A Constitution for the Socialist Commonwealth*, p. 155.
17. For a contemporary rendition of some of these arguments see T. Clarke, "Industrial Democracy: The Institutionalised Suppression of Industrial Conflict", in T. Clarke & L. Clements (eds), *Trade Unions Under Capitalism* (London: Fontana, 1977).

demise of capitalist firms is highest and their birth rate lowest, and die through their transformation to CFs [capitalist firms] during economic upswings when the rate of demise is lowest and the birth rate is highest for CFs".[18] In part, this was a consequence of the rise and fall of employment opportunities, the desire for alternatives being most potent when conventional employment opportunities diminished. However, there were also strong theoretical grounds for suggesting that in periods of prosperity, when a PC was doing well, its members would maximize their net revenue by employing wage labour rather than extending membership. For, as noted in the previous chapter, this would allow members to secure for themselves the quasi-rents which arose when demand and prices increased. So, in this way, prosperity militated in favour of actions which undermined co-operative principles. Where self-interest remained a powerful motivating force, therefore, the likelihood was that membership would be diluted in periods of prosperity and the PC would increasingly replicate the salient features of its capitalist counterparts.[19] What would occur, in effect, was a process of "bourgeoisification: the nucleus of genuine members hires ancillary employees, and so concerts itself into a kind of capitalist employer".[20] To the extent that this occurred, the PC would suffer death by corruption. Furthermore, to the extent that this was indeed its life cycle, those who saw PCs as a means of incrementally transforming a capitalist into a decentralized socialist economy were clearly doomed to disappointment. Self-interest could not be packaged in a co-operative form that allowed the PC's socialist attributes to be retained. Co-operative principles would not triumph by a process of demonstrative percolation but, rather, would yield to the osmosis of capitalist practice and values.

In addition to those who conceptualized the degenerative life cycle of PCs in essentially economic terms, there were those whose articulation of this idea was rooted in a "strong tradition of pessimism in the social sciences concerning the efficiency of democratic organisations and their susceptibility to oligarchic tendencies".[21] Whatever the organization, be it political party, public corporation or PC, it was argued that power would eventually come to be concentrated in the hands of a few. In part, this was seen as a consequence of the division of labour, with specialization extending to the task of management. In part, it was viewed as a function of size. Thus "large co-operatives, in particular, were vulnerable to the iron law of oligarchy . . . co-operatives are constrained by efficiency considerations which can make extensive participation impractical".

---

18. Ben-ner, "Comparative Empirical Observations", p. 7
19. For two among many renditions of this argument see P. Blumberg, *Industrial Democracy: The Sociology of Participation* (New York: Schocken, 1968) and A. Ben-ner, "On the Stability of the Co-operative Form of Organization", *Journal of Comparative Economics* **8** (1984), pp. 247–60.
20. P. Wiles, *Economic Institutions Compared*, p. 134.
21. Cornforth *et al.*, *Developing Successful Workers' Co-operatives*, p. 7.

Or, as Estrin put it, "in practice co-operatives tend either to remain small and ultimately disappear, or, in growing, to abandon the co-operative structure in favour of the traditional capitalist form".[22]

There were also those who, like the socialist writers noted above, saw the economic imperatives of capitalism, and not just those of large organizational structures, as eroding the co-operative emphasis on democracy and participation. Here the argument was that noted in the previous chapter: that enterprises organized according to such principles were incapable of effective decision-making in a competitive and volatile capitalist economy. As such, it was contended, there would ultimately be an overriding need to resort to "traditional organisational patterns. Data suggest that market forces pressurise co-operative ventures to return to traditional capitalist forms where certain information is the preserve of a small, separate and influential group, and where the alternative is to risk collapse."[23] So, to survive, co-operators would eventually be forced to sanction the apotheosis of the expert and the manager to positions of largely unmediated authority.[24]

There was in this life-cycle literature all the pathos and pessimism integral to an organic metaphor which, of its very nature, assumes decomposition as the inevitable end of all things. There were also some of the inflections of a Victorian moral melodrama with virtue fated to corruption by worldly temptation: "Touch not pitch lest ye be defiled" or, in more modern parlance, "enter not competitive spot labour markets" lest ye be "assimilated to the entrepreneurial *modus operandi* in the long run".[25] This was certainly the great fear of early-nineteenth-century communitarian socialists when they expressed the autarkic desire to remove themselves from "the competition and struggles of worldly traffic".[26]

However, without dismissing the substance of much of the work pursuing the life-cycle theme, it is salutary to note here Batstone's reservations about "the risks of broad generalisations such as those typical of degeneration theses which take no account either of details of co-operative organization or of the nature of the society in which co-operatives are located".[27] If life cycles were a characteristic feature of PCs, they were nevertheless seen by some as unlikely to follow a uniform pattern but to be particular to PC origins, constitution, size, location, product, sector, mode of finance and the homogeneity and aspirations of their workforces. Rather than an inevitable progression from robust and principled

22. Elster & Moene, "Introduction", p. 25; Estrin, "Workers' Co-operatives", p. 182.
23. K. Bradley, "A Comparative Analysis of Producer Co-operatives: Some Theoretical and Empirical Implications", *British Journal of Industrial Relations* **18** (1980), p. 157.
24. In this context Bradley gives the example of the *Scottish Daily News*, *ibid.*, p. 161.
25. H. Miyazaki, "On Success and Dissolution of the Labor-Managed Firm in the Capitalist Economy', *Journal of Political Economy* **92** (1984), p. 909.
26. *The New Age*, 6 May 1843 – a publication of the Ham Common Concordists.
27. Batstone, "Organization and Orientation", p. 157.

youth to degenerate and vicious senescence, it was more likely, as Cornforth suggested, that "a number of alternative patterns or life-cycles, determined partly by internal or external forces and constraints and partly by the choices of co-operators", would eventuate.[28]

It was also suggested that it was possible for management to become a specialist function without the iron law of oligarchy prevailing. Management functions could be centralized at the same time as information was widely disseminated and the workforce exercised final control through the appointment and monitoring of managers. Admittedly, there were dangers implicit in such a delegation of power but, as one writer has put it, "as long as members do not abdicate their fundamental right to govern the enterprise", delegation of managerial authority need not undermine the *raison d'être* of co-operative firms.[29]

Moreover, it was argued that while, in certain circumstances, there were undoubtedly incentives to keep down the size of membership and expand the waged workforce, it was illegitimate to assume that the membership of PCs would necessarily adopt this course of action. To do so was to view members as invariably conforming to the individualistic and economistic presuppositions of neo-classical economics. Of course, on occasion, such self-seeking, individualistic, utility-maximizing behaviour on the part of members of co-operatives was all too apparent. In this regard there was, for example, the episode of the *Scottish Daily News*, when "the direction and principal motivation of the workforce seem[ed] to be overwhelmingly economistic" – a motivation which furnished "a foundation for market forces to induce organisational changes away from co-operativism, where workers have access [to] and control of information, towards a more traditional structure in which such access is the preserve of management".[30] But many counter-instances of solidaristic behaviour blocking such developments could be, and were, cited.

Finally here, as Tomlinson has perceptively noted, much Left criticism of the degeneration of PCs was based on the assumption "that the form of enterprise management is an effect of operating in a capitalist economy, and therefore a co-operative, whatever its intentions and formal internal organisation, would have to operate in a similar way to survive".[31] But there was, clearly, no simple deterministic relationship between the organizational form assumed by enterprises in a capitalist economy and their success. Capitalist firms varied considerably in terms of the kind of management practices, organization and forms of decision-making that brought them success. There was, therefore, no single organizational stereotype to which a capitalist economy would ensure

28. Cornforth *et al.*, *Developing Successful Workers' Co-operatives*, p. 205.
29. Elster & Moene, "Introduction", p. 25.
30. Bradley, "A Comparative Analysis", p. 161.
31. J. Tomlinson, "British Politics and Co-operatives", *Capital and Class* **12** (1981), p. 59.

that successful PCs conformed. Once that was acknowledged, the argument that to survive and prosper PCs had necessarily to accept some non-democratic, non-participatory, quintessentially capitalist form of enterprise management was vitiated.

While the proponents of PCs were therefore agreed that capitalism created a problematic environment for their survival, one constantly threatening to corrupt the participatory, humanistic and egalitarian principles by which their formation was inspired and by which they sought to live, they nonetheless vigorously rebutted the arguments of those who proclaimed the inevitable degeneration and demise of co-operative enterprises. Even so, as with much of the critique of such firms, while this theoretical counter-attack was in many respects impressive, substantial cause for concern remained as both regards the developmental trajectory of existing PCs and their likely final fate.

But to what extent did the actual experience and behaviour of such enterprises in the 1970s and 1980s help to fuel such concern? To what extent did PCs in fact succumb to capitalist pressures and imperatives in relation to their number, longevity, performance, democratic practice, adherence to egalitarian principles and the quality of working life which they offered to their workforces?

The number of PCs throughout this period was small, and their general economic significance remained marginal. Italy, the country with by far the largest PC sector of western industrialized nations, had, by one undoubtedly generous estimate, around 12,000 co-operatives employing roughly half a million workers in the late 1980s.[32] Yet even that represented only around 3% of the non-agricultural labour force. In France, possessing the second largest co-operative sector in Western Europe, around 1,000 PCs employed some 40,000 workers in the early 1980s, a mere 0.2% of the non-agricultural working population;[33] while in Britain the number of co-operative employees in the early 1980s was around 10,000, representing a negligible proportion of the non-agricultural workforce of around 0.03%.[34] This leaves the most successful PC complex, Mondragon. For all its success, even after 25 years it comprised only some 100 co-operatives employing around 20,000 employees.[35] This is not in any sense to disparage what Mondragon and the PCs in other countries achieved, still less the formidable efforts that were made to secure whatever success they enjoyed. But it calls decidedly into question the view that such organizations could do anything more, in the foreseeable future, than play an

32. Estrin, "Workers' Co-operatives", p. 167.
33. Estrin & Svejnar, "The Productivity Effects of Worker Participation", p. 46; Ben-ner, "Producer Co-operatives", p. 442.
34. Estrin, "Workers' Co-operatives", p. 166; Ben-ner, "Producer Co-operatives", p. 442; for UK producer co-operatives, see also S. Estrin & V. Perotin, "Co-operatives and Participatory Firms in Great Britain", *International Review of Applied Economics* **1** (1987), pp. 152–76.
35. Mygind, "From the Illyrian Firm", p. 100.

ephemeral role in the construction of an economically feasible socialism. In the 1980s, PCs may have been flavour of the month, and in some genres of democratic socialist political economy they remained so into the 1990s, but their popularity in such quarters belied their economic insignificance. In this respect, on the basis of past and current experience, any democratic socialist political economy which would give them a fundamental transformative role would seem to be driven more by aspiration than by a dispassionate consideration of their actual achievements in the post-war period.

As to their survival and longevity compared with their capitalist rivals, the data are contradictory. For the UK, Cornforth *et al.* insisted that, for the 1975–86 period, it was not the case, despite claims of their proponents to the contrary, "that co-operatives [had] much better survival rates than small businesses",[36] even if it were possible to point to a small number of long-lived co-operative enterprises.[37] Similarly, for the United States, it was contended that despite a "persistent belief" in the capacity of US PCs to survive, "data demonstrate . . . that belief has little basis in fact".[38] Reviewing the available evidence in 1980 one commentator found that, "for American PCs, only in plywood [did] the median lifespan exceed twenty years".[39] For France, however, while the infant mortality rate of PCs was high (a characteristic experience of most countries), a study conducted in the early 1980s concluded that "French co-operatives tended to survive as long as, and probably longer than, capitalist enterprises".[40] On balance, however, this evidence lent credence to the theoretical and practical doubts about the viability of PCs that had been expressed by many commentators.

But what of the performance and competitiveness of those PCs that did survive for a significant period of time? In the wake of the growing theoretical interest in the economics of PCs in the 1970s and 1980s, there followed a considerable number of empirical studies which sought to establish, first, whether such enterprises enjoyed higher labour productivity than their capitalist counterparts and, secondly, whether, and to what extent, any productivity gains were a function of participation in management decision-making or the ownership of enterprise capital or profit-sharing. What emerged unambiguously from such investigations was, first, that where comparative studies were possible, PCs performed as well, and usually better in terms of labour productivity, than their capitalist rivals. To touch on just five examples: US plywood co-operatives enjoyed markedly higher rates of productivity than capitalist equivalents even if the differential appeared to narrow over time;[41] a study of

---

36. Cornforth *et al.*, *Developing Successful Workers' Co-operatives*, p. 38.
37. Oakeshott, *The Case for Workers' Co-operatives*, p. 73.
38. Jones, "The United States of America", p. 144.
39. D. Jones, "Producer Co-operatives in Western Industrialised Economies", *British Journal of Industrial Relations* **18** (1980), p. 344.
40. Batstone, "Organization and Orientation", p. 143.
41. Jones, "The United States of America", p. 62.

Israeli kibbutz co-operatives over the period 1954–65 showed a rate of growth of labour productivity which, at 6.2%, was significantly higher than that for the Israeli economy as a whole;[42] in Italy, "in terms of total factor productivity, PCs in fact perform better than do capitalist firms" and they also enjoyed a higher rate of profit;[43] in France, if one takes value-added per unit of labour as a measure of efficiency, then the performance of French PCs in the construction and printing industries was comparable with capitalist firms in the early 1980s;[44] finally, Mondragon co-operatives, whether compared with large, medium or small Spanish capitalist enterprises, showed, across the board, a higher rate of labour productivity and profitability in the 1970s and early 1980s.[45] It is also interesting to note here the findings of a study by Dow which showed marked labour productivity gains in those PCs which emerged from transmogrified capitalist enterprises.[46]

Of course, all of this empirical evidence raised the question of which of the characteristic features of PCs was decisive as regards their productivity performance. As noted above, three in particular were considered – participation in decision-making, the nature of worker ownership (collective or individual) and the extent of profit-sharing. Again, only a sample of studies can be noticed, but it is significant that the general conclusions of these were broadly similar. In this regard, they showed that there existed positive correlations between productivity and effective participation and between productivity and profit-sharing.[47] As regards ownership, a study of US plywood firms indicated that productivity was higher, the higher the ratio of worker–owners to all owners and the higher the ratio of worker–owners to the workforce.[48] However, other studies suggested that the effect of capital ownership was usually small or negligible,[49] while a number concluded that where positive productivity effects could be correlated with ownership, it was in those cases where ownership took an individual rather than a collective form.[50]

---

42. H. Barkai, *Growth Patterns of the Kibbutz Economy* (New York: North-Holland, 1977).
43. Zevi, "The Performance of Italian Producer Co-operatives", pp. 244–5.
44. Batstone, "France", p. 113.
45. H. Thomas, "The Performance of the Mondragon Co-operatives", in Jones & Svejnar, *Participatory and Self-managed Firms*, p. 149.
46. Dow, "Democracy versus Appropriability", p. 215.
47. On participation, profit-sharing and productivity see, for example, Elster & Moene, "Introduction", p. 30; Estrin & Svejnar, "The Productivity Effects of Worker Participation", p. 40; D. Jones & J. Svejnar, "Participation, Profit-Sharing, Worker Ownership and Efficiency in Italian Producer Co-operatives", *Economica* 52 (1985), p. 460; M. Conte, "Participation and Performance in US Labor-Managed Firms", in Jones & Svejnar (eds), *Participatory and Self-Managed Firms*. Specifically on profit-sharing and productivity see also Defourney *et al.*, "The Effects of Worker Participation", p. 200.
48. Elster & Moene, "Introduction", p. 30.
49. Estrin & Svejnar, "The Productivity Effects of Worker Participation", p. 40; Jones & Svejnar, "Participation, Profit-Sharing, Worker Ownership and Efficiency", p. 460.
50. For evidence of the negative effects of collective ownership on productivity see Estrin & Svejnar, "The Productivity Effects of Worker Participation", p. 40.

One important conclusion drawn from the above was, of course, that all the productivity benefits of the PC form of enterprise could be secured by conventionally capitalist firms if they were willing to institute a measure of industrial democracy and the requisite system of profit-sharing. The key to co-operative productivity gains could be seen as the reduction, or elimination, of the antagonistic attitudes and alienation that stemmed from hierarchical, non-participatory decision-making and, in so far as expedients making for their diminution could be replicated in the context of the capitalist firm, there was no reason, at least on performance-enhancing grounds, to effect a radical alteration in property rights. All the benefits of co-operative social relations of production could be had without the pain of effecting a fundamental alteration in the existing forms of ownership. As one commentator put it, "limited gain or profit-sharing and shop-floor level participation seem to provide adequate motivational bases, and do so without posing a threat to control by non-worker owners".[51]

As regards the capacity of PCs to compete with their capitalist rivals, in Italy the bigger construction and civil engineering PCs certainly did just that – and with considerable success. Further, in the 1980s, they began to make inroads into overseas markets.[52] Mondragon co-operatives were also competitively successful both within and outside Spain,[53] as were US plywood co-operatives in their competition with capitalist firms.[54] In contrast, a study of British PCs, published in 1980, suggested a less than impressive performance; however, it was shown that where successful enterprises were given to their workers, they did tend to outperform their rivals in the sector in which they operated.[55]

Yet despite these favourable indicators of performance in general, and competitive performance in particular, PCs remained few in number and accounted for only an infinitesimal fraction of both workforce and output in western industrial economies. Given this, and what was known about performance, it was clear to many commentators that, whatever else, the economic playing field upon which PCs competed with their capitalist rivals was far from level. This in turn raised the question of what could be done about this and whether it was reasonable to expect that any levelling could be achieved in a dominantly capitalist context. If PCs failed to multiply in a world which was not of their own making, what expectation could there legitimately be that that world might be made anew, or sufficiently anew, to effect a significant alteration in the relative preponderance of PCs and capitalist firms? This was again an

51. Putterman, "After the Employment Relation", p. 142.
52. Earle, *The Italian Co-operative Movement*, p. 205.
53. See, for example, Oakeshott, *The Case for Workers' Co-operatives*, p. 185 and, more generally, Thomas & Logan, *Mondragon: An Economic Analysis*.
54. Conte, "Participation and Performance".
55. Jones, "Producer Co-operatives in Western Industrialised Economies", p. 146; Oakeshott, *The Case for Workers' Co-operatives*, p. 75.

important question for those who wished to place PCs at the heart of their democratic socialist political economy and it is one which will be considered in the concluding paragraphs of this chapter.

Before doing so, however, the evidence on life-cycle degeneracy must be briefly reviewed. First, as regards the retention of co-operative principles, it is interesting at the outset to note that the work of the Webbs on the supposedly degenerative trajectory of PCs, as regards their democratic structures, came in for considerable criticism. As one writer put it, "with respect to participation, the Webbs both misinterpreted the situation that existed when they wrote and . . . their expectations for the future were not fulfilled . . . the tendency even between 1890 and 1913 was toward increased average participation".[56] However, it should also be noted that this critique of the Webbs was in its turn subjected to vigorous refutation.[57]

On the basis of more modern evidence, a number of commentators noted a tendency for "worker-owned firms . . . to transform into capitalist firms when they prove[d] successful":[58] a haemorrhage from co-operative ranks of just those enterprises which might have imparted the kind of dynamism to the co-operative sector which would justify a measure of optimism about its future significance. With respect to Italy, for example, one writer remarked on the loss of "ideological inspiration" by "the big co-ops" and, for that reason, in the early 1980s, the *Lega* "expressed concern over the developing crisis of democracy in co-operatives".[59] In general, too, successful Italian PCs showed a preparedness "to employ trained managers, sometimes with market salaries".[60] In France, while PCs did not always adhere rigorously to participatory and democratic practices, nor did they "simply develop into democracies of small capitalists".[61] Further, as regards Mondragon, "the democratic, self-governing and bottom-upwards character [of PCs] [was] . . . ensured by provisions and by articles which defined who [we]re to be its members".[62] Participatory and democratic decision-making structures were therefore often put in place and maintained in such a manner as to ensure, for the most part, democratic control over enterprise policy. At the same time daily management was left to professional managers: managers whose position was ultimately dependent upon democratic endorsement. So there is no evidence here of inevitable and unambiguous

56. D. Jones, "British Producer Co-operatives and the View of the Webbs on Participation and the Ability to Survive", *Annals of Public and Co-operative Economy* **46** (1975), p. 37.
57. M. Fairclough, "Conditional Degeneration and Producer Co-operatives: A Reappraisal of the Socialist Tradition", in *Proceedings of the National Conference on Research on Workers' Co-operatives* (Milton Keynes: Co-operatives Research Unit, Open University, 1986).
58. Ben-ner, "Comparative Empirical Observations", p. 20.
59. Earle, *The Italian Co-operative Movement*, p. 204, Thornley, "Workers' Co-operatives and Trade Unions", p. 328.
60. *Ibid.*, p. 327.
61. Batstone, "France", p. 120.
62. Oakeshott, *The Case for Workers' Co-operatives*, p. 187.

degeneration, although there is enough to bolster a pessimistic view of the developmental direction of those PCs that proved successful in the competitive race.

As regards the maintenance of egalitarian principles, studies indicated more cause for optimism that PCs could resist the siren call of capitalist values. In France, they showed that, in the early 1980s, income differentials in such enterprises were much smaller than across the whole of industry generally.[63] In the UK the "internal income ratios" of PCs "do not exceed three or four to one".[64] Similarly, in Mondragon, income differentials were comparatively low.

Finally, there is the matter of the quality of working life that PCs sustained. Here the argument for PCs was that the kind of social relations of production which they engendered would ensure an emphasis on humanizing work and reducing labour alienation. As Miller put it,

> where work is organised co-operatively and the profits of enterprises are shared among all the members, there is no reason for work to be monotonous or physically unpleasant, nor will workers be estranged from their products, given that they benefit directly from the sale of these products in the market-place.[65]

Here there was certainly evidence, for example from the US plywood co-operatives, that "working shareholders show a much greater propensity to rotate jobs . . . and to care about the quality of the final plywood product than do workers in conventional plywood firms".[66] In Danish co-operatives "special attention to working conditions is reported in most of the firms. Piece work has been abolished and the quality of the working process has been taken into consideration."[67] Yet there was also considerable evidence, particularly from UK PCs, of the self-exploitation and deteriorating terms and conditions of service that eventuated where, in the context of competitive capitalism, they had to struggle to survive. Also, as one commentator pointed out, working for PCs was "no guarantee of less alienating job designs"; while "non employee-owned firms" (Volvo and Proctor and Gamble among others) were, in the 1980s, at least as innovative in the design of non-alienating jobs as were PCs, many of which were "relatively conventional in these respects".[68] Moreover, for the future, some writers believed that the "increasing level of income and education, and more comprehensive social security nets which reduce the

63. Batstone, "France", p. 110.
64. D. Miller & S. Estrin, "Market Socialism: A Policy for Socialists", in I. Forbes (ed.), *Market Socialism*, p. 15.
65. *Ibid.*, p. 205.
66. Greenberg, "Industrial Democracy", p. 971.
67. Mygind, "From the Illyrian Firm", p. 96.
68. Putterman, "After the Employment Relation", p. 142.

disciplinary impact of the threat of dismissal", would be likely to "induce [capitalist] firms to seek more intrinsic ways of motivating their workers", so "leading to the increasing incidence of less alienating work modes in many countries".[69] Here again it seemed possible that essentially capitalist firms might offer many of the benefits which gave PCs their *raison d'être*.

In this and the previous chapter an attempt has been made to review some of the theoretical literature on, and empirical studies of, PCs that have emerged over the last three decades. In part, this has been done to elucidate some of the salient theoretical themes in this area of the recent history of socialist economic thought, but it has also been an attempt to assess the strength of the position of those who would put such enterprises at the heart of their democratic socialist political economy. For such firms have been seen, by some, as constituting the characteristic productive units of an economically dynamic socialist commonwealth and as the transformative means to that objective. In keeping with the overarching objective of this volume, therefore, the aim has been to consider whether we have here a road out of the wilderness for Left political economy in Britain or yet another grand detour on the road to nowhere.

Of course, the dust has not yet settled on the debate over the merits and demerits of such democratically constituted enterprises and it is unlikely to do so for some considerable time to come. But a number of conclusions seem to have emerged from the theoretical war of attrition which has taken place. First, even pursuing the conflict on essentially neo-classical terrain, the proponents of PCs have made good their claim that, for the most part, such firms can, theoretically, be expected to utilize resources with a considerable measure of efficiency and behave in an economically rational manner. Also, once certain neo-classical assumptions are relaxed and capitalist firms and the capitalist economy are made, in theoretical models, to approximate more nearly to the reality of imperfect competition, incomplete markets, intra-enterprise conflict and the relative or total ignorance of market participants, the case for PCs, on most measures of efficiency and performance, is considerably strengthened. In addition, when crude assumptions about the individualistic, self-interested, maximizing motivation and behaviour of those who establish and participate in PCs are relaxed or abandoned, and the more realistic notion that their members have the capacity to act in a solidaristic, if not altruistic, manner is introduced, the case for the economic virtues of these enterprises can be considerably strengthened.

Yet, all that said, and much more could be, fundamental problems particular to PCs have emerged in the course of theoretical discussion. The limitations on the kinds and volume of finance available, the lack of managerial and technical expertise, the generally hostile nature of the socio-economic environment which they have confronted, the intensity of the competitive pressures making

---

69. *Ibid.*, p. 145.

for failure, and the corrupting imperatives and temptations involved in the pursuit and attainment of success: all these have clearly presented formidable obstacles to the formation and growth of PCs and go some way to explain what can only be seen as the relatively bleak picture which emerges from the empirical evidence we have on the numbers, longevity, behaviour and developmental trajectory of PCs.

In this context, what has become apparent, in part through the theoretical debate and in some measure from the actual experience of PCs, is that there are good reasons for believing that such enterprises will not, through their own unaided efforts, assume a significant position in the economic life of western industrial nations. Some will undoubtedly prosper and some will combine that success with a determined adherence to co-operative principles, but the numbers in the latter category will be small and, therefore, of negligible macroeconomic significance. *Ceteris paribus*, left to themselves, PCs will remain a rare, if not an endangered species and, except in microcosm, will not in the foreseeable future effect any significant or widespread change in the social relations of production.

Realistically, therefore, PCs can only be put at the heart of a democratic socialist political economy if one assumes (i) that an extensive institutional support structure can be constructed sufficient to allow them to circumvent or counter those factors which put them at a competitive disadvantage vis-à-vis their capitalist rivals or (ii) that the transition to an essentially socialist economy has already largely been made – the theoretical starting point, as we shall see, of many of those who have given to PCs a prominent, if not dominant, role in their political economy of market socialism. The consequences and problems of formulating a democratic socialist political economy on the basis of (ii) will be considered in the next chapter. As to (i), those who would give to PCs a crucial, transformative role need to be clear just how extensive an institutional support structure would be required to enable them to fulfil it. What would be needed to remedy the financial deficiencies of such firms has already been touched on. Whether that remedy is conceived of in terms of regional co-operative banks,[70] state financing,[71] co-operative consortia,[72] or new finan-cial instruments tapping private savings, or holding companies,[73] it presupposes the creation of a formidable institutional infrastructure and, consequently, a radical sea change in the political attitudes to interventionism which dominated the 1980s and, on both sides of the political divide, continued to prevail in the 1990s. This is to say nothing of the threat which such institutions could themselves pose to enterprise adherence to co-operative principles.

---

70. Defourney *et al.*, "The Effects of Worker Participation", p. 215.
71. Dow, "Democracy versus Appropriability", p. 193
72. Thornley, *Workers' Co-operatives: Jobs and Dreams*, p. 332ff.
73. Estrin, "Workers' Co-operatives", p. 187.

That a supportive institutional framework may be achieved in microcosm by the efforts of co-operatives themselves has been proven. The *Caja Laboral* is the obvious example, but the *Lega*'s financial arm, *Fincooper*, while not directly providing loans, both underwrote and secured them for Italian PCs at favourable rates. But these are isolated examples. They would have to be replicated many times over to make any significant impact on western industrial economies and, with respect to the unique achievements of Mondragon, an extensive secondary literature has made plain that the problems of repeating such success elsewhere are, to say the least, formidable.

As regards PC self-help, there was and is the problem, in most countries, of critical mass. In Mondragon and the Emilia Romagna, there did exist a concentration of PCs sufficient to permit the collective provision of a supportive institutional infrastructure. However, where, as in Britain and most other western industrialized economies, PCs represented a small fraction of the workforce, there was little chance of achieving the scale of co-operative co-ordination required to furnish this. Nothing succeeds like success – but the problem with the co-operative movement in Britain and other countries is that the converse is equally true. And, in default of the co-operative movement itself providing the remedy to problems such as the deficiency of finance, there only remained the state – local or national. Chapter 2 has already highlighted the limitations of the former in the British case and, as to the latter, there are no indications that the political will is there, even where social democratic governments have secured the requisite political power, to embark on the wholesale creation of a national and/or regional financial infrastructure geared to the support of an expanding PC sector. The fact is, at least in Britain, that the political tide which flowed in favour of co-operatives in the 1970s ebbed strongly in the 1980s, and those who looked to a social democratic government to lay the basis of a strong PC sector, let alone a decentralized, PC-dominated, socialist economic commonwealth, have been left like flotsam on the foreshore.

But, finance aside, what other PC deficiencies require mitigation by institutional support and with what assurance can it be expected to be forthcoming? Most obviously there are the problems of high-quality management, technical expertise and support services, such as marketing, where units of production are relatively small. Here it is conceivable that the co-operative movement itself could purchase or collectively provide those services that they need. Managerial and other expertise might be bought in on a consultancy basis. Consortia, such as in Italy, might collectively furnish a range of services and expertise not within the financial scope of the individual PC. There, for example, they "undert[ook] a variety of common functions on behalf of their member co-operatives. They purchase[d] supplies, arrange[d] financing at a set rate for all co-operatives in the consortia, [and] act[ed] as general contractors in the construction industry by managing the contract and dividing the work between the various co-operatives."[74] In addition, "groups of co-operatives from different sectors" took the opportunity to "plan together and become established in new markets".[75] With such centrally provided support services, Italian co-operatives had at least the opportunity of "captur[ing] the respective advantages of being large and small".[76]

But, for this to happen, a critical mass or concentration of PCs is again required. And, in Britain in particular, that is manifestly absent and is likely to remain so. Nor, in Britain, is there the political will or political forces required to provide what the co-operative movement itself is unable to furnish. No significant state reordering of the economic world can therefore be anticipated which will make it an environment less hostile to PCs. As at present, so for the future, the economic playing field is likely to remain sharply tilted in favour of capitalist enterprises. In the light of all this, those who continue to insist not just on the socialist virtues of PCs but also on their transformative capacity are fantasists and the prisoners of a political economy that owes everything to hope and nothing to the clinical assessment of the lessons of historical experience and those to be derived from the theoretical debate which has unfolded over the last three decades. In giving to PCs a central place in their imagined socialist commonwealths, both theory and practice suggest they are building on friable foundations.

74. J. Jordan, "A System of Interdependent Firms as a Development Strategy", in Jansson & Hellmark (eds), *Labor-Owned Firms*, p. 110.
75. Earle, *The Italian Co-operative Movement*, p. 213.
76. Jordan, "A System of Interdependent Firms", p. 107.

Chapter 6

The political economy of
market socialism

The market socialism expounded by writers in the 1980s and 1990s looked to the creation of an economy in which PCs played an important, if not a dominant, productive role; in which those public corporations which were retained were thoroughly democratized as regards both their workforce and their responsiveness to those whom they served; in which it was primarily the market that mediated the demands of the nation's citizens; in which that market was truly competitive, purged of the concentrations of oligopoly and monopoly power that distorted and corrupted its operations under contemporary capitalism; in which, therefore, consumer sovereignty with respect to the public, private and co-operative sectors was a meaningful concept; and in which the market played a genuinely integrative socio-economic role in the manner that classical and neo-classical political economists since Adam Smith had anticipated it would.

Integral to this vision was a critique of Keynesian social democracy and its legacy. The extent of redistribution, it was argued, had been negligible, the major benefits of the welfare state had accrued to the middle classes, the tools of macroeconomic management had been blunted by the behaviour of transnational corporations (TNCs) and their misuse had, on occasion, damaged economic performance, while the extension of public ownership had failed on egalitarian, efficiency and democratic grounds. For the future, therefore, as one market socialist saw it, a continued adherence to a "social-democratic programme" carried with it the "danger . . . that it may lead merely to an expanded state sector, with a corresponding increase in the tax burden carried by nearly all social groups but without any very appreciable increase in social equality".[1]

As to this state sector, it was considered that its expansion under Keynesian social democracy had proceeded with both a lack of clarity as to objectives and a patent absence of industrial democracy, the latter precluding workforce involvement in the formulation of policy and thence its identification with the goals of public corporations. Further, there had been political interference in the decision-making processes of these corporations – something that had obscured, where it had not hindered, the pursuit of efficiency and dynamism and had also resulted in the creation of powerful lobbies and interest groups which had frequently dictated behaviour different from that which would have eventuated had a concern solely for economic rationality prevailed. What had emerged in "most western countries", therefore, was a public sector which was "typically, a ragbag of utilities, public service corporations, defence contractors, oil companies, previously bankrupt capitalist firms and miscellaneous others";[2] one that operated inefficiently on the basis of conflicting and arbitrarily altered objectives and that employed an alienated workforce denied democratic involvement in the setting of enterprise goals. Small wonder, therefore, that "market socialism set itself against nationalisation" and what was referred to as "the narrow economism of Clause Four advocacy".[3]

Also, as regards the redistributive component of Keynesian social democracy, not only had policy proved largely ineffectual, but it had also produced a level of taxation that had reached the limits of the politically tolerable. This was particularly problematic in a climate of opinion increasingly characterized by possessive individualism and a concomitant antipathy to the direct taxation of earned income. Certainly by the 1980s, as Roemer phrased it,

> in a market economy, I think people tend to believe they have earned, [their remuneration] in a moral sense, through selling their talents on the market . . . If so, this places a political limit on the degree of redistribution that can be accomplished by social democratic methods: an economic mechanism, at least in a democracy, cannot be stable if it rewards people in disproportion to what they believe they deserve.[4]

---

1. Miller, *Market, State and Community*, p. 9.
2. S. Estrin & J. Le Grand, "Introduction", in Le Grand & Estrin (eds), *Market Socialism*, p. 14.
3. I. Forbes, "Introduction", in I. Forbes (ed.), *Market Socialism*, pp. 1, 2.
4. J. Roemer, *A Future for Socialism* (London: Verso, 1994), p. 119.

In such circumstances, it was argued, the egalitarian aspirations of socialism would have to be realized by other than traditional social democratic, fiscal means.

What market socialism offered, therefore, in the context of the crisis of Keynesian social democracy, was a way of pursuing and attaining the traditional objectives of extended social ownership and greater equality which avoided expedients that had both failed and alienated their democratic socialist supporters. But more than that, it offered to combine the pursuit of these goals with that of enhancing economic efficiency and transforming the nation's economic performance, reversing the secular trend of relative economic decline which, by the 1980s, threatened rapid deindustrialization and endemic mass unemployment.

This economic transformation was to be accomplished in a number of ways. Most obviously, in the tradition of an earlier democratic socialist economics,[5] market socialists offered to realize, to a considerable degree, the neo-classical ideal of perfectly competitive markets generating a full and efficient utilization of resources – an ideal from which capitalism was increasingly departing. The view of Vanek that "on grounds of several arguments" an economy dominated by LMFs could "be expected . . . to yield market structures more competitive than any other free economy", has already been noted.[6] Similarly, Miller insisted that "provided . . . adequate arrangements are made to facilitate the creation of new PCs, a market socialist economy should come closer to fulfilling the requirements of competition than its capitalist counterpart".[7] In place of an increasingly sclerotic economy dominated by monopolistic behaviour and oligopolistic collusion, market socialists offered one that was truly competitive, which would therefore stimulate innovation and would also provide the requisite incentives to effect an efficient utilization of resources and ensure that producers were rewarded more nearly in accordance with their actual contribution to the production process.

"The reasons why the market [had] fail[ed] to secure the efficient allocation of resources ha[d] to do with the gap between the real and hypothetical functioning of the mechanism of market competition, with imperfections growing over time."[8] What market socialism would do was bring the former back into line with the latter, reconstructing the economy so that it approximated more closely to the neo-classical ideal. As Stiglitz put it,

one of the motivations behind market socialism was the belief that, in modern industrial economies, nothing approaching the perfect

5. See, for example, the work of Oskar Lange, Abba Lerner and Fred Taylor in the 1930s.
6. Vanek, "Decentralisation Under Workers' Management", p. 335.
7. Miller, *Market, State and Community*, p. 109.
8. W. Brus, "Socialism – Feasible or Viable?", *New Left Review* **153** (1985), p. 159.

competition ideal was possible. A market socialist economy could replicate the behaviour of an idealized perfect competition economy – something not achievable under capitalism.[9]

Just as Marx in the *Communist Manifesto* waxed lyrical on the material achievements of nascent industrial capitalism, so market socialists proved equally eloquent on what might be accomplished by the authentically competitive markets that socialism could create, particularly with respect to the economic dynamism which a market-induced efflorescence of innovative activity would engender.[10]

Such socialists also stressed the capacity of markets to co-ordinate economic decision-making in ways that avoided the wasteful bureaucracy, and the distortion of economic decision-making by political interests, that attended central planning and, for that matter, the conduct of the social democratic nationalized corporation. For Estrin and Le Grand, "the market mechanism [was] the most efficient way of co-ordinating decentralized economic decision-making", "eschewing [as it did] the tendency to centralised intervention as an economic characteristic of socialist parties".[11]

Such a decentralization of economic decision-making would also serve to disentangle political from economic power in a manner that would purge the polity of the undemocratic consequences of that corporatism which, in Britain and elsewhere, had resulted from their interpenetration. At the same time, a decentralization of economic decision-making would relieve governments of that "overload" which the New Right had been quick to use as part of its rationale for privatization. In these respects, in the words of Miller, "to confine the economic role of the state", in the way that market socialists suggested, "makes democratic government feasible".[12]

On the imperative pursuit of the dispersal of power market socialists were emphatic, particularly in the 1980s, when the New Right were rapidly occupying the libertarian high ground and threatening to make the language of freedom their own. In respect of this, market socialism offered the opportunity for counter-attack on a number of fronts. Like those whose democratic socialist political economy was derived more exclusively from the doctrines and anticipated triumph of flexible specialization, market socialists generally applauded the freedom involved in the market's extension of consumer sovereignty. Market socialism would furnish genuine choice to the consumer

---

9. J. Stiglitz, *Whither Socialism? Perspectives from the Economics of Information*, Wicksell Lectures (Cambridge, Mass.: MIT Press, 1994), p. 15.
10. On the necessary link between competition and innovation see, for example, Roemer, *A Future for Socialism*, pp. 44, 125.
11. Estrin & Le Grand, "Introduction", p. 1.
12. Miller, *Market, State and Community*, p. 9.

in contrast to its denial by socialist central planning and its spurious offer in a monopolistic/oligopolistic capitalist context in which, in any case, the consumer power of many was attenuated by labour exploitation. The aim of market socialism was, therefore, "the rolling back of [the] non-market provision" of the central planners "to allow competitive forces to increase efficiency *and choice*" and, in the context of contemporary capitalism, "to root out [the] monopolistic abuse" of consumers.[13] Socialism should break its "identification" in the popular mind "with bureaucratic sloth and restrictions upon choice", an identification which was seen as having "arisen as a consequence of the Left's distrust of markets . . . in favour of the planned allocation of resources . . . and of goods and services".[14] Indeed, along with efficiency and social justice, freedom of choice was an integral element of the mantra most often chanted by market socialists to exorcise the New Right's appeal and, for that matter, that of the Old Left. "A socialist market economy . . . can reasonably promise freedom of choice of personal consumption, freedom of choice in work and freedom of expression."[15]

Freedom as regards consumer choice was on offer, but there was also a new kind of freedom in the context of the workplace. Participatory democracy was, of course, built into the concept of the PC and, to the extent that PCs were to play a prominent role in a market socialist economy, the freedoms associated with non-authoritative, enterprise decision-making would also be a salient feature. But even where a major economic role was given to public corporations, emphasis was placed on the need for these to be democratized in ways which would preclude any re-emergence of past authoritarian practice. So market socialism tapped into, articulated and proposed to assuage the discontents felt by many on the Left with what were seen as modes of public enterprise decision-making that had contributed fundamentally to the nation's disenchantment with social ownership; modes that engendered labour alienation, managerial arrogance, failures of communication and a level of industrial unrest that had materially and adversely affected economic performance.

Market socialists also purported to offer a way forward for the "many" who "wish[ed] to escape the inherent chauvinism of . . . class analysis";[16] here again they were attempting to distance themselves from the shibboleths of the "Old Left". They proposed not the abolition of private ownership but its generalization, either directly through the individual share ownership of PCs or, more often, through such intermediaries as holding companies and investment

---

13. S. Estrin & D. Winter, "Planning in a Market Socialist Economy", in Le Grand & Estrin (eds), *Market Socialism*, p. 105.
14. P. Abell, "An Equitarian Market Socialism", in Le Grand & Estrin (eds), *Market Socialism*, pp. 79–80.
15. D. Miller, "Why Markets?", in Le Grand & Estrin (eds), *Market Socialism*, p. 35.
16. Forbes, "Introduction", p. 1.

banks. The forms of ownership and control proposed for a market socialist economy will be considered at greater length below. But here one can see market socialism as a mirror image of the political economy of the New Right which, under the slogan of popular capitalism, had also claimed to dissolve the antagonistic juxtaposition of capital and labour by giving the working class, through privatization, the opportunity to acquire a stake in the nation's capital stock. However, while privatization could be dismissed as offering the shadow and retaining the substance, market socialists purported, through the combination of individual capital stakeholding and industrial democracy, to effect a real dispersal of economic and decision-making power. In such circumstances, class antagonism would be dissipated and the chauvinism of class analysis rendered redundant.

In this context, the point should also be made that, as for Adam Smith, so for many market socialists, the market was seen as playing a socially integrative role. For Smith, the centrifugal forces of competition were countered by the centripetal pressures of the growing interdependence that the progressive division of labour engendered. Similarly, for some market socialists, "markets, in that *all ordinary people are involved in them*, are seen as providing a sense of overall community throughout society. To that extent they potentially constitute a kind of political democratic mechanism."[17] What could turn that potential for social integration and community into a reality was the involvement of all in enterprise decision-making, in particular through the proliferation of PCs and the democratization of public corporations. So "instead of the iron fist of the state" enforcing communitarian values, "the velvety glove of participatory democracy [would] envelop[e] the invisible hand of the free market",[18] steering the members of a society to a recognition of their interdependence and thence the communality of their interests. The market, under socialism, would thereby achieve an integrative end that was no part of the original intent of those who pursued their self-interest within it.

An attempt to realize the socialist desire for an enhanced sense of community was therefore central to market socialism. Community and fellowship were viewed in traditional socialist terms as of profound value in themselves. But they were also regarded as a means to an economic end, because the elimination of social antagonism was seen as reinforcing all those efficiency advantages which stemmed from participatory democracy and the socialization of ownership. In this regard a growing awareness and recognition of communality would serve to strengthen the overall competitiveness of the market socialist economy. So when Roemer and others wrote oxymoronically

---

17. *Ibid.*, p. 2, my emphasis.
18. *Ibid.*, p. 2; but see Miller's view that a sense of nationality must be drawn on to engender and/ or bolster the sense of community necessary for a welfarism based on need, Miller, *Market, State and Community*, pp. 237–8.

of "competitive socialism", or about the effectiveness of co-operative competition, they sought to convey not just the inherently competitive nature of market socialism but also the competitive edge that the efficiency gains, emanating in part from a growing sense of *social* unity and *social* harmony, would give it.

In relation to their critique of Keynesian social democracy, market socialists were quick to highlight the tension between the pursuit of distributive equity and the maintenance of an effective incentive structure. As already noted, market socialists argued that the kind of "egalitarianism" practised under social democratic auspices and by traditional social democratic means had undoubtedly had deleterious repercussions for the economy, as well, of course, as proving ineffectual in promoting social and economic justice. However, market socialism would "obtain the efficiency advantages of markets in the production of most goods and services" *and* "bring about a more equal distribution of primary income".[19] Under its auspices, economic justice and economic efficiency would be reconciled. This was where market socialists believed they scored over the egalitarianism of Keynesian social democracy. That had sought to achieve its egalitarian objectives *ex post*, aiming to remedy the injustices involved in marked disparities of income after they had been earned. For market socialists, that was a recipe for social resentment, with all the material diseconomies and disincentives that such disaffection could engender. In contrast, where PCs and democratized public corporations predominated, the situation would be markedly different. Wages and salaries might vary, although not to the same extent as in enterprises devoid of participative and democratic decision-making procedures, but, importantly, "market socialism tend[ed] to spread the windfall gains of economic success more widely, since profits are shared throughout the membership of each enterprise and . . . they are unlikely to be concerted into capital investment in succeeding periods".[20] For Roemer, what distinguished contemporary models of market socialism,[21] indeed what allowed them to claim to be socialist at all, was not their adherence to any traditional notion of public ownership, but rather "the relatively egalitarian distribution of profits they hope to implement and their abrogation of the right to the massive accumulation of private property in the means of production".[22] This "relatively egalitarian" distribution of profits resulting from the social nature of capital ownership was of the essence. But so too was the assumption that whatever disparities in income remained would not become cumulative because the capacity, inclination and opportunity to reinvest would be circumscribed and this in turn would reduce the scope for the well-paid to

---

19. Miller, *Market, State and Community*, p. 9.
20. *Ibid.*, p. 171.
21. What he referred to as "fifth generation models of socialism", Roemer, *A Future for Socialism*, p. 34.
22. *Ibid.*, p. 34.

generate, from ownership, an income stream markedly different from that of their fellow workers.

"Thus", wrote Miller,

> market socialism seems likely to correspond more closely to the football league model than existing capitalist markets, for which, if we are looking for a games analogy, the most appropriate might be Monopoly, where the player who gets ahead in the early rounds usually moves inexorably towards complete domination of the game.[23]

It was not always made clear though, in market socialist literature, whether it was the *capacity* to invest or the circumscribed (legally or otherwise) *opportunities* to invest which would ensure that no individual, group of individuals, company or collective could purchase Mayfair *and* Park Lane. Also, it was not immediately apparent why initial success, through the purchase of key resources and infrastructure, could not lay the basis for subsequent and cumulative competitive triumphs of PCs so favoured. But these matters will be considered at greater length later in the chapter. The point to make here, in terms of the appeal of market socialism, is that it did purport to reconcile egalitarianism and efficiency, social harmony and competitiveness, social justice and self-interest. While adhering to quintessentially socialist distributive and redistributive objectives, it could therefore purport to offer a supply-side solution to Britain's relative economic decline, a solution which, like that of the New Right, could also claim to have harnessed market imperatives to the transformative task, while avoiding the increasingly manifest diseconomies of the social atomism which New Right political economy praised, presumed and precipitated.

The appeal of market socialism in the West was that it appeared to provide an answer to the crisis of contemporary democratic socialism: a response to the urgent "need for a radical review of the socialist idea itself, as a political project in the late twentieth century". "The Left was no longer in the vanguard of intellectual radicalism; rather it was the so-called New Right that was producing radical ideas for social reform and change, ideas to which the Left could only respond with a limp defence."[24] Market socialism claimed to have recaptured the agenda for radical change. It had taken what was of potency and of worth in the appeal of the New Right project – libertarianism, efficiency, reward commensurate with effort – and iterated it in terms that embraced socialism's traditional objectives of freedom, equality and community.

However, one further aspect of the contemporary appeal of market socialism should be noted. For market socialism also seemed to offer an agenda for

---

23. Miller, *Market, State and Community*, p. 171.
24. *Ibid.*, p. 1; S. Estrin & J. Le Grand, "Preface", in Le Grand & Estrin (eds), *Market Socialism*.

radical change as regards Central and Eastern Europe and one that, until 1989, and for a short time thereafter, seemed in harmony with the dynamic of development in many communist countries. Since Yugoslavia had pursued the ideal of a labour-managed economy in the late 1950s, market socialism had had not just its theorists but also its practitioners in communist ranks. Further, in Hungary in the 1960s, and later in Poland, economic reforms were instituted that gave an increasing, if still decidedly constrained, role to market forces. Ideas began to circulate, such as those of the Hungarian economist Tibor Liska, who proposed the idea of an "entrepreneurial socialism" in which state assets were auctioned to the highest bidder, who in turn would assume "responsibility for failure and reward for success".[25] For many on the Left, these and comparable ideas seemed to intimate the shape of things to come for communism, and market socialism could therefore claim to be not only a radical economic philosophy that challenged a disintegrating social democracy in the West but also one with the imminent possibility of realization in the East.

Of course, if this added to its persuasive power, it also meant that the political economy of market socialism sometimes seemed to be, consciously or unconsciously, predicated upon what was emerging in Eastern Europe in the wake of economic reform. Indeed, Frankel wrote of Nove's *Economics of Feasible Socialism* (1983), that he "regard[ed] [it] as a response to the developments in Eastern Europe rather than an adequate alternative to existing capitalist societies".[26] And he viewed it thus because it proceeded on the assumption that the social ownership of the means of production was a *fait accompli*. This is an important point, as Nove was not alone in theorizing his market socialism on this basis, and it is a point that will be considered again when the prescriptive and practical limitations of market socialism are discussed later in this chapter. At this juncture, however, it is necessary to consider in greater detail the lineaments and structures of those economies that market socialists envisioned.

To begin with, there were the forms of ownership by which the market socialist economy would be characterized. On ownership in general, all would have agreed with Roemer's "claim" that while "markets [we]re necessary to achieve an efficient and vigorous economy . . . private ownership [wa]s not necessary for the successful operation of markets".[27] It was, in fact, this "failure of both right and left to disambiguate the concepts of private ownership and market equilibrium that ha[d] led to the premature obituaries for socialism".[28]

---

25. On this see W. Brus & K. Laski, *From Marx to the Market: Socialism in Search of an Economic System* (Oxford: Oxford University Press, 1989), p. 146.
26. B. Frankel, "The Historical Obsolescence of Market Socialism – A Reply to Alec Nove", *Radical Philosophy* **39** (1985), p. 28.
27. J. Roemer, "The Possibility of Market Socialism", in D. Copp, J. Hampton & J. Roemer (eds), *The Idea of Democracy* (Cambridge: Cambridge University Press), p. 243.
28. D. Winter, "Market Socialism and the Reform of Capitalism", in Le Grand & Estrin, *Market Socialism*, pp. 162–3.

All would also have concurred that "a socialist economy [would] have to abandon the private ownership of the means of production as the *principal* form of ownership in the economy".[29] Miller, for example, theorized an economy in which "all productive enterprises ... [were] constituted as worker's co-operatives, leasing their operating capital from an outside investment agency".[30] Yet there was also a fairly general recognition that certain sectors and certain kinds of enterprise were not particularly amenable to a workers' co-operative form of organization. In this context, mention was made of some of those deficiencies of PCs, which have already been discussed in the two previous chapters, and it was accepted that for high-risk and technologically innovative firms and, in particular, for those enjoying considerable economies of scale, this form of enterprise might well prove inappropriate.[31]

As regards such firms, it was considered that state ownership was often to be preferred. In addition, it was believed by some that where positive or negative externalities were significant and where the public service aspect of an activity predominated, then, once again, PCs operating according to market imperatives were probably inappropriate and some form of state ownership, or at least regulation or control, might be required. As Nove saw it,

> there are important sectors in our economy that by reason of monopoly, size, the importance of externalities or the dominance of the public-service aspect, even under modern capitalism, are either publicly owned or in some important respect publicly regulated, or subsidised, or implicitly or explicitly guaranteed against bankruptcy. These are sectors that a "market socialist" economy would place under state control.[32]

For some, "market socialism could even be compatible with co-operatives being in a minority". But even those who adhered to such a position were adamant that PCs could still be expected to "interact to form a substantial co-operative bloc in the economy".[33]

As to private enterprise, most versions of market socialism confined it to an ephemeral role, although some gave it a greater importance. Roemer, for example, saw the existence of a market socialist private sector as usefully "provid[ing] almost the same incentives that exist in capitalism for those who

---

29. *Ibid.*, p. 162.
30. Miller, *Market, State and Community*, p. 12; for a similar view see also D. Miller & S. Estrin, "Market Socialism: A Policy for Socialists", p. 8. On this see too Bardhan & Roemer, "Market Socialism: A Case for Rejuvenation?", p. 101.
31. PCs were also considered inappropriate for those industries, such as banking and insurance, in which a small number of highly skilled personnel played a pivotal role.
32. A. Nove, "The Role of Central Planning under Capitalism and Market Socialism", in Elster & Moene (eds), *Alternatives to Capitalism*, p. 102.
33. *Ibid.*

form *new firms* in order to bring innovations to market". Thus, in this context, private enterprise was seen as imparting an innovative dynamism at the fringes of market socialism which it might otherwise lack. Capitalist firms could exist, but only "up to a certain size".[34] Nove, for example, wrote of the necessary "predominance of state, social and co-operative property and the absence of any large-scale private ownership".[35] This was in order to prevent the emergence of a class of capitalists capable of wielding any significant degree of economic and political power. Once private firms arrived at a certain size, therefore, market socialists considered that they should usually be taken into public ownership or transformed into PCs.[36] Certainly "the bulk of ownership [could] not be private in a socialist society".[37]

So what emerged from the minds of most theorists (usually the sole locus for the existence of market socialism in the 1980s and 1990s) was a vision of a pluralistic socialist economy with a general preponderance of PCs. Nove, for example, envisaged an economy composed of "state enterprises, centrally controlled and administered, . . . state-owned (or socially owned) enterprises with full autonomy and a management responsible to the workforce, [and] . . . co-operative enterprises",[38] the first category of enterprise being subjected to democratic controls by the state, the workforce and their consumers. Put another way, what was offered were imagined economies constructed on the basis of a form of enterprise of negligible significance outside the "Third Italy" and the Basque region and the kind of state corporations that, in the 1980s, were being systematically dismantled by privatization. Thus, while market socialists in the 1970s and 1980s could be seen as swimming with a tide of opinion that set store by the choice, autonomy, economic pluralism and the accountability to consumers which the market purportedly created, the institutional framework within which they anticipated the realization of their vision increasingly lacked a basis other than the aspirational and imaginative.

However, before developing some of these points further, specifically in relation to the political economy of transition that market socialists articulated, it is important to consider in more detail the differing conceptions of ownership and control that they advanced. All, of course, were predicated upon the prior existence of a market socialist economy which was up and running. So the only limits to what was proposed were those of the general principles by which it was conceived market socialist economies *should* operate, the internal theoretical consistency of the model constructed

---

34. Roemer, *A Future for Socialism*, p. 78; Estrin & Le Grand, "Introduction", p. 15. On this see also, for example, Miller & Estrin, "Market Socialism: A Policy for Socialists", p. 8.
35. A. Nove, *The Economics of Feasible Socialism* (London: Allen & Unwin, 1983), p. 227.
36. Roemer, *A Future for Socialism*, p. 78.
37. Estrin & Le Grand, "Introduction", p. 15.
38. Nove, *The Economics of Feasible Socialism*, p. 200.

and the imaginative creativity of the theorists themselves, the latter never acting as a severe constraint.

Most suggestions as to the form that enterprise ownership and control should take were centred on the key entity of the PC and aimed to counter the various potential difficulties that such enterprises confronted and that have been noted in the two preceding chapters. In particular, on a systemic basis, market socialists aimed to address the problems of lack of risk-taking, the absence of innovation, underinvestment, the general limitations of self-financing and the monitoring of managerial performance. With respect to these problems, most market socialists insisted upon the external provision of finance. This was seen as a primary means of dealing with the problem of sub-optimal risk-taking and unwillingness to innovate which, some believed, characterized self-financed PCs. Various means of external financing were suggested. One proposal was for "labour–capital partnerships" that would "spread the risk of variations in income between both the providers of capital and providers of labour. Both [workers and capitalists] [would] possess share certificates which [would] entitle the holder to a dividend in net income."[39] Another proposal was borrowed from the practice in post-war Japan of establishing *keiretsu*. These were corporate groupings, usually with a main bank at their core. Articulated in market socialist terms, these became groups of joint stock companies, partly worker-owned, but also financed by other share-owning enterprises in the group. It would be the bank, however, that would furnish the nucleus of the corporate conglomerate, operating as the major conduit for investment, with the majority of its shares owned by the state.[40] Such interdependence would, in theory, spread the risks of investment and also provide substantial scope for new funding when required. Another suggestion was for the leasing of capital from outside investment agencies or banks.[41] In addition to solving the problem of "conservative" business practice in the light of the concentrated risk consequent upon self-financing, such expedients were also deemed to provide a solution to the problem of underinvestment along similar lines.

Such financial expedients, in conjunction with other practices, were also considered as providing the basis for monitoring corporate performance – an activity that was considered essential if scarce resources were to be disbursed among the competing ends of a market socialist economy in the most efficient manner. In Anglo-American capitalism, the problem of ensuring an efficient use

---

39. Abell, "An Equitarian Market Socialism", p. 98.
40. Bardhan & Roemer, "Market Socialism: A Case for Rejuvenation", pp. 106–7. Although they go on to suggest that "some significant fraction of the shares will be owned by pension funds, insurance companies and other banks, to allow for some diversification of interest in, and professional control of, bank lending operations", *ibid.*, p. 113.
41. Miller, *Market, State and Community*, pp. 10, 310-11; Roemer, *A Future for Socialism*, p. 49.

of resources by companies was seen as being effected by the threat and actuality of takeovers and a competitive market for managers. However, the notion of a stock market was clearly problematic for many market socialists, threatening, as some saw it, the re-emergence of coercive aggregations of wealth and economic power. Yet with certain constraints on share ownership, purchase and sale, and within an apposite institutional framework, a market socialist stock exchange was deemed by some to provide a means of assessing the efficiency of PCs and other socialist enterprises, along with the quality of their management.

Thus, in the case of "labour–capital partnerships", "capital shares [would be] tradeable on the market though labour shares are not".[42] So there would be a market in income-bearing assets, the value of which would rise or fall with the earnings/profits of the company. In this manner, an objective judgement on the efficiency of enterprises could be made, with appropriate signals sent to both management and workforce. As regards market socialist *keiretsu*, it was considered that shares in these corporate enterprises should be tradable. However, "while citizens would be free to trade their stock in mutual funds for stock in other mutual funds, they could not liquidate their portfolios . . . We might call this a clamshell economy."[43] They would, in effect, be trading rights over income streams without ever realizing or liquidating their capital value. Such expedients, it was believed, would exert a quasi-stock-market discipline over firms and corporate groupings while, at the same time, the nature of the "stock market" created "would prevent the concentration of [the] ownership of firms in the hands of a small class".[44] It would, though, be the core bank which would play the crucial monitoring role as the major owner of stock and it would be expected to respond to the signals which the quasi-stock market sent out by effecting or inducing the reorganization or closure of ailing firms. It would, therefore, be these public banks and agencies that, in the final analysis, would be responsible for monitoring enterprise management and, so ensuring an efficient use of public resources.

The idea was also mooted of entitlement to profit-sharing by individual shareholders through the distribution of ownership "coupons" that could only be traded against each other. Once again there was the notion of a clamshell economy, in which superior performance would be indicated by a rise in coupon value but where there would be no opportunity for concentration of ownership with all the deleterious distributional and power implications which would ensue. Further, "everyone's coupon portfolio would return to the public treasury at death".[45] Coupon value would be indicative of performance and this

---

42. Abell, "An Equitarian Market Socialism", p. 98.
43. Bardhan & Roemer, "Market Socialism: A Case for Rejuvenation", p. 110.
44. *Ibid.*
45. Roemer, *A Future for Socialism*, p. 49.

would be monitored by the providers of finance, the banks. And if, as was anticipated, "banks monitor firms aggressively and firms must depend on banks for finance, and if the doors to international trade are open, firms will innovate".[46] This last point is also worth remarking on because, almost without exception, market socialists emphasized the positive consequences of an open economy where enterprises would be subjected to the full rigours of foreign competition. This was seen as yet another means by which efficient performance could be ensured. What had to be avoided, of course, where external finance came directly or indirectly from the state, was what Janos Kornai termed a soft budget constraint, under which enterprises in a socialist economy came to rely upon the public purse as an inexhaustible source of finance regardless of their performance. Socialist enterprises had to be free to fail. This was the inevitable corollary of an efficient utilization of available resources.

So how should we view such solutions to some of the investment-related weaknesses in a market socialist economy in which PCs played a pivotal role? To begin with, one can note that they were only available once the transition to a fully fledged market socialist economy had occurred, and the whole question of how that transition was to be effected therefore assumes, or should have assumed, a fundamental significance in market socialist political economy. In addition, there was the whole issue of where these proposals for external funding would leave the autonomy of PCs. Certainly, once recourse was had to any of them, the notion of the pristine WOF made its exit from the market socialist stage. Further, if we take, for example, the proposal for "labour–capital enterprises", the idea was for "ultimate control" to lie "in the hands of the board of directors elected in equal numbers by labour and capital"; so here even labour management or worker control would be diluted if not altogether abrogated.[47] Moreover, the tradability of "capital shares" would also be likely to impose definite external constraints on worker/capital management of a kind likely to impinge more on the former's power to determine how the enterprise should be managed than the latter's. Thus where, as with market socialist *keiretsu*, the greater part of the shares was to be owned by the investment bank and other public firms, the autonomy of the enterprise was likely to be severely constrained and the idea of worker control would become distinctly problematic. Similarly, where public banks were seen as the major source of finance and monitored performance aggressively, and where ownership resided with a coupon-holding public, autonomy and self-management would again be severely circumscribed. In short, these kinds of solution to the problems of sub-optimal risk-taking, underinvestment and lack of innovative zeal not only seemed to preclude the emergence of WOFs but also called into question, in

---

46. *Ibid.*, p. 78.
47. Abell, "An Equitarian Market Socialism", p. 98.

crucial ways, the notion of an LMF. Thus many of the salient characteristics of the LMF – its autonomy, its democratic and participatory decision-making structures, its horizontal patterns of communication – would be partially subverted or even wholly compromised by what many market socialists proposed. Much of what proponents of a decentralized socialism considered to be of worth in both a narrow economic and a broader human sense would be lost; a high price, in terms of lost socialist aspirations, would be paid to circumvent the difficulties which self-financing was believed to create. Also, as regards constraints on autonomy, there were the problems likely to arise from the directive role which many believed should be assumed by the state and planners in a market socialist economy. However, this will be considered in more detail below.

What one also sees in these speculative forays to counter the anticipated difficulties of enterprises in an imagined market socialist commonwealth is the eidetic refurbishment of the institutions and mechanisms that impose order, and monitor performance, in a capitalist economy. Thus, we have the socialist joint stock company, the socialist corporate finance grouping or holding company, the market socialist bank and the market socialist stock market with its socialist shareholders. In effect, in order to counter difficulties, as regards efficiency and dynamism, that would emerge with the effective elimination of private property in the means of production, market socialists seemed to have believed it necessary to establish structures and mechanisms that would approximate closely to those which generated the imperatives and incentives in a capitalist economy. Thus it has been suggested that what was offered by market socialists was capitalism *faute de mieux*. As one writer put it, "in many respects market socialism seems remarkably similar to what we have at present",[48] and this raises the question of the socialist worth of replicating what capitalism did so much better – something that will be discussed at greater length when the deficiencies of market socialism are more fully considered.

Before doing so, however, it is important to understand how market socialists envisaged the role of the state and the nature and function of central planning. Here what strikes the reader is the familiarity of much of what they tended to offer. All accepted, for example, the need for macroeconomic management to attain the traditional objectives of full employment and stable prices. Thus, for Nove, "Keynes d[id] not cease to be right under market socialism".[49] Aggregate demand must be managed to ensure that "labour and capital stocks [we]re as far as possible fully employed",[50] and to secure the objective of non-inflationary full employment many market socialists accepted,

---

48. K. Beuret & D. Coole, "Rethinking the Present", in Forbes, *Market Socialism*, p. 21.
49. Nove, "The Role of Central Planning", p. 105.
50. Miller, *Market, State and Community*, p. 296.

with Nove, that "an incomes policy bec[ame] an essential central responsibility".[51] "It is clear that in any socialist economy worthy of the name there would have to be regulation of incomes, as a pre-condition for achieving something close to full employment, while avoiding continuous conflict and accelerating inflation."[52] Thus, for many market socialists, the nettle of an incomes policy had to be grasped, although it could reasonably be anticipated that in a (market) socialist context, the social and political ambience would be more favourable to a resolution of those conflicts between the state and organized labour which, in Britain, had done so much damage to the viability and credibility of Keynesian social democracy.

In addition, as we have seen, it was anticipated that the state would own, or failing that would certainly control, important sectors of the economy in which natural monopolies, economies of scale, the public-service nature of the enterprise or the existence of significant externalities made it economically rational and socially imperative for it to do so.[53] Also, even where the PC sector was envisaged as dominant, it was anticipated that the state, directly or through a range of financial intermediaries, would also have a significant ownership stake in many private enterprises, giving it potential leverage on such concerns. Further, most market socialists were agreed that it would be the responsibility of the state directly or through intermediaries, to provide services such as health and education on a non-market basis. So simply in terms of macroeconomic management, ownership, control and the direct provision of public goods and services, the role of the state under market socialism was clearly seen as substantial.

The state was also envisaged as having a crucial role to play in making, maintaining, monitoring and regulating markets. As regards the labour market, if full employment were to be secured and maintained, then the structural rigidities resulting from immobility and the absence of desired skills would have to be rectified.[54] It was also anticipated that the state would act to prevent the growth of enterprises wielding monopoly power or having the capacity to indulge in non-competitive oligopolistic behaviour. Thus it would deploy "powers to promote competitive conditions, monitoring the development of particular markets to pre-empt exploitation".[55] It would also have a monitoring role, noted above, in ensuring that enterprises responded efficiently to market imperatives; "stimulating", where necessary, "changes in sectors where supply adjustments to demand changes are relatively low".[56] Thus the kind of

---

51. Nove, "The Role of Central Planning, p. 108.
52. Nove, *The Economics of Feasible Socialism*, pp. 172–3; on this see also, for example, Winter, "Market Socialism", p. 163.
53. Nove, "The Role of Central Planning", p. 102.
54. Winter, "Market Socialism", p. 163.
55. Abell, "An Equitarian Market Socialism", p. 80; Miller, *Market, State and Community*, p. 296.
56. Estrin & Winter, "Planning in a Market Socialist Economy", p. 112.

"economic pluralism" envisaged by market socialists did not carry with it the corollary of laissez-faire. As even neo-liberals were finding in the 1980s, the maintenance of free markets required, and market socialists accepted this, a strong and interventionist state – *"pluralism would have to be cultivated as a matter of policy* and supported by the appropriate regulatory and investment agencies".[57]

Of primary importance, too, given the egalitarian claims for market socialism, was the state's redistributive function; all the more so as it was recognized, both in theoretical terms, and in consequence of the practical experience of self-management in a Yugoslav context, that market socialism had a tendency both to generate and then to accentuate material inequalities.[58] An incomes policy might form part of such a redistributive strategy but also, as under traditional social democracy, "a tough progressive tax system would be needed to avoid (minimise) what could be regarded as excessive and unreasonable income differentials".[59] It would also be necessary at the outset to institute a redistributive system that "largely abolishes previously inherited economic privileges".[60] Of course, the problem here, as market socialists recognized, was that of how "to ensure that . . . outcomes are ethically acceptable without destroying the very mechanisms that enable them [markets] to work effectively".[61] In an important sense, it was a question of how far income differentials might be narrowed without attenuating the effectiveness of market stimuli, and this was something which, manifestly, could only be determined once a market socialist economy had come into being.

Finally, the economic responsibilities of the state were further extended in those situations where the need for some sort of state planning was accepted. Again, views varied as to the forms and the extent of the planning required. For some, the emphasis was on indicative planning of the kind which had characterized the French economy in the post-war period. Such planning, involving "a decentralised and democratic process of consultation and discussion to devise a guide to medium-term economic development",[62] was deemed to be consistent with the market socialist emphasis on participatory decision-making, enterprise autonomy and the dispersal of economic power. This "decentralized and potentially democratic version of planning", "allow[ing] a wider social involvement in the allocation of resources",[63] was more about facilitating the effective transmission of information to permit

57. Miller & Estrin, "Market Socialism", pp. 8–9, my emphasis.
58. See, for example, S. Estrin, "Income Dispersion in a Self-Managed Economy", *Economica* **47** (1980), pp. 181–94.
59. Nove, "The Role of Central Planning", p. 103.
60. Estrin & Winter, "Planning in a Market Socialist Economy", p. 113; see also, for example, Miller, *Market, State and Community*, p. 296.
61. *Ibid.*, pp. 294–5.
62. Estrin & Le Grand, "Introduction", p. 11.
63. Estrin & Winter, "Planning in a Market Socialist Economy", pp. 119, 118.

rational, informed and decentralized economic decision-making, than about the central coercive and directive exercise of power. As such, it was in keeping with the spirit of market socialism.[64]

But, for others, there was clearly to be more to planning in a market socialist economy than this. In particular, some stressed the need for some kind of planning of investment. Thus "its aggregate magnitude would surely be a major central-planning task in a market socialist economy. It is difficult to see how the time preference of the community can be expressed other than by and through political organs."[65] In addition, many believed that major investments, whether in infrastructure or strategic industries, should also be subject to central direction. Nove, for example, wrote of the need for "conscious planning, by an authority responsible to an elected assembly, of major investments of structural significance".[66] Yet he and others went further. As he saw it, it was also necessary that central planners should influence and "monitor decentralised investments, conscious of the need to avoid duplication and the financing of plainly unsound projects".[67] Likewise Roemer envisaged investment planning as taking a disaggregated form, with planners "providing incentives for firms to invest in particular sectors or regions",[68] these incentives or disincentives taking the form "of interest rate discounts and surcharges".[69] Roemer was adamant that such an approach to planning and guidance did not entail the kind of intrusive and coercive intervention characteristic of traditional socialist central planning but was, rather, planning of an "indirect", non-bureaucratic and non-authoritarian kind. That said, the scope for state intervention and the range of state economic responsibilities would, once again, be considerable, even where planning took this indirect or indicative form.

Such disaggregated "popular political control over investment" was seen by Roemer and others as vital. Much might be left to be determined by market forces, but investment was something which did not fall into that category. According to Roemer,

> If . . . there were a full set of futures markets, if externalities associated with investment were small, and if people's preferences were formed under conditions of equal opportunity, I would have little objection to determination of investment by the market, that is, by citizens in the

---

64. *Ibid.*, p. 110; Miller refers, for example, to "economic forecasts to allow enterprises to plan their future activities", *Market, State and Community*, p. 296.
65. Nove, "The Role of Central Planning", p. 106; "there will be the quite basic task of determining the share of total GNP to devote to investment, as distinct from current consumption", Nove, *The Economics of Feasible Socialism*, p. 208.
66. *Ibid.*, p. 227.
67. *Ibid.*, p. 207.
68. Roemer, *A Future of Socialism*, p. 90.
69. *Ibid.*, p. 103.

economy determining the rate of investment as a consequence of individual responses to prices and interest rates.[70]

But none of these conditions applied. In the absence of the requisite futures markets, uncertainty and ignorance would be likely to produce a sub-optimal level of investment and one whose direction was ill-judged. Further, it was clear that the positive and negative externalities of a wide range of investments in social and industrial infrastructure and in productive activity were considerable, while the possibility of time preferences being formed under conditions of equal opportunity was simply visionary.

As regards Roemer's views on planning, one final point should be made in relation to the direction of investment in a market socialist economy. This relates to his admiration for the economic achievements of the South Asian tigers such as Taiwan and South Korea where, as he saw it, state-directed investment had played a crucial part in generating the high growth rates that they enjoyed. In the light of this, he clearly had sympathy for the notion of the state playing a comparable role with respect to strategic decisions that would affect the productive base and thence the overall performance of a market socialist economy. Such strategic intervention was viewed as all the more needful when market socialist economies were viewed as having to confront the full force of competition from South Asian tigers and other capitalist powers in international markets.

What purportedly distinguished market socialism from Keynesian social democracy was, first, the more extensive social ownership of the means of production it proposed; secondly, its insistence that the extension of public ownership must take a plurality of forms; and thirdly, its particular emphasis on WOFs and LMFs because of the dispersal of economic power which they allowed, the producer autonomy they permitted and the democratic practice they embodied. What supposedly distinguished it from the central planning, Clause IV and AES Left was, again, its emphasis on the decentralization of power and decision-making. Yet the wide range of responsibilities that market socialists acknowledged had to be assumed by the state blurred these distinctions. The state would have a full range of Keynesian macroeconomic management functions; it would have, for many market socialists, directly or indirectly, a substantial ownership stake in the economy; what it did not own it would often regulate, either directly or through intermediaries; it would determine the level and, for some, the direction and use of investment; it would provide a range of non-marketable public goods, and it would, if indicatively, plan the economy. So to get a market socialist economy up and to keep it running, there would need to be a considerable concentration of power in the

---

70. *Ibid.*, p. 21.

hands of the state and its intermediaries. In such circumstances the distinctively market socialist goals of autonomy, democracy, participation and decentralization of decision-making began to look profoundly compromised or threatened. In effect, market socialists seemed to have been drawn back by diverse and devious routes to the notion that the effective performance of a socialist economy required a strong and interventionist state.

Of course, given these common features, many of the problems of Keynesian social democracy, Clause IV and AES socialism came back into play, problems of a kind which have already been discussed in Chapters 1 and 2. Most obviously, there were the problems of using macroeconomic policy to maintain full employment and of implementing an incomes policy to secure price stability. Here it was not immediately apparent what market socialists believed could or should be done to circumvent past failures. Nor was it made clear how the limitations imposed on a full employment strategy by an increasingly open international economy could be avoided. Indeed, in general, discussion of the exogenous pressures and constraints on a future market socialist economy was limited. For the most part, market socialists embraced the idea of free trade and even, on occasion, saw it as a necessary means of ensuring the efficiency of socialized and, in particular, state-funded enterprises. But there was negligible consideration of the difficulties that trade liberalization would create for the kind of macroeconomic management and planning which they proposed, or of the hostile response such planning would provoke from international financial interests.

In addition, in relation to the international dimension, Frankel was to ask Nove in particular, but market socialists more generally, "how . . . socialist planning [could] be effective in a socialist economy whose major enterprises were already locked into transnational component production?"[71] This and related difficulties generated by the existence of TNCs, were issues which, again, were not discussed at length in the market socialist literature of the period. Further, as regards the production of goods for global markets, the question arose as to whether market socialist enterprises would conform to socialist standards as regards issues such as the environment, working conditions, safety standards and minimum wage levels, or whether such standards would be trimmed to accommodate the need for competitive survival.[72] Only if it were assumed that adherence to socialist ethics must also enhance economic competitiveness could this question be legitimately elided. A failure to address satisfactorily the international implications of constructing a market socialist economy therefore left, to put it kindly, a number of major theoretical and prescriptive gaps in its political economy.

---

71. Frankel, "The Historical Obsolescence of Market Socialism", p. 31.
72. On this see *ibid*., p. 32.

Other deficiencies were noted by commentators, particularly on the Left. To begin with, the notion that market socialism could combine equality with efficiency was subjected to critical attack. It was argued that market forces made for cumulative inequality and those measures which might be implemented to blunt them could also adversely affect their role in inducing effort and ensuring an efficient utilization of resources. Against this the microcosm of Mondragon, and for that matter the example of the Scandinavian economies, suggested that income differentials could indeed be narrowed considerably without such adverse consequences; though it is interesting to note Roemer's doubts as to "the limited degree of equality that I think market socialism can achieve . . . due in the main to my skepticism concerning the existence of alternatives to a competitive labour market for allocating labor in an efficient manner".[73]

If the labour market could not be interfered with to effect a narrowing of income differentials, that left the tax system. But, as Roemer accepted, the popular view that one deserves to retain what one has earned "places a political limit on the degree of redistribution that can be accomplished by social democratic methods".[74] In effect, as with macroeconomic management, so with redistribution, market socialists had once again to confront many of the same difficulties which had constrained the aspirations of Keynesian social democracy.

There was also the criticism of market socialism, emanating largely from the Hard Left, that focused on the market *per se*: specifically, on the nature of the social relations which a market economy fostered and the kind of values which it engendered and endorsed. Thus, for some socialists, "an acceptance of markets appear[ed] to endorse current capitalist values like competition, inequality, avarice, insatiability of appetite and materialism in general".[75] Utilizing the market would, it was argued, inevitably taint the socialist project. Taking just one example from such literature,

> although the advocates of market socialism envisage a welfare system based on need rather than ability to pay, it seems unlikely that these two areas of the social structure could happily coexist since they are based on such a very different ethic and logic. Of course, temporary balances might be struck, but *where competition and profit remain rampant, the welfare sector is always at risk of being sucked in or squeezed*.[76]

Or, as Frankel phrased it, "*the logic of market mechanisms is* in many respects *incompatible with values of solidarity, equality and care*".[77]

---

73. Roemer, *A Future of Socialism*, p. 120.
74. *Ibid.*, p. 119.
75. Beuret & Coole, "Rethinking the Present", p. 18.
76. *Ibid.*, p. 19, my emphasis.
77. Frankel, "The Historical Obsolescence of Market Socialism", p. 32, my emphasis.

Such criticisms of the market had a long socialist history. They can be traced back, in Britain, to the early nineteenth century and, indeed, little of substance and nothing in terms of rhetorical eloquence has been added since that period. Then too the market was condemned for the narrowly materialistic selfishness, the duplicity and deceit, the antagonistic and predatory social relations, the angst and insecurity and the dehumanizing intellectual atrophy that corrupted its participants.[78] For many market socialists there was some substance in these views, but they were also adamant that a marketless socialism was not, even in the nineteenth century, and certainly not in the twentieth, a feasible socialism. Yet if such a riposte was fair, the fact remained that certain social, psychological and ethical diseconomies *did* undoubtedly emanate from social relationships and values constructed in a market nexus. These might be seen by market socialists as representing the necessary price to be paid for a mechanism that furnished the least worst way of effecting the relatively efficient provision of a wide range of goods and services in a socialist context. But such diseconomies nonetheless represented substantial obstacles in the way of realizing socialist objectives and ensuring the hegemony of socialist values.

More serious, though, in terms of its deficiencies, was market socialism's intrinsic utopianism. Certainly one does not have to delve far into the writings of its proponents to unearth admissions that they had little idea as to how they would get to where they wanted to go. "This paper is about blueprints", wrote Bardhan and Roemer, "and not so much about their implementation"; though these writers "did not harbour illusions about the formidable problems, political and economic, of the possible transition to our proposed system of market socialism."[79] Nove was, if anything, more brutally honest. It "has been pointed out", he wrote in *The Economics of Feasible Socialism*, "that there is a yawning gap in my argument. Part 4, labelled 'Transition', abounds in warnings against extremist policies . . . But then how is one to move towards the socialism of Part 5? The gap is indeed wide. The reason is: *I really have no idea how to bridge it!*"[80] Similarly Miller, in his work on "the theoretical foundations of market socialism", disavowed the "intention . . . to start drawing up manifestos for market socialists . . . My aim in general has been to show that market socialism embodies in a coherent way a range of values that stand up to *theoretical* scrutiny."[81]

Now this is all well and good. But what of the transition to the kind of economy market socialists envisioned? Here it must be said that however much one admires the theoretical sophistication of the New Jerusalems which they

---

78. On this see N. Thompson, *The Market and its Critics: Socialist Political Economy in Nineteenth Century Britain* (London: Routledge, 1988), pp. 58–79.
79. Bardhan & Roemer, "Market Socialism", p. 115.
80. Nove, *The Economics of Feasible Socialism*, p. xi, my emphasis.
81. Miller, *Market, State and Community*, p. 336.

constructed, it would not seem unreasonable to have expected some suggestions as to how progress might be made from the capitalist slough of despond to the Celestial City. Yet, as to this transition, market socialists usually had recourse to little else than that last best expedient of utopians and model builders – the "let-us-assume" approach to the business of radical change. "Let us proceed by way of *a thought experiment*", suggested Miller, and *"suppose"* that the threshold to socialism has been crossed, and that people, now consciously controlling their future existence in a democratic manner, have to decide what economic relations to establish."[82] *"Suppose"*, wrote Estrin, "a market socialist government were elected to office, with an unambiguous mandate to transform relations in the production sphere. All productive enterprises would have to be transformed into self-managed firms and a system of holding companies created to administer the social capital."[83] And what was used to furnish a general solution to the problem of transition was also used to tackle particular difficulties. Addressing the problem of how to equalize post-tax incomes without dulling incentives to effort, Carens, for example, supposed, in a manner peculiarly redolent of Owenite socialism, that "individuals be taught during late childhood and early adolescence that they have a social obligation to earn as much pre-tax income as they can" – that done the problem, and others, would be solved.[84] Like Dick Barton and Batman, just when escape seemed impossible and the forces of darkness threatened defeat, market socialists "supposed" and with one bound they were free – free certainly from many of those constraints which, historically, had obstructed progress to a socialist transformation of society. Pilgrim attains his goal without the trials and tribulations of the journey; though one must wonder what effect this might have upon his (socialist) soul.

Market socialists aimed to transfer the greater part of all productive assets to one kind or another of social ownership; institute effective systems of participatory, workplace democracy; substantially reduce income differentials and severely limit accumulations of personal wealth. Yet although one seeks it with thimbles and seeks it with care, any allusion to the likely widespread social conflict precipitated by the pursuit of such objectives, or how that conflict could be resolved, remained snarkly elusive in the market socialist literature of the period. One is all for bloodless social revolutions; but the market socialist recourse to "suppose" rendered the revolution they offered not bloodless but anaemic. After all, as Frankel, like many a socialist before him, pertinently asked, "which capitalist class is going to peacefully tolerate the overthrow of large sectors of private property?"[85]

---

82. *Ibid.*, p. 220, my emphasis.
83. Estrin, "Workers' Co-operatives", p. 191, my emphasis.
84. J. Carens, *Equality, Moral Incentives and the Market: An Essay in Utopian Politico-Economic Theory* (Chicago: University of Chicago Press, 1981).
85. Frankel, "The Historical Obsolescence of Market Socialism", p. 32.

We are, indeed, occasionally teased with the prospect of something more. The expectations of the reader are momentarily raised when Miller avers that "a defence of market socialism must . . . address the question of how these desirable policies may be achieved";[86] but then he proceeds to examine the political structures and practices which would be consistent with and supportive of market socialism *once it had come into being*, the discussion presupposing the transition has already occurred, rather than addressing the complexities of the transition process. At another point the reader is again tantalized with the question as to whether market socialism "is . . . any more than an attractive sounding pipe dream",[87] although here at least some tentative suggestions are made as to how it might be rendered more than that. Thus the possibility of a growing sense of "nationality" instilling the kind of "common identity that makes it possible for [people] to conceive of shaping their world together" was mooted as a conceivable psychological/aspirational basis upon which market socialism might be constructed.[88]

Further, market socialists did cite evidence in Britain and elsewhere indicating support for greater self-direction at work, for a greater say in government and for a fairer society, using it to suggest a potential groundswell of opinion sympathetic to market socialist principles. But, as the authors of that evidence frequently made plain,[89] support for increasing self-management and the greater democratization of the economy and society did not necessarily create or lead on to the egalitarian attitudes that could form a basis for socialist advance. Nevertheless, Miller built on this evidence a belief in a kind of incremental market socialist advance redolent of an idealist Fabian gradualism,[90] although a gradualism lacking the historical dynamic that gave Fabian socialism its prescriptive force and persuasive power. For the Webbs, the economic efficiency and thence the competitive superiority of publicly owned enterprises would ensure the eventual practical triumph of the principle of social ownership; no comparable agency or dynamic was suggested by those who founded their faith in the incremental triumph of market socialism on a growing popular predilection for self-management.

Roemer also hinted at a gradualist transition. "The transition to a society based on co-operation", he wrote, "will take a long time and, tritely, must begin with people as they are."[91] But even accepting that the longest journey must begin with the first step, there was no indication as to what would set the transition in motion. Historical experience suggested that it would not occur

---

86. Miller, *Market, State and Community*, p. 227.
87. *Ibid.*, p. 322.
88. *Ibid.*, p. 245.
89. E. Greenberg, "Industrial Democracy", pp. 964–81 and C. Hanson & P. Rathkey, "Industrial Democracy: A Post-Bullock Shopfloor View", *British Journal of Industrial Relations* **22** (1984), pp. 154–68.
90. Miller, *Market, State and Community*, p. 336.
91. Roemer, "The Possibility of Market Socialism", p. 365.

spontaneously. Nor did market socialists themselves identify a transitional dynamic inherent in contemporary capitalism, unless one counts passing reference to the shaky economic logic of flexible specialization, with its expectation that the small and democratic must ultimately triumph in an economic world of transient desires. Further, if a gradual transition were to be engineered, the means of effecting that were unlikely to exist until *after* the socialist cause had already made considerable advances and the political will for such developments had already emerged. As regards the transition to socialism, therefore, the market socialists of the 1980s and 1990s seemed to find it more intellectually and psychologically congenial to travel in hope than to arrive.

There is, of course, utility in utopianism and model building. The former has often served an inspirational and the latter a clarificatory function. As Bardhan and Roemer have stated, "designing blueprints for [market] socialism" is one way of showing that it "can achieve production efficiency roughly similar to that of capitalism".[92] For another writer, such models were a way of meeting "the challenge for contemporary socialists" involved in "formulat[ing] a normative model of society which can serve as a template against which proposed policies may be assessed".[93] Further, "such models . . . offer a vocabulary within which the issues at stake may be rationally discussed . . . Equitarian market socialism should be seen in this light."[94]

It was argued, therefore, that market socialist models provided the theoretical constructs and systems, the conceptual apparatus and economic discourse, in terms of which a feasible socialism could be articulated and defended against the criticisms of neo-classical and other writers. Writing of Vanek's model of an economy comprising labour-managed enterprises pursuing the goal of dividend maximization, Bonin and Putterman, while conceding that it failed to "capture the richness of the organizational goals and sub-goals of real enterprises", nonetheless stated that such "simple models are the starting point for understanding the complex issues of real-world organizations".[95]

All this is true as far as it goes. Such market socialist models did have the worth and some of the attributes that such apologiae suggested. But the fact remained that market socialists claimed to be in the business of changing the world as well as interpreting it, building the New Jerusalem as well as inspiring others to reach it. And, in the absence of a political economy of transition, market socialists had little to offer prescriptively as regards the former. They were clear, or reasonably so, as to the destination, but had little to say as to the route. Too often they seemed more enthused by the thrill of the intellectual chase than where that pursuit was leading.

---

92. Bardhan & Roemer, "Market Socialism: A Case for Rejuvenation", p. 103.
93. Abell, "An Equitarian Market Socialism", p. 78.
94. *Ibid.*, p. 79.
95. Bonin & Putterman, *The Economics of Cooperation*, p. 21.

As to the inspiration which utopias can provide, that function has been nicely rendered by E. P. Thompson as the "education of desire" – something that could indeed, in the fullness of time, have a socially transformative effect. But while, in market socialist model building, there was much to satisfy the intellect, there was little, in the Thompsonian sense, to educate popular desire. What we have, in the 1980s and 1990s, is the mathematically sophisticated Left talking to themselves or, more accurately perhaps, exchanging simultaneous equations. What they offered was *News from Nowhere* for the cognoscenti, something which would seem to contradict the more general inspirational purpose of most utopian literature. Market socialist thought seemed less interested in educating the desire of the many than it was in exercising the logical faculties of the few.

There is, though, or rather was, one important qualification to be made here: not with respect to what market socialists had to say as regards the transition to socialism in western industrial capitalist economies, but in relation to the situation that prevailed before and after the 1989 revolutions in the communist bloc. For what Central and Eastern Europe offered market socialists, for a time at least, was essentially two things. First, it provided an area in which the transition to public ownership had been effected, so debate could focus on questions such as the most efficient, democratic and equitable forms that social ownership should assume and the most effective allocative and distributive mechanisms which might be put in place, in an economy already socialist, to stimulate and integrate economic activity. In effect, here the problem of transition could legitimately be assumed to have already been solved with no need to "suppose". Secondly, in the 1980s, and for a short time after 1989, communist economies seemed to be heading, at an accelerating rate, down the market socialist road. History was solving the problem of transition.

Some market socialists, such as Brus, wrote with developments in Central and Eastern Europe very much in mind.[96] Others, such as Nove, were implicitly extrapolating from such developments to the structures and mechanisms of the feasible socialism which they outlined for western industrial economies.[97] Still others, such as Roemer, quite clearly saw the East rather than the West as more likely to progress in a market socialist direction.[98] However, as a springboard for the realization of market socialism and as a source of aspiration and inspiration for market socialists, the East became increasingly worthless, with the fears of some commentators that market socialism would prove "simply a stage on [the] road to capitalism" being rapidly realized. As

---

96. Brus, "Socialism – Feasible or Viable?", pp. 43–62.
97. On this see, for example, Frankel, "The Historical Obsolescence of Market Socialism", p. 28.
98. "The countries where the opportunity costs of adopting market socialism are the least are, I believe, those that have formed in Eastern/Central Europe and out of the Soviet Union since 1989 . . . I think the transformation of market socialism is least likely, in the foreseeable future, in advanced, democratic capitalism, for here the laws and institutions that guarantee private property are stable", Roemer, *A Future for Socialism*, pp. 126–7, 128.

Brus and Laski saw it, writing in the late 1980s, "the more 'real socialism' mature[ed] the more it [was] compelled to borrow from the capitalist armoury".[99] For Kornai, the idea of market socialism as state property + market co-ordination had "simply fizzled out" by the early 1990s – "Yugoslavia, Hungary, China, the Soviet Union, and Poland bear witness to its fiasco."[100] With regard to the possible emergence of a market socialism on the basis of a different type of social ownership, he doubted strongly that PCs were likely to "multiply" in the economic circumstances that were emerging.[101]

As regards Yugoslavia, hopes that it might provide a model for the emergence of other self-managed economies evaporated in the 1970s and 1980s as its economic performance deteriorated,[102] income differentials widened,[103] investment slumped[104] and its LMFs confirmed the predictions of Ward's Illyria, at least as far as workforce antipathy to their expansion was concerned.[105] Of course, it could be, and was, argued by market socialists that Yugoslavia had not adhered to market socialist principles or implemented them with sufficient energy. Stiglitz, for example, wrote that

> not too much should be read into the failures of the worker-managed firms in the former Yugoslavia, for these involved peculiar (and obviously unsatisfactory) arrangements with respect to the transfer of property rights, as well as other institutional details which, both *ex ante* and in hindsight, were not conducive to success.[106]

Yet the apologetic reaction of market socialists to Yugoslav failure was all too often reminiscent of that of Robert Owen to the collapse of communitarian experiments, with fault being imputed not to his political economy, but to a failure to adhere to the principles it embodied and that *should* have informed its prescriptive implementation. With the reality of practice departing markedly from the ideal, it could be argued that the latter remained untainted and, even in 1989, it seemed possible to write that "if we try to estimate the performance of a co-operative economy in the real world, the difficulty is that we have no full scale examples to consult".[107] Here, of course, we have the final fall-back position of those who would defend their *nostra* from empirical refutation: market socialism has not succeeded because it had never truly been tried.

99. Brus & Laski, *From Marx to the Market*, p. 151.
100. J. Kornai, *The Road to Freedom* (New York: Norton, 1990), p. 58.
101. *Ibid.*, p. 96.
102. Brus & Laski, *From Marx to the Market*, p. 192.
103. See, for example, S. Estrin & W. Bartlett, "The Effects of Enterprise Self-Management in Yugoslavia: An Empirical Survey", in Jones & Svejnar (eds), *Participatory and Self-Managed Firms*.
104. Brus & Laski, *From Marx to the Market*, p. 88.
105. Nove, *The Economics of Feasible Socialism*, p. 217.
106. Stiglitz, *Whither Socialism?*, p. 277.
107. Miller, *Market, State and Community*, p. 14.

Chapter 7

Whatever happened to Keynesian social democracy?

In the mid-1970s Keynesian social democracy fell prey to the combined pressures of a sterling crisis, the IMF and the US Federal Reserve and was jettisoned by many of its erstwhile supporters within the Labour Party. What remained of an intellectual and political commitment to government-initiated expansionary policies was swept aside and a "punk monetarism",[1] to use Peter Kellner's term, was embraced by the prime minister and others within the Labour leadership, with varying degrees of sincerity. Meanwhile, as we have seen in the previous chapters of this book, the 1970s also witnessed an impressive theoretical assault from the Left that damaged the hegemony that Keynesian social democracy had exercised within the Labour Party in the previous two decades. Yet, as regards some of its key components, its obituaries, and there was no shortage of these, were premature. Many of the rats of the social democratic Right might have deserted what they had convinced themselves was a sinking ship; many on the Left had never been convinced of its capacity to float in the first place, but, for some, the essential elements of Keynesian social democracy, with a little reconfiguration, could still be combined to construct a craft which was economically and politically seaworthy.

---

1. P. Kellner, "The Economic Consequences of Jim", *New Statesman*, 17 October 1980.

It had, of course, been the case, even in those years when the AES Left was setting the terms of economic debate within the Labour Party and "punk monetarism" had infected its upper echelons, that the *core* of the economic strategy offered to the electorate was essentially Keynesian. Despite Callaghan's "candid" 1976 rejection of the notion that you could spend your way out of depression, the 1979 manifesto, *The Labour Way is the Better Way*, proposed increased expenditure through the National Enterprise Board, aids to investment, job creation programmes and "an expansion in housing, the health service, education and other social services *which have such a crucial part to play in providing jobs*".[2] *The New Hope for Britain*, Labour's 1983 manifesto, while clearly dominated by the thinking of the AES Left, which established the overarching ideological framework in which its macroeconomic policies were set, nevertheless had as its centrepiece an

> expan[sion] of the economy, by . . . a strong and measured increase in spending. Spending money creates jobs . . . More spending means that the economy will begin to expand: and growth will provide the new wealth for higher wages and better living standards, the right climate for industry to invest, and more resources for the public services.[3]

Here the thrust and theoretical underpinning are distinctively Keynesian, even if the more general analytical and prescriptive context are not. Indeed, some on the Left of the Party condemned "the presentation of our strategy as, in essence, little more than a Keynesian state spending programme".[4]

Of course Tony Benn was correct to see the 1983 election as having been "fought on the basis of an openly socialist manifesto",[5] even if he was wrong to suggest that the extent of the subsequent electoral support for the Labour Party indicated that there were 8.5 million socialists in Britain. Certainly, set in the wider policy framework on offer, the policies of employment expansion became part of something qualitatively different from what Keynesian social democracy had previously offered the electorate. That said, a number of points can be made. To begin with, there were clearly those within the party whose continued support for Labour was predicated upon the Keynesianism of its short-run strategy rather than the longer-term socialist transformation envisaged by the AES. And even the 1983 manifesto provided enough for them to believe that they were keeping faith with the salient elements of Keynesian

---

2. Labour Party, *The Labour Way is the Better Way* (London: Labour Party, 1979), p. 11, my emphasis.
3. Labour Party, *The New Hope for Britain*, p. 8.
4. R. Green, "Going Forward", *New Statesman*, 23 September 1983.
5. Quoted from P. Kellner, "Are there really 8.5 Million Socialists in Britain?", *New Statesman*, 24 June 1983.

social democracy. Moreover, as support for the AES began to ebb, as it did even before 1983, and with gathering pace thereafter, and as the distinctively radical elements of the AES began to be jettisoned in the party's efforts to become electorally viable, salient components of Keynesian social democracy were to assume a greater, if short-lived, prominence in Labour Party literature.

It was also the case that economic circumstances, and in particular those that had eventuated from the pursuit of deflationary monetarist policies, gave Keynesianism a powerful resonance and relevance in the early 1980s. At full or near-full employment, the force of moral and economic imperatives to pursue expansionary, employment-creating policies was inevitably lessened. But the failure of Conservative economic policy had put mass unemployment back on the political agenda, thereby giving new life to the arguments and policies of those who offered an alternative to a passive reliance on the equilibrating properties of market forces.

Further, the credibility of monetarist predictions as to the dire consequences of policies involving increased public expenditure was significantly damaged in the early 1980s. Specifically, the view that increased public expenditure would crowd out private enterprise from access to productive resources looked increasingly suspect. As one commentator put it in 1980, "when there are one and a half million people unemployed, it makes little sense to be cutting down public sector employment to free workers for jobs in industry which do not exist".[6] In any case, as critics of monetarism pointed out, the notion that public expenditure had spiralled destructively out of control had little empirical basis. As one noted, "if we look at the volume of public spending using constant prices over the . . . [1962/3–1978/9] period, it actually fell as a share of output by 0.9 percentage points".[7] So it appeared that scope did exist for an increase in public expenditure which would not threaten either to bankrupt the nation or to deny the private sector the resources it required.

Despite this, in the early 1980s in particular, the Conservative government persisted with its policy objective of reducing such expenditure. The result, argued Keynesians and others, was the wholesale decay of the nation's social and industrial infrastructure. "Pressing needs in industrial regeneration, housing, education, health and urban renewal" now "co-exist[ed] with massive unemployment of workers and resources".[8] The Keynesian case for matching the one with the other therefore seemed to have regained a pertinent and compelling force.

As to previous constraints, the threat of inflation was reduced as economic depression freed up resources. In any case, it was argued, increased utilization

6. C. Atkinson, "Introduction", in D. Blake & P. Ormerod (eds), *The Economics of Prosperity: Social Priorities in the Eighties* (London: Grant & Macintyre, 1980), p. 4.
7. *Ibid.*, p. 25.
8. A. Mitchell, "Political Aspects of Unemployment: The Alternative Policy", in B. Crick (ed.), *Unemployment* (London: Methuen, 1981), p. 49.

of plant and equipment was likely to lower unit labour costs and thence prices,[9] while the manifestly weakened state of the trade union movement now rendered it amenable to policies that would prevent inflationary wage settlements. As to balance of payments difficulties, these were certainly exacerbated by the massive destruction of industrial capacity, but at the same time North Sea oil was seen as mitigating this problem for the foreseeable future and, for some Keynesians, this reopened "the prospect of [demand-driven] sustained economic growth".[10]

All in all, therefore, by the early 1980s, Keynesianism seemed to be an idea whose time had come – again. For Mitchell,

> mass unemployment, widening gaps in society, increasingly inadequate provision, a threatened industrial base, a welfare system that is creaking and undermined . . . all make it necessary for Labour to resume its task . . . with the re-emergence of the old problems, there is even greater need for the old Labour Party.[11]

And the policies of the "old [post-war] Labour Party", like those propounded by Mitchell, had, of course, been informed by Keynesian social democracy.

Other factors combined to give Keynesian social democracy a brief efflorescence. To begin with, in the early 1980s, the monetarism that had sapped some of its support within the Labour Party and destroyed its hegemony in the corridors of power itself came in for a severe pummelling. The work of Hendry, Ericson, Kaldor, Desai and the National Institute of Economic and Social Research effectively destroyed the empirical basis of the notion that there was a clear causal connection between changes in the money supply and the general level of prices;[12] while a *Report* [on monetary policy] *of the Treasury and Civil Service Commission* (1981), exposed both the theoretical flaws and the practical deficiencies in the strategy of monetary control that the Conservative government was pursuing.[13] As one contemporary commentator saw it,

> the Committee's report shows that there is no simple way of controlling the money supply, no single measure that can tell you whether money supply is under control, and no point in setting a rigid target one year

9. On this see *ibid.*, p. 47.
10. *Ibid.*, p. 45.
11. A. Mitchell, *The Case for Labour* (London: Longman, 1983), p. 50.
12. See, for example, D. Hendry & N. Ericson, *Monetary Trends in the* UK, paper no. 22 (London: Bank of England Panel of Academic Consultants, 1983), which delivered a devastating critique of M. Friedman & A. Schwartz, *Monetary Trends in the United States and the United Kingdom* (Chicago: University of Chicago Press, 1982). See also here M. Desai, *Testing Monetarism* (London: Pinter, 1981).
13. *Report from the Treasury and Civil Service Commission*, London, House of Commons Paper 163-1 (London: HMSO, 1981).

ahead – let alone four years ahead as the government's Medium Term Financial Strategy did last spring.[14]

Further, as Goodhart's Law[15] intimated, when the government sought to control what it defined as an appropriate measure of the money supply, it provoked a response from financial intermediaries that destroyed the appropriateness of the measure being used.

Other elements of monetarist theory and its associated policy prescriptions were also made to look empirically suspect in this period. For the monetarist Right, burgeoning public expenditure and an associated explosion of taxation had not only denied the private sector the resources it craved, but had also throttled the spirit of enterprise. As they saw it, three decades of Keynesianism had involved the pursuit of fiscal policies that imposed an increasing tax burden on the nation and denied the energetically creative and entrepreneurially talented their just desserts. In fact, as contemporary commentators pointed out, "if countries are ranked by their position in the tax league, we slid down from fifth in 1970 to twelfth in 1977". Moreover, before the VAT increases of 1980, "the proportion of total government revenue coming from taxes on expenditure in Britain [wa]s about average for industrial nations as a whole".[16]

More generally within academic circles, while monetarism had its devotees and institutional citadels, there were many within the economics profession who continued to adhere to a theoretical and prescriptive position on macroeconomic questions, such as unemployment, that was essentially Keynesian.[17] Not all those 364 economists who, after Geoffrey Howe's "hairshirt budget" of 1981, signed a letter to the *Times* condemning government economic policy could be so labelled. And of those who could, many would have eschewed a Keynesian *social democrat* tag. But others would have accepted both categorizations and these continued to subscribe to and iterate a distinctively Keynesian political economy during the bleak days of the late 1970s and the early 1980s.

On empirical, theoretical and prescriptive grounds, therefore, monetarism was not so much on the ropes as bouncing repeatedly off the canvas by the early 1980s[18] and, for these and the other reasons noted, the times seemed particularly propitious for the resurrection of a revamped and reinvigorated Keynesian social democracy. Yet although it continued to have its adherents

---

14. P. Kellner, "Monetarism: The Fight Starts Here", *New Statesman*, 6 March 1981.
15. Named after C. A. E. Goodhart, Cambridge University and Bank of England economist.
16. O. McDonald, "Will Taxes Go Up?", in Blake & Ormerod (eds), *The Economics of Prosperity*, pp. 37, 38.
17. Most obviously in Cambridge. For a contemporary Keynesian critique of monetarism see, for example, N. Kaldor, "The New Monetarism" (1976), in C. Johnson (ed.), *Monetarism and Keynesians* (London: Pinter, 1991), pp. 79–100.
18. For an account of the fate of monetarism in Britain see D. Smith, *The Rise and Fall of Monetarism: The Theory and Politics of an Economic Experiment* (Harmondsworth: Penguin, 1987).

throughout the 1980s, after the AES and the onset of Thatcherism it can be argued that Keynesian social democracy was never really quite the same again. After 1981, and the emergence of the SDP, support for it was politically split and, within the Labour Party, it was never subsequently to achieve the ideological hegemony that it had enjoyed in the 1950s and 1960s. Moreover, running through the Keynesian social democracy of the 1980s were the leitmotifs of other political economies. In the early part of the decade, there were the lingering cadences of the AES and then, from the mid-1980s onwards, there were the increasingly strident tones of supply-side socialism.[19] So while, during the decade, Keynesian social democracy did exert a measure of ideological influence within the Left, it was of a relatively short-lived and increasingly qualified nature and was diminished by its fusion with political economies whose ethos and objectives were not its own.

Furthermore, proponents of the central Keynesian notion of a public-expenditure-driven reflation and recovery were divided not only in the political sense just noted, but also in terms of what they saw as the necessary adjuncts to the successful pursuit of an expansionary fiscal and monetary strategy. These divisions concerned issues such as prices and incomes policies, the necessity of extending social ownership, the relative importance of trade protection, exchange control and devaluation, the necessity, nature and extent of planning and the role of the trade union movement. Of course, on many of these issues, a division of opinion, or at least a difference of emphasis, had always been a characteristic of Keynesian social democracy, even in its golden age. Indeed, its monolithic nature has almost always been overstated in accounts of the history of the post-war years.

In addition, although Keynesian macroeconomics lived on in Left thinking in the 1980s, as the decade progressed there was an increasing awareness, even among its proponents, of the profound and growing external constraints upon the unilateral pursuit of an unreconstructed Keynesian strategy, as international flows of goods and money increased both in volume and in terms of their relative importance to national economies. Moreover, as the economic power and resources of TNCs continued to expand rapidly in the 1980s, so the pertinence of the earlier AES critique of Keynesian social democracy became all too apparent. Such developments signally eroded the confidence of many of the latter's adherents and helped to pave the way for the effective demise of its influence within those elements of the democratic socialist Left which had been its traditional constituency.

To illustrate and amplify some of these and other weaknesses of Keynesian social democracy in the 1980s, it is important to focus in particular on its

---

19. The term was originally used in the Campaign for Labour Party Democracy's *The Case for Public Ownership* (London: CLPD, 1986). On this see N. Costello, J. Michie & S. Milne, *Beyond the Casino Economy* (London: Verso, 1990), p. 14.

central, macroeconomic component – namely, the belief that the goal of full employment, and much besides, might be obtained through the use of fiscal and monetary policy to manage the level of aggregate demand. And here it is useful to consider, albeit in a rather cursory manner, a small sample of the macroeconomic strategies that, in the 1980s, had at their core the fiscally driven, expansionary dimension of Keynesian social democracy.

In 1980, for example, a group of Fabian economists proposed a four-year programme of increasing public expenditure. Expenditure was to be £1bn a year above the "group's forecast of what the present government were planning to do".[20] It would be accompanied by a 10% tariff on all imports of manu-factures and semi-manufactures, together with a 10% devaluation of sterling, and it would be financed by the taxation of the corporate sector. After running this programme through the Treasury model, they concluded that it would create 1.6m jobs, have a positive impact on the balance of payments and leave inflation some 3–4% per annum higher.[21] With "moderate pay settlements" the growth in output and employment would be even greater.

In 1981 the TUC proposed a £8.3bn package of public expenditure on capital programmes, pensions, social benefits, training programmes, the NHS and industrial aid that would generate 677,000 jobs, increase inflation by around 1.1% and, according to the Treasury model, would pay for itself by increased tax receipts, reduced unemployment-related expenditure and revenue from import tariffs.[22] Again, it was accepted that a measure of pay restraint would increase the salutary employment consequences of the programme but there was *no* mention of an incomes policy.

As regards the Labour Party, its *Programme for Recovery, 1982*, proposed a substantial increase in public expenditure, together with a devaluation of sterling by 30% over two years. Price controls, together with cuts in VAT, interest rates and national insurance contributions, would offset any infla-tionary consequences, as would a measure of moderation in pay settlements. Again, in 1983, the general expansionary thrust of *The New Hope for Britain* was similar, with a substantial employment-creating increase in public investment and social welfare expenditure mooted. Counter-inflationary measures were to take a comparable form to those proposed in *Programme, 1982* and were to be considered in the context of a "national economic assessment . . . to be agreed each year with the trade unions"[23] – the nearest the manifesto got to any allusion to the exercise of effective control over incomes.

Finally, as late as 1986–7, Neil Kinnock and the Labour Party were propos-ing a two-year emergency programme of increased public investment

---

20. Atkinson, "Introduction", p. 13.
21. *Ibid.*, p. 14.
22. TUC, *Plan for Growth* (London: TUC, 1981).
23. Labour Party, *The New Hope for Britain*, p. 11.

expenditure on roads, housebuilding, railways and the caring services. Running it through the Treasury model, one of the great indoor Keynesian social democratic pastimes of the period, suggested it would reduce the number of registered unemployed by about 2 million.[24]

The theoretical and practical case made out for these employment-creating strategies was, with a few embellishments, conventionally Keynesian. Increased public expenditure created jobs, "if directed carefully it [could] channel a greater degree of extra prosperity to those most in need"[25] and it "played a positive role in ensuring growth"[26] and, therefore, in creating the kind of buoyant climate that facilitated necessary and beneficial structural change – "the whole balance of the economy . . . [being] tilted in favour of those sectors which offer the greatest chance of employment and productivity gains".[27] Further, on the last point, demand-induced expansion would "allow us to change and improve, to phase out the old and in the new, to invest and increase productivity in the only climate in which it will take hold, one of expansion".[28] Indeed, some believed, "the overall economic climate [was] . . . the most important single determinant of trends in productivity".[29] In that respect, a demand-led expansion could be, and was seen as providing, a necessary stimulus to enhanced competitive performance in the international sphere. In addition, it would, in itself, be an antidote to inflation, reducing unit labour costs both by raising productivity directly and through the elimination of excess capacity.[30] Here again, Britain's competitive position would be improved.

Yet this apparent unanimity in terms of the content and theoretical justification of Keynesian expansionary strategies belies a marked divergence of views on the adjuncts considered necessary to make them effective. In this regard, there were differences both of emphasis and of substance. It is important to discuss these because they expose some of the potential faultlines in the Keynesian position that contributed, in some considerable measure, to the eventual disintegration of Keynesian social democracy, and the eclipse of Keynesian ideas in social democratic ranks, by the late 1980s and early 1990s.

As we have seen from the sample of strategies discussed, in order to get some kind of Keynesian show back on the road most accepted the need for a variety of supporting acts. In particular, there was a fairly general recognition of the need for some kind of counter-inflationary policy on incomes.[31] There were dissenters. It was sometimes the case, as Kellner put it, that an "understandable

24. N. Kinnock, *Making Our Way* (Oxford: Blackwell, 1986), p. 46.
25. Atkinson, "Introduction", p. 15.
26. *Ibid.*, p. 4.
27. B. Gould, J. Mills & S. Stewart, *Monetarism or Prosperity?* (London: Macmillan, 1981), p. 193.
28. Mitchell, "Political Aspects of Unemployment", p. 45.
29. Gould *et al.*, *Monetarism or Prosperity?*, p. 10.
30. Mitchell, *The Case for Labour*, p. 100; Gould *et al.*, *Monetarism or Prosperity?*, p. 193.
31. It was also generally agreed this was to be of a non-statutory kind.

opposition to bad incomes policies" could "slide over into intellectually dishonest opposition to all incomes policies".[32] Policy statements such as the TUC's *Plan for Growth* (1981), for example, said nothing about incomes policy, even if it did embody some kind of implicit recognition that wage moderation did have implications for the employment-generating consequences of an expansionary fiscal policy.[33]

Also, for many, a rose by another name did not smell as sweet and the term "incomes policy" was regarded as having a particularly fetid historical odour. As Hattersley put it, the "experiences" of the 1974–9 period "so prejudiced the Labour Party against incomes policy that socialists who believed in that system had to search desperately for another name with which to describe the object of their enthusiasm".[34] Hattersley himself wrote of the need for "a measure of *planning for earnings*", others of the "orderly *growth of incomes*" and of "*collective agreement* by the unions to lower the 'going rate'".[35] Such were the weasel words, circumlocutions and euphemisms necessary to negotiate the political mine-fields sown by the collapse of the Social Contract.

However, if some denied the need for an incomes policy and others eschewed use of the term, there was, by the early 1980s, a fairly general recognition on the democratic socialist Left that it was, in non-statutory form, a necessary concomitant if fiscally induced expansion was to deliver the goods. However, a fairly general adherence to the principle, if not the rhetoric and terminology, of an incomes policy can still give a misleading impression of unanimity on this issue. Proposals for a policy on incomes were almost always advanced in conjunction with a range of trade-offs or *quid pro quos*[36] and here there were important differences of opinion as to what these should be and what they implied. This is something that warrants further consideration, not least because a lack of unanimity here may be seen as touching on the eventual evaporation of support on the Left for the demand-managed full employment component of Keynesian social democracy.

One of the key policy constructs in relation to which these trade-offs were articulated and discussed was the National Economic Assessment (NEA). This emerged in the early 1980s and was to provide a conceptual and institutional

---

32. P. Kellner, "Plan for Growth", *New Statesman*, 6 February 1981.
33. On this see, for example, P. Kellner, "But What Exactly is Labour's Alternative?', *New Statesman*, 3 July 1981.
34. R. Hattersley, *Choose Freedom: The Future for Democratic Socialism* (Harmondsworth: Penguin, 1987), p. 237.
35. R. Hattersley, *Labour's Choices*, Fabian Tract 489 (London: Fabian Society, 1983), p. 13, my emphasis; D. Roy, "The Problem of Rising Prices", in Blake & Ormerod (eds), *The Economics of Prosperity*, p. 54, my emphasis.
36. Of course, there were exceptions. Wilfred Beckerman, for example, clearly saw "the failure to include a genuine and effective incomes policy" as the fundamental reason for the failure of an expansionary Keynesian demand management strategy, "A New Realism", *New Statesman*, 2 December 1983.

framework within which macroeconomic issues relating to the successful pursuit of an expansionary strategy could be considered. For some, the NEA was simply a necessary, counter-inflationary device to control income growth during periods of government-induced expansion. For others on the Left, the NEA was a framework within which genuine macroeconomic planning of the economy, incomes included, might take place. Yet others saw it as the means by which any ground conceded over the control of incomes could be made to yield fundamental concessions on the distribution of macro- and micro-economic decision-making power. In short, for some, NEA read AES.

Taking examples of the latter position first, the Labour Party/TUC Liaison Committee's *Partners in Rebuilding Britain* (1983) saw the NEA as a means by which national economic priorities could be established at union conferences, in corporatist forums such as a National Economic Planning Council and within Parliament. Wage norms would not be part of this, but prioritization could take the form of giving precedence to jobs over wage increases and to the interests of the low paid over other workers. In addition, and in line with the AES, under the auspices of the NEA, there should be a radical extension of industrial democracy. This would take the form not only of giving trade unions a vital input to the discussion of economic priorities at a national level, but also, at enterprise level, of giving workers an active and potentially decisive say in decisions over investment, marketing, the organization and direction of production, expansion and contraction, the location of plant and remuneration. Collective bargaining, constrained at a national level by the iteration of national economic priorities, would be extended at a microeconomic level to encompass whole areas of decision-making previously seen as the prerogative of management. This would, as one commentator put it, "signal an end to the basic principle that management's job is to manage the company in the ultimate interest of the owners".[37] Here the notion of encroaching control was clearly expressed.[38]

Similarly, while an AES supporter such as Meacher could argue that "unions and professional and managerial associations" should "accept a firm policy on incomes so that the huge job-creating potential of this exercise [expansionary policy] is not dissipated in a pay spiral", he nonetheless considered that this should elicit "a genuine and substantial *quid pro quo*".[39] Among other things, this should encompass an acceptance of "joint control at company and plant level between local management and trade union/worker representatives over all those industrial decisions now unilaterally determined by management outside the current scope of collective bargaining".[40]

---

37. Editorial, *New Statesman*, 22 July 1983.
38. Such views can also be found in the Labour Party's *Economic Planning and Industrial Democracy* (London: Labour Party, 1982).
39. M. Meacher, "Models not Rhetoric", *New Statesman*, 14 August 1981.
40. *Ibid.*; such views were amplified in his *Socialism with a Human Face*.

However, for others, any extension of economic democracy as a *quid pro quo* for the control of incomes required to make Keynesian expansion work should occur within an essentially corporatist framework. Consistent with this, there was a particular emphasis on the macroeconomic dimension and a marked coolness towards the idea of extending economic democracy at enterprise level to any extent that significantly impinged on managerial prerogatives. For Mitchell, writing in 1983, the NEA was about the trade unions, government, employers and representatives of nationalized industries establishing an "annual norm for wage increases, investment, profits and taxes, as well as the social dividend of benefit and transfer payments".[41] This was to occur under the auspices of a proposed National Planning Authority and by way of an extended role for that most corporatist of post-war institutions, the National Economic Development Council (NEDC).[42] In essence, the NEA was to be about high-level corporatist decision-making to determine the broad divisions of the national product. As Pimlott put it at the time, a "national economic summit" would provide "a means of restoring the severed connections of tripartism".[43] For Kinnock also, and thence for Labour Party in the mid-1980s,

> the National Economic Assessment [would] involve government, man-
> agement and trades unions in deliberation about the distribution of
> national production among private consumption, social consumption . . .
> and investment. Gaining and maintaining a national consensus on the
> distribution of our national product will have clear implications for wages
> and profits and it will establish a direct link between the achievement of
> targets in investment, output and job creation.[44]

Kinnock also looked to an extension of the functions of the NEDC, anticipating its development "into a decentralized participatory planning institution".[45]

Meanwhile, in addition, the party's *Planning for Full Employment* (1985) proposed a reconstitution of the tripartite sector working parties of the NEDC.[46] But this fell a long way short of what many on the Left had anticipated should be the substantial and prior concessions on industrial democracy that the labour movement's acquiescence to a policy on incomes merited.

Clearly, then, there were fundamental divisions between the supporters of a Keynesian expansionary strategy as regards the nature, objectives and trade-offs

---

41. Mitchell, *The Case for Labour*, p. 104.
42. *Ibid.*, p. 108.
43. B. Pimlott, "Introduction", in B. Pimlott (ed.), *Labour's First Hundred Days*, Fabian Tract 519 (London: Fabian Society, 1987), p. 6.
44. Kinnock, *Making Our Way*, p. 55.
45. *Ibid.*, pp. 108–9.
46. For a critical assessment of the capacity of trade unions to play the microeconomic role allotted to them see T. Lane, "Fit for Active Service?", *Marxism Today* (February 1987), p. 20.

of any policy on incomes. This in itself gave an impression of incoherence that did nothing to win, or even maintain, support for the cause. In addition, those who insisted on linking the NEA to a fundamental assault on capitalist power were seen by many as irremediably tainting Keynesianism with AES Leftism. As a result, Keynesian social democrats could be seen as keeping dubious company – something that endangered the support that an expansionary Keynesianism might hope to elicit.

It was of course the case that, by the late 1980s, the NEA, as discussed in Labour Party literature, had shed most of the AES trappings by which it had previously been distinguished. It had ceased to be informed by an overriding concern to redistribute power, wealth and income but it had also become less focused on providing a counter-inflationary adjunct to policies of Keynesian expansion. Indeed, as regards the latter, the rapidly diminishing power of the trade union movement was rendering the idea of the need to restrain income growth largely redundant. As it was put in a Fabian tract published in 1987, "Kinnock's union partners have lost their power and their ambitions have shrunk commensurately".[47] Rather, by that date, the NEA was increasingly being seen as providing a forum for considering the means by which national economic competitiveness and growth might be enhanced. Discussion of its nature and purpose might still reverberate with the language of democratization and full employment, but the primary objective that it was seen as serving was, by then, radically different. Further, the notion of democratization was, by then, increasingly discussed with reference to its contribution to the transformation of Britain's economic performance, rather than in terms of its effecting a social transformation through the redistribution of power.

From the late 1980s, the rhetoric and aspirations of a new supply-side socialism were beginning to leave their mark on the discourse and aspirations of democratic socialists and the Labour Party. As early as 1986 Kinnock wrote that "the National Economic Assessment stands at the core of the planning system. The distribution of resources among investment and consumption and various categories of government expenditure will be considered *in the light of the objectives of industrial policy*."[48] As for the extension of industrial democracy, "the participation of the workforce in the management of industrial development" was now to be *"the key ingredient of an efficient economic strategy"*.[49] Like the NEA, of which it was and continued to be an integral part, the extension of industrial democracy was ceasing to be primarily about a fundamental shift in the balance of power in favour of working people and their families, but was trumpeted rather as a means of reversing Britain's relative economic decline. At the same

---

47. J. Lloyd, "Unions and Economic Management", in Pimlott (ed.), *Labour's First Hundred Days*, p. 17.
48. Kinnock, *Making Our Way*, p. 160, my emphasis.
49. *Ibid.*, my emphasis.

time, therefore, as the residual elements of AES socialism were being excised from party literature, the NEA began to be purveyed more in terms of a supply-side-oriented economic strategy and less in terms of one that regarded the solution to Britain's macroeconomic difficulties, and in particular unemployment, as amenable to Keynesian demand-side solutions. No sooner, therefore, had Keynesian social democracy liberated itself from the AES Left than those from whom it might have expected support were being seduced by the siren call of another political economy. But more will be said about the nature and substance of that supply-side socialism in the next chapter.

So even if we consider only the "incomes-policy" adjunct to the effective pursuit of full employment, it is clear that the Keynesian social democracy of the 1980s rested on fractured and shifting political and theoretical foundations. Yet some kind of policy on incomes was seen as only *one* of the complementary policies required if Keynesian social democracy was to deliver its promised solution to the problem of mass unemployment. For throughout the post-war period, it was recognized by Keynesian social democrats that expansionary fiscal and monetary policies would, at least in the short run, engender balance of payments difficulties on both the current and capital accounts, as part of the increased purchasing power created leaked abroad by way of a rise in imports and increased overseas investment. The regular balance of payments and sterling crises that had afflicted the post-war economy with increasing intensity in periods of rising aggregate demand provided ample evidence of this. Four expedients were therefore mooted to circumvent the problem – devaluation, protection, exchange control and internationally concerted expansion.

With variations of detail, emphasis and prioritization all of these expedients were put forward by Keynesian social democrats as necessary complements to policies of expansion in the 1970s and 1980s. As regards devaluation, geology and the Conservative government conspired to give substance to the Keynesian argument. A combination of a tight monetary policy and North Sea oil's transmutation of sterling into a petro-currency accelerated an exchange rate appreciation that had begun under the previous Labour government. As Gould and others saw it, writing in 1981, "the pound's overvaluation has, in effect, imposed a tax of at least 45% on exports and provided a subsidy of more than 30% to imports".[50] Significant scope existed, therefore, for a substantial devaluation, which, through its impact on the relative price competitiveness of British exports and foreign imports, would give considerable balance of payments leeway for an employment-creating expansionary strategy. Gould *et al.* proposed an immediate 35% devaluation. Thereafter, the exchange rate should be allowed to move to whatever level would allow the economy to "be run at full capacity . . . without running into the balance of payments

---

50. Gould *et al.*, *Monetarism or Prosperity?*, p. 185.

problems which have inhibited us in the past".[51] Writing in the same year, Mitchell proposed a devaluation of 45% with the exchange rate allowed to move to the level deemed necessary to ensure what he termed "constant competitiveness".[52]

Historical precedents were favourable. For Mitchell, the "Barber boom" had created 760,000 jobs in 21 months and raised manufacturing output by 15.6% in the 18 months before political nerve had failed.[53] Others alluded to the dramatic recovery of the British economy from a comparable position of mass unemployment after an effective devaluation of 30% in 1932; while one commentator pointed out that devaluation, in combination with an incomes policy, had succeeded in making the economy more competitive in the 1975–7 period.[54] Mention of an incomes policy is significant here because it is indicative of a general recognition by Keynesian social democrats that if devaluation was to conjure up the competitive space required, unions would have to be induced not to respond to higher import prices by increased wage claims – at least in the short run. So adherence to the policy expedient of devaluation necessarily enmeshed its proponents in many of the practical, political and theoretical quagmires noted above.

Devaluation was also usually seen as being pursued in conjunction with import and exchange controls. Again, the rationale was the same: insulating the British economy from the surge in imports and the outflow of funds that might otherwise be expected when purchasing power was increased and credit expanded. As we saw in Chapter 1, such attempts at insulation were an integral part of the AES, with the Cambridge Economic Policy Group suggesting import quotas and variable general tariffs, which would be highest on finished manufactures and lowest on services. However, the favoured nostrum for those in the Keynesian social democratic tradition was selective import controls bearing on particular manufactures and semi-manufactures;[55] controls that would complement devaluation in providing respite from balance of payments concerns that could otherwise be addressed only by unemployment-creating deflation.

Protection was also to be pursued in conjunction with exchange control. This was a measure that the Conservative government had rejuvenated as a political issue through its abolition shortly after coming into office in 1979. Keynesian social democrats and other democratic socialists argued that this severely limited

---

51. *Ibid.*, p. 198.
52. Mitchell, *The Case for Labour*, p. 91.
53. *Ibid.*, p. 95.
54. P. Holmes, "Economic Growth and Unemployment", in D. Bell (ed.), *Labour into the Eighties* (Beckenham: Croom Helm, 1980), p. 28.
55. On this see, for example, Atkinson, "Introduction", p. 13, Gould *et al.*, *Monetarism or Prosperity?*, pp. 204–6, Mitchell, "Political Aspects of Unemployment", and M. Rees, in G. Kaufman (ed.), *Labour's Britain in the 1980s* (Harmondsworth: Penguin, 1983), p. 44.

any government's freedom of policy manoeuvre and there was general agreement among them that an expansionary policy "must be backed by [the reintroduction of] exchange controls".[56] "The idea that Britain alone can stick out against and beat the constraints of international [capital] markets seems to me to be pure fantasy", wrote Hattersley. It was, however, possible to "insulate ourselves from them to a degree. The exchange controls scheme is one of the ways of stopping a run on the pound [together with] . . . limited import controls."[57] To this end the then deputy leader of the Labour Party proposed a "scheme intended to deflect the investment destination of 10% of any [investment] portfolio",[58] while the tax system would be used to encourage pension funds, insurance companies, unit trusts and other investors to repatriate a proportion of their overseas investments. This would, in addition, be a means of furnishing part of the investment capital necessary for expansion.[59] "Industrial development requires that capital resources in Britain are used in Britain . . . Labour's capital repatriation scheme is designed to do exactly that." But such controls would also be "one of the ways of stopping a run on the pound".[60]

So, in principle, and with respect to means (if not the detail of those means), the early 1980s saw considerable agreement among Keynesian social democrats on the need to insulate the domestic economy from external pressures, such insulation being viewed as a *sine qua non* of the transformative Keynesian expansion which the British economy required. However, here the problem was not so much division of opinion but rather the rapidly growing obstacles in the way of constructing and operating an effective insulatory regime. The major institutional obstacle at this time was the EEC. As Mitchell put it in 1983, "EEC rules either specifically prohibit, or inhibit, many of the necessary strategies of industrial regeneration",[61] including devaluation, import management, aid for industry, low interest loans and regional employment premiums. Further, with the emergence of the Exchange Rate Mechanism (ERM) later in the decade and the possibility of sterling joining it, there was the danger not simply of constraints on the implementation of an exchange rate policy, in particular devaluation, but an absolute prohibition on its use to achieve macroeconomic objectives. In such circumstances, when sterling came under pressure, "the only available mechanism to stabilize the system would be interest rates and massive currency purchases and the arrangement would leave us with either a very unstable currency or very unstable interest rates".[62] So, with the ERM,

---

56. See, for example, Mitchell, *The Case for Labour*, p. 93.
57. Interview with Roy Hattersley, "An Alternative to the Alternative: Labour's Economic Strategy', *Marxism Today* (October 1985), p. 30.
58. R. Hattersley, "Exchange Control", *New Statesman*, 22 February 1985.
59. Kinnock, *Making Our Way*, p. 102.
60. Hattersley, "An Alternative to the Alternative", p. 30.
61. Mitchell, *The Case for Labour*, pp. 126–7.
62. Kinnock, *Making Our Way*, p. 166.

there was the prospect of Britain returning to a gold standard era, when monetary and fiscal policies were determined by considerations other than the general level of employment and output.

For some, the obvious solution was to cut off the European shackles and "to withdraw from the selfish club of the Common Market".[63] This would give back into the hands of policy-makers the power to introduce the adjuncts necessary for the success of a full employment strategy. Britain would re-assume the "power currently exercised by the EEC of negotiating our own trade arrangements";[64] it would eliminate the "heavy drain on the balance of payments" which "the Market imposes";[65] it would permit devaluation as and when required by the macroeconomic circumstances of the British economy; it would in itself have a positive net effect on the level of employment – "the propaganda claim that millions of jobs will be lost as a result of withdrawal takes no account of the greater gain in jobs from the replacement of their exports in our market, because our tariffs going back against them would be higher than theirs against us".[66]

The problem was, as Hattersley put it in 1983, that "no one believes that British withdrawal from the EEC will be a major feature of the next general election campaign".[67] Of course, this was an exaggeration. There were those who did continue to believe that withdrawal was a live issue that could be forced back onto the political agenda. But, in a strict sense, he was correct. Withdrawal was not a major issue in 1987 and became even less of one subsequently. Membership of the EMS and the ERM was a different kettle of fish, but by the late 1980s there were few serious politicians who did not accept Britain's membership of the EEC as a *fait accompli* and along with that acceptance there went the inevitable corollary that some of the complementary policies necessary for the effective pursuit of full employment were no longer available to a British government.

However, not all of the constraints upon the use of adjuncts necessary to render employment-creating, performance-transforming policies effective emanated from the European Community. As regards devaluation and import and exchange controls, other economic and institutional developments in the 1970s and 1980s were also rapidly diminishing the possibility of their use. The demise of Bretton Woods and the emergence of a regime of floating exchange rates in the early 1970s had seemed to open up the possibility of a greater degree of policy autonomy, with exchange rates adjusting automatically to eliminate imbalances in the external current account. In such circumstances, it was believed, expansionary policies would no longer fall victim to those external

63. Mitchell, *The Case for Labour*, p. 122.
64. Gould *et al.*, *Monetarism or Prosperity?*, p. 205.
65. *Ibid.*, p. 125.
66. *Ibid.*, p. 129.
67. Hattersley, *Labour's Choices*, p. 5.

pressures resulting from mounting balance of payments deficits which, when combined with an intransigent unwillingness to devalue, had, for example, destroyed the Wilson government's National Plan for growth. As it turned out, however, floating exchange rates created considerably more problems for policy-makers than they solved, because speculative movement of capital produced an unsettling volatility in foreign currency markets that proved less and less amenable to unilateral countervailing action.[68] Also, and of particular importance as regards policy autonomy, with the advent of floating exchange rates it was increasingly the case that markets became the main arbiters of the exchange rate implications of macroeconomic strategies. As one commentator put it, "markets (rather than official institutions) became the main mechanisms for adjusting conflicts between national policies" with "th[is] role further enhanc[ing] their position relative to individual national governments".[69]

As regards capital movements, developments were again of a kind to reduce the freedom of policy manoeuvre that governments had enjoyed prior to the demise of Bretton Woods and to magnify the external pressures they confronted. Since 1932 Britain had possessed a system of exchange control that had allowed action to be taken to prevent, or at least reduce, the destabilizing consequences of capital flows. For many, this system could, potentially, provide the economy with a significant measure of insulation from those external, capital-account pressures which invariably threatened the international value of sterling when a growth-oriented, employment-creating strategy was pursued. As noted above, it was also regarded by some as furnishing additional revenue that could be used to boost domestic investment.

However, the United States removed capital controls in 1974, and Britain followed suit in 1979. By 1988, as part of the move towards the Single European Market of 1992, all European Community countries agreed to remove their controls completely within the next two to four years.[70] In 1989–90 Scandinavian governments similarly committed themselves to ending controls. Outside the EC, Japan progressively dismantled its capital controls throughout the 1980s.[71] Similarly, worldwide, "the OECD countries agreed in May 1989 to extend the OECD Code of Liberalization of Capital Movements to cover *all* international capital movements, including short-term fiscal transactions".[72] The result of all this was a massive expansion in the economic importance of

68. On the expectations and reality of floating exchanges see, for example, E. Helleiner, *States and the Emergence of Global Finance: From Bretton Woods to the 1990s* (Ithaca: Cornell University Press, 1994), p. 123.
69. G. Epstein & H. Gintis, "International Capital Markets and the Limits of National Economic Policy", in T. Banuri & J. Schor (eds), *Financial Openness and National Autonomy: Opportunities and Constraints* (Oxford: Clarendon, 1992), p. 101.
70. See Helleiner, *States and the Emergence of Global Finance*, p. 9.
71. *Ibid.*, p. 146.
72. *Ibid.*, p. 166, author's emphasis.

both exchange trading and international capital flows. The daily value of the former, which totalled some $150 billion in 1985, had risen by the late 1990s to $1.2 trillion, almost 50 times that of international trade; international bank lending grew from $265 billion to $4.2 trillion in the 20 years after 1975, and in the same period the value of foreign direct investment rose from $21.5 billion to $400 billiob.[73]

The pressures to move in the direction of liberalizing capital flows in the 1970s and 1980s were considerable, cumulative and militated heavily and increasingly against any return to control as part of a strategy of economic insulation pursued by national governments. There was, for example, considerable pressure from the City to eschew exchange controls as these would threaten its dominance of the lucrative Eurodollar and Eurobond markets that had expanded rapidly in the 1970s and 1980s. Further, the international diversification of portfolios by financial institutions[74] and the attendant increasing scope for internationalizing the provision of financial services led them to seek to convince governments of the need to remove the remaining barriers to outward investment.[75] Complementary pressures eventuated from the "Big Bang" in October 1986 which, among other things, opened up the London Stock Exchange to foreign securities firms. In addition, as is obvious from the Cecchini Report (1988), those pushing for a Single European Market also tended to emphasize the necessity and benefits of integrating financial markets. The political pressures pushing forward the former project therefore also tended to make for progress on the latter issue.[76]

There was also a domino effect as regards the liberalization of financial markets. Deregulation had a competitive dynamic. "When one state began to deregulate and liberalize its financial markets, other states were forced to follow its lead if they hoped to remain competitive in attracting footloose funds and financial business."[77] In effect, after the US deregulation of their financial markets and services in the 1970s and 1980s, there was "an imperative need", on the part of the global financial community, "to follow the US example".[78] The process was also cumulative in another respect, for once exchange controls were abolished the facility with which industrial corporations could internationalize, or further

---

73. On this see S. Caulkin, "Third Way Loses its Bearings", *Observer*, 6 February 2000; S. Strange, *Casino Capitalism* (Oxford: Blackwell, 1986), p. 11; Helleiner, *States and the Emergence of Global Finance*, p. 1.
74. Among other factors the privatization of state-run assets "contributed towards the internationalisation of finance because shares in privatised utilities were designed to attract foreign investors", J. Coakley & L. Harris, "Financial Globalisation and Deregulation", in J. Michie (ed.), *The Economic Legacy, 1979–1992* (London: Academic Press, 1992), p. 51.
75. Epstein & Gintis, "International Capital Markets", p. 100.
76. Considerable pressure for the Single Market had built up by the mid-1980s. On this see, for example, J. Lloyd, "Europeans by Default", *Marxism Today* (October 1990), p. 39.
77. Helleiner, *States and the Emergence of Global Finance*, p. 167.
78. Strange, *Casino Capitalism*, p. 54.

internationalize, their operations was increased.[79] The rapid growth in the scale and power of TNCs that resulted created a formidable financial and economic constituency in favour of the maintenance and extension of capital market liberalization.[80] By way of contrast, there was no major social or economic constituency opposed to the abolition of exchange control. For while the beneficial effects of the liberalization of financial markets were high profile and could be portrayed as distributing cheaper financial commodities throughout society, its adverse impact upon the autonomy of macroeconomic policy was less transparent and, therefore, difficult to turn into a major political issue.

In short, therefore, by the 1980s the liberalization of global financial markets had become increasingly rapid, cumulative and, for many contemporary commentators, irreversible.[81] This irreversibility was manifest in a number of ways: the financial sector of any national economy that bucked the trend would be heavily penalized; the damage to international confidence in a currency that was once again made subject to exchange control would have deleterious repercussions for the economy as a whole; the economic constituency in favour of liberalization – the financial community and transnational capital – dwarfed in terms of its economic power any possible combination of forces that could be mustered in favour of the idea of re-regulation in pursuit of a measure of economic policy autonomy.[82] Finally, it was irreversible also in that should such an alliance be created, the practical political and economic difficulties of re-regulation would still prove formidable, not least in Britain's case, given its position within the EC.

As we have seen in Chapter 1, in the 1970s Holland, Barrett Brown and others on the AES Left had highlighted the extent to which the internationalization of economic activity, through the rapid growth of TNCs, was serving to limit the efficacy of economic policy-making informed by Keynesian perspectives and objectives. But the degree of impotence imputed to national economic policy-making in consequence of the globalization of finance and trade in the 1980s and 1990s was qualitatively different. John Gray, for one, put it succinctly and brutally: "it is no exaggeration to say that the global freedom of capital effectively demolishes the economic foundation of social democracy".[83] Gray wrote in

---

79. A spate of mergers, takeovers and joint ventures also intensified the international integration of firms in the 1980s, see Costello *et al.*, *Beyond the Casino Economy*, pp. 27–8.
80. ". . . a key catalyst for the 1992 initiative was the formation of the European roundtable, a coalition of big European transnational companies", S. Gill, "The Emerging World Order and European Change: The Political Economy of the European Union", *Socialist Register, 1992* (London: Merlin, 1992), p. 165.
81. "The institutional changes that have made the world market the sole relevant frame of reference for capital investors seem to be irreversible", F. Scharpf, *Crisis and Choice in European Social Democracy* (London: Sage, 1991), p. 258.
82. A major obstacle in the way of introducing something like the Tobin Tax which some have suggested might restore a measure of autonomy to national economic policy-making.
83. J. Gray, *After Social Democracy* (London: Demos, 1996), p. 26.

1996, but more than a decade earlier the general secretary of the West German SPD had made a similar if more general point that "due to the rise of transnational financial markets . . . The scope of action open to national governments and central banks ha[d] not been reduced to zero, but . . . [wa]s painfully small."[84] A nation's monetary and fiscal policy had to harmonize with those pursued by the major economic powers or financial markets exacted a price by way of capital flight and the destabilization of the exchange rate.[85] Thus if in 1976 it had been the IMF that had penalized and curbed departures from fiscal and monetary orthodoxy, by the 1980s, and "following the abolition of exchange controls", such penalties were "more likely to be administered by the markets".[86]

Further, if the use of fiscal and monetary policy to achieve macroeconomic objectives was constrained by the prospect of capital flight and the danger of a balance of payments haemorrhage to which the tourniquet of import controls could no longer be applied, many on the Left, by the late 1980s and early 1990s, had also come to accept that the use of taxation to finance the pursuit of social welfare strategies was increasingly limited by the growing mobility of capital and labour. Capital, if subject to increased taxation, would decamp in search of a superior rate of return; skilled labour likewise would bid not-so-fond farewells in pursuit of higher post-tax remuneration. In this context, too, it was argued that, in the 1980s, the downward revision of what was deemed a socially tolerable level of taxation had also narrowed the margins within which tax rates could be manipulated before precipitating an adverse public response.[87] Indeed, concern with the impact of fiscal policy on incentive effects was regarded as one reason why "the move towards capital liberalisation in Europe necessarily implies a shift in the structure of taxation, towards a larger revenue burden falling on indirect, regressive forms of taxation, such as VAT".[88] This was one of the consequences of that narrowly self-interested "culture of contentment" that the Thatcherite New Right had so assiduously and so successfully fostered in the 1980s and that many on the Left now felt they had to accommodate. So, in the 1980s, both the expansionary *and redistributive* objectives of Keynesian social democratic fiscal policy were being rendered nugatory and it seemed, as Scharpf put it in 1991, that "there [was] now no economically plausible Keynesian strategy that would allow the full realization of democratic goals within a national context without violating the functional imperatives of the capitalist economy".[89]

84. P. Glotz, "Europe – The Helpless and Silent Continent", *New Statesman*, 20/27 December 1985. For another early rendition of this argument see Scharpf, *Crisis and Choice*, p. 258 and R. Pecchioli, *The Internationalization of Banking* (Paris: OECD, 1983).
85. Epstein & Gintis, "International Capital Markets", p. 102.
86. Editorial, *Financial Times*, 13 January 1996.
87. On this see, for example, Gray, *After Social Democracy*, p. 32 and Epstein & Gintis, "International Capital Markets", p. 102.
88. Gill, "The Emerging World Order", p. 172.
89. Scharpf, *Crisis and Choice*, p. 274.

On the theme of prescriptive impotence, it was also considered that membership of the EC not only eliminated the national use of fiscal and monetary policy to achieve broad, macroeconomic objectives, but also ruled out the implementation of an industrial policy designed to improve performance. Thus "the 1992 programme", in particular, was seen as "demolish[ing] many of the instruments through which nation states have implemented industrial policies in the past, and will make national industrial policies impossible".[90] But, of course, such views pointed not just to the impotence of Keynesian social democracy but also to that of a radical, interventionist supply-side socialism, something that will be discussed at greater length in the following chapter.[91]

Finally here, as regards the growing constraints on the prescriptive aspects of Keynesian social democracy, some further, brief mention must be made of TNCs. At the core of the 1970s AES critique of Keynesian social democracy was the argument that their growth resulted in the emergence of entities that had the economic power to act to undermine government economic policy, where that policy was deemed to run contrary to their material interests. In the 1980s there was, clearly, a further increase in that power as the trend towards industrial globalization encouraged TNCs to engage in mergers, takeovers and joint ventures. Writing in 1984, Holland pointed out that "today, 140 companies account for a third of Gross Domestic Product in EEC countries. They dominate not only trade payments and smaller firms but also governments and community institutions."[92] By the late 1980s, it was pointed out that "the world's top 200 transnational corporations now have an annual turnover of US$6 trillions, equivalent to about 30% of the gross world product",[93] while the late 1990s saw the emergence of trillion-dollar corporations, corporations whose wealth and revenue dwarfed that of most medium-sized nation states. The 1990s was also characterized by an intensification of merger and takeover activity that led to further aggregation and concentration of TNC economic power.

Inevitably, the actions of such giants had a profound impact on employment, investment, research, technological innovation and value added within any nation state. They manifestly did possess the potential to act in the manner that

---

90. D. Marquand, "The Irresistible Tide of Europeanisation", in Jacques & Hall (eds), *New Times*, p. 214.
91. It was also argued that if supply-side socialism was endangered by globalization, that phenomenon also threatened the emasculation of social democracy in general. Some, of course, broadened the argument to suggest that economic globalization threatened not just social democracy but the democratic process *per se*. See, for example, D. Held, "Democracy, the Nation State and the Global System", *Economy and Society* **20** (1991), p. 166. On the anti-democratic implications of the Delors Report, 1989, see Gill, "The Emerging World Order", p. 169
92. S. Holland, "Out of Crisis – International Economic Recovery", in J. Curran (ed.), *The Future of the Left* (Cambridge: Polity, 1984), p. 243.
93. Costello *et al.*, *Beyond the Casino Economy*, p. 39.

Holland and others had feared, and they clearly would perceive any policies that endangered the increasingly free flow of goods, services and capital as something contrary to their economic interests. It would, therefore, be a brave or foolhardy government, or one whose economy was unusually independent of TNCs, that would have recourse to import and exchange controls, or for that matter to fiscal policies whose revenue-raising implications threatened to erode TNC profitability. Indeed, as has been noted, TNC influence in the 1980s was one factor driving forward the international liberalization of trade and capital markets. The Single European Market, in particular, represented the fruition of the efforts of "a transnational alliance . . . involving the European Commission, pan-European TNCs and neo-liberal governments within the twelve".[94] For them, it was "the realisation of their original post-war dream of a Western Europe for themselves" and it drove the final nail into the coffin of unilateral Keynesianism.[95] That did, of course, leave open the possibility of a multilateral variant, but consideration of proposals for this, and their viability, must wait until the final chapter.

Lastly, what was increasingly accepted at a theoretical level – namely, the insuperable obstacles to the national pursuit of employment objectives – seemed, in the 1980s, to be empirically verified by the fate of a number of European democratic socialist governments but, in particular, that of Mitterrand in France. As we have seen in Chapter 1, the Mitterrand experiment had more in common with the AES than Keynesian social democracy. However, its failure was taken by many as proof positive that the classic, employment-creating policy instruments of the latter were now largely ineffectual, creating external pressures greater than any internal problems they solved. The demise of the Common Programme, while not the last, was nonetheless a substantial nail in the coffin of a Keynesian social democracy that could claim the attributes of a feasible socialism.

Its influence within the Labour Party, or at least certain elements of the party, did linger on into the 1990s. Wickham-Jones has argued that a commitment to the pursuit of full employment was jettisoned shortly after the Policy Review of 1987–9, succumbing to the logical imperatives consequent upon the party leadership's embrace of the ERM and European Monetary Union (EMU).[96] But, as Anderson and Mann have noted, even after that there still existed within the party a considerable number who believed in the possibility of a macro-economic strategy that would deliver full or near-full employment.[97] A Full

---

94. Gill, "The Emerging World Order", p. 165.
95. Costello *et al.*, *Beyond the Casino Economy*, p. 45.
96. M. Wickham-Jones, "Anticipating Social Democracy, Pre-empting Anticipations: Economic Policy-Making in the British Labour Party, 1987–1992", *Politics and Society* **23** (1995), pp. 465–94.
97. P. Anderson & N. Mann, *Safety First: The Making of New Labour* (London: Granta, 1997), pp. 88–90.

Employment Forum was set up by Bryan Gould in 1993. This group was supported by Tribunites such as Peter Hain and Derek Fatchett, by Austin Mitchell and, almost inevitably, by a number of Cambridge economists. More-over, *Labour's Economic Approach*, published by the party in the same year, supported the pursuit of a high and stable level of employment, while John Smith, in a speech to the TUC Congress in September 1993, stated that "the goal of full employment remains at the heart of Labour's strategy".[98] But, in retrospect, these seem no more than the British death throes of Keynesianism in one country.

---

98. See *ibid*.

Chapter 8

The apotheosis of labour: knowledge-driven, supply-side socialism

Much by way of statistical evidence has been deployed to highlight the economic topography of globalization and it is only necessary here to identify some salient features before considering their implications for democratic socialist political economy and its evolution in Britain in the last decade of the twentieth century.[1] Most frequently cited have been figures for direct investment flows, short-term capital movements, international trade and the significance of TNCs, with these being used to point to the quantitative and qualitative changes in the degree of interdependence that have characterized the post-war international economy.

Between 1983 and 1990 foreign direct investment increased at an average annual rate of 34%, expanding almost four times as rapidly as merchandise trade over the same period.[2] For many commentators it had, by the early 1990s,

1. For a critical review of some of this statistical evidence see D. Baker, G. Epstein & R. Pollin, "Introduction", in D. Baker, G. Epstein & R. Pollin (eds), *Globalization and Progressive Economic Policy* (Cambridge: Cambridge University Press, 1998), pp. 1–17.
2. On this see, among others, P. Hirst & G. Thompson, *Globalization in Question: The International Economy and the Possibilities of Governance* (Cambridge: Polity, 1996), pp. 54–5; J. Dunning, *The Globalization of Business: The Challenge of the 1990s* (London: Routledge, 1993), pp. 286–7 and J. Goodman & L. Pauly, "The Obsolescence of Capital Controls? Economic Management in the Age of Global Markets", *World Politics* **46** (1993), p. 57.

"reached [a] threshold where [it] create[d] a qualitatively different set of linkages amongst advanced economies",[3] locking them and the major corporations of which they were composed into a complex system of international networks and economic relationships.[4] All this was, of course, part of a more general expansion of capital flows in the international economy that left the stock of international bank and bond lending at 25% of the aggregate GNP of western industrialized nations by 1989, as against 5% in 1973.[5]

As regards short-term capital movements, with the abandonment of exchange controls by the United States, Britain, Germany and Japan in the late 1970s and early 1980s and France and Italy in the late 1980s, the last two decades of the twentieth century witnessed their dramatic increase. By the early 1990s, the daily volume of trading in foreign currency markets was already exceeding $1 trillion – greater than the combined foreign reserve holdings of the leading central banks – and by the late 1990s that figure had doubled.[6] In such circumstances a serious attack on a currency could not be repulsed even with the co-operation of the major economic powers.

As to the importance of international trade for Organization for Economic Cooperation and Development (OECD) countries the ratio of exports to GDP more than doubled in the three decades after 1960 while, by the mid-1980s, trade had expanded to the point where exports and imports together constituted over 50% of GDP for most western industrial nations.[7] Further, post-1989, with the collapse of Comecon and the consequent liberalization of trade policy by its erstwhile members, the trade/GDP ratios of many Eastern European economies rose to above 50%.[8] Moreover, although the business of global trade liberalization proceeded haltingly in the 1980s and 1990s, with the problematic negotiations of the GATT Uruguay Round, intra-regional trade liberalization proceeded apace with the expansion of the North American Free Trade Agreement (NAFTA), the creation of the Single European Market in 1992 and

3. D. Julius, *Global Companies and Public Policies: The Challenge of the New Economic Linkages* (London: Chatham House, 1989), p. 35.
4. R. Wade, "Globalisation and its Limits: Reports of the Death of the National Economy are Greatly Exaggerated", in S. Berger & R. Dore (eds), *National Diversity and Global Capitalism* (Ithaca: Cornell University Press, 1996), p. 63.
5. J. Frieden, "Invested Interests: The Politics of National Economic Policies in a World of Global Finance", *International Organization* **45** (1991), p. 428.
6. M. Webb, "International Economic Structures, Government Interests and International Co-ordination of Macroeconomic Adjustment Policies", *International Organization* **45** (1991), p. 319.
7. G. Garrett & P. Lange, "Political Responses to Interdependence: What's Left for the Left?", *International Organization* **45** (1991), p. 542. On this see also A. Maddison, *Monitoring the World Economy* (Paris: OECD Development Centre, 1995). However, as A. Glyn has pointed out, assessing "the impact of internationalization through trade is quite complicated", "Internal and External Constraints on Egalitarian Policies", in Baker *et al.* (eds), *Globalization and Progressive Economic Policy*, p. 401.
8. J. Perraton, D. Goldblatt, D. Held & A. McGrew, "The Globalization of Economic Activity", *New Political Economy* **2** (1997), p. 261.

the enlargement of the European Union. Here again, with this extension and strengthening of trading links, evidence pointed to an increasingly interdependent global economy.

Finally, there was the increase in the size and relative importance of TNCs. The total value of real assets "attributable to foreign ownership or TNCs" "increased from \$67bn in 1960 to \$42.7 trillion in 1995".[9] By the 1990s they accounted for approximately 75% of international trade, of which just under 50% took place within individual corporations,[10] while "MNE [multinational enterprise] intensity of economic activity (measured as the percentage of inward plus outward investment stake to GNP) ha[d] risen from generally being of marginal, to being of very considerable significance" by the early 1990s, the figure for the UK being over 40% in 1990.[11] In addition, as noted above, merger waves of increasing amplitude in the 1980s and 1990s significantly increased the size and relative importance of individual TNCs,[12] while these decades also saw an increasing number of alliances between TNCs that again added considerably to their global economic muscle.

For some, this globalization of economic activity had, by the 1990s, precipitated a fundamental erosion of state power, calling into question the whole notion of national sovereignty, the future of the nation state as an accountable source and locus of economic and social policy[13] and thence the process of democracy itself.[14] As one contemporary commentator put it, "politicians are in charge of a declining industry: the governance of the nation state".[15] In this view, national economic policy was seen as increasingly determined by the needs of global capital, with any deviation from these being punished by the response of TNCs, multinational financial intermediaries and the market forces they set in motion. Thus, as regards the location strategy of TNCs, this was seen as driven by their preoccupation with reducing transactions costs. To induce TNCs to come, and to stay once they had arrived, it was considered vital that

9. P. Tolentino, "Transnational Rules for Transnational Corporations", in J. Michie & J. Grieve Smith (eds), *Global Instability: The Political Economy of World Economic Governance* (London: Routledge, 1999), p. 171.
10. Dunning, *The Globalization of Business*, p. 303.
11. *Ibid.*, p. 382.
12. In the first quarter of 2000 merger and acquisition activity reached \$1,166 billion according to Thomson Financial Services Data. See M. Skapinker, "Governance Responds to Globalisation", *Financial Times*, 2 June 2000.
13. As early as 1969 Kindleberger had opined that "the state is about over as an economic unit", C. Kindleberger, *American Business Abroad: Six Lectures on Direct Investment* (Cambridge, Mass.: MIT Press, 1969), p. 207.
14. See, for example, D. Held, "Democracy, the Nation-State and the Global System", pp. 138–72; D. Held, "Farewell Nation State", *Marxism Today* (December 1988); D. Held, *Democracy and the Global Order: From the Modern State to Cosmopolitan Governance* (Cambridge: Polity, 1995).
15. C. Leadbeater, "What's the Big Idea?", *Observer*, 4 August 1996; on this see in particular K. Ohmae, *The End of the Nation State: The Rise of Regional Economies* (London: HarperCollins, 1995).

governments accommodated this objective. On pain of failure or threat of TNC exit, governments were therefore forced to adhere to policies consistent with the interests of global capitalist players.[16] In practice this meant, it was argued, a diminution in taxation to eliminate fiscal disincentives to investment and work, a consequent reduction in, or curb upon, social welfare expenditure, the provision of a flexible, mobile and highly skilled labour force, cost-reducing infrastructural investment, a deregulated economic environment, the privatization of public corporations, an institutional and economic environment that facilitated and financed R&D activity[17] and the removal of barriers to the free flow of goods, services, capital and people.

Conformity with these objectives, it was argued, would make for an inflow of capital investment, the rapid expansion of employment, participation in a lucrative international division of labour, the influx of technologically innovative transnational industries, an increase in technology and skill transfer throughout the economy and the penetration of expanding global markets. Deviance, it was claimed, would inevitably bring problems on both the current and capital account. TNCs would exit or fight shy of committing or expanding investment and, in consequence, a nation's penetration of world markets would falter; there would be an outflow of mobile capital investment in search of more congenial berths; interest rates would rise as international finance attached risk premia to aberrant policies and, consequently, there would be a diminution in the level of economic activity and an attenuation of the nation's revenue base. Such developments, it was suggested, would of themselves furnish a remedy for policy deviance. But, either willingly or unwillingly, consciously or unconsciously, national governments would be brought to heel, with policy convergence an inevitable consequence. As one commentator put it in the mid-1980s, "international trade is conventionally thought of in terms of the movement of goods and services across national borders. Alongside such trade there is also a transfer of public policies across national borders that takes on increasing importance during the present supranational period."[18] In effect, the interventionist role of government was coming to be largely confined to the elimination of market and hierarchical failures that threatened an increase of enterprise transactions costs,[19] with the primary objective of national economic policy becoming that of creating what some referred to as a "national competition state" – competitive in the context of the global economy but competitive

16. On this see, among other literature, J. Stopford & S. Strange, *Rival States, Rival Firms: Competition for World Market Shares* (Cambridge: Cambridge University Press, 1991).
17. On this see Tolentino, "Transnational Rules", pp. 171–2.
18. H. Wachtel, *The Money Mandarins: The Making of a New Supranational Economic Order* (New York: Pantheon, 1986), p. 211.
19. On this see, for example, Dunning, *The Globalization of Business*, p. 372 and P. Evans, "The Eclipse of the State? Reflections on Stateness in an Era of Globalization", *World Politics* **50** (1997), p. 76.

also in terms of its relative attractiveness to foreign direct investment and as regards the location of key global economic players.

As regards long- and short-term international capital movements, similar consequences were seen as resulting for national economic policy. To begin with, if a nation's financial sector was to retain or expand the invisible earnings that came from being a major participant in global financial markets, policies had to be pursued that were consistent with the free inflow and outflow of such funds. In addition, there was pressure from corporations with global aspirations which found that the free flow of capital allowed a more effective pursuit of policies of tax avoidance and exit.[20] Given, as we have noted, the crucial contribution that could be made by such entities to national success or failure in global markets, it was believed by many that capital controls could no longer be deployed as an instrument of national economic policy. Further, given freely flowing international capital, the resultant vulnerability of national economies to the "animal spirits" of the international financial community would again necessitate macro- and mesoeconomic strategies consistent with its view of the economic good. Deviance would be swiftly punished by capital flight and, given the speed and volume of the flow of funds, a rapid market check would be given to deviant policies.[21] As one commentator put it, "the volume of capital that can flow internationally in response to macroeconomic policies is enormous and governments are not able to lend to each other on a large enough scale to permit 'management' of . . . cross-national macroeconomic policy differentials".[22] The failed Mitterrand experiment of 1981–3 was frequently cited as indicative of this for the early 1980s and the effective collapse of the hegemony and reform programme of Swedish social democracy was seen as providing evidence for the late 1980s and early 1990s.[23]

This narrative of globalization could be, and has been, read in a number of ways: as the final triumph of economic rationality over the dysfunctional interventions of states prey to vested interests determined to extend their own authority and unable to accommodate the notion of a borderless world;[24] as the enlightened diffusion of best policy practice on the part of states whose economic success was coterminous with that of the transnational enterprises which they sought competitively to attract;[25] and as the ineluctable convergence

20. Goodman & Pauly, "The Obsolescence of Capital Controls?", p. 51.
21. What was seen as having occurred was "an enormous increase in gross mobility of short-term financial capital", G. Epstein, "International Capital Mobility and the Scope for National Economic Management", in R. Boyer & D. Drache (eds), *States Against Markets: The Limits of Globalization* (London: Routledge, 1996), p. 214.
22. Webb, "International Economic Structures", p. 319.
23. On this see, for example, J. Pontusson, *The Limits of Social Democracy: Investment Politics in Sweden* (Ithaca: Cornell University Press, 1992).
24. See, for example, K. Ohmae, *The Borderless World: Power and Strategy in the Inter-Linked Economy* (London: HarperCollins, 1990).

of national policy-making on a putatively optimum policy cluster under the irresistible pressure of market forces.[26] Yet, however the plot was read, the dénouement remained the same – the loss of national economic policy autonomy and the prescriptive impotence of the state. As regards economic policy, it was contended, these states were being "condemned to tinkering around the edges"; "state power to make policy independent of a country's major trading partners" [was] "being progressively eroded as countries find themselves trapped into a seamless web of interdependence"; "politics [had] yielded to economics"; "the impersonal forces of world markets . . . [were] now more powerful than the states to whom ultimate political authority over society and economy is supposed to belong".[27] In this scheme of things the notion of a national economy and the idea of national economic management were being rendered meaningless.[28]

Seen in this way, the constraints imposed by globalization on state policy in general were doubly applicable to any states that sought to pursue a democratic socialist agenda. Thus what might be tolerable in terms of "tinkering at the margins" from a right-of-centre government would be deemed absolutely impermissible by international finance and TNCs if resorted to by governments of the Left.[29] Policies guided, and institutions informed, by the principles of equity, fraternity and justice would inevitably be viewed as threatening the prioritization of growth, efficiency and profitability and, thence, national economic performance. In consequence, they were simply not affordable in the context of intensifying global competition. They added to costs, they limited entrepreneurial freedom of manoeuvre and they jeopardized the possibilities of gain. As far as global corporations and international financial capital were concerned, they were, in short, actually or potentially dysfunctional.

Inimical as they were to democratic socialist principles, the economic instincts and corporate behaviour privileged by globalization, and the forces it unleashed, were also seen as playing an active part in eroding and dissipating what remained of the Keynesian social democratic legacy. As one commentator

---

25. "World governments have to compete against one another by seeking more efficient policies in order to retain the physical and human capital that is now so crucial to modern productive processes and the tax bases upon which governments depend", R. McKenzie & D. Lee, *Quicksilver Capital: How the Rapid Movement of Wealth has Changed the World* (New York: Free Press, 1991), p. xi.
26. For a discussion of different notions of convergence see S. Berger, "Introduction", in Berger & Dore (eds), *National Diversity*, p. 16.
27. P. Cerny, "Globalization and the Changing Logic of Collective Action", *International Organization* **49** (1995), p. 611; D. Drache, "From Keynes to K-mart: Competitiveness in a Corporate Age" in Boyer & Drache (eds), *States Against Markets*, p. 50; McKenzie & Lee, *Quicksilver Capital*, p. 174; S. Strange, *The Retreat of the State: The Diffusion of Power in the World Economy* (Cambridge: Cambridge University Press, 1998), p. 4.
28. L. Weiss, *The Myth of the Powerless State: Governing the Economy in a Global Era* (Cambridge: Polity, 1998), pp. 2–3, provides a rendition of this view prior to its vigorous critique.
29. Perraton *et al.*, "The Globalization of Economic Activity", p. 270.

put it, "issues related to globalization such as international competitiveness, capital flight and the credit rating of governments by financial institutions have provided new ammunition to call into question many of the fundamental notions underpinning the welfare state".[30] And, indeed, in the 1980s and 1990s, these "issues" gave New Right conservatism an intellectual and popular momentum that allowed it to destroy, or substantially erode, the achievements of the social welfarism that, for some three decades after 1945, had been an integral part of the Keynesian social democratic hegemony. De-prioritizing the expansion of social expenditure, eroding the principle of univeralism, lowering or allowing inflation to whittle away the value of social benefits, the incremental privatization of social welfare provision and the replacement of the principle of social service by that of self-interest and by the imperatives of the market, were all indicative of this onslaught and of a democratic socialist retreat which bid fair to become a rout. For this was an onslaught which, while ideologically underpinned by an unreconstructed neo-classicism, was materially driven by the fiscal consequences of the increasingly competitive provision of low-cost corporate environments. Thus for a nation to acquire the corporate base that would enable it to perform effectively in global markets, it required, as one writer put it, "a competitive downgrading of welfare and citizenship rights",[31] a market-induced gravitation towards a lowest common denominator of welfare rights and social expenditure.[32] Not only did democratic socialism in the 1980s and 1990s seem to be losing the agency of a prescriptively autonomous nation state that could transmute its vision into reality; it also appeared to be losing whatever foundation for future socialist advance three decades of Keynesian social democracy had established.

Yet there were those, particularly on the Left, who challenged the notion that what was termed "globalization" did in fact involve a unique threat to the nation state's integrity as regards the formulation and implementation of economic policy. Such writers often compared contemporary developments with the international trading system that had emerged on the basis of the gold standard in the period 1870–1914. In this regard, they suggested that, on virtually all measures, what existed prior to 1914 represented a more open and integrated economic regime than that which had emerged in the last three decades of the twentieth century. Gross figures for the ratios of trade and capital flows to output, overseas investment as a percentage of global GDP, and transnational securities trading as a percentage of total securities trading, all pointed to this conclusion.[33] Admittedly, the contemporary speed, volume and

---

30. R. Mishra, "The Welfare of Nations", in Boyer & Drache (eds), *States Against Markets*, p. 316.
31. Berger, "Introduction", p. 12.
32. *Ibid.*; on this see also Mishra, "The Welfare of Nations", p. 319.
33. On this see R. Zevin, "Are World Financial Markets More Open? If So, Why and With What Effects?", in Banuri & Schor (eds), *Financial Openness*, pp. 51–2.
34. Wade, "Globalisation and its Limits", p. 75.

volatility of short-term international capital flows were considerably greater than the pre-1914 period. But even here the destabilizing consequences of these were not historically unique. It could be argued too that, as regards the speed of transmission of investment decisions, late-twentieth-century technology did not perform any more efficiently than the electric telegraph. Moreover, if late-twentieth-century globalization was historically unique, one might also have expected a greater international uniformity of short-term interest rates than had previously been the case. In fact, "the differences in real interest rates between countries today are probably not so different from the differences forty and even 100 years ago".[34]

Evidence could also be cited that called more generally into question the importance of the international as against the domestic dimension of industrial economies. Thus, despite the increase in global economic interdependence that had manifestly occurred in the last three decades of the twentieth century, by far the greater part of production in western industrial nations was still for the domestic market.[35] In addition, "domestic investment by domestic capital easily dominated both direct investment overseas and foreign investment at home".[36] In any case, it was pointed out, foreign direct investment (FDI) as a percentage of long-term capital flows fell in the early 1990s, as against the 1980s, while much FDI flowed into non-manufacturing activity and the acquisition of existing assets and therefore had "minimal significance for the transnationalization of production".[37]

Commentators also questioned the degree of interdependence and integration that characterized the contemporary international economy on other grounds. For example, despite the obvious mobility of short-term capital, the "degree of international diversification of [long-term] investments [was] surprisingly low". Thus "in December 1989, US investors held 94% of their stock market wealth in their home country . . . UK investors 82%". Nor, according to a study by Epstein, had the elimination of exchange controls and the freeing of capital movements resulted in a greater sensitivity of US foreign direct investment to profit differentials in the international economy.[38] There was also evidence to suggest that the diminution in national savings/investment correlations that should have eventuated with global liberalization of capital markets had not materialized. The fact was that "domestic saving and investment rates remained highly correlated among OECD countries"; rather than "drawing freely" on the savings of other countries, "domestic investment in the OECD was still mainly financed out of domestic savings".[39]

---

35. Weiss, *The Myth of the Powerless State*, p. 176; Wade, "Globalisation and its Limits", p. 61.
36. *Ibid.*, p. 70; see also Weiss, *The Myth of the Powerless State*, p. 174.
37. *Ibid.*, p. 175.
38. Epstein, "International Capital Mobility", p. 213; as Epstein saw it, it was enforcement not transactions costs which were crucial and as these had remained unaffected by liberalization there was no reason why sensitivity should have increased.
39. Wade, "Globalisation and its Limits", p. 74; Weiss, *The Myth of the Powerless State*, p. 179.

Nor, it was argued, had there been any "major tendency to the growth of truly international companies", something that was also confirmed by one of the major gurus of the "internationally linked economy".[40] "International businesses", it was pointed out, were "still heavily committed to their home territory in terms of capital investment, R&D, their overall business activity and the location of strategic decision-making; they remain[ed] 'nationally embedded' and continue[d] to be MNCs [*multinational* corporations], rather than TNCs [*transnational* corporations]".[41] The notion of TNCs shifting rapidly and relatively costlessly about the globe in predatory pursuit of open markets, minimal social overheads and a low-waged labour force was, therefore, largely mythical.[42] Most TNCs, for all their global nature, were, it was argued, still shackled by commitments, in terms of investment and organizational structure, to their country of origin. They were also tied by the need for high-quality rather than low-cost labour, for high-grade social and industrial infrastructure and for political stability and the relationships of trust and reliability imperative for the effective operation of "just-in-time" production methods.[43] Certainly, FDI figures did not suggest any major North–South flows in search of cheap labour – hardly surprising when "labour costs typically represent no more than 20% of the cost of the final product in manufacturing in advanced countries".[44] Indeed, during the FDI boom of the 1980s, the South's share of such investment fell from 25% to 19%, while "as of 1991, a good 81% of world stock of FDI was located in high wage (and relatively high tax) countries".[45]

In short, the argument was that the contemporary international economy was no more integrated than that which had existed prior to 1914; that, for most western industrial nations, the national economy and national economic circumstances were overwhelmingly more important than the international context; and, finally, that in important respects the global economy was still not integrated to any significant degree. It was argued, therefore, that there had been a tendency to overemphasize the uniqueness and importance of contemporary tendencies making for increased global economic interdependence. Further, it was suggested that this was an overemphasis that had had pernicious consequences. For, all too often, it had been, and was being, used as an excuse for policy inertia and a pusillanimous willingness on the part of governments to

---

40. Hirst & Thompson, *Globalization in Question*, p. 2; Ohmae, *The Borderless World*, p. 95.
41. Hirst & Thompson, *Globalization in Question*, p. 98. On this see also H. Chang, "Globalization, Transnational Corporations and Economic Development", in Baker *et al.* (eds), *Globalization and Progressive Economi Policy*, pp. 97–113 and W. Pauly & S. Reich, "National Structures and Multinational Corporate Behaviour: Enduring Differences in the Age of Globalization", *International Organization* **51** (1997), pp. 1–30.
42. See, for example, Perraton *et al.*, "The Globalization of Economic Activity", p. 273.
43. Wade, "Globalisation and its Limits", p. 81.
44. Hirst & Thompson, *Globalization in Question*, p. 117.
45. Wade, "Globalisation and its Limits", p. 70; Weiss, *The Myth of the Powerless State*, p. 186.

pursue the policy line of least resistance, a line determined more often than not by what international capital perceived as its interests.

To question the extent and importance of globalization was, therefore, as these writers saw it, to challenge the current apologia for inertia and to imagine a policy space that could be exploited by national governments. Once the exaggerated uniqueness of contemporary economic circumstances had been exposed, and once the true extent of international economic interdependence had been made clear, the scope for policy autonomy could be more realistically assessed. That done, some of the economic policies that a misconceived globalization had seemed to render redundant could be returned to the agenda of a feasible democratic socialism.

However, a number of points can be made here. First, even if the historical uniqueness of contemporary globalization could be questioned, the fact remained that, by the late twentieth century, the global economy, by any measure, was characterized by a much higher degree of economic interdependence than at any time in the post-war period. Secondly, the policy autonomy possessed by the governments of industrial nations prior to 1914 was, in significant measure, a function of a protectionism that, by the late twentieth century, had been decisively abandoned. Thirdly, even accepting that a comparable degree of economic interdependence characterized the global economy prior to 1914, this did not weaken arguments stressing the constraints that the current situation imposed on contemporary governments of a democratic socialist hue. Fourthly, the speed and volume of short-term capital movements undoubtedly imposed *unique* and severe constraints on the freedom of manoeuvre which policy-makers possessed. Fifthly, while for the major industrial economies domestically oriented economic activity was certainly more significant than that which was internationally oriented, in all major industrial economies trade as a percentage of GDP underwent a massive and rapid increase in the post-war period that continued into the last two decades of the century. Sixthly, while TNCs might still be heavily committed to their home territory, and were less mobile than some suggested, policy-makers could not be insensitive to possibilities of entry and threats of exit – all the more so as the increasing size of such enterprises magnified the scale of the benefits they could bring and the problems this departure could cause. Seventhly, TNCs certainly did possess, and in this period added to, their capacities to undermine or neutralize policy initiatives. And finally, while in the major industrial economies indigenous investment was much greater than inward direct investment, the significance of the latter, in terms of employment creation, multiplier effects and technology transfer, was nonetheless considerable for medium-sized industrial economies such as that of Britain.[46]

---

46. Recent British experience with Ford, BMW and Corus (2000/01) has shown just how considerable the loss of such investment can be.

Moreover, even if it were accepted that globalization was not as significant as many commentators suggested and that the economic policy autonomy of medium-sized nation states was greater than those sold on the notion of globalization opined, it was not immediately apparent what that meant in terms of the policy options available to democratic socialists. Nor were those who called into question the uniqueness and degree of globalization altogether forthcoming in this regard. If there was greater room for policy manoeuvre than suggested by those for whom globalization was a given, neither the nature nor the extent of that space, nor how it was to be filled to democratic socialist or even centre-left effect, were ever clearly delineated. In so far as such possibilities were discussed, it was very much in terms of the "old" strategies that had macroeconomic management and expansion as their centrepiece. And what came to the fore in such discussion was the recognition of the need for the "old" prerequisities if such a strategies were to be effective. Thus for Glyn an "expansionary egalitarian strategy" had to be pursued in the context of "a convincing institutional framework within which to resolve the conflicts generated by high unemployment"[47] – that is, a framework within which some kind of incomes policy could be formulated and implemented to maximize employment creation. Likewise, Pollin intimated the need for an incomes policy, capital controls and, possibly, a dual exchange rate if an egalitarian/ expansionary strategy was to be successful – a revisiting of the policy terrain on which Keynesian social democracy had been routed in the 1980s.[48] In any case, despite the arguments of those sceptical of the notion of globalization, the fact was that many democratic socialists in the 1980s, and even more in the 1990s, came to accept that, to a greater or lesser extent, increasing international economic interdependence had indeed fundamentally altered the rules of the policy ball game. And, on that premise, they set about radically reconfiguring the democratic socialist political economy that they articulated. These reconfigurations assumed a number of forms but, for the most part, they tended to be variants on a supply-side socialist theme.

There was, of course, nothing new in the idea of utilizing supply-side measures both to transform an ailing capitalism and to lay the basis for socialist advance. But not since the Fabianism of the inter-war period had supply-side

---

47. Glyn, "Internal and External Constraints", p. 396.
48. Pollin, "Can Domestic Expansionary Policy Succeed in a Globally Integrated Environment? An Examination of Alternatives", in Baker *et al.*, *Globalization and Progressive Economic Policy*, pp. 436, 443. He also referred to the need for a "permanent framework for regulating financial markets" and a transactions tax on foreign currency dealing along the lines of that proposed by James Tobin. The case for the efficacy of the Tobin Tax in enhancing national policy autonomy is made in P. Arestis & M. Sawyer, "What Role for the Tobin Tax in World Economic Governance?", in Michie & Grieve Smith (eds), *Global Instability*, pp. 151–70. However, grave doubts as to its practicability have been expressed, see, for example, R. Kurdle, "Market Globalization and the Future Policies of the Industrial State", in A. Prakash & J. Hart (eds), *Globalization and Governance* (London: Routledge, 1999), p. 219.

ideas captured Left political economy as completely as they did in the 1980s and 1990s. An awareness of the constraints imposed by the internationalization of economic activity upon Keynesian social democracy and other forms of democratic socialism was one reason for this. But there was also the seeming acceleration of Britain's relative economic decline in the 1970s and 1980s and the manifest triumphs and sustained political success of the economic ideology of a New Right that offered its own supply-side revolution and the prospect of a transformation of economic performance driven by untrammelled market forces. All this appeared to signal to the Left the imperative need for a political economy that would increase the flow, enhance the quality and secure a more efficient utilization of factor inputs in increasingly competitive and internationalized markets.

The problem was how the attainment of such objectives, clearly needful for economic survival and success in the light of intensifying global competition, could be integrated with distinctively socialist goals. The Fabians had done so by predicating their supply-side strategy on a wholesale extension of public ownership that would permit the planned, efficient mobilization of economic resources, while simultaneously allowing the social use of the massively increased economic surplus that would eventuate. AES supply-sideism looked to a transformation of Britain's economic performance by means of a radical extension of the social control of economic activity, through both public ownership and the democratization of enterprise decision-making. However, when the Labour Party stated in 1993 that "any attempt to regenerate Britain's economy by pulling the levers of demand management is doomed to failure unless it also tackles . . . problems on the supply side",[49] its prioritization of competitive efficiency was linked with the democratic socialist agenda in a different way.

To begin with, drawing inspiration from American writers such as Reich and Pfeffer,[50] many social democrats began to give a pre-eminence to labour in their view of things which it had not had since nineteenth-century socialists formulated their diverse renditions of the labour theory of value. The argument they constructed ran thus. While all other factors of production were mobile, while they could be readily acquired and were, therefore, unlikely to give nations a significant or permanent comparative advantage, the same was not true of high-quality labour. As Reich put it, "money, plants, information and equipment [we]re footloose, along with corporate logos. Brains, however, [we]re far less mobile internationally"; "the only value that [could] not be easily replicated worldwide [was] . . . the specialized research, engineering, and

---

49. Labour Party, *Labour's Economic Approach* (London: Labour Party, 1993), p. 6.
50. R. Reich, *The Work of Nations* (New York: Simon & Schuster, 1993); J. Pfeffer, *Competitive Advantage Through People* (Boston, Mass.: Harvard Business School Press, 1994).

design services necessary to solve problems; and the specialized strategic, financial, and management services for brokering the first two".[51]

So "skills" became "the true determinant of national competitive advantage", with "capital more than ever a global commodity, highly skilled labour is now finally acknowledged to be the critical resource".[52] In an increasingly knowledge-based economy, high-level skills would allow the production of a high-value output. They would enable Britain to avoid a low-wage, "bargain-basement" solution to its economic ills, with all the social diseconomies which that would entail.[53] Skills enhanced adaptability; they facilitated that acceleration of change that was imperative in servicing the rapidly evolving markets for technologically sophisticated products. "Competitive strength" now came "from cost-effective production, continued product and process innovation, the flexibility of a highly skilled workforce and the ability to translate the achievements of modern science into commercially viable projects."[54] Also, interwoven with such arguments, was the rhetoric of "new times" and the detritus of post-Fordist socialism. Certainly, there were those prepared to fuse recycled post-Fordist notions with the idea of a human-capital-driven supply-side revolution.

Now the socialist virtue of all this was that the "high-road approach" to competitive success clearly implied that "investing in people [wa]s probably the single best thing that a government [could] do in a global economy".[55] And, from a socialist perspective, this creation of skills was seen not only as having an impact on economic performance, but also as furnishing the "key . . . to the realisation of individual potential" and "rais[ing] people's capacity to . . . .take charge of their own lives".[56] The realization of creative potentialities, the material affluence of a high-wage economy, greater individual autonomy, the social apotheosis of a substantial cohort of the working class, together with a transformation of the nation's economic prospects: all were on offer when the requisite investment was made in human capital. What was needed, therefore, as the Labour Party saw it in 1992, was a "national training programme" with "all employers, except for very small businesses . . . obliged to invest a minimum amount on training their workforce or make a contribution to a local

51. Reich, *The Work of Nations*, pp. 163, 85; for a New Labour rendition of this argument see G. Brown, *Fair is Efficient: A Socialist Agenda for Fairness*, Fabian Pamphlet 563 (London: Fabian Society, 1994), p. 1.
52. Labour Party, *Labour's Economic Approach*, pp. 8–9.
53. Gordon Brown wrote of "a pile 'em high and sell 'em cheap approach to the unemployed . . . a closing sale in a bargain basement", *Fair is Efficient*, p. 18.
54. Labour Party, *Made in Britain: A New Economic Policy for the 1990s* (London: Labour Party, 1991), p. 3.
55. G. Betcherman, "Globalization and Labour Markets", in Boyer & Drache, *States Against Markets*, p. 261.
56. Labour Party, *Labour's Economic Approach*, p. 9; Commission on Social Justice, *Social Justice: Strategies for a National Renewal* (London: Vintage, 1994), p. 77.

or national training effort".[57] And, in the early 1990s, the party proposed a 0.5% payroll tax on major corporations to finance this proposal.

Human resource investment established the basis for a non-alienated, well-remunerated workforce and thence for the social stability and social solidarity that socialists had traditionally seen as among the distinguishing characteristics of a democratic socialist society. And, in so doing, it created a well-educated, continually re-skilled and therefore occupationally flexible workforce that could accommodate the constant structural change which was the inevitable consequence of a relentless pursuit of competitiveness – a workforce that would give society a stable core that would enable it to escape the social diseconomies, tensions and fragmentation which such change had historically engendered.

Further, a society with social inequities mitigated if not removed, and with social rights clearly articulated and financially underpinned, would, by engendering a sense of cohesion, security and stability, foster that social acceptance of rapid change that was crucial if the rapids of globalized competition were to be negotiated with a minimum of social disruption.[58] As one writer put it,

> the insatiable drive for innovation and higher quality which is the motor of modern industrial economies requires citizens to adapt and change. This they won't or can't do without the security that can be found only in cohesive solidaristic societies which both protect all citizens and enable them to achieve their potential.[59]

Only if the costs and dangers implicit in rapid structural change were mitigated by society's adherence to solidaristic principles, only if citizens could be assured that the short-term costs of long-term benefits would be met or minimized by concerted action, could a society expect the wholehearted commitment to the notion of change that was necessary for sustained economic growth. And, for some, "only socialism's commitment to a fair distribution of wealth and income [could] create a workable consensus for necessary changes".[60] The success to be had from mutability required the embrace of mutuality.

It was also the case, as many social democrats and others saw it, that this social cohesion made for a "framework of civic responsibility and values" without which markets would not operate efficiently. For, unless participants were to be perpetually embroiled in self-interested and often disruptive negotiation and/or litigation, it was necessary that a commercial society should operate

---

57. Labour Party, *It's Time to Get Britain Working Again* (London: Labour Party, 1992), p. 13.
58. On this see, for example, M. Albert, *Capitalism Against Capitalism* (London: Whurr, 1993), p. 167.
59. P. Hain, *Ayes to the Left* (London: Lawrence & Wishart, 1995), p. 125.
60. *Ibid.*

according to certain commonly accepted rules and norms of behaviour. Social cohesion made for the emergence of these and served to underpin them; social antagonism threatened their erosion and eventual destruction. The trust that followed from the former was increasingly seen by many commentators in the 1990s as vital to economic success; its absence represented a major obstacle to enhancing economic performance.[61] Only market economies which rested on a basis of social justice could therefore expect to be economically successful, at least in the long run. And, for some, only social democracy could deliver and maintain that basis.

Social equity and social solidarity, as well as being laudable by-products of productivity-enhancing human capital investment, could therefore be seen as economic assets in their own right. As the report of the Labour Party's Commission on Social Justice put it, "the rich social fabric that allows people to live well enables business to do well too; social capital is as important to economic performance as human capital".[62] In this view, a more equitable distribution of income and wealth became complementary to a dynamic economy because of the social costs it obviated and the non-alienated labour it produced.[63] Or, as Tony Blair put it, with his sights on Middle England, "inequality is expensive. Social justice is in every taxpayers' interest."[64] It was in just such terms too that the case for a European Social Charter was made in the 1980s and early 1990s. Thus "the Commission saw social policy as contributing to, rather than hampering, economic efficiency. It argued that social consensus, along with market competition, was a vital ingredient of sustained economic growth and job creation."[65]

In support of such arguments it was pointed out that the two most successful economies of the post-war period, Japan and Germany, were also among the most equal societies in terms of income distribution, with the income disparities between the richest and poorest 20% of the population markedly lower than more poorly performing economies such as those of Britain and the United States. "Growth with equity . . . developmental and distributive capacities combined" therefore "appear[ed] to offer a robust alternative to the socially and economically unambitious model of neo-liberal political economy."[66] And,

---

61. See here F. Fukuyama, *Trust: The Social Virtues and the Creation of Prosperity* (New York: Free Press, 1995).
62. Commission on Social Justice, *Social Justice*, p. 98; the 1990s saw the emergence of a considerable American literature on the importance of social capital which seems to have impinged on Left thinking in Britain. See here, for example, R. Putnam, "Bowling Alone: America's Declining Social Capital", *Journal of Democracy* **6** (1995), pp. 65–78.
63. *Ibid.*
64. Quoted from S. Fielding, *Labour: Decline and Renewal* (Manchester: Baseline, 1995), p. 87.
65. M. Wise & R. Gibb, "A Social Charter for a European Social Market", in M. Ugur (ed.), *Policy Issues in the European Union: A Reader in the Political Economy of European Integration* (Dartford: Greenwich University Press, 1995), p. 250.
66. Weiss, *The Myth of the Powerless State*, p. 156.

of course, in that regard, a human-resource, supply-side socialism might be used to defend the welfare state from New Right criticisms that it added to costs and attenuated flexibility. For only with an adequately financed welfare state could that sense of security be created that would enable the working population to accommodate positively and constructively the notion of rapid and accelerating change. In this scheme of things, the welfare state was seen not just, and indeed not primarily, as a safety net but as a "fitness centre, to make possible the extension of life chances" in the bracingly competitive air of a globalized economy.[67]

So, after all, socialism and globalization could be reconciled. Socialist values and objectives were consistent with, indeed implied, policies that inevitably impacted on the supply side in a favourable manner. "As the century ends", opined Gordon Brown, in millennially reflective mood, "we are leaving behind the old British conflicts between a left that undervalued enterprise and a right that undervalued fairness to build", predictably, "an enterprising *and* fair Britain."[68] Likewise the economic growth that a polyvalent working population and an upgraded educational and social infrastructure would bring would engender further social progress, setting in motion an economically and socially virtuous upward spiral. Globalization did not spell the triumph of neo-liberalism; it did not entail competition with predatory East Asian tigers on their terms of low-cost, malleable labour and the minimization of social welfare expenditure. On the contrary, supply-side socialism pointed to the conclusion that only democratic socialism could lay the basis for success in a global context. Circles could be squared and socialist virtues reconciled with economic expediency. Such was the view of things that was articulated by an increasing number on the Left and that was embraced by the Labour Party in the late 1980s and the 1990s. Seldom have social democrats whistled in the dark with such tuneful anticipation.

Yet there were also those on the Left who saw major problems with such a human-resource-based, social democratic, supply-side strategy. To begin with, investment in human capital, while admirable as regards both its social and economic intent, was unlikely, on its own, to effect that marked increase in labour productivity that would hone a nation's competitive edge to the sharpness necessary to attract footloose corporate capital and ensure success in global markets.[69] As one commentator put it, in relation to what he termed the "training myth", "it obscures the fact that competitiveness and efficiency are primarily

67. Commission on Social Justice, *Social Justice*, p. 104.
68. G. Brown, "Enterprise and Fairness", in G. Kelly (ed.), *Is New Labour Working?* (London: Fabian Society, 1999), p. 49, my emphasis.
69. On this see F. Vandenbroucke, "Globalization, Inequality and Social Democracy", in R. Cuperus & J. Kandel (eds), *European Social Democracy: Transformation in Progress* (Amsterdam: Wiardi-Beckman Stichting, 1998), p. 109.

socially, not individually based".[70] Investment in training might be a necessary, but it was certainly not a sufficient, condition for competitive success. How labour was organized, the attitudes it brought to its work, its relationship to management, the quality of the capital equipment that it utilized and the circumstances of the industries in which it was deployed, were all germane to its effective utilization and, thence, to its contribution to economic performance.

Further, looked at in terms of the socialist goal of greater social equity, a number of critical points could be made. There were, for example, definite limitations on the number of highly trained, polyvalent labourers that even industrialized nations could absorb. Only some sections of the working population might therefore expect any significant increase in income as a consequence of such a strategy.[71] Also, to the extent that many nations pursued policies involving investment to upgrade human capital, global competition would be likely to operate in such a way as to reduce the remuneration of even the highly skilled.[72]

It was also the case that what was proposed was clearly a high-cost, long-term strategy. As Reich himself wrote, "good education and training . . . will be costly"[73] but, as noted above, the expectations of global economic actors as regards the conduct of fiscal and monetary policy would be likely, in the short run, to constrain such expenditure severely, however admirable its intent and however beneficial its longer-term competitive consequences.

Nor could the indigenous private sector be relied upon to fund and direct a training programme of the magnitude that a skills-driven, supply-side economic revolution required. To begin with, unless corporate funding of such a programme was mandatory, there would be the problem of "free riders". Also, as capital investment in human resources would not immediately generate a significant financial return and as corporations were never going to fund a national programme from some sense of social obligation, there was little likelihood that they would take the initiative in upgrading a nation's human capital stock. There was too a recognition, even by its proponents, that there would be problems persuading private citizens to accept the increase in taxation necessary to fund the social investment the strategy required. "Financial constraints were bound to get in the way of good intentions because the fortunate few were never going to fund a huge national training effort [just] out of some sense of social obligation."[74] There were, therefore, major financial

70. M. Bienefeld, "Is a Strong National Economy a Utopian Goal at the End of the Twentieth Century?", in Boyer & Drache, *States Against Markets*, p. 429.
71. D. Marquand, has, for example, called into question the idea "that a mixture of training, education and moral suasion [could] transform the entire society into winners", "The Blair Paradox", *Prospect*, 19/22 May 1998.
72. Bienefeld, "Is a Strong National Economy a Utopian Goal?", pp. 430–1.
73. Reich, *The Work of Nations*, p. 250.
74. Bienefeld, "Is a Strong National Economy a Utopian Goal?", p. 430.

obstacles in the way of either public or private actors pursuing the high-skill, human-resource-investment road to the supply-side revolution that Britain was deemed to require.

Another matter to address was the question of the direction which any training effort should take. Thus, unless what was envisaged was general investment in high-level transferable skills and the creation of a polyvalent labour force able to respond flexibly to *whatever* imperatives emanated from the market, then some assessment of future demand for particular skills would be required.[75] But, in this regard, rapid change itself precluded accurate estimates of this kind and few were prepared to embrace, even notionally, the *dirigisme* of manpower planning.

There were also substantial problems with the argument that the competitive advantages fostered by a social cohesion, underpinned by increased social welfare expenditure, would persuade global capital of the merits of such spending. Thus, from the perspective of global capital, only a low level of social cohesion was required for the untroubled pursuit of its objectives. In terms of the general social environment in which they operated, TNCs could clearly live with a level of social antagonism that stopped short of disruptive social conflict. For, as social microcosms in themselves, they could create sufficient harmony for efficient production at the microeconomic level without needing, or wanting, to sign up to the fiscal consequences of welfare expenditure designed to promote social cohesion at the level of the nation state. They could function effectively in a 40–30–30 society. Costs would rarely be raised and operational efficiency seldom jeopardized by the existence of a burgeoning underclass, certainly not in the way they would be by the tax hikes required to furnish the level of social expenditure necessary for that group's elimination.[76]

As to the argument that "fair is efficient", while it might be accepted that public expenditure, that made for a healthier, less-alienated and less-impoverished population, would enable society to avoid many of those diseconomies that drained the public purse in ways which were singularly unproductive, and while it could legitimately be contended that fairness did, in some instances, though often only in the long run, make for efficiency, the difficulty, as many democratic socialists recognized, was that on occasion it clearly did not. And when, in that regard, socialist principle could not be reconciled with economic expediency,[77] as Swedish social democrats had found to their cost in the late 1980s and early 1990s, global market forces would be likely to inflict severe penalties if social justice was seen to be prioritized at the expense of efficiency and profitability. Therefore, any tension between the

---

75. "... no one actually [knows] what training [is] needed', *ibid.*, p. 431.
76. As the experience of Sweden in the late 1980s and early 1990s would seem to suggest.
77. For a fuller exposition of these arguments see N. Thompson, "Supply Side Socialism: The Political Economy of New Labour", *New Left Review* **216** (1996), pp. 47–8.

commitment of resources to the pursuit of social equity and the accommo-dation of the interests of global capital would almost certainly have to be resolved in favour of the latter. Here again, there were clearly major problems with a democratic socialist political economy whose *modus operandi* was a human-capital and social-justice-driven, supply-side revolution.

For some democratic socialists and social democrats it was therefore necessary to formulate a supply-side socialism that encompassed more than just a happy, healthy, educationally enriched, perpetually retrained, polyvalent, secure, welfare-state-invigorated, socially cohesive workforce. For them, it had also to entail a fundamental change in the nature of the relationships and the balance of power between employers and employees, management and workforce, capital and labour, that had traditionally prevailed in British industry. To the fore here was the political economy of what can be termed radical stakeholderism, articulated with particular energy by writers such as Will Hutton and John Kay in the 1990s[78] and influential for a short time within the Labour Party in the early part of that decade. It is the substance and fate of this that will be discussed in the following chapter.

---

78. For Hutton see *The State We're In* (London: Vintage, 1996) and for Kay's views on the need for a reformation in corporate governance see J. Kay, *The Foundations of Corporate Success* (Oxford: Oxford University Press, 1993) and *The Business of Economics* (Oxford: Oxford University Press, 1996). For other later renditions of radical stakeholderism see, for example, D. Bailey & J. Clancy, "Stakeholder Capitalism via Venture Socialism", *Renewal* **5** (1997), pp. 49–60 and J. Callaghan, "Stakeholding and the Scottish Parliament", *Renewal* **5** (1997), pp. 59–65.

Chapter 9

Embracing the Anglo-American model, or, whatever happened to radical stakeholderism?

Although it came to public prominence in the late 1990s, key elements of the radical stakeholder critique of contemporary British capitalism and the policy prescriptions that were derived from this had deep historical roots in the thinking of the British Left. These roots were particularly apparent in its discussion of the short-termism that distinguished the Anglo-American model of corporate finance, a short-termism that was seen as constraining the time horizons of British entrepreneurs and managers through the lack of long-term involvement and commitment to industry on the part of corporate investors.[1] Here it had long been argued on the Left that, historically, the British banking system had, for the most part, provided British industrialists with only short-term finance, finance which gave bankers liquidity and diminished risk, while its recipients avoided the dilution of control which long-term borrowing and

---

1. This was a concern that had long been a staple of the Left's explanation of Britain's relative decline and, as a number of commentators have pointed out, the ideas of Hutton paralleled here the Nairn/Anderson thesis on British exceptionalism, while other renditions of this critique of the short-termism of the relationship between finance and industry, pre-dating Hutton, can be found in the work of writers such as L. Harris & B. Fine, *The Peculiarities of the British Economy* (London: Lawrence & Wishart, 1985) and G. Ingham, *Capitalism Divided? The City and Industry in British Social Development* (London: Macmillan, 1984).

investment might have threatened.[2] And what had been historically the case remained so into the late twentieth century. Thus "one of the few international comparisons available, from 1992, shows that 58% of all lending to British small and medium-sized companies was in the form of overdrafts, compared with 14% for Germany, 31% for France and 35% for Italy".[3] Of course, this had allowed those companies to retain a kind of autonomy from financial intermediaries not enjoyed in countries, such as Germany, where the relationship between finance and industry was more intimate. But the price of this was that British industry often lacked the finance necessary to fund the long-term, fixed capital investment that technological innovation and expanding markets made increasingly imperative and lacked too an agent, comparable to the German banking system, to effect the industrial reorganization, restructuring and diversification that the rapid evolution of the contemporary global economy now increasingly required.[4]

In addition, like the proponents of stakeholderism, there were those on the Left who had long argued that the emphasis of the City on maintaining sterling's role as a global currency had resulted in government policy prioritizing the stability of its international value;[5] something which often eventuated in "continual short-term adjustments in monetary policy" that frequently "clash[ed] with the longer term financial requirements of British industry".[6] Indeed, some on the Left suggested that the "City ha[d] actively blocked the development of state policies which [we]re progressive for industrial capital" in addition to "fail[ing] to stimulate industrial growth".[7] So neither the state nor financial institutions played, or were in a position to play, the directive, modernizing and restructuring role which, from the late nineteenth century onwards, British industry had required.[8] To all of this analysis Hutton and other radical stakeholders subscribed.

Further, as Hutton saw it, to the extent that British industrialists relied not on assured, long-term funding, but on short- and medium-term loans, they had to meet both stringent security requirements and high expected rates of return. So if there was the absence of a long-term perspective furnished from outside the industrial sector, that sector had also been subjected to pressures that militated in favour of a short-termism that looked to quick and high returns to meet the kind of financial obligations that it had contracted. Banks

---

2. Hutton, *The State We're In*, pp. 121–31; on this see also Harris & Fine, *The Peculiarities of the British Economy*, p. 39.
3. Hutton, *The State We're In*, p. 150.
4. For one of the many discussions of this see G. Ingham, "Commercial Capital and British Development", *New Left Review* **172** (1988), pp. 61ff.
5. On this see, for example, Hutton, *The State We're In*, p. 123 and Ingham, *Capitalism Divided?*, p. 5.
6. *Ibid.*, p. 10.
7. Harris & Fine, *The Peculiarities of the British Economy*, p. 49.
8. *Ibid.*, p. 123; Ingham, "Commercial Capital", p. 51.

ha[d] to make returns to satisfy their own investors . . . [had] to maintain a high margin between funds they borrow and lend, to charge high fees for loans, to take the maximum property collateral, and to retain the capacity to switch the[ir] . . . lending to more profitable operations. The demand for quick profits is fundamental to their relationship with industry.[9]

But, as regards culpability for Britain's relative economic decline, the political economy of radical stakeholderism also emphasized the short-termism in entrepreneurial decision-making and corporate behaviour that many on the Left had traditionally seen as resulting from the mediation of finance/industry relations by the Stock Exchange. Specifically, it was argued that the kind of "active market for corporate control", which the British stock market created, ensured that "the short-term perspective of financial institutions impinged decisively on the perspective of industry".[10] In this active market for corporate ownership, investment fund managers became the key players, players who were essentially concerned with the rapid realization of short-term gains through high dividends and the favourable movement of share prices.[11] "To retain the loyalty of [their] otherwise febrile shareholders", the primary objective had to be quick gains rather than long-term returns and the trading of existing ownership rather than investment in new capacity.[12] Here share price and dividends become the transmission belt between fund managers and corporate executives. The focus of the former on such short-term performance measures ensured that the latter were forced to make decisions with these indicators in mind.[13] If they did not, the penalty could be swift and decisive; a falling share price and squeezed dividends would lay the basis for a change in corporate control through takeover, so corporate policy had to be focused on avoiding both. "Owners make their desires for short-term profit known by insisting on companies performing well against short-term measures", so company resources were shifted into dividend payments rather than, for example, research or long-term capital investment.[14] As the Labour Party literature of the early 1990s emphasized, there was, therefore, a constant

9. Hutton, *The State We're In*, p. 153.
10. K. Cowling, "The Strategic Approach to Economic and Industrial Policy", in K. Cowling & R. Sugden (eds), *A New Economic Policy for Britain* (Manchester: Manchester University Press, 1990), p. 14.
11. Hutton, *The State We're In*, pp. 156–7.
12. *Ibid.*, pp. 163–5; on this theme see also Ingham, *Capitalism Divided?*, p. 62; Labour Party, *Winning for Britain: Labour's Strategy for Economic Success* (London: Labour Party, 1994), p. 7.
13. "The day to day fluctuations of the value of company shares on the Stock Exchange . . . encourage a concern with short-run ephemera to the detriment of the long run and so to the detriment of investment and growth", J. Eatwell, *Whatever Happened to Britain? The Economics of Decline* (London: Duckworth, 1983), p. 159.
14. D. Pitt-Watson, *Economic Short Termism: A Cause of the British Disease*, Fabian pamphlet 547 (London: Fabian Society, 1991), p. 3; for Hutton on this see, for example, *The State We're In*, p. 166.

"pressure in British companies to maintain short-term dividends". And in that period, as Hutton pointed out, "dividends in Japan as a proportion of industrial companies' profits [were] a quarter, and even in the US r[an] at half of British levels".[15] Even in a period of recession, such as the late 1980s and early 1990s, dividends actually increased despite deteriorating company performance, with investment crowded out in consequence.[16]

In such a context, long-term investment was eschewed because, by definiton, its benefits took some time to accrue and, in the interim, both dividends and share price might be adversely affected. "Investment capital appears to be impatient and footloose and does not encourage long-term investment planning, while dividend payout ratios are much higher in Britain than in other countries and have risen sharply over the 1980s."[17] As Hutton put it, "the threat of takeover" created "a 'spectre effect' in which firms cut back on all those expenditures that are vital for their long-term health but which lower short-term profits and dividends".[18]

Moreover, takeovers and mergers were used pre-emptively to ward off the threat of losing corporate control and as a means of conveying an illusion of growth and dynamism, while the long-term investment necessary to deliver the reality of both remained absent. Such recourse to takeovers had made for acquisitive companies and conservative managers. Necessary structural change, long-term investment, reorganization and long-term corporate planning had been eschewed in favour of the "quick fix". In consequence, as one commentator saw it, "the takeover activity of the 1980s has probably seriously damaged the economy. Such studies as have been done suggest that more than half the companies involved in takeover bids subsequently underperformed over the next ten years."[19] In this view of things,

> a high level of takeover activity [wa]s the symptom of an economy that [wa]s functioning badly rather than well. It signifie[d] an economy in which corporate progress [wa]s made, not through investment in new productive capacity, innovation and greater competitiveness but through increasing market share by acquisition and by eliminating competitors.[20]

Further, in such a takeover culture, "there [was] no hint of anything resembling a [long-term] industrial strategy in the machinations of the corporate

---

15. Labour Party, *Rebuilding the Economy* (London: Labour Party, 1994), p. 18; Hutton, *The State We're In*, p. 160.
16. On this see, for example, Labour Party, *Winning for Britain*, p. 7.
17. Labour Party, *A New Economic Future for Britain* (London: Labour Party, 1995), p. 30.
18. W. Hutton, "Fool's Gold", *Observer*, 2 June 1996; see also *The State We're In*, p. 157.
19. A. Hilton, *City Within a State: A Portrait of Britain's Financial World* (London: Tauris, 1987), p. 177.
20. B. Gould, *A Future for Socialism* (London: Cape, 1989), p. 162.

raiders". For the "sole concern" of both predators and prey was "immediate profit".[21]

For Hutton, as had been the case for many on the Left, "the story of British capitalism" was "at heart th[is] peculiar history of the destructive relationship between British finance and industry", a relationship that entailed "British companies not only suffer[ing] one of the highest costs of capital in the world" but in which a "febrile stock market compel[led] them to earn a very big mark up over even the cost of capital to fend off the threat of takeover and keep their shareholder base stable".[22] It was a story of lack of commitment, rapid disengagement and predatory behaviour that militated against the emergence of those stable and committed relationships between finance and industry that, as the economic fate of Germany and Japan made plain, were integral to industrial success in increasingly competitive global markets. "British companies with their footloose shareholders hungry for ever higher dividends and their arm's length bankers who keep them on a short lease with short-term loans on onerous terms" were, "by comparison, at a permanent disadvantage in an increasingly cutthroat international marketplace"[23] and the results of this were there for all to see in Britain's relative economic decline in the post-war period.

So, for proponents of radical stakeholderism, "an important focus for reform" had to be "the way the stockmarket, ownership structures and corporate governance interlock". "New means [had] to be found of encouraging more committed, long-term and responsible ownership."[24] As the Labour Party's *Winning for Britain* (1993) put it, "a key objective of . . . reforms must be to create the structures that produce a large number of committed owners supporting a longer-term view of the company's future".[25] Or, as Gordon Brown phrased it in 1989, measures had to be implemented which prevented the damage which, historically, the City's "speculative concerns" and "whims" had inflicted on British industry.[26]

For Hutton, "the great challenge of the twentieth century . . . [was] to create a new financial architecture in which private decisions produce a less degenerate capitalism", something that would require a "transformation" of the "constitution, mission and values of the Bank of England" so that it would become the apex of a financial system that delivered cheap, long-term finance to British industry.[27] To this end, he proposed the creation of a "framework of regional public banks" that, backed by the Bank of England, would furnish

---

21. Albert, *Capitalism Against Capitalism*, p. 72.
22. Hutton, *The State We're In*, pp. 112, 157.
23. W. Hutton, *The Stakeholding Society: Writings on Economics and Politics* (Cambridge: Polity, 1999), p. 53; *ibid.*, p. 91.
24. *Ibid*.
25. Labour Party, *Winning for Britain*, p. 11.
26. Quoted in Wickham-Jones, "Anticipating Social Democracy", p. 479.
27. Hutton, *The State We're In*, p. 298.

such finance and whose directors would constitute the Bank's Court.[28] He also suggested that, as in other countries such as Germany and Japan, Britain should "create a public agency that will act as a financial intermediary collecting longer term deposits and channelling them to lending institutions".[29] It should be noted though that even prior to the publication of *The State We're In* (1996), the Labour Party, and others on the Left, had proposed a number of such expedients to foster the provision of long-term, committed finance. To this end, proposals had been made for "long-term investment agreements between financial institutions and industrial companies"; for "encouraging an investment culture which support[ed] long-term relationships between government, managers, shareholders and employees"; for the provision of long-term venture capital in the form of industrial bonds in which pension funds would invest; and for differential interest rates as a directive influence upon industrial investment.[30] In addition, as regards pension funds, it had been proposed that greater powers should be given to trustees and that they should receive training "so that they [would be] able to consider the best long-term interests of the pensioners they represent[ed]". Power, at present in the "hands of a handful investment managers residing in the City", could in this way be transmuted into a democratic "expression of the investment power of millions of small savers".[31]

Recognizing though that "the most important factor in reducing the cost of capital for banks and businesses generally is shareholder commitment", Hutton also proposed reforms in corporate governance that would ensure the representation of banks, financial institutions and other investors in a manner that would ensure a more committed, long-term, stakeholder attitude to enterprise performance.[32] He suggested too the introduction of a "penal, short-term capital gains tax" to discourage a speculative, short-termist attitude to share purchase.[33] Also, with respect to takeovers, proposals were made by Hutton, and had already been made by others, to diminish the pressures that frequently forced managers to pursue short-term goals. Here the idea of "shifting the burden of proof" was mooted, "so that the bidding company [would have to] demonstrate that the takeovers would increase efficiency and advance the public interest".[34] Given this, the onus would no longer be on the Monopolies and Mergers Commission to prove that they were inimical to the national

28. *Ibid.*
29. *Ibid.*, p. 300.
30. Labour Party, *Labour's Economic Approach*, p. 16; *A New Economic Future for Britain*, p. 31; and *Making Britain's Future* (London: Labour Party, 1993), p. 12.
31. Gould, *A Future for Socialism*, p. 154.
32. Hutton, *The State We're In*, p. 302.
33. *Ibid.*, 303.
34. Labour Party, *A New Economic Future for Britain*, p. 33; see also Gould, *A Future for Socialism*, pp. 162–3.

interest before they were halted. Here too it had already been suggested by some that there should be an absolute ban on mergers within the top 100 British companies, with the additional proposal that the ban should also encompass mergers that projected the resultant company into that top 100.[35]

Underpinning all such policy prescriptions was the aim of ensuring that companies saw investment, innovation, restructuring and the drive for efficiency, rather than simply company acquisition, as the path to growth. The objective was to create an economic ambience in which corporate managers could think and plan on a long-term basis and to persuade institutional investors to think in terms of a long-term stakeholder commitment rather than short-term speculative gain. The policy prescriptions that related to investment were designed to eliminate short-termism, to forge new and qualitatively different links between finance and industry and to alter the motivation and objectives of corporate managers. And they were seen by some as indicative of how a supply-side socialism, responsive to the competitive pressures engendered by globalization and with a radically transformative intent, might be formulated. Of course, such a stakeholder political economy owed a considerable debt to a particular reading of the success of the German and Japanese models of industrial capitalism. But, in terms of its determination to transform the investment ethos that permeated City institutions, constrain the speculative activity of fund managers, democratize pension fund decision-making and limit the acquisitive behaviour of corporate giants, it was recognizably in the democratic socialist tradition. It was concerned *not just* with a transformation of industrial performance through qualitative and quantitative alterations in the supply of investment, although that was of fundamental importance; it also sought to curb, regulate and democratize the irresponsible power of British financial capital.

As regards the democratization of economic activity, radical stakeholderism also articulated a conception of the firm in which ownership was not absolute and, therefore, the claims and interests of shareholders not necessarily paramount. Rather, the firm was seen as embodying a cluster of claims and prerogatives with employees, customers, suppliers and local communities all having a stake in its fortunes. Further, it was argued, the most successful firms were those that accommodated these disparate stakeholder interests in their decision-making structures; enterprises that acknowledged the social nexus and networks of which they were a part and which, in tandem with their own efforts, determined their economic fate. Such an institutional accommodation of stakeholders made, it was argued, for the continuity and stability of economic relationships and this was an essential prerequisite for that flexibility, trust, co-

---

35. K. Cowling & M. Sawyer, "Merger and Monopoly Policy", in Cowling & Sugden (eds), *A New Economic Policy*, pp. 82–3.

operation and workforce commitment necessary for corporate survival in the context of rapidly changing and increasingly competitive markets.[36]

So, in a manner consistent with democratic socialist ideals, the political economy of radical stakeholderism sought to challenge and change the balance of decision-making power within the companies driving the national economy and, in doing so, lay the basis for a transformation of Britain's economic performance. Moreover, in so far as what they proposed represented a version of the Rhine model (of capitalism), this was a model where, as Albert put it, "the interests of the group are generally felt to take precedence over narrow individual interests" – a principle to which most democratic socialists would have been only too happy to subscribe.[37] In addition, in its emphasis on employees as stakeholders with a right to participate in enterprise decision-making, radical stakeholderism clearly raised issues relating to the status, rights and dignity of labour that had been integral to powerful currents within twentieth-century British democratic socialist political economy. It also pointed to a resolution of these issues that was clearly socialist in tenor. In these respects, therefore, radical stakeholderism offered the basis for a reconfigured democratic socialist political economy.

For radical stakeholders the state should play a crucial developmental role. It would do so, most obviously, by setting corporate governance on a radically altered legal basis and by effecting a fundamental change in the arm's-length, short-termist, Anglo-American model of corporate finance. But more than this, it should also play an important part in creating the institutional and value framework necessary to foster and maintain the social solidarity and co-operative ethos that was seen as lying at the heart of the Rhine model and its success. In particular, it needed to provide a significant measure of social protection for participants in the market economy.

Radical stakeholders such as Hutton mounted a vigorous attack upon the widening of social divisions, the marketization and thence deterioration of public services, the attenuation of social welfare provision, the decay of social infrastructure, the scaling down of employment regulation and the erosion of social sensibilities that had eventuated from an adherence to the principles and practice of neo-liberalism. For a large part of the population, these developments had destroyed the material basis for active citizenship.[38] They were

36. On this see, for example, the work of S. Fernie & D. Metcalf, "Participation, Contingent Pay, Representation and Workplace Performance: Evidence from Great Britain", *Discussion Paper No. 232* (London: Centre for Economic Performance, 1995).
37. Albert, *Capitalism Against Capitalism*, p. 124. A. Gamble & G. Kelly wrote of the "idea of stakeholder capitalism" as appealing to "core Labour values", "Stakeholder Capitalism and One Nation Socialism", *Renewal* 4 (1996), p. 23. C. Hay, in reviewing Hutton's *The State We're In*, wrote of him as providing "a genuinely original and radical programme for [a] centre-left administration", "A State of Disarray: Huttonomics, New Labour and the Contemporary British Impasse", *Renewal* 4 (1996), p. 46.
38. For this see Hutton, *The State We're In*, pp. 193–225.

ethically indefensible and, moreover, economically inexpedient. As regards the latter, "the case linking inequality and the economy [could be] simply put. Inequality between classes and regions adversely affects both demand and supply. Demand becomes more volatile and unbalanced while supply is affected by underinvestment and neglect of human capital."[39] Further, the regressive cuts in direct taxation that had been effected during a decade of Thatcherism had failed to induce that increase in labour supply/effort that, in theory, was to have restored the dynamism of the British economy.[40]

A rejuvenation of the welfare state was therefore an important element of radical stakeholderism. Hutton, for example, wrote of the need for its "democratization",[41] by which he meant that its development should be informed and directed by decisions that came out of the democratic process, rather than by purely economic imperatives. The welfare state should become an expression of social citizenship. It should be informed by the need for social inclusivity and, therefore, become an engine of the social cohesion and social co-operation that he, like many others, saw as central to national economic success as well as social harmony and social justice. "What is in reality required from the welfare system is that it provides boundaries to the operation of markets, underwrites social cohesion and helps produce the values that sustain the co-operation without which successful economies cannot flourish."[42] To this end, Hutton and other radical stakeholders were adamant that there must be some measure of redistribution both to provide the necessary funds and, crucially, "to bind the top third of our society into a system that embodies a morality of citizenship".[43] Redistribution must therefore once again be put at the heart of the centre-left political agenda. In this respect, as in others, there was in radical stakeholderism echoes of the political economy of Keynesian social democracy.

Only a commitment to redistributive measures would mitigate the social inequalities that Thatcherism had produced and that had gone some considerable way to undermine the solidaristic and co-operative attitudes necessary for economic success; only such policies would construct a material basis for active and responsible citizenship; only the social protection that an adequately resourced social welfare system furnished would instil that commitment to corporate change and innovation that successful enterprises required; only increased expenditure on public services would furnish the adaptable, responsive, skilled workforce necessary for high-value-added economic activity; only the demarketization of public services would reverse "the collapse of social cohesion that comes when the market is allowed to rip through society".[44]

39. *Ibid.*, p. 176.
40. *Ibid.*, pp. 182–3.
41. *Ibid.*, p. 306.
42. *Ibid.*, p. 307.
43. *Ibid.*, p. 309.
44. *Ibid.*, p. 175.

Radical stakeholderism looked, therefore, to an active, interventionist role for the state – a state that would furnish the social, cultural, institutional and legal infrastructure necessary for firms to seize the competitive initiative in global markets. But in order to fulfil that role effectively and deliver the policy agenda of radical stakeholderism, it would also be necessary, Hutton believed, to encompass its fundamental reform. In particular, it would be necessary to give constitutional and institutional expression to the principle of subsidiarity and disperse power away from central government. It would be necessary too to underpin active citizenship with a bill of rights. The creation of what radical stakeholders envisaged as a developmental state therefore also required a fundamental political reconfiguration, or, more accurately, democratization, of the highly centralized and authoritarian political state we were in.

For Hutton, the international dimension was also of fundamental importance as regards the success of the stakeholder project. As he saw it, the effective implementation of radical stakeholder policies required the EU in particular to assume a range of macroeconomic responsibilities of a Keynesian social democratic kind. The EU, Hutton believed, had "the power to regulate financial markets and control capital flows".[45] It had "the potential jointly to manage demand . . . without having [its] policies blown off course by the capital markets" and "through the ERM, and possibly monetary union, [it had] the capacity to construct a system of international financial order". Moreover, "Europe can insist on common social rights across the continent, so that multinational firms cannot play one state off against another in an effort to bid down wages and working conditions" and Europe could also "set common environmental standards, and common regimes of corporate governance, establishing the concept of a stakeholder company".[46] The policy autonomy that had been lost at a national level could be retrieved at the European level, a view to which others on the Left came to subscribe in the 1980s and 1990s, as we shall see in the final chapter.

For a time, the political economy of radical stakeholderism had purchase on the Left, both within and outside the Labour Party.[47] For there was in stake-holderism the potential for what some have termed an egalitarian or socialist politics of production,[48] a politics which challenged the existing loci of power and decision-making and which called into question existing notions of the hierarchical exercise of authority, traditional conceptions of ownership and the

---

45. *Ibid.*, p. 315.
46. *Ibid.*, p. 316.
47. As regards Labour, even if the concept itself was not deployed overtly until the mid-1990s, much of the critical analysis of radical stakeholderism, and many of its supply-side/industrial strategy policy prescriptions, were to be found in the economic literature produced both during its "Policy Review" of 1987–9 and its immediate aftermath.
48. J. Rodgers & W. Streeck, "Productive Solidarities: Economic Strategy and Left Politics", in D. miliband (ed.), *Reinventing the Left* (Cambridge: Polity, 1994), p. 138; for the expression of similar views see M. Rocard, "Social Solidarity in a Mixed Economy", in Miliband (ed.), *Reinventing the Left*, p. 159.

relationship of ownership to power. The democratization of decision-making, the diffusion of power and the values of co-operation, community, trust, commitment and social cohesion all found a place in the political economy of radical stakeholderism and gave it a distinctively socialist resonance, as did its frequent recourse to the language of social egalitarianism.

That said, it was an essentially productivist political economy, articulated very much in the language of economic performance. The institutional and social changes it implied might have merit, even socialist merit, but they tended to be justified more often than not in terms of their contribution to productivity, efficiency and growth. The crucial point was that there was profit to be had from virtue; or as it was phrased, "virtuous social institutions" were a *sine qua non* for the "progress [of] an advanced economy".[49] What, in the past, the Left saw as ends in themselves, what they saw as integral elements of the good society or good life, were, in the context of radical stakeholderism, viewed and portrayed as economic assets and engines of economic advance. As one commentator put it, "a productivist Left political economic policy conceives equality and democratic participation not as consumptive benefits taken out of an efficient economy by distributive politics but as a source of productive progress".[50] Here again, we have the argument that socialist values and objectives could be squared with competitive success in increasingly globalized markets.

Radical stakeholders might fight shy of their political economy being labelled "socialist", often preferring, as did Hutton, a "left-centre" categorization. Yet what they offered embraced much of the agenda and many of the aspirations traditionally associated with post-war democratic socialism. They deployed too a conceptual rhetoric that was either recognizably socialist or possessed markedly socialist inflections; they articulated an agenda in which greater social equity and social cohesion were prominent; they stressed the importance of raising *pari passu* the responsibilities and status of labour; they gave to the state an important role in the realization of socio-economic objectives, while emphasizing its facilitative rather than directive role. Above all, they focused on questions of economic power: how it was distributed, how it was used and to what effect, in terms of economic progress and the improvement of the material well-being of the working classes. In the case of Hutton and others it could be said too that they articulated their radical stakeholderism in ways that accommodated traditional Keynesian social democratic concerns with full employment and redistribution. In the 1990s, therefore, radical stakeholderism offered a basis on which a democratic socialist economy could be reconstructed and rejuvenated. But what became of all this?

---

49. Rodgers & Streeck, "Productive Solidarities", p. 139.
50. *Ibid.*, p. 138.

As it was conceived of by writers such as Hutton, Kay and others, the idea of stakeholding formed the conceptual core of a political economy that aimed to transform both the economy and polity of British capitalism. And central to this transformation, as we have seen, was the notion of a "development" state: a state that through macroeconomic management, infrastructural and human capital investment, reform of corporate governance, the demarketization of public service provision and its role as investor, regulator and facilitator would effect a rejuvenation in the fortunes of British capitalism and equip it to cope with the intensification of competitive pressure unleashed by globalization. In particular, radical stakeholders saw the state as creating an institutional basis that militated against the short-termism that had so disadvantaged British capitalism in the post-war period. Although sometimes accused of doing so, radical stakeholderism did not advocate the uncritical importation of the German or Japanese models of corporate finance and corporate governance, or the kind of developmental state of which they were a part.[51] Yet the notion of *a* "developmental state" was clearly central to the realization of its objectives.[52]

In contrast, when, in the mid-1990s, Blair and New Labour took the concept of stakeholderism overtly on board, they did so in a manner consistent with the principles and ideals of a "competition" state and the Anglo-American model of capitalism: a state that aimed to hone the economy's competitive edge in global markets but, unlike its "development" counterpart, to do so in a manner that did not alter or threaten existing modes of corporate governance and finance and thence the existing distribution of economic decision-making power. While radical stakeholderism therefore articulated the need for a reconfiguration of corporate power relations and the relationship between finance and industry, those who articulated their stakeholderism in terms of the competition state were, on such matters, essentially silent. They sought to preserve the lineaments of the Anglo-American model, accepting the existing distribution of economic power, while seeking to secure the smoother and more flexible operation of markets, particularly the market for labour.[53] As Hutton put it, "The British now define the political task as adapting to market forces whatever the social cost: the Europeans see the task as shaping market forces to sustain dearly held social and cultural values."[54] The different readings of the concept of stakeholderism that emerged in the mid-1990s were integrally related to these competing conceptions of what capitalism was and could become.

---

51. For one such accusation from within New Labour ranks see M. Smith, "Understanding the 'Politics of Catch-up': The Modernization of the Labour Party", *Political Studies* **42** (1994), p. 713.
52. See, for example, Gamble & Kelly, "Stakeholder Capitalism", p. 23ff.
53. For a critical, though generally positive discussion of what the first New Labour government see S. Ludlam & M. Smith (eds), *New Labour in Government* (London: Macmillan, 2001).
54. Hutton, *The Stakeholding Society*, p. 148.

Thus, with its embrace of the Anglo-American model, New Labour's explication of stakeholderism, in the mid-1990s, shifted the emphasis from the corporation, corporate relationships, the developmental role of the state, and thence the stakeholder as part of *collective* entities, to the role of markets and the place of stakeholders, as *individuals*, within them. As Mandelson and Liddle saw it, a "stakeholder society . . . [was] not primarily about companies and how they are run" but "about giving every individual a stake in society".[55] For Leadbeater and Mulgan, the "focus" should be "on employees rather than companies".[56] Thus the individual and individual endeavour, not collective entities and action, were put centre stage. As Blair saw it, "the stakeholder economy" was "not about giving power to corporations or unions or interest groups. It is about giving power to *you* the individual. It is about giving you the chances that help you get on."[57] An individualist articulation of the concept of stakeholderism also loomed large in Blair's reading of it as meritocratic and infused with the notion of "enlightened self-interest".[58] "A stakeholder economy", in his Singapore speech of January 1996, was about giving individuals the opportunity for "self-improvement" and "a chance to earn and get on"; "it is a stakeholder economy in which opportunity is available to all [and] advancement is through merit".[59] As one commentator has remarked, in that speech "the complex link between equalising opportunity and economic success for Britain [wa]s made through metaphorically extending the everyday language of individual success to Britain – you 'getting on' leads to Britain 'getting on'".[60] The ideal was an atomistic one: a bourgeois utopia where all would participate, and all were able to participate, in the competitive cut and thrust of an acquisitive society, and where their self-interested activity would redound to the nation's economic advantage. New Labour's stakeholderism was, therefore, a political economy that took seriously the New Right aspiration of creating a truly popular capitalism.

This reading of stakeholderism found particular expression in the idea of employee share ownership. Thus Alistair Darling, amplifying the ideas contained in Blair's Singapore speech, "called for a big increase in employee share ownership", arguing that this was something that in giving individuals a stake in their company would provide both "motivation and reward for [corporate]

---

55. P. Mandelson & R. Liddle, "Come the Revolution", *Guardian*, 27 March 1996.
56. C. Leadbeater & G. Mulgan, *Mistakeholding: Whatever Happened to Labour's Big Idea?* (London: Demos, 1998), p. 1.
57. T. Blair, speech at the Derby Assembly Rooms, 18 January 1996 in T. Blair, *New Britain: My Vision of a Young Country* (London: Fourth Estate, 1996), p. 57, my emphasis.
58. On this see J. Kampfner, "Politics of the Possible", *Financial Times* 14 December 1995.
59. Blair, *New Britain*, p. 58.
60. N. Fairclough, *New Labour, New Language?* (London: Routledge, 2000), p. 86. Fairclough's work provides an excellent discussion of the discursive construction and reconstruction of the New Labour agenda through the elaboration of the concept of stakeholderism, see *ibid.*, pp. 83–93.

success", without "more laws, more rules or more regulation".[61] Gordon Brown too applied the sobriquet "stakeholder" to proposals for the introduction of employee stock-ownership plans,[62] while Leadbeater and Mulgan in rejecting the "Hutton–Kay idea of stakeholding" as having "too many major flaws", sought to replace it with one that had the extension of share ownership at its core.[63]

For Mulgan and Leadbeater,

> stakeholding Hutton–Kay style would not fit into the very different culture of British capitalism. It would not help Britain to create jobs in the industries of the future and it would not have anything like the political appeal of its 1980s New Right equivalent: the promise that people could have a stake through owning their home and some shares.

For them, stakeholding should be rather the banner under which "to reinvigorate the idea of a share-owning democracy" and "a new Labour government should encourage not just employee share-ownership plans but also experiments with consumer share-ownership schemes ... and even related-enterprise share-ownership plans to underpin networks of suppliers, assemblers and distributors."[64] There was in their proposals a faint and distorted echo of radical stakeholderism. Like Hutton and Kay, they sought to confirm and therefore to reinforce the interdependencies upon which economic success was built. An extension of share ownership of the kind they proposed would, as they saw it, encourage a more responsible and thence a more long-term attitude to economic interrelationships: one more productive of trust and certainty. That said, their proposals were avowedly in harmony with the shareholder-centred, Anglo-American model[65] and they rejected what they saw as radical stakeholderism's attempt to promote "Byzantine reforms to corporate governance". What "people" wanted was "real shares" in their companies and not "an ill-defined voice" in decision-making.[66]

The existing scheme of things where "companies [were] accountable to their shareholders" and sought to "deliver shareholder value" should be retained. Government should simply be in the business of broadening the shareholder base. Such a view of things was consistent with the idea of a

61. P. Wintour, "Blair Insists", *Guardian*, 19 January 1996.
62. W. Hutton, "Now Gordon", *Observer*, 8 November 1998.
63. C. Leadbeater & G. Mulgan, "Stakeholding: Nice Ideas, Shame about the Reality", *Observer*, 6 October 1996.
64. *Ibid.*; the idea was taken from J. Womack & D. Jones, *Lean Thinking: Banish Waste and Create Wealth in Your Corporation* (New York: Simon & Schuster, 1996).
65. Leadbeater & Mulgan, *Mistakeholding*, p. 5.
66. *Ibid.*; it is interesting to juxtapose this to Leadbeater's earlier view that the Left should be in the business of "offering some alternative to this [Conservative] individual form of share owning" such as the Swedish Left's Meidner plan, C. Leadbeater, "The Sid in Us All", *Marxism Today* (January 1987), p. 21.

competition state and antipathetic to its development rival. On this, Mulgan and Leadbeater were explicit. For them, contemporary corporate success stories were not to be found in Germany or Japan.[67] They were not a function of the Rhenish model and the development state. On the contrary, "all the big new companies of the 1990s, such as Microsoft, Netscape and Oracle", came from "the entrepreneurial culture of the United States".[68] "Rather than forlornly searching the Rhineland or suburban Nagoya for models of the future, British policy-makers would do better to look at the fleet-footed information, entertainment and software companies on the US west coast." That was the kind of business culture that Britain should seek to replicate: an approach to stakeholding tailored to the Anglo-American model of capitalism.[69]

As Hutton saw it, the Leadbeater/Mulgan proposals simply sought the wider extension of what would remain "obligation-less property rights". "British business" would still remain "yoked to maximising shareholder value for those uncommitted owners."[70] It would still, therefore, be characterized by short-termism and the failings that followed from that. So their proposals would not effect the radical reconfiguration of power relations within British capitalism that radical stakeholders saw as fundamental. But it was the Leadbeater/Mulgan position that represented the stance of New Labour in the late 1990s.

Those who configured stakeholderism in such a way as to render it consistent with the Anglo-American model did accept the need for a change in the ethos of corporations. In pursuit of "more precision . . . about what we mean by stakeholderism in business", for example, Mandelson and Liddle argued the need for firms "to show commitment to employees, adopt an egalitarian and open style of management, build long-term relations with suppliers and customers" and to become "actively involved in their local communities". But, at the same time, they were quick to stress that "responsibility to stakeholders [did] not mean accountability to them". In the final analysis, company "boards should be accountable to shareholders; only shareholders can replace the management or sell their shares to someone else who will".[71] Mandelson and Liddle admitted that the besetting sin of short-termism had indeed characterized the shareholder-centred model of British capitalism, but they were equally adamant that "the solution [was] not heavy-handed legislation".[72] Rather, what was needed was a "cultural change

---

67. *Ibid.*
68. Except, presumably, for those companies – such as Nokia and Ericsson – that didn't! C. Leadbeater & G. Mulgan, "Labour's Forgotten Idea", *Financial Times*, 2 October 1996.
69. *Ibid.*
70. W. Hutton & J. Kay, "Only Working Together", *Observer*, 13 October 1996.
71. Mandelson & Liddle, "Come the Revolution".
72. *Ibid.*

... in the relationship between boards and shareholders".[73] Further, whatever reforms were necessary "to make institutional investors more effective custodians of the enormous economic power they wield[ed]", "these reforms should not be seen as a high-profile campaign against the City of London", not least because "the problem of short-termism in the UK owe[d] far more to our chronic failures of economic management" than it did to the behaviour and activity of the City, and the solution to these was macroeconomic fiscal rectitude of a kind that the Conservatives preached but rarely practised.[74] Also, as regards takeovers, while it might be necessary to "re-balanc[e] the rules of the takeover process", "we must not throw so much grit in the wheels that bad management is artificially protected".[75]

In contrast to the economic philosophy of radical stakeholderism, therefore, the Mandelson/Liddle rendition left the City, the institutional heart of the Anglo-American model, untouched. "New Labour should aim for a robust model of capitalism" but a model that was "dynamic and competitive" as well as "civilised": a model that would allow Britain to survive "the rigours of the global market". For these writers, the model would be "an adaptation of market capitalism", that is to say, an adaptation of the Anglo-American model, and "not the radical alternative to it for which some are still searching".[76]

The language of stakeholderism was also used to articulate the New Labour agenda of social inclusion, skills and labour flexibility.[77] Thus, in Blair's Singapore speech, stakeholding "meant a commitment by the Government to tackle long-term unemployment, help the underclass out of poverty, reform the Welfare State, provide quality education for all [and] spread the benefits of new technology".[78] Similarly, the "idea of a stakeholder economy . . . [was] not a code for the import of the German economic model; rather . . . it builds on the commonsense insight that a community based on inclusion will be stronger than one with a whole class set apart".[79] Read in this way, stakeholderism became the conceptual springboard for notions such as "welfare to work" and an emphasis on the centrality of skills to economic success.

Educate, educate, educate: the inculcation of skills was to be the means by which labour would be given a stake in the future prosperity of British capitalism. As Blair put it in a speech at Derby in January 1996, "the stakeholder economy is

---

73. *Ibid.*; in Alistair Darling's view too what was needed, as regards the reform of corporate governance, was not legislation but "change [in] people's behaviour and attitudes", quoted from W. Lewis & D. Wighton, "Labour Softens on Stakeholding", *Financial Times,* 26 June 1996.
74. Mandelson & Liddle, "Come the Revolution".
75. *Ibid.*
76. *Ibid.*
77. See, in particular, Leadbeater & Mulgan, *Mistakeholding.*
78. Editorial, "Trust Me says Blair", *Observer,* 14 January 1996.
79. T. Blair, "Switch on the Bright Ideas", *Guardian,* 27 May 1996.

the key to preparing our people and business for vast economic and technological change".[80] Similarly, in a speech to the British American Chamber of Commerce in New York in April 1996, Blair argued for a revolution in skills linked to technology, while Leadbeater and Mulgan saw the creation of "an individually based knowledge investment fund" as a key component in their view of a stakeholderism that "buil[t] on the strengths of the Anglo-American model".[81] It was this knowledge-driven, supply-side socialism that constituted Blair's concept of "a stakeholder economy"; an economy that "grant[ed] all our people a stake in the nation's future, empowering them to develop their potential to the full, in education, technology and – for the unemployed – the world of work".[82] For where labour was perceived as the key factor input (and this was an idea that New Labour enthusiastically embraced) then the "competition" state had a key role to play in making it available as freely and cheaply to employers as possible, not least to those multinational corporations (MNCs) whose inward investment was seen as central to the retention of global competitiveness. And the notion of *freely* available was certainly reinforced by the abandonment, after 1997, of New Labour's previous commitment to taxing firms to provide a national training fund.

As to propelling the unemployed from welfare to work, this was, of course, a key prescriptive nexus where stakeholderism fused with New Labour's views on social exclusion and labour flexibility. In the words of Tony Blair, social welfare provision "should be a platform of opportunity not a recipe for dependency".[83] Entry, or rapid re-entry, to the labour market was a key opportunity/stake that New Labour (and others) believed the state should be in the business of providing. As Mulgan put it, "for most people a job is a far more important symbol of citizenship even than a vote or constitutional rights".[84] However, with respect to the "welfare-to-work" gospel, there was more than a little substance in the view that in "encouraging" entry to the labour market, "Labour's welfare to work proposals [were] rooted in a view of the unemployed as potential knaves who face sanctions if they refuse to do something about their own position."[85]

Also, to ensure its employment stake, it was argued that labour needed to be flexible. Mulgan and Leadbeater emphasized the need for "a much more flexible and entrepreneurial model of stakeholding" than that offered by

80. Wintour, "Blair Insists".
81. Leadbeater & Mulgan, *Mistakeholding*, p. 7.
82. Quoted from R. Smithers, "Blair Woos US", *Guardian*, 12 April 1996.
83. T. Blair, *The Third Way: A New Politics for the New Century*, Fabian Pamphlet 558 (London: Fabian Society, 1998), p. 11; Gordon Brown wrote of using social security rules as a "springboard for new employment", "The Politics of Potential: A New Agenda for Labour", in Miliband (ed.), *Reinventing the Left*, pp. 120–1.
84. G. Mulgan, "A High Stake Society", *Guardian*, 30 January 1996.
85. S. Driver & L. Martel, *New Labour: Politics After Thatcherism* (Cambridge: Polity, 1998), p. 92.

Hutton and Kay. Indeed, an emphasis on the necessity of labour market flexibility was a distinguishing feature of New Labour literature in the run-up to the 1997 election and remained a central theme in New Labour's explication and conduct of policy thereafter.[86] As regards minimum wage legislation, "commitment to minimum labour standards" was fine "provided they don't lead to rigidity or inflexibility in the labour market".[87] What was wanted was "a *sensible* national minimum wage".[88] As to the Social Chapter of the Maastricht Treaty, Blair pledged to oppose those aspects of it that threatened labour flexibility.[89] In a lecture to the City in April 1997, he insisted that New Labour "would seek to extend flexible labour markets to the rest of Europe", rather than "import Eurosclerosis".[90] Europe should conform to the Anglo-American model. "Europe's aim should be to match the dynamism of the single market of the US . . . Europe need[ed] to pursue economic reforms to make its product, labour and capital markets more flexible . . . to create new jobs."[91] Similarly, in a speech to European socialists shortly after the 1997 election, he insisted that to become and remain competitive, "knowledge, skills, technology and enterprise are the keys, *not rigidity, unnecessary regulation and old-style intervention*",[92] an economic verity that was to be iterated on a number of subsequent occasions. And, in a foreword to a White Paper on *Fairness at Work* (1998), Blair applauded the fact that even after implementing the proposals it contained, "Britain [would] still remain the most lightly regulated labour market of any leading economy in the world".[93] Here, as elsewhere, he iterated New Labour's belief that "the task of government is to make the market more dynamic".[94]

Blair and New Labour also spoke the stakeholder language of partnership and social cohesion. "Partnership", as Blair himself saw it, was "critical to national prosperity." "A high level of social cohesion is not just urgent in itself, it is essential for an efficient, prosperous economy." Similarly, "a culture of respect, trust and co-operation and teamworking" was to be valued for its "essential" contribution "to productive and competitive industry".[95] Stakeholderism should therefore be about creating a "recognition of a mutual

86. Leadbeater & Mulgan, *Mistakeholding*, p. 6.
87. L. Elliott, "In Place of Fear", *Guardian*, 13 January 1997, on Blair's Singapore lecture.
88. NEC Statement to the Labour Party Annual Conference, *Labour in Government: Delivering Our Contract to the People* (London: Labour Party, 1997), p. 9, my emphasis.
89. See Fielding, *Labour: Decline and Renewal*, p. 101.
90. Quoted in M. Marqusee, "New Labour and its Discontents", *New Left Review* **224** (1997), p. 128.
91. Blair, *The Third Way*, p. 19.
92. Quoted in Fielding, *Labour: Decline and Renewal*, p. 102, my emphasis.
93. *Ibid.*, p. 103; when in 1998 the minimum wage was set at £3.60 for adult workers, considerably lower that the level sought by the TUC and benefiting, in most cases marginally, only 10% of the workforce, it was argued that a higher level would threaten the flexibility required at the lower end of the labour market.
94. Speech, April 1996, quoted in R. Heffernan, *New Labour and Thatcherism: Political Change in Britain* (New York: St Martin's Press, 2000), p. vii; on this see also Labour Party, *New Labour: Because Britain Deserves Better* (London: Labour Party, 1997).

purpose for which we work together and in which we all benefit".[96] "The stakeholder economy [wa]s about making us one nation again", "binding all parts of the community to a common national enterprise".[97] In building prosperity on the basis of social cohesion a stakeholding economy would also render redundant that Old Left politics that had been informed by notions of social antagonism and class division. So whereas social cohesion was seen by Hutton *et al.* as something to be created by the dispersal of power and the greater democratization of decision-making, for New Labour it was seen more as an attitude of mind or something that could be engendered without any substantial interference with, or alteration in, existing economic interests and power relations. In that regard, as Fairclough has rightly argued, "stakeholding" was "what link[ed] together the two great themes of New Labour, its Thatcherite legacy and its communitarianism".[98]

Moreover, in the New Labour view of things, it was business that was constructed as *its* partner and ally, while Labour's traditional constituency was usually seen as an obstacle to realizing the New Labour vision of a prosperous and business-friendly Britain. Thus when John Monks suggested trade unions as the representative institutions through which workers could claim and utilize their stake in corporate management, the Labour leadership was quick to distance itself from his remarks. When John Edmonds of the GMB union saw stakeholderism as entailing new legal rights of job security, the response was equally cool.[99] In addition, under Tony Blair, the party shifted its position on the universal right to trade union membership (some 5 million employees were not subject to the legislation on trade union recognition that New Labour produced) and on secondary picketing, and also came to insist on public and binding arbitration for all public sector workers involved in the provision of essential services.[100] Further, presumably for the benefit of potential inward investors, Blair was insistent (1998) that New Labour changes to trade union legislation, proposed or implemented, "would still leave British law the most restrictive on trade unions in the Western world".[101] Again, as with the "most

---

95. Blair, *The Third Way*, p. 8; T. Blair, "My Vision for Britain", in G. Radice (ed.), *What Needs to Change: New Visions for Britain* (London: HarperCollins, 1996), p. 12; see also T. Blair, "Power for a Purpose", *Renewal* **3** (1995), p. 11.
96. Blair, *New Britain*, p. 58.
97. Speech at the Derby Assembly Rooms and Singapore, as reported in the *Guardian*, 19 January 1996 and commentary on Blair's Singapore speech, N. Cumming-Bruce & M. White, "Blair Unveils Economic 'Big Idea'", *Guardian* 8 January 1996.
98. Fairclough, *New Labour*, p. 91.
99. W. Hutton, "Raising the Stakes", *Observer* 17 January 1996; D. Marquand, "A Stake Through the Heart of Old Simplicities", *Independent* 15 January 1996.
100. C. Hay, *The Political Economy of New Labour: Labouring Under False Pretences* (Manchester: Manchester University Press, 2000), p. 110.
101. Quoted in *ibid.*, p. 111; for the Labour Party's evolving relationship with the trade unions, and in particular the new trade unionism of the 1980s and 1990s, see D. Farnham, "New Labour, the New Unions and the New Labour Market", *Parliamentary Affairs* **49** (1996), pp. 584–98.

lightly regulated labour market", the lodestar of policy was clearly the needs of the competition state.

Mandelson's remark that "the filthy rich" should feel at ease with New Labour might have proved an embarrassment to colleagues, but it reflected how far New Labour had travelled during the 1990s in its quest to accommodate the capitalist entrepreneur and how far it proposed to distance itself from the agenda of radical stakeholderism. In a review of New Labour's pre-election literature, Fairclough pointed to no less than "195 instances" of the mention of "business in the New Labour corpus" of which "a total of 48 . . . in collocations which relate to partnership or co-operation between business and government".[102] Gordon Brown declared that his "vision" was "of a Britain . . . which is business friendly".[103] As one commentator saw it, prior to the 1997 election, "the Federation of Small Businesses seem[ed] to be exercising more influence over Labour's employment policy than the trade unions" and during the election itself Blair presented himself as "the entrepreneur's champion".[104] It was not surprising, therefore, that on coming to power, it was leading entrepreneurs and City figures who were appointed to guide many of New Labour's policy reviews and key policy-making committees. Nor that, in 1998, the then chair of the CBI, Sir Colin Marshall, could declare that Tony Blair and the leaders of business shared "a largely mutual philosophy",[105] a view exemplified by the reduction of corporation tax from 33% to 31% (23% to 21% for small businesses) shortly after New Labour came to office. This was trumpeted in the NEC Statement to the Labour Party Annual Conference in 1997 as a key element in a "major reform of the corporate tax system provid[ing] a low-tax environment for companies . . . and maintaining an attractive environment for inward investment".[106] Here is not the place to discuss the whiff of corruption that periodically tainted the air in the corridors of power after Labour's 1997 election victory, but it can be noted in passing that, almost without exception, the odour emanated from New Labour's intimacy with business.

With regard to the legislation on corporate governance that would have been necessary to give substance to a radical stakeholder vision, it is clear that Blair's Singapore speech did have Huttonian inflections, intimating the need to "shift the emphasis in corporate ethos from the company being *a mere vehicle for the capital market* – to be traded bought and sold as a commodity – towards the vision of the company as a community or partnership in which each employee

---

102. Fairclough, *New Labour*, p. 30. It is interesting here to note such titles as the Labour Party's *New Labour: A Government for Entrepreneurs* (London: Labour Party, 1997).
103. Brown, "Enterprise and Fairness", p. 54.
104. R. Taylor, "Change of Tack", *Financial Times*, 9 July 1996; Heffernan, *New Labour and Thatcherism*, p. 74.
105. *Guardian*, 28 May 1998.
106. Labour Party, *Labour in Government*, p. 8.

has a stake".[107] However, it was significant that in that speech Blair was adamant that "we cannot by legislation guarantee that a company will behave in a way conducive to trust and long-term commitment" and it was the case that no specific legislative proposals as regards corporate governance were made in the run-up to the 1997 election.[108] Nor was there any attempt to articulate the kind of merger and takeover policy that radical stakeholders had advocated.

In 1996 New Labour had committed itself to a review of the legal framework of corporate governance, proposing to establish an "Expert Panel", though Alistair Darling qualified this commitment by stating that "there [was] a limit to how many of Britain's corporate ills [could] be resolved by legislation. What we are trying to do is change people's attitudes."[109] It was decided further that it would be established only after the report on corporate governance of a committee chaired by Sir Ronald Hampel, chairman of ICI, a report that, when published in 1998, refused to accept the general argument that corporations had obligations as well as rights.[110] In 1998, however, a Company Law Steering Group, under the chairmanship of Sir Stuart Hampson and composed mainly of industrialists and institutional shareholders, was duly established by Margaret Beckett. A first consultation report, published in March 1999, gave some support to the stakeholder idea, although the language was anodyne rather than radical, with references to the need for businesses to operate as teams and for managers to recognize the interests of the wider community. It did, though, adumbrate the possibility of what it termed a "pluralist" approach to stakeholding with progress being made through the creation of a legislative regime "in which directors are permitted – or required – to balance shareholder interests against those of others". However, this so-called "pluralist" approach had effectively been jettisoned by October of that year in favour of an "enlightened (stakeholder) approach" that "relie[d] on progress under today's [legal] principles", with any legal changes focused on "broaden[ing] the information given by companies to the public".[111] The discourse of stakeholding therefore lingered on, but in anaemic form devoid of radical content. And when the group finally reported in early 2000, it was seen as having "backed off from radical proposals to revolutionise Victorian statutes", with its views eliciting the comment that "Victorian company law look[ed] set to stay".[112]

As Hutton saw it, to implement a radical stakeholder merger, takeover and corporate governance strategy would "require national leaders to take on the rich

---

107. T. Blair, *The Times*, 18 September 1995, my emphasis.
108. G. Davies, "Tony Blair puts Meat on the Stakeholder Bones", *Independent*, 15 January 1996.
109. On this see W. Lewis & D. Wighton, "Labour Softens on Stakeholding"; for a similar view from a Labour frontbench adviser see P. Metcalf, "Stakeholding Versus Competition", *Renewal* 4 (1996), p. 78.
110. On this see W. Hutton, "It's Stakeholding not Sclerosis Stupid", *Observer*, 1 March 1998.
111. J. Kelly, "An Era of Broader Interests", *Financial Times*, 19 March 1999.
112. R. Cowe, "Stakeholder Rights", *Guardian*, 9 March 2000.

and powerful" and that was something which, given New Labour's embrace of the Anglo-American model, was simply inconceivable.[113] Indeed, as early as 1996, New Labour was regarded as "flinch[ing] from the implications of a break-out from the straightjacket of Britain's shareholder capitalism. Shifting the entire political economy on to a different course – and that is what adopting the stake-holder model would involve – . . . [was regarded by them as] a slow, difficult, risky and sometimes painful business" and "it would", they believed, "be much easier to take the shareholder model as given".[114] Taking it as given was clearly the line that New Labour pursued, with any aspiration for a Huttonian "stakeholder economy" decidedly displaced by the desire to create, in Gordon Brown's words, "an enterprise culture for all".[115] By late 1999, Tony Blair was stressing the moribund nature of the Rhenish model of capitalism and exhorting his European partners to embrace its Anglo-American rival; and, by that date, too, Will Hutton had emerged as one of New Labour's more perceptive and trenchant critics.[116]

Stakeholding largely disappeared from the political vocabulary of politicians, pundits and most journalists only months after being unveiled as New Labour's big idea.[117] As early as October 1996, well before the general election, commentators were remarking that "Tony Blair has abandoned his big idea" and that he had been "scared off the idea of the stakeholder economy that he launched so buoyantly a few months back".[118] By December 1996, one commentator could write that "like the pop group 'Blur', stakeholding blazed a trail across the media's firmament, leaving behind little sign that it had ever existed".[119] And indeed, in a speech in the autumn of 1996 to the Labour Party Annual Conference, Blair did not even mention stakeholding. Thus he seems to have come to view the idea as being too tainted with the corporatism of Old Labour[120] and as having the potential to alienate the corporate sector whose support New Labour had been so assiduously cultivating.[121]

---

113. Hutton, *The Stakeholding Society*, p. 118.
114. D. Marquand & T. Wright, "Labour and the Intellectuals", *Political Quarterly* **67** (1996), p. 3.
115. Brown, "Enterprise and Fairness", p. 50.
116. Even before this date, Hutton was being dismissed by New Labour leaders as "a well-liked, useful, free thinker but not a great influence". See A. Grice, "Has Stakeholding Shrunk to a Slogan?", *Sunday Times*, 21 January 1996. However, it should be noted that Hutton did express some support for New Labour's putative agenda before its second term.
117. Although there were subsequent sporadic attempts to breathe some prescriptive life back into the concept. See, for example, S. White, "Interpreting the 'Third Way'", *Renewal* **6** (1998), pp. 17–33, R. Prabhakar, "Social Capital, Stakeholding Capitalism and the Third Way", *Renewal* **7** (1999), pp. 84–8 and J. Plender, *A Stake in the Future: The Stakeholding Solution* (London: Brealey, 1997).
118. Leadbeater & Mulgan, "Stakeholding"; P. Doyle, "From the Top", *Guardian*, 19 October 1996.
119. *Financial Times*, 2 October 1996; *ibid*. 27 December 1996.
120. On this see Heffernan, *New Labour and Thatcherism*, p. 22. This was an accusation that the Conservatives were quick to make, see D. Willetts, *Blair's Gurus: An Examination of Labour Rhetoric* (London: Centre for Policy Studies, 1996).
121. On this see the interview with Adair Turner, the director general of the CBI, in the *New Statesman*, 19 January 1996, in which he expressed antipathy to the idea of stakeholding and concern as to how it might be developed.

Yet such commentary obscures what actually occurred and the light it throws on the political economy of New Labour and the current state of democratic socialist political economy in Britain. Certainly, the process of abandonment was swift, but it was a process rather than an event.[122] *Radical* stakeholderism was indeed *immediately* jettisoned. Tony Blair soon made clear that stakeholderism was "not a code for the import of the German model" and, as we have seen, there were many in the ranks of New Labour who were quick to reject "stakeholding, Hutton–Kay style", as inimical to "the very different culture of British capitalism".[123] Such a stance was also reinforced by a view of Rhenish capitalism as increasingly sclerotic and as outperformed by the economies that adhered to the Anglo-American model. But stakeholderism *per se* did not die a quick death; rather, it was refined and reconfigured to form a conceptual basis for a political economy that accommodated the Anglo-American model. Thus "as deployed by the Labour leader" it became "a slogan, a soundbite, a portmanteau in which to carry the many soft-Right aspirations he is offering the electorate."[124] In this context it is also interesting to note its appropriation by BT in February 2000, when that company's mission statement opined that "to continue to provide *an excellent return on shareholder investment*, we must also take into account the expectations of all stakeholders". Here in its general commitment "to sustainable development *and stakeholding*", BT showed the extent to which the concept had, by that date, been made an integral element of the shareholder model that it had originally been formulated to critique.[125] Thus a concept that might have provided the basis for a centre-left, or democratic socialist, political economy was stripped of its radical content and connotations, reconfigured to harmonize with the principles and practice of Anglo-American capitalism, then jettisoned from the official discourse of New Labour before, finally, being appropriated by the purveyors of corporate pabulum. Nothing could so graphically symbolize the death of British democratic socialism and New Labour's embrace of an Anglo-American model fundamentally inimical to its resurrection.[126]

122. As Fairclough has phrased it, "the political discourse of New Labour is a process rather than a finished product", *New Labour*, p. 93.
123. T. Blair, "Switch on the Bright Ideas"; Leadbeater & Mulgan, "Stakeholding".
124. J. Rogaly, "Right Still Calls the Tune", *Financial Times*, 27 January 1996.
125. Caulkin, "Third Way Loses its Bearings", my emphasis.
126. For a prescient anticipation of this ideological trajectory see Hay, "A State of Disarray", p. 48.

Chapter 10

Multinational socialism

With national governments impotent to act or, at least, constrained to behave in ways largely consistent with the interests of international capital, it seemed to some British democratic socialists in the 1980s and 1990s that only a multinational pursuit of their objectives was feasible. To assume otherwise was "to cling to national sovereignty [and] in practice, to hand sovereignty over to the global marketplace".[1] In Britain, this attitude of mind became particularly widespread in the 1980s and was reinforced by the manifest failure of the Mitterrand experiment that seemed to confirm that the policy autonomy of the nation state was now severely circumscribed. The conclusion that many inevitably drew from this was that what was no longer feasible nationally had now to be pursued at an international level and, in particular, within a European framework. "Social democracy and democratic socialism", argued one writer, "can only be achieved today as European concepts; in national terms these ideals become more illusory and hopeless every day."[2] A unilateral Keynesian assault on unemployment had failed in France because of

---

1. C. Crouch and D. Marquand, "Introduction", in Crouch and Marquand (eds), *Reinventing Collective Action: From the Global to the Local* (Oxford: Blackwell, 1995), p. 13.
2. Glotz, "Europe – The Helpless and Silent Continent".

capital flight, growing current account deficits and pressures on the franc. But a multilateral Keynesianism would not have to confront balance of payments and exchange rate pressures and would have the international financial support necessary to cope with whatever capital flight was provoked. For some it seemed obvious, therefore, that "Keynesians must try to re-establish on an international level the institutional capability to control economic processes that they have lost on a national level";[3] that Keynesian social democrats, and for that matter other democratic socialists, should now "concentrate their hopes of the chance of regaining Keynesian options on the international level, either on the high road of macroeconomic coordination between the United States, Japan and Western Europe or on the low road of economic policy integration in the European Community".[4]

In the 1980s there were, for example, those who advocated a European socialist economic strategy based on the AES. Stuart Holland's *Out of Crisis: A Programme for European Recovery* (1983) came from the work of "a group of socialist economists in the main Western European countries who had met . . . over a period of up to ten years" and proposed to tackle on a continental basis, by concerted European reflation, the problem of 15 million European unemployed. And what it suggested was a multinational strategy that was to be combined with "a restructuring of power and redistribution of resources"[5] in order to ensure a truly socialist resolution of capitalism's contemporary crisis.

By the late 1980s, the notion of using European institutions as a means of implementing a democratic socialist strategy and repairing the damage inflicted by a decade of Thatcherism had gathered considerable momentum. Neil Kinnock's speech to the Socialist Group of the European Parliament, in September 1988, clearly indicated a fundamental change in the erstwhile anti-Europeanism of the Labour Party; the favourable reception of Jacques Delors' speech to the TUC Conference at Bournemouth in 1988 was indicative of a similar shift of opinion on the part of the trade union movement. And, within the labour movement more generally, it was increasingly believed that once Europe was embraced, the realm of feasible socialism, both prescriptively and geographically, could be much expanded. European co-operation might be used to render any expansionary policies "less vulnerable to speculative flight". A "common European currency policy", and even more so the creation of a single European currency,[6] could give Europe a degree of autonomy from the actions

---

3. Scharpf, *Crisis and Choice*, p. 294.
4. *Ibid.*, p. 249; see also Glotz, "Europe – The Helpless and Silent Continent".
5. S. Holland, *Out of Crisis: A Programme for European Recovery* (Nottingham: Spokesman Books, 1983), p. 215; the policies advanced in the programme had originally been "sponsored by members of the incoming socialist government in France".
6. For example, Strange wrote in 1989 that its creation would "involve some loss of national autonomy in the management of the national economy. Yet the opportunities it would open to the Europeans for economic diplomacy . . . would be tremendous", *Casino Capital*, p. 189.

of the US Federal Reserve which individual European states could never possess.[7] Co-operation in an EEC context also opened up the prospect of co-ordinating fiscal policies in a European-wide onslaught upon unemployment that would no longer be imperiled by balance of payments leakages.[8] Variations on these central themes by British writers became increasingly evident from the mid-1980s onwards. The idea of a Euro Bretton Woods, which would "take initiatives to harness multinational finance capital . . . [and] achieve the conditions for modern full employment policies in Europe", was mooted.[9] And it was also pointed out that "the Common Market [did], potentially . . . have the institutions to conduct an effective quasi-regional policy between countries".[10] The possibility of a "black pound" to give European industry the kind of protection that the "green pound" provided for agriculture was also suggested.[11]

Even many erstwhile Eurosceptics and proponents of Britain's withdrawal from the EEC now argued that it was "time that left-wing members regarded the European Community as a stunning opportunity";[12] that "the situation in the European Community" had "brought together the most promising set of circumstances for establishing transnational policies that we shall see for some time".[13] Or, as Michael Barrett Brown phrased it,

> for many of us the nation state and the power of national association, and particularly of organised labour, offered the only realisable countervailing power. Now, however, such national resources are no longer adequate. In the face of the concentrated power of the organisations of capital in the giant European corporations, nothing less will do but that European-wide structures – both political and economic – should be built and maintained and European-wide social policies should be conceived and fought for.[14]

For some, of course, the geographical basis of a multilateral socialism had to be broader still. In effect, it had to be global. "The struggle for freedom, welfare and democracy, and for human rights" could "only be strategically and effectively fought out on a global plane. Globalized capital necessitate[d] a

---

7. Scharpf, *Crisis and Choice*, p. 264.
8. On these themes see Scharpf, *Crisis and Choice*, pp. 264–5.
9. N. Kinnock, "A New Deal for Europe", in J. Curran (ed.), *The Future of the Left* (Cambridge: Polity, 1984), p. 232.
10. R. Rowthorn, "An Interview with Wynne Godley", *Marxism Today* (July 1981).
11. *Ibid.*
12. "The Tale of Two Parties", *The Economist*, 23 June 1990.
13. G. Ross, "The European Community and Social Policy: Regional Blocs and a Humane Social Order", *Studies in Political Economy* **40** (1993), p. 41.
14. M. B. Brown, *European Union: Fortress or Democracy?* (Nottingham: Spokesman Books, 1991), p. 1.

world-wide and internationally intertwined democratic movement of resistance" if it was to be effective.[15] "It [was] clear that the Left [needed] to have its own international economic strategy"; that "instead of wringing our hands at the loss of power of national governments", the aim should be "to set in place regional and global structures, which will give us the ability to control our economic environment".[16]

Of course, the internationalization and Europeanization of the socialist project were not, for the most part, seen as mutually exclusive. The regional and global dimensions of the pursuit of socialism were interlinked. The "new collectivism" was to be "pluralistic, diverse and internationalist. It look[ed] outwards to the institutions of global economic governance and to the supranational institutions of the European Union."[17] For some too this pluralism should also accommodate greater and more effective decision-making by local communities as regards those economic and social matters that touched them directly. Here the European Community was seen as providing an institutional framework within which greater mutual co-operation between municipalities and regions might be fostered. With the doughty socialist deeds of the GLC still fresh in mind, one writer looked to "linkages between municipalities across Europe to build co-operation from the ground up". "The Left's programme for further development of the Community should therefore consist" not only in "a demand for stronger and more representative Community institutions, capable of managing economic policy and providing a co-ordinated monetary framework" but also "an increased stress on resource transfers to support local investment and development at the regional or city level".[18] In the late 1980s, such views were also frequently infused with the decentralist rhetoric of flexible specialization and local socialism.

By curbing and controlling global market forces and constraining and regulating the power wielded by TNCs, multilateral socialism would, paradoxically, rejuvenate local and national democracy by reinvesting it with the capacity for the effective implementation of policy. It would permit "popularly elected local authorities and national governments to establish their authority over the major processes of production and finance in the longer term".[19] The "dominant problems of economic governance" might "lie in the international

---

15. J. Hirsch, "Globalization of Capital: Nation-States and Democracy", *Studies in Political Economy* **54** (1997), p. 53.
16. J. Michie, "Introduction", in J. Michie & J. Smith (eds), *Global Instability: The Political Economy of World Economic Governance* (London: Routledge, 2000), p. 1.
17. Crouch & Marquand, in *Reinventing Collective Action*, p. 5.
18. K. Coates, "Time for a New Internationalism?", in K. Coates (ed.), *Joint Action for Jobs: A New Internationalism* (Nottingham: Spokesman Books, 1985), p. 30; F. Cripps & T. Ward, "Employment Creation", in K. Coates & M. B. Brown (eds), *The Regulation of International Banking* (Cambridge: Woodhead/Faulkner, 1985), p. 97.
19. M.B. Brown, "Can European Workers Cope with Transnational Capital?", in Coates (ed.), *Joint Action*, p. 49.

domain" but if these were successfully addressed then national economic "routes to economic stability and prosperity" would once again become a possibility.[20] So, in a European context, such proponents of pluralism envisaged not the creation of a European superstate, but "a division of labour across national and regional governments co-operating with Union institutions with considerable power but limited functions".[21] Not all might have agreed with the specifics of this vision, but many did see the emergence of a multilateral socialism as the key to the retrieval of the power of effective policy-making at national and sub-national levels.

But what, specifically, was it believed could be achieved, given the requisite forms of international co-operation and concomitant institutional frameworks? To begin with, and of particular importance, those on the Left who looked to some form of multilateral socialism as a means of escaping the emasculation of national economic policy were agreed in seeing it as once again allowing the pursuit of full employment. This was at the core of *Out of Crisis*, and it was central to the macroeconomic strategy proposed by many on the Left in the late 1980s and early 1990s. A full employment strategy was "now a matter for joint action between governments as well as the European community".[22] It should involve increased employment-creating public expenditure "to save energy and to develop new sources and to provide education, health, recreation and cultural facilities".[23] It should aim to promote social cohesion as well as economic regeneration. It should be financed both by the Community and by individual nation states. As to the former, ideas such as a five-year European recovery bond were mooted, with institutions such as the European Investment Fund being seen as having "potential as an instrument for Keynesian expenditure policies".[24] As to the latter, ideas such as a "framework for the conduct of fiscal policy across the Community" were suggested, to "ensure support for [national] governments whose borrowing needs are increased as a result of downturns in activity".[25] For "if recovery is both to occur and be sustained the Community should be able to support development deficits in those countries which need major long term expenditure".[26] Further, if Community unanimity on these matters was not attainable, it was believed that it should still be possible for "progress to full employment" to "be pioneered by those countries [that were] willing to counter the crisis through joint action".[27]

20. Hirst & Thompson, *Globalization in Question*, p. 53.
21. *Ibid.*, p. 157.
22. K. Coates, "The Spectre of Unemployment", in K. Coates & M. B. Brown (eds), *A European Recovery Programme* (Nottingham: Spokesman Books, 1993), p. 2.
23. Cripps & Ward, "Employment Creation", p. 100.
24. Holland, *Out of Crisis*, p. 69.
25. Cripps & Ward, "Employment Creation", p. 102.
26. S. Holland, "An Alternative Economic Strategy", in Coates (ed.), *Joint Action*, p. 220.
27. *Ibid.*, p. 229.

An automatic fiscal stabilizer was also proposed which would cut in "to provide insurance against country-specific shocks".[28] Here one suggestion was that the Community might finance a part of national unemployment insurance schemes, receiving in return a part of the employer/employee contributions. What would result would be an employment-stabilizing transfer of funds from nations with below-average to those with above-average levels of unemployment.

Such prescriptions were given political impetus and credibility in the early 1990s by the European Commission president, Jacques Delors. In 1989, Delors had declared that the EU would be "the theatre in which social democracy accomplishes its mission".[29] Thus, in 1992, he argued the need for an ambitious programme of European infrastructural investment not only to enhance the competitiveness of European economies, but also to effect a substantial reduction in the level of European unemployment. Indeed, it was in this context that Stuart Holland, then working for Delors, "produced a plan for expanding the Delors proposals ... into an ambitious counter-cyclical programme".[30] This drew support from a number of MEPs, trade unions such as the GMB and MSF and from Leftist periodicals such as *Tribune* and the *New Statesman*, and was articulated at some length in publications such as Coates and Barratt Brown's *A European Recovery Programme* (1993), and Holland and Coates's *Full Employment for Europe* (1995). "The unemployed", wrote Coates in the latter, "are the excluded people ... To will a cure for their plague of adversities, we must choose rational forms of political action. *In modern Europe this implies joint action, by all sides of the European Community*, co-ordinated and urged forward by their common institutions."[31] Such ideas also infused New Labour literature in the early 1990s, with pamphlets such as *Labour's Economic Approach* (1993) stressing the importance of institutions such as the European Investment Bank and its investment fund as instruments for creating jobs. In a similar vein, *Economic Renewal in the European Community* (1993) proposed the creation of a contra-cyclical, employment-creating role for a European Recovery Fund.

It was also considered that monetary policy could be used in pursuit of employment objectives at a European level. To begin with, if a speculative attack on a national currency were to be provoked by a radical expansionary strategy,

---

28. D. Gros & N. Thygsen, "The Relationship between Economic and Monetary Integration: EMU and National Fiscal Policy", in Crouch & Marquand (eds), *Reinventing Collective Action*, p. 193.
29. J. Delors, "A New Frontier for Social Democracy", in P. Dankert & A. Koopman (eds), *Europe Without Frontiers: Socialists on the Future of the European Community* (London: Cassell, 1989), p. 32.
30. This was done in the summer of 1992. On this see Anderson & Mann, *Safety First*, p. 94.
31. S. Holland & K. Coates, *Full Employment for Europe* (Nottingham: Spokesman Books, 1995), afterword, my emphasis.

it was believed that the financial resources that could be mobilized on a European basis might be such as to permit its effective defence. Further, some on the Left enthused over the possibilities opened up by a *single* European currency. Individual currencies might be vulnerable to speculative attack in foreign currency markets in a context of unilateral expansion, but the possibility of such an assault was diminished where a community of European nations shared the same currency.[32] "A dramatically accelerated monetary union" was therefore seen by some on the Left as the prerequisite for greater national macroeconomic policy autonomy and, more generally, as permitting a major EC budgetary expansion.[33] As Coates put it, "if governments [were] ever to recover the capacity to plan for higher levels of investment, they will need to work together while moving towards the strength of a single currency".[34] In place of a nominal sovereignty, a single currency would "deliver to European states a real measure of collective and, therefore, effective, sovereignty within the context of the global economy".[35]

It was also suggested by some on the Left that the constitution proposed for the European Central Bank, as part of the Maastricht agreement, opened up the possibility of using it to attain socialist objectives. As Holland saw it, that constitution obliged "the ECB . . . not simply to pursue a monetary policy *consistent* with the general policies of the Community but 'to contribute to the achievement of the objectives'". Nor did those objectives "simply include price stability or monetary union but also a high degree of economic convergence, *a high level of employment and social protection* and the raising of the standard of living".[36] Given the requisite political control of the Commission and Parliament, therefore, the ECB could be used to expedite the pursuit of such democratic socialist goals.

More generally, a single European currency or, simply, more effective monetary integration, would make for a haven of stability in a turbulent economic world. The former, by definition, would eliminate the problem of exchange rate movements within the Community; the latter, it was believed, would reduce intra-European fluctuations to a point that would allow macroeconomic policy at national and Community level to be focused on matters other than countering or accommodating the exogenous shocks emanating from the foreign currency maelstrom. Such stability would also help to create the kind of economic certainty that would allow more rational, long-term,

---

32. On this see, for example, K. Coates, "The Dimensions of Recovery", in Coates & Brown (eds), *A European Recovery Programme*, p. 10.

33. A. Marvell, "Funding the Recovery Programme", in *ibid.*, p. 62.

34. Coates, "Dimensions of Recovery", p. 10.

35. A. Leyshon & N. Thrift, "European Financial Integration: The Search for an 'Island of Monetary Stability' in the Seas of Global Financial Turbulence", in S. Hardy *et al.* (eds), *An Enlarged Europe: Regions in Competition?* (London: Kingsley, 1995), p. 118.

36. Holland, "Planning the Recovery", p. 73, my emphasis.

economic decision-making at both micro- and macroeconomic levels. In effect, for many democratic socialists, it seemed to retrieve the possibility of economic planning.

However, if European institutions could be used to tame global market forces in such a manner as to open up space for the pursuit of democratic socialist policies, what control could they exercise over global corporate players? Some indication of the growing importance and size of TNCs in the 1980s and 1990s has been given earlier in this book. At a European level this was particularly manifest, when the prospect, and then the advent, of the Single European Market precipitated a wave of mergers between Europe's biggest companies. Thus European Commission data for Europe's 1,000 largest firms pointed to a growth from 117 involved in merger activity in 1982–3 to 492 by 1988–9. In consequence, as one commentator put it, "for the first time, European integration was extended to the production level".[37]

The Single European Market therefore furnished a milieu that fostered the further aggregation of TNC power. It confirmed, if confirmation was needed, the pivotal role of TNCs in national and European economies. The worst fears of the AES Left were being rapidly realized or surpassed. The emergence of socially irresponsible, footloose corporations with the determination and capacity to subvert democratic policy-making and eradicate even the most tentative of socialist initiatives was writ large in these developments. Yet, for some, the European Union also possessed the institutional potential to exercise control over these organizations. It was argued, for example, that national monitoring of the consequences of inward investment made possible the construction of an EU-wide social accounting framework, one that would itemize its social costs and benefits with a view to minimizing the former and maximizing the latter. Such a framework might also furnish a basis for laying down codes of conduct and social responsibility protocols to which TNCs would have to adhere. This would not preclude national initiatives, but the whole business of ensuring social responsibility and social accountability "would be more effective if it were part of a wider European process".[38] As one writer saw it, "a crucial dimension of European economic management" should be "the determination of the economic and social responsibilities of those large – which means transnational – enterprises . . . Single countries have not had the ability to handle the terms of that development dialogue with the world's multinationals; the emerging Economic Community will have."[39] Indeed, it

37. L. Tsoukalis, *The New European Economy: The Politics and Economics of Integration* (Oxford: Oxford University Press, 1991), p. 64.
38. J. Hughes, "The Dole Economy: Can We Plan Our Way Out?", in Coates (ed.), *Joint Action*, p. 156; on this see also Hirst & Thompson, *Globalization in Question*, p. 140.
39. J. Hughes, *The Social Charter and the Single European Market: Towards a Socially Responsible Community* (Nottingham: Spokesman Books, 1991), p. 4.

was only within such a transnational framework that TNCs could be subjected to any effective kind of social constraint. For some too such a framework also opened up the possibility of this control being exercised along AES lines. The notion of planning agreements and the extension of public ownership, while admittedly moribund in a purely national context, could be rejuvenated in a European one. Such was certainly the expectation of the author of *Out of Crisis* and such notions were current throughout the 1980s.[40] So, in place of the competitive pursuit of TNC inward investment, which threatened the abrogation of labour rights and the excision of socially responsible behaviour and public accountability from the corporate agenda, the EU, through monitoring and enforcement, would ensure the dissemination and implementation of best corporate practice in all these respects.

It was with these objectives in mind that some on the Left supported and stressed the potentialities of the Social Charter and then the Social Chapter of the Maastricht Treaty. As they saw it, Charter and Chapter indicated the emphasis that was increasingly being placed on social issues and, in particular, on the likely deleterious social consequences of the acceleration in economic integration, and consequent structural adjustments, which the Single Market would effect.

> Taking it all in all, the Commission [was] clearly not going to leave the Social Charter as a mere element in gesture politics. Behind the scatter of measures one can see some clear principles of social protection and harmonisation . . . European social policy is coming in from the margins, and may even occupy centre stage.[41]

The Social Chapter gave the Commission the means of preventing the kind of social dumping which the competitive pursuit of inward investment could create. Among other things, such "dumping" could precipitate the abrogation or dilution of individual and collective employment rights, the abandonment of minimum levels of remuneration and an end to controls over hours and working conditions. All these were possible outcomes of competitive bidding for TNC favours and would involve national connivance in the corporate evasion of social responsibilities to workforces and communities. However, transnational EU directives could, it was believed, prevent complicity in social dumping by investment-hungry nation states. This view that European

---

40. On this see also J. Palmer, "A Common Programme for Europe's Left?", in Coates (ed.), *Joint Action*, p. 55.
41. Hughes, *The Social Charter*, p. 26. Note also Gold's remark that "recent developments, such as the Social Charter and moves behind the Social Chapter, have been aimed at consolidating the social dimension and speeding up the adoption of measures associated with it", M. Gold "Introduction", in M. Gold (ed.), *The Social Dimension: Employment Policy in the European Community* (London: Macmillan, 1993), p. 3.

integration created opportunities for social protection from the pressures of globalization, transnational corporatism and neo-liberalism was certainly one that was argued powerfully by Jacques Delors in the early 1990s.[42]

In addition, it was stressed by many British as well as European democratic socialists that an active European social policy was vital to prevent the social disintegration, and its attendant costs, which the increasing liberalization of market forces threatened to unleash.[43] As Lionel Jospin stated at a Congress of the Party of European Socialists in 1997,

> à la globalisation de l'économie . . . nous devons répondre par la coordina-
> tion, par la construction d'un cadre économique, sociale et politique
> commun, par la volonté de la régulation. Sinon, les forces de marché,
> libres de tout contrôle, ménaceront notre conception même de la civil-
> isation.[44]

The intensification of competition would precipitate rapid structural change with the multiplication of winners and losers an inevitable consequence. "The proposals for European Economic and Monetary Union and for a single market by 1992" might well "provide the discipline which will relate growth of income to productivity and wipe out inefficient producers", but for that very reason "these proposals need[ed] to be balanced by fiscal measures to relax taxation and increase spending for groups and regions which have fallen behind and will suffer from the new discipline of competition".[45] Thus it seemed to some that those nationally based, redistributive and regional policies that had made for social cohesion but had fallen victim, in the 1970s and 1980s, to the "crisis" of public expenditure, the onslaught of the New Right and the punitive action of international finance could be rejuvenated at an EU level. Further, it was argued, just as "national insurance, social security, public education and socialized medicine were . . . powerful symbols of national solidarity . . . a supranational welfare state would provide an equally strong demonstration of [and basis for] Europe-wide solidarity".[46] Again, it was believed that many of the essential components of democratic socialism, which could no longer be implemented in a purely national context, might furnish the basis for social cohesion and solidarity within a European framework.

Of course, there was a non-socialist argument from expediency here, as well as one from socialist principle. The need for socially ameliorative expenditure

---

42. R. Cuperus & J. Kandel, "Introduction", in Cuperus & Kandel (eds), *European Social Democracy*, p. 21.
43. Though this was not an argument exclusive to the Left.
44. Vandenbroucke, "Globalization, Inequality and Social Democracy", in *ibid*., p. 95.
45. Brown, *European Union*, p. 47.
46. G. Majone, "The European Community: Between Social Policy and Social Regulation", in Ugur (ed.), *Policy Issues in the European Union*, p. 232.

was embraced by those for whom it was quite clearly a palliative to prevent the diseconomies attendant upon a burgeoning underclass of losers and dispossessed. It could also be, and indeed was, justified, on the pragmatic grounds that it contributed to economic efficiency, making for a "social consensus [which] along with market competition, was a vital ingredient of sustained economic growth and job creation". This was the language of "productive social policy" in which an emphasis on "investment training and improved working conditions as elements of social policy leading directly to increased economic efficiency" loomed particularly large.[47] It was very much the language of the authors of the Social Charter but, for many on the Left, it encompassed only one, circumscribed aspect of the possibilities which the Charter and the Chapter held out – possibilities of an egalitarian, socially transformative, in short, socialist nature.

What was needed to realize those possibilities was new "sources of taxation for an expanded budget for development" and the extension of a democratically elected European Parliament's control over that budget. In fact, the late 1980s and early 1990s did see just such a significant increase in funds to ease the process of structural adjustment and at least a putative adherence to the principle of additionality on the part of recipients.[48] Further, there was an increasing "acceptance of the redistributive function of the EC budget and hence the link between economic integration and solidarity across national frontiers". And although "certainly limited compared with the size of inter-regional redistribution of resources inside member countries and federal systems outside the EC", its redistributive role was, by this period, regarded by some as "no longer negligible".[49] In addition, in the 1990s, the European Parliament did, in some respects, begin to play the role which the Left wished it to assume, consistently stressing as it did the need for more resources to be committed to regional and social policy and also campaigning for bigger budgets to be used in a more decidedly redistributive fashion. It was also the case that during this period the socialists formed the largest group in the European Parliament and were able to interpret the concept of "Social Europe" in ways that highlighted its redistributive, egalitarian and socially cohesive potential.

So, clearly, a number of democratic socialist writers in the 1980s and 1990s believed it was possible to pursue their macroeconomic, social and redistributive objectives within the political and institutional framework provided by the EU. In particular, they took seriously the concept of a Social Europe designed to mitigate, if not to eliminate, the deleterious socio-economic

47. Wise & Gibb, "A Social Charter", p. 250.
48. R. Barnett & V. Barooah, "The Additionality (or Otherwise) of European Community Structural Funds", in Hardy *et al.* (eds), *An Enlarged Europe*, p. 190.
49. Tsoukalis, *The New European Economy*, pp. 233, 244.

consequences of the accelerating process of EU economic integration, something that found expression in the Social Charter and the Social Chapter of the Maastricht Treaty. Of course, it was recognized that such a commitment to a Social Europe was often proffered by those who saw it purely in ameliorative terms, but, for all that, some democratic socialists nonetheless believed it could be made the basis for the pursuit of overtly socialist objectives.

There were, however, major obstacles in the way of realizing such aspirations. In particular, there were the constraints imposed by the European budget. Thus, as late as 1997, EU expenditure was only 3% of the total expenditure of its member states, while throughout the 1990s the EU budget remained less than 1% of Community GDP.[50] As regards the mitigation of regional disparities, in the late 1980s, assistance coming from the European Regional Development Fund was only 0.09% of Community GDP and 0.46% of gross domestic capital formation. Structural adjustment funds were doubled in the 1990s, together with an attempt to increase their effectiveness, but, for the most part, they remained of marginal significance as far as regional economies were concerned.[51] Further, there was, in the 1980s, little evidence that expenditure by the European Social Fund was indeed additional to what would have been undertaken in any case by member states; although there was a definite attempt in the 1990s to ensure adherence to the principle of additionality. However, in these circumstances, with a minimal commitment of resources, it was always likely that Social Europe would fail to evolve in ways that would allow even the partial realization of the expectations with which it had been invested by its democratic socialist supporters. The budget was, and was likely to remain, "clearly inadequate to support a Community-wide policy even on a modest scale".[52]

This deficiency of resources was, of course, indicative of a more general attitude that militated against the possible development of a significant social dimension in EU policy-making. While member states were prepared to concede considerable autonomy as regards their conduct of monetary, fiscal and exchange rate policy, such concessions did not extend to any area of policy that required substantial public expenditure. To relinquish power and responsibility of that kind would be likely to entail a significant transfer of funds from national to Community coffers. For that reason alone, the effective implementation of a comprehensive European social welfare policy was never likely to be high on the political agenda.

It was also the case that while the liberalization of EU trade and capital movements proceeded, for the most part, on the basis of an ideological consen-

---

50. J. Delors, "The Scope and Limits of Community Action", in Coates & Brown, *A European Recovery Programme*, p. 46; R. Mackay, "European Integration and Public Finance: The Political Economy of Regional Support", in Hardy *et al.* (eds), *An Enlarged Europe*, p. 170.
51. Tsoukalis, *The New European Economy*, pp. 212, 217.
52. Majone, "The European Community", p. 233.

sus, "the social dimension of the EC" was, and has remained, "an ideological battleground", something which, as many saw it, clearly obstructed "advancement in adopting social programmes or standards across the Community".[53] More generally, it can be said that the concept of a Social Europe emerged and existed in an uncongenial ideological ambience. As commentators on the Left had pointed out from the time of the formation of the EEC, the essence of its constitution and rationale were the principles of free market liberalism. It was with reference to such principles that progress was measured and it was the imperatives they generated which were the engine of integration. Thus even if, by the late 1980s and 1990s, the "measures proposed by the Commission in the social field" "no longer [had] to be justified in functional terms", they had still to "be compatible with the 'economic constitution' of the community, that is, with the principles of a liberal economic order. This requirement creates an ideological climate quite unlike that which made possible the development of the welfare state in the Member States."[54] As the same commentator put it, in such an ideological context the rationale advanced for social dimension expenditure was one that was increasingly couched in "efficiency-improving", "supply-side", rather than ethical/distributional terms. Of course, where fair could be deemed to be efficient, then the same rhetorical squaring of circles evident in New Labour literature could be iterated at an EU level.

There was also the problem of giving substance to the "social dimension" where there already existed such a diversity of national social policies. States differed both in their commitment to social justice and, more obviously, in the manner in which they gave practical effect to it.[55] This reflected national historical traditions of welfare provision, the economic circumstances and stage of development that characterized member states and their different political and legal systems and structures.[56] While, therefore, "the Social Charter was intended to lay a foundation for the European social dimension by establishing a set of rights systematically applicable to all workers and to certain groups of marginalised people across member countries", the problem was, and remains, that of translating this intention into a coherent Community-wide programme.[57] For, leaving aside the unwillingness to cede the national sovereignty and to yield the resources necessary to implement it, the fact that "national historical traditions [had already] created a dense web of welfare institutions covering most citizens", threw up the problem of how and on what basis to

---

53. M. Danson, "The Spatial Impact of the Social Chapter", in Hardy *et al.* (eds), *An Enlarged Europe*, p. 84.
54. Majone, "The European Community", p. 229.
55. B. Hettne, "The Double Movement: Global Market Versus Regionalism", in R. Cox (ed.), *The New Realism: Perspectives on Multilateralism and World Order* (London: Macmillan, 1997), p. 223.
56. Majone, "The European Community", pp. 229, 239.
57. Gold, "Introduction", p. 10.

strive for European uniformity.[58] Harmonization upwards on matters such as wages, social provision and working conditions would create major competitive difficulties for those nations at a lower level of economic development. On the other hand, lowest-common-denominator harmonization was politically unacceptable (and not just for those on the Left) to nations that were more economically developed and enjoyed the benefits of extensive social welfare expenditure. What Ed Balls wrote in a Fabian discussion paper in 1992 has remained largely the case. "For now the necessary degree of social and political cohesion required to run a federal tax and transfer system does not exist."[59] And, given this, only symbolic acts, exhortation and the general enunciation of social-dimension principles were and are left to save the blushes of those democratic socialists with egalitarian or even social welfarist aspirations. It has also been suggested that, in any case, the much-cited principle of subsidiarity has pointed in the direction of national sovereignty rather than EU action as regards the implementation of effective social welfare programmes.[60]

So there would seem to be little grist here for the mill of the multilateral socialists. On the contrary, there was much in the experience of the 1980s and 1990s to substantiate the view of some that the social programmes proposed under the Charter were "not to be introduced for their own worth but for their role in ensuring public acceptance of the expansion of profit through the completion of the single, integrated market across Europe". At best, it could be argued the Social Charter was never intended as more than the basis for "an amelioration to the effects of 1992".[61] At worst, the much-trumpeted social dimension was, as one Irish MEP put it in 1990, "a placebo to placate workers and their representatives and lead them to believe they are not being left behind in the drive towards the single market". Certainly, as regards the relative progress of "liberalization" and "social" agendas in the 1980s and 1990s, the former was fast tracked while the latter languished in a cul-de-sac.[62] "The programme to create a single market has surged ahead on the basis of concrete EC law, whilst the proposals to build a Social Europe have dragged behind and encountered the utmost difficulty in being translated into legislative action."[63] There was little basis for socialist advance here, but rather every indication of a profound asymmetry between the determination to liberalize and the commitment to cope effectively with the socio-economic consequences of that process.[64]

58. Majone, "The European Community", p. 229.
59. E. Balls, *Euro-Monetarism: Why Britain was Ensnared and How it Should Escape it* (London: Fabian Society, 1992).
60. On this see, for example, Ross, "The European Community", pp. 61, 42.
61. Danson, "The Spatial Impact", p. 88.
62. Wise & Gibb, "A Social Charter", p. 262.
63. *Ibid.*, p. 257.
64. For example, as one commentator has pointed out, "the Union's convergence criteria and competition rules do not enjoin countries not to exceed a maximum level of unemployment, or to provide for a minimum level of social protection", W. Streeck, "Public Power, Beyond

Nor did New Labour seek to alter the relative emphasis. On the contrary, it warned against the costs involved in implementing a number of EU Social Chapter provisions.[65] Indeed, since 1997, a consistent New Labour refrain has been its criticism of the costs of the "European-style over-regulation" with which a Social Europe threatens the economic dynamism of European economies.[66] Moreover, while Jospin and the French socialists might call for "l'Europe sociale"[67] and the Swedish social democrats might seek to use the EU to defend their national model of social protection,[68] there was a tendency on the part of a number of social democratic governments in the late 1990s, in addition to that of New Labour, to succumb to a neo-liberalism fundamentally inimical to any meaningful vision of a Social Europe[69] – a function no doubt of the increasing dominance of the Anglo-American model of capitalism within continental Europe. Britain aside, this was particularly the case in Spain and in Germany where "Schroeder advocate[d] flexibility . . . deregulation [and] trimming social costs".[70]

So much for a European, democratic socialist social policy, but what socialist possibilities existed in the sphere of multilateral macroeconomic management? After the exchange rate volatility of the 1970s, attempts were made towards the end of the decade, and into the 1980s, to secure greater stability within the European Community – first, through the European Monetary System and the creation of the Ecu and then by means of the Exchange Rate Mechanism. In effect, this meant the creation of a Deutschmark zone, with the Bundesbank pursuing a monetary policy geared, primarily, to the objective of price stability and with other central banks adjusting domestic policies to maintain the requisite exchange rate against the German currency, something which, on occasion, involved adherence to restrictive, anti-inflationary, unemployment-generating monetary policies.[71] As one commentator put it, "the Bundesbank became the *de facto* European Central Bank"; while, as another wrote, "there seem[ed] to be little doubt amongst central bankers as to who [was] the leader in the European game".[72]

But if the national monetary policies of European nation states were constrained by the EMS and the ERM, and if the creation of a European single

the Nation State: The Case of the European Community", in Boyer & Drache (eds), *States Against Markets*, pp. 309–10.
65. Such as, for example, the establishment of works councils.
66. On this see, for example, Hay, *The Political Economy of New Labour*, pp. 111–12.
67. His 1997 Malmo speech.
68. S. Lightfoot, "Prospects of a Euro-socialism", *Renewal* 7 (1999), p. 11.
69. G. Grunberg, "Socialism and Liberalism", in Cuperus & Kandel (eds), *European Social Democracy*, p. 62.
70. Lightfoot, "Prospects", p. 13.
71. On this see, for example, J. Goodman, *Monetary Sovereignty: The Politics of Central Banking in Western Europe* (Ithaca: Cornell University Press, 1992), pp. 195, 200 and Strange, *The Retreat of the State*, p. 177.
72. Streeck, "Public Power", 307; Tsoukalis, *The New European Economy*, p. 181.

currency was ultimately to make the whole notion of *national* policies decidedly and irrevocably redundant, there remained the question of whether European institutions could be used for the pursuit of a European monetary policy which facilitated or expedited the pursuit of socialist goals. Here, as many writers recognized, a key question was the role to be played by a European Central Bank. Where the Bundesbank had effectively assumed that role, its insulation from *political* pressures ensured that the principles governing the conduct of monetary policy were those that conformed to the pressures exerted by international capital markets. This *de facto* co-ordination of the monetary policies of European states had, therefore, nothing to do with the retrieval of democratic control over economic policy and everything to do with conformity to market forces and the interests of international capital.

As to the potentialities of an actual European Central Bank, democratic socialist writers fantasized (though less so after its formation) about a bank that would operate according to guidelines established by the European Parliament and the Commission and that would report annually to those bodies, with "any serious divergence from what should be moderately expansionary goals . . . necessarily involv[ing] the threat of disciplinary action for the governor".[73] In effect, it was hoped that the bank could be made subject to close democratic control and could therefore be used as an instrument to advance a democratic socialist macroeconomic strategy where this enjoyed majority support within the Parliament and the Commission. But there were a number of problems with this. First, the Maastricht Treaty embodied the blueprint for the creation of an independent central bank strongly resembling the Bundesbank model. Secondly, to secure the kind of political control over a European Central Bank that some democratic socialists envisaged, it was recognized that a European central government would be required in order to exert it. However, while, as noted, Maastricht made provision for the former, "there is no blueprint for the establishment and *modus operandi* of the analogue in Community terms, of a central government".[74] As it was conceived at Maastricht, the Council of the ECB would be responsible for the formulation of monetary policy *independently* of direction from national governments and Community institutions. It was certainly considered that it should act in support of whatever general economic policy, if any, was formulated at Community level but always subject to the overriding objective of price stability. There was little room for macroeconomic manoeuvre here, and little space either for the exercise of democratic control, let alone its effective exercise with socialist intent. And so it has turned out. Indeed, far from opening up politico-economic possibilities for democratic socialists to grasp, one writer has suggested, with respect to the ECB, that "in the

---

73. Coates, "Dimensions of Recovery", p. 34.
74. W. Godley, "A Federal Government?", in Coates & Brown (eds), *A European Recovery Programme*, p. 80.

future European monetary union, issues of macroeconomic management that have been the lifeblood of western politics, determin[ing] the rise and fall of governments and affect[ing] the fate of national economies, [would now] be decided by politically independent experts".[75] And it is interesting to note here that, at a national level, New Labour moved swiftly on taking office in 1997 to put the conduct of monetary policy into the hands of *independent* experts, giving autonomy to the Monetary Policy Committee of the Bank of England when it came to setting interest rates in relation to an inflation target. The principle of the independence of central banks from political pressures was, in this regard, enthusiastically endorsed.

What could also be added, in relation to the Bundesbank experience, is that "*independent* expertise", whether at a national or ECB level, invariably showed itself acutely sensitive to the imperatives emanating from international capital markets and the major players in them.[76] It is these that proved most likely to determine the monetary policy agenda, with "independent experts" responding like marionettes to the strings pulled by international financial capital. In this regard it has become clear, as one commentator anticipated, that "the logic of deflationary adjustment to which the planned European Central Bank will be wedded, along the lines of the Bundesbank, will do [no]thing to unfreeze the geography of uneven development in Europe following EMU".[77]

This leaves the use of Community fiscal policy as a means of achieving the macroeconomic objectives of democratic socialists. Here most were agreed that the Community budget itself was insufficiently large to have any significant effect upon the level of economic activity within the EU.[78] It could not, therefore, "provide the stimulus for Euro-Keynesian policies without coincident fiscal and monetary policies in at least the majority of the member states".[79] As to the Delors plan noted above, this ran into major difficulties after 1993 and New Labour's flirtation with the kind of Euro-Keynesianism it embodied had died a death by the mid-1990s. Thus, as one writer has it, "there was not even of whiff of Euro-Keynesianism" in *New Labour: New Life for Britain*, the party's 1996 draft manifesto. Further, at the EU Summit in Amsterdam in June 1997, Tony Blair was at pains to emphasize that employment creation "would not come from the EU injecting demand into the continent's depressed economies but from *Europe-wide encouragement of labour*

75. G. Majone, "Introduction", in G. Majone (ed.), *Regulating Europe* (London: Routledge, 1996), p. 40. On this see also W. Nicholl, "Maastricht Revisited: A Critical Analysis of the Treaty of European Union", in A. Cafruny & G. Rosenthal (eds), *The State of the European Union*, 2 vols (Boulder: Lynne Rienner Publishers, 1994), vol. 2, pp. 19–34 and Hirst & Thompson, *Globalization in Question*, p. 162.
76. Tsoukalis, *The New European Economy*, p. 182.
77. Leyshon & Thrift, "European Financial Integration", p. 139.
78. Holland, "An Alternative European Strategy", p. 219.
79. Hirst & Thompson, *Globalization in Question*, p. 165.

market flexibility".[80] Debt reduction, he believed, should remain as the top EU priority, rather than the launch of any new spending programmes.[81] Adhering to such notions, he effectively blocked an attempted Euro-Keynesian initiative by Lionel Jospin.[82]

Of course, there remained two other ways in which a European, employment-creating strategy could be pursued other than by centrally directed expenditure. On the one hand, there was the possibility of formulating and implementing complementary fiscal policies to secure common employment objectives. On the other, some writers suggested that, given the existence of a single currency, the opportunity arose for unilateral assaults on rising unemployment that would no longer fall prey to the kind of capital flight which had previously undermined them.

Taking the latter possibility first, it was generally agreed that, given a single currency, individual countries would be unable to conduct fiscal policy in Keynesian, employment-creating fashion without some reaction from other member states. Thus, unless the nation state concerned was small, budget deficits would be likely to have Union-wide effects on the value of the Euro and thence interest rates. So the Union as a whole would have to pay an interest rate risk premium on assets denominated in terms of the European currency. In such circumstances it would be likely that action would be taken to eliminate this "free rider" problem – action that would impinge on the fiscal autonomy of the state concerned. There seems little possibility, therefore, that individual democratic socialist governments would be able to exploit, unilaterally, the putative fiscal policy space furnished by the single currency.[83] As many commentators have argued, far from providing greater autonomy, "a European monetary system must sooner or later mean reasonably uniform fiscal policies, which must sooner or later lead to congruence, if not convergence, in substantive policies financed by public expenditure".[84] And, clearly, in the run-up to the creation of a single European currency, fiscal convergence criteria were applied, with greater or lesser rigour, to aspirant members, the targets to be aimed at being budget deficits of no more than 3% and government debt of no more than 60% of GDP. It is also interesting to note in this context that Ireland was taken to task in February 2001, by the collective of European finance ministers, for what was seen as an inflation-generating economic strategy.

---

80. On this see Anderson & Mann, *Safety First*, p. 97, my emphasis.
81. On this see A. Prakash & J. Hart, "Globalization and Governance: An Introduction", in A. Prakash & J. Hart (eds), *Globalization and Governance* (London: Routledge, 1999), p. 7.
82. Lightfoot, "Prospects", p. 12.
83. On this see, for example, Gros & Thygsen, "The Relationship Between Economic and Monetary Integration", pp. 179–85.
84. D. Marquand & C. Crouch, "Introduction", in D. Marquand & C. Crouch (eds), *The Politics of 1992: Beyond the Single European Market* (Oxford: Blackwell, 1990), p. ix.

As to multilateral Keynesianism, leaving aside the powerful constraints which would, inevitably, be imposed by an independent European Central Bank pathologically focused on the goal of price stability, there were the formidable obstacles in the way of co-ordinating such a strategy if it were to be successfully implemented. Currie, Holtham and Hallett summarized the results of a number of studies on the difficulties and possible benefits of effective policy co-ordination. Such studies suggested that there would be problems involved in securing and maintaining co-ordination agreements; that there would be particular difficulties where co-ordination took place among nations "with differential political leverage – the politically more powerful countries . . . find[ing] it convenient to push other countries to take action that would reduce the pressures on the former to put their houses in order"; that "the gains from full coordination [we]re likely to be small"; and that "it [wa]s not clear how these gains were to be distributed across countries".[85] There was also the question of how much genuine control the makers of co-ordinated policy would have over the instruments of economic policy required to give it effect, and, in addition, there was the whole problem of ceding control over the macroeconomic policy instruments traditionally seen as integral to national sovereignty.[86] Further, any multilateral pursuit of democratic socialist objectives would involve the additional and substantial difficulty of creating and maintaining the necessary ideological unity or commitment required to under-pin and drive the project forward. Barring some unprecedented, concerted, European-wide swing to the Left, the best that could be hoped for here would be partial co-ordination. Yet, even among the ideologically empathetic, there would be likely to be different views as to the desirability of particular policies, based both on genuine disagreements over consequences and the perceived relative importance of different sets of trade-offs.[87] These might not be insuperable obstacles to the formulation of a prescriptive macroeconomics for multilateral socialism, but they would clearly be substantial and there is little evidence that they will be overcome in the foreseeable future or that there is likely to be the political will to do so.

Interwoven with all these difficulties was the problem of agency: just who or what was to do the co-ordinating? And here, once again, there were acute problems for those democratic socialists who wished to use the EU to pursue a concerted socialist economic programme. Specifically, there was the absence of

85. D. Currie, G. Holtham & A. Hallett, "The Theory and Practice of International Policy Co-ordination", in R. Bryant *et al.* (eds), *Macroeconomic Policies in an Interdependent World* (Washington: Brookings Institute, IMF and Center for Economic Policy Research, 1989), p. 48. On the limited nature of the gains see Gros & Thygsen, "The Relationship Between Economic and Monetary Integration", p. 181.
86. Currie *et al.*, "The Theory and Practice", p. 49.
87. More generally on disagreements of this kind see Webb, "International Economic Structures", pp. 320–1.

institutions subject to the kind of democratic pressures and control that might be used to implement policies of a socialist hue. This was something that had been appreciated for some time within the Left. Indeed, as early as the 1960s and 1970s it was an essential tenet of the anti-EEC stance that many then assumed. Those who sought to use European institutions to attain what could no longer be pursued by way of national strategies had, therefore, as a *sine qua non* of what they proposed, to "demand . . . stronger and more representative Community institutions capable of managing economic policy" and to press for "sufficient democratic control and accountability of decision-making at the Community level to provide the basis of co-ordination of economic policy that is essential for the effective pursuit of adequate rates of economic growth and employment creation".[88] There was, therefore, a need for "new agencies, new procedures, more transparency and the extension of democratic accountability", as far as European institutions were concerned.[89] Or, as another commentator put it,

> the democratic deficit concerns the weakness of the power of European representatives as agents of deliberation, legislation and control; the lack of vigilance and grip of national parliaments in European affairs, and the absence of a truly European civil society with European party mobilization and public opinion. So the first priority of social democrats should be the fundamental democratization of Europe.[90]

This was particularly needful for social democratic policies with redistributive intentions that required legitimation at a European level to engender and maintain the political pressure essential for their effective implementation.

But, of course, the "democratic deficit", identified as early as the 1960s and 1970s, has persisted. And there has been no indication that it is likely to be eliminated. The hopes that were invested by some on the Left in the European Parliament have not borne fruit, or at least fruit with any democratic succulence. While directly elected, it lacked, and continues to lack, any real power over the European Council and the European Commission. It has been, and remains, a "talking shop for second-eleven teams of politicians who mostly would much rather have been elected to national parliaments".[91] That this is so seems to have been intuitively appreciated by national electorates – an appreciation that in part must account for the failure of European elections, in most member states, but particularly Britain, to secure more than derisory turnouts. Electorates have seemed to understand that, in a European context, there is a

88. Cripps & Ward, "Employment Creation", pp. 97, 101.
89. Hughes, *The Social Charter*, p. 4.
90. J. de Beus, "Modernized Social Democracy and the Fundamental Democratization of Europe", in Cuperus & Kandel (eds), *European Social Democracy*, p. 221.
91. Strange, *The Retreat of the State*, p. 175.

major disjuncture between the socio-economic programmes of political parties
and the means available to realize them. And a popular awareness of this
disjuncture has itself damaged the possibility of pursuing democratic socialist
economic and social policies at an EU level.

Yet the problem of democratic accountability did not simply stem from the
fact that the European Parliament lacked power over the executive. What was
also absent was a "mandate to use that power in any particular manner".[92] And
this occurred, in large measure, because MEPs were elected not by reference to
European issues, but with reference to policy differences in national arenas.[93]
There was no such thing as a European popular politics. There were no
European political parties, but rather parties that "generally treated European
elections as opportunities to test their own relative popularity in the national
arena". Small wonder, therefore, that, as one writer put it in 1996, "the idea of
a European socialist party is in abeyance".[94] In the absence of parties with a
popular mandate there was a concomitant absence of democratic accountability
and the possibility of democratic control over European affairs and, without
that, there was, and there is, little realistic prospect of a popularly driven
European democratic socialist strategy.

As many writers pointed out, what the EC did, and what the EU continues to
do, was constrain national economic policy-making without adding to the
capacity to undertake economic management at a supranational level. It
liberated market forces without strengthening institutions that might have
subjected them to political control for social ends.[95] Or, as one commentator
saw it, "today the battle on the political economy of European Union is over . . .
Thatcher won and Delors lost and that is very likely irreversible".[96] The EU
was, and is, in the business of unfettering market forces and then responding to
the increasingly powerful imperatives that they have created, not in that of
enhancing public power to pursue concerted, EU socio-economic objectives.
Further, the EU "has over the years, accumulated an institutional legacy – a *de
facto* constitution as embodied in the revised treaties and in international custom
and practice – that effectively precludes such development for the foreseeable
future".[97] Of course, for New Labour, with its adherence to an Anglo-

---

92. C. van der Eijk & M. Franklin, "The Problem: Representation and Democracy in the
European Union", in C. van de Eijk & M. Franklin (eds), *Choosing Europe* (Ann Arbor:
University of Michigan Press, 1996), p. 7.
93. On this see C. van der Eijk, M. Franklin & M. Marsh, "Conclusions: The Electoral
Connection and the Democratic Deficit", in *ibid.*, p. 369.
94. M. B. Brown and K. Coates, *The Blair Revolution: Deliverance for Whom?* (Nottingham:
Spokesman Books, 1996), p. 163.
95. K. Livingstone, "Planning on a European Scale?", in Coates (ed.), *Joint Action*, p. 138.
96. Streeck, "Public Power", p. 302.
97. *Ibid.*; some would also argue, of course, that "no supranational authority has yet been
designed to replace a highly efficient system of national government", Drache, "From Keynes
to K-Mart", p. 55.

American model of capitalism, this has been a cause for celebration rather than regret.

And if there has been no central authority and complementary institutional framework by means of which policies that embodied and articulated the concept of a Social (let alone a socialist) Europe could be effectively pursued, neither has there been anything like a common industrial policy, despite some European initiatives to promote collaboration and co-ordination between European firms in relation to research. The EU did construct a regulatory framework that could be applied to cross-border mergers involving large corporations; such mega-mergers were to be scrutinized with respect, in particular, to the emergence of monopoly power. But it did not have the instruments and powers required to develop "Euro-champions" (even if that had been thought advisable) capable of competing at a global level. Here again, with respect to industrial policy, there was an atrophy of powers at a national level, but no comparable aggregation of authority at a European level to compensate. "National governments become increasingly unable to perform such a [strategic] role, while EC institutions lack[ed] the legitimacy and political power to fill the vacuum."[98] An interventionist industrial policy formulated along AES or other socialist lines was, therefore, like so much else on offer from multilateral European socialists, a subject for speculation rather than active practical politics.[99] As even those who favour a rejuvenation of socialism in a European context admitted, in so far as there was a European industrial policy, "the present aim of the European Commission can be characterised as providing a better organised clientele for the transnationals".[100]

But if the EU could not deliver, what might be achieved by the concerted action of the European trade union movement, in particular in relation to protecting the interests of labour in an economic environment dominated by TNCs? Here again, the experience of the 1980s and 1990s suggested that, for the future, it would be unwise to be sanguine. For example, there were, and continue to be, major divisive factors which have obstructed the emergence of an effective multinational unionism. There was the reluctance of trade union leaders to cede the control they exercised to a supranational organization; there was a long tradition of inward-looking nationalism that distinguished many trade union movements, but particularly that in Britain; there were the ideological differences that characterized national trade union movements and also inhibited greater international unity; there were the diverse legal positions of trade unions in different countries; and there was, and continues to be, the hostility of TNCs to any form of concerted international organization and

---

98. Tsoukalis, *The New European Economy*, p. 104.
99. Similarly with transport and energy policy, see Majone "Introduction", p. 63.
100. Brown & Coates, *The Blair Revolution*, p. 173.

action by trade unions.[101] In addition, for much of the 1980s, and on into the 1990s, the British and other trade union movements were profoundly weakened by high levels of unemployment, declining union membership and, in some instances, an assault upon their legal position. In Britain, the period saw wages drop as a share of GDP, while the level of strike activity in many countries fell to historically low levels. With unions under threat in a national context, these were not propitious times for forging international links and embarking on multinational collective action.[102]

That said, the 1980s and early 1990s did witness an attempt to give institutional substance and practical effect to international unionism. European-wide shop stewards' combines were established to oversee the activity of companies such as Kodak, Ford, Phillips and Lucas.[103] In addition, despite the considerable obstacles to such concerted action, the European Trade Union Council produced its own Social Charter in the late 1980s that secured the support of its 36 member confederations. The Charter included calls for uniform, Europe-wide, collective bargaining, for standard and strictly enforced health and safety minima and for information and participation rights such as those embodied in the Vredling proposals.[104] From a British perspective, it was also the case that, in the late 1980s, the General Council of the TUC abandoned its previous anti-EC stance, gave vigorous support to the social programme advanced by the ETUC and accepted the need "to make the most of the opportunities for advancing trade union policies and defending the working people" that Europe provided.[105]

In the 1980s there also existed multinational company councils that had been established by International Trade Secretariats in the 1960s and 1970s to monitor the activity of major TNCs. These, it was hoped, would evolve and eventually provide an organizational basis for international collective bargaining, thereby curbing the exploitative and coercive behaviour of TNCs with respect to the greater part of their labour force.

However, the ETUC's "Social Charter" did little to advance the cause of Social Europe. Certainly, it did not prevent the Social Chapter of the Maastricht Treaty from assuming an anaemic form that provided little basis for the kind of

---

101. S. Silvia, "The Social Charter of the European Community: A Defeat for European Labour", *Industrial and Labour Relations Review* **44** (1991), p. 627; Brown, *European Union*, p. 23.
102. On the economic fundamentals see Tsoukalis, *The New European Economy*, p. 153 and Silvia, "The Social Charter", p. 630. The decline of union membership occurred in every country except Denmark, *ibid.*, p. 630.
103. For an optimistic account of what might be expected from this activity, given the requisite local authority and national government backing, see Palmer, "A Common Programme", pp. 53–4 and Livingstone, "Planning on a European Scale?", p. 142.
104. Silvia, "The Social Charter", p. 634; on the Vredling proposals and their fate see, for example, Tsoukalis, *The New European Economy*, p. 154.
105. TUC, *Maximising the Benefits, Minimising the Costs: TUC Report on Europe 1992* (London: TUC, 1988), p. 187.

substantial, well-funded social programme which was needed to rectify the marked disparities of income and wealth between and within member countries. Also, multinational shop stewards' combines, while a noble effort to establish some labour leverage upon the activities of TNCs, had a negligible effect upon the treatment of their labour forces and, crucially, the modes and basis of decision-making within these corporations. As for multinational company councils, these, "despite high initial expectations . . . proved disappointing to labor by the 1980s. The councils neither strengthened the hand of individual unions in talks with multinational employers nor served in practice as a first step towards international collective bargaining."[106] Specifically, they were never used to put effective pressure on TNCs through industrial action and were, in consequence, largely ignored by them.[107]

Throughout the 1980s and 1990s, therefore, there were those who looked to the creation of a multinational socialism that would match and ultimately master the increasingly transnational character of global capitalism. Specifically, there were those who saw in the EU the institutional and political vehicle for the realization of such an objective. Yet the obstacles were clearly formidable. Most obviously, there was the absence of a democratically accountable, supranational body that could initiate and implement radical economic and social policies – one mandated by a *European electorate* and therefore enjoying the kind of political authority requisite to elicit the necessary resourcing from national governments and to counter the opposition that such policies would be likely to provoke. In the absence of such an entity economic liberalization was the default position of most EU institutions and was likely to determine the broad trajectory of the EU's evolution. Thus, while considerable progress undoubtedly was made in the 1990s in removing the remaining barriers to the free flow of goods, investment and services, in the creation of a single European currency and in the establishment of a politically independent European Central Bank, no significant advances were made in realizing the vision of a Social Europe embodying the principles of social solidarity and equity. On the contrary, those who held such a vision, such as Jacques Delors, became increasingly marginalized in the EU scheme of things; and those who sought to act upon it, such as Jospin, had their best efforts blocked by devotees of the Anglo-American model.

Moreover, many of those social democratic parties that might have been expected to take the lead in the realization of this vision themselves came to embrace, with greater or lesser fervour, many of the principles of neo-liberalism. In 1998, a sympathetic commentator could interpret "the outstanding victory of Tony Blair's New Labour, the recent upswing of the French

106. Silvia, "The Social Charter", p. 628.
107. *Ibid*.

socialists led by Lionel Jospin, the comeback of the German SPD, the Dutch social-liberal experiment under social-democratic leadership, the resurrection of the Swedish social-democratic government and the Italian Olive coalition" as "impressively refut[ing] the idea of the end of social democracy".[108] But like the female rabbit which, when threatened by a predator, eats her young to "protect" them, so the ideological, economic and political threat posed by neo-liberalism and transnational capitalism would seem to have led many social democrats to devour most of those principles and policies that, for a century, had given social democracy its *raison d'être*.

In an EU context there were, therefore, neither the institutional structures, nor the political organizations, nor the political will, nor the shared, definitively socialist ideology necessary to give international substance to a democratic socialist project that could no longer be realized at the level of the nation state. There was, and is, little possibility of using the EU to set in motion forces that might threaten the hegemony that neo-liberalism has hitherto enjoyed within it. If, as one commentator has it, "European social democracy shall be European or it shall not be", its prospects look bleak indeed.[109]

---

108. P. Kalma & T. Meyer, "Foreword", in Cuperus & Kandel, *European Social Democracy*, p. 7.
109. Kandel & Cuperus, "Introduction", in *ibid.*, p. 23.

Conclusion

Post-war British democratic socialism has tended to define itself in relation to the changing nature of the capitalism in which it has been embedded. In the period from 1945 to the early 1970s that capitalism was of an organized or managed kind. It was a capitalism that had emerged chastened from the trauma of the inter-war period. Bretton Woods, Keynes and Beveridge were all embraced with greater or lesser enthusiasm and market forces constrained, channelled and sometimes abrogated in ways that opened up space for the articulation and pursuit of democratic socialist programmes. In large measure that space was occupied by Keynesian social democracy, with its pursuit of full employment, its commitment to redistribution, its extension of social welfare provision and its adherence to the notion of a mixed economy.

In the 1970s the demise of Bretton Woods, the onset of stagflation, the re-emergence of mass unemployment, the seeming inefficacy of Keynesian instruments of macroeconomic management and the increasingly self-confident iteration of a free market ideology combined to usher in a different kind of capitalism – a disorganized capitalism no longer informed by a belief in the need for the state to pursue an equilibrating and redistributive role if it was to survive. The Anglo-American capitalist model had never been as ethically, structurally, institutionally or culturally constrained as its Nordic, Rhenish or

Japanese variants,[1] but the economic crisis of the 1970s allowed it to cast off most of what had previously restrained it. And that in turn demanded a radical reconfiguration of the political economy of democratic socialism. In this context, an Enlightenment faith in Humanity's rational capacity to manage and control the economic variables that determined its material fate was to yield to a celebration of the *sturm und drang* and Schumpeterian creative destruction of market forces. Keynes gave way to Hayek and Friedman, and Beveridge succumbed to a "culture of contentment" where greed was good, where there was no such thing as society and where, by implication, there was no such thing as social obligations. In such a hostile ideological climate there was also, inevitably, an attenuation of those values and expectations that had inspired and informed the post-war welfare state.

In this context, the AES may be seen as a last desperate attempt to translate Enlightenment optimism into a practical economics of social transformation, one that defined itself dialectically in relation to an ascendant Anglo-American model. The conscious planning and structuring of economic activity was counterposed to the increasingly unfettered nature of market forces. Protection and exchange control would retrieve a measure of autonomy for policy-makers at a national level. The extension of social ownership would address the prescriptive impotence of democratic socialism in the face of the burgeoning power of international corporations. Planning agreements would ensure the embrace of democratically determined social and economic objectives by industrial corporations. Greater industrial democracy would effect an extension of enterprise goals beyond the monopolistic/oligopolistic pursuit of profit maximization. An acquisitive, amoral society driven by a possessive consumerist individualism would be infused with a spirit of mutuality and conscious social purpose. In short, the Enlightenment faith in the rational ordering of the material world, en route to the perfectibility of human society, would be made to triumph over the self-seeking fatalism inherent in the Anglo-American model. In Britain, such hubris was shortlived, with nemesis following the onset of the Thatcherite dispensation.

If the AES represented British democratic socialism's last dialectical riposte to the increasing dominance of the Anglo-American model, post-Fordist socialism sought to negotiate and reconfigure, for socialist purposes, the powerful economic and ideological currents which that model had set in motion, articulating the individualism and consumerism of the age in ways which connected with the New Left libertarianism of earlier decades. Consumerism was translated into a language of empowerment and social transformation. This

---

1. For a discussion of the Nordic variant, see G. Esping-Andersen, *The Three Worlds of Welfare Capitalism* (Cambridge: Polity, 1990) and E. Lindberg, "The Rise and Fall of the Swedish Model", *Journal of Economic Literature* **23** (1985), pp. 1–36.

was empowerment through the extension of the rights and privileges of the consumer into the public sphere, with bureaucratic, paternalistic and authoritarian provision being replaced by an iterative interaction between provider and beneficiary that democratized decision-making and delivery, and social transformation through the discriminating consumer's generation of employment opportunities for polyvalent labour in creative, high-value-added areas of productive activity, where the distinction between conception and execution was blurred; productive activity that also demanded participative, decision-making structures to accommodate the increasingly volatile and evanescent nature of demand. So, while Thatcherism celebrated the consumer as a rational, utility-maximizing guarantor of allocative efficiency, post-Fordist socialism embraced him/her as the source of imperatives that would encompass a democratization and transformation of both the public and private spheres. Both used the language of freedom. With Thatcherism, it had the negative inflections of the absence of external or public constraints; with post-Fordist socialism, it had the positive libertarian connotations of democratized decision-making and non-alienated labour.

Yet, as we have seen, the Mephistopheles of consumerism demanded nothing less than the soul of socialism. The consumer wanted cheapness as well as quality. The consumer discriminated, but all too often with exploitative consequences. The age of Fordism, and all that post-Fordists believed it entailed, was not dead. Production processes did not, or only rarely, or only for a few, assume Morrisian characteristics. The consumer might wish for the useful and the beautiful, but the consumer also wanted them at the lowest possible price and if that sometimes entailed the use of polyvalent creative labour it as often made for an unrelenting helotism. Ethical was but rarely reconciled with utility-maximizing consumption. And, as the empowered consumer of fuel has recently shown, where the two were at odds, the maximization of consumer utility usually prevailed: cheapness being preferred to environmentalism, and price competitiveness to fulfilling and creative labour. Far from being a source of democratizing and ethical imperatives, the consumer continued to behave in ways that were coercive, exploitative and destructive.

Post-Fordist socialism anticipated the late-twentieth-century emergence of an economic ambience favourable to firms that could accommodate demands that were becoming more volatile and particular; firms that could display a sensitivity and responsiveness to market forces; firms distinguished by workforce involvement in enterprise decision-making and thence commitment to the enterprise strategy which emerged from this process. These were qualities particularly associated with producer co-operatives and, indeed, post-Fordist socialists envisaged their proliferation in the context of contemporary capitalism. The proponents and theoreticians of producer co-operatives certainly believed they had the capacity to compete and thrive, even in an increasingly predatory economic world. If socialism increasingly lacked a macroeconomics, it was nonetheless seen by these writers as possessing, in the form of producer co-operatives, a microeconomic ideal that, in the context of Anglo-American capitalism, could prove itself more Catholic than the Pope. Producer co-operatives would be more committed to competitive success, because that success would be in the interests of all; more focused on what was needed to achieve it, because they would be less constrained by hierarchy and have a workforce motivated by the embrace of co-operative ideals; more responsive to rapidly changing consumer demand, because of the effective communication and flexibility that flatter hierarchies would allow. Producer co-operatives could therefore be expected to leave their capitalist rivals floundering in their competitive wake. Thus social transformation when it came would be a transformation from within, the culmination of a process, a long process, of competitive osmosis.

In many respects, the socialist political economy of producer co-operatives can be seen as going with the flow of Anglo-American capitalism. Like post-Fordist socialism (of which it sometimes formed a part), it was adaptive rather than combative. In so far as it challenged capitalism its challenge was that of example. It offered the new moral world in microcosm, and though engaged in the sordid business of capitalist commerce its adherents were seen as remaining untainted by possessive individualism. They would pursue profit, but over them the self-interested pursuit of gain would have no dominion. In so far as they engaged antagonistically with capitalism, they would do so in the market place. They did not seek the expropriation of the expropriators, but their bankruptcy.

The dangers of such a stance have been made plain. The process of osmosis can, and has, worked both ways. Co-operative values and ideals can be corrupted by the pursuit of profit; survival and success have required them to be both compromised and abandoned; self-interest cannot easily be left at the producer co-operative's gate. Where an economic ambience more favourable to their survival can be created, when they can be furnished with the requisite institutional and political support and where they achieve a critical mass, this process of demoralization may be arrested or obviated. But such has not been the case in Britain and, given the dominance and ethos of the Anglo-American capitalist model, there is no reason to believe that such preconditions for success and survival will emerge in the foreseeable future. Producer co-operatives may indeed continue to exist in the interstices of contemporary capitalism, but their political economy can no longer be seen as pregnant with transformative socialist possibilities or intent.

As to the political economy of market socialism, little need be said. If co-operators aimed to implant socialist microcosms into a world not of their own making, market socialists were involved in an imaginative, mathematical (and, indeed, mathematically imaginative) construction of that world to accommodate producer co-operatives and other forms of democratized socialist enterprise. Where the political economy of producer co-operatives aimed to engage with the Anglo-American model by embracing its competitive logic (while rejecting the moral philosophy of its atomistic individualism), market socialism wished it away to offer a truly competitive market mechanism sanitized and of use for socialist purposes. Where the microeconomic socialism of producer co-operatives confronted the brutal realities of the hostile and ruthlessly competitive economic world of Anglo-American capitalism, the macroeconomics of market socialism turned its back on the phenomenon, constructing idealized institutional frameworks and economic game rules that ensured that competition and constrained maximization would deliver economic efficiency and distributive justice. Seldom since the Battle of Copenhagen has the blind eye been deployed with such bravura. And though, for a time, before and after 1989, it looked as if history, or at least Central and Eastern European history, might be on the market socialists' side, the determined enthusiasm for the market evinced by erstwhile communist countries was to render this particular historical moment shortlived.

Throughout the 1980s and early 1990s Keynesian social democrats continued to try to show how the genie of Anglo-American capitalism could be confined within the structures that had contained it prior to the early 1970s. Such attempts were articulated in both unilateral and multilateral terms; although the former with diminishing conviction as the experience of France and then the Scandinavian economies, the manifest growth of international economic interdependence, the proliferation and expansion of TNCs and the increasing importance of the EU were seen to compromise the policy-making autonomy of national governments. Full employment, greater distributive equity, enhanced social welfare provision and the constant upgrading of social infrastructure remained primary policy objectives for social democrats but, in the 1980s and 1990s, many came to accept that their effective pursuit required concerted international action. The global nature and ambitions of Anglo-American capitalism had to be matched by a comparably global apparatus of institutions and constraints if social democracy was to have a future. For many, the EU was the favoured framework. But aspiration and reality rarely connected. The EU was built with different purposes in mind. It was infused with a different ethos. It was constructed to accommodate and celebrate multinational capitalism, rather than to direct it to purposes that were no part of its original intent. Nor was there the political basis, institutions or political will necessary for its transformation into a vehicle for the pursuit of democratic socialist objectives.

It is in the context of this theoretical exhaustion of the political economy of democratic socialism that the idea of stakeholderism took root. In its Huttonian rendition, its aim was to reopen the possibility of social democratic advance by changing the nature of the capitalism that British social democracy confronted. That such possibilities were there, even in the context of a globalized capitalism, the Rhenish and Nordic models made apparent. They might be circumscribed but they existed. They existed in relation to the nature and kinds of enterprise decision-making that such models of capitalism encouraged; in the scope they gave for long-term economic and social planning; in the widening of enterprise goals which they demanded of corporate decision-makers; in the concept of social and corporate solidarity which they fostered; in the co-operative, non-predatory, often solidaristic nature of their conception of how competitive success was to be achieved. These were capitalisms with which democratic socialism could do business. They provided prescriptive possibilities that social democracy could exploit and they recognized the worth (if sometimes only the economic worth) of many of the values that democratic socialists embraced.

The political economy of radical stakeholderism represented British social democracy's last serious fling of the ideological dice. It offered a supply-side transformation of the British economy, a profound alteration of the relationship between finance and industry, but, above all, from a social democratic perspective, it proposed a radical reconfiguration of power relations in the British economy and polity. In short, it eschewed the Anglo-American model in favour of the construction of a capitalism that would allow the possibility of social democratic progress. The things that were Caesar's had to be rendered unto Caesar, but many of the values and objectives of post-war social democracy could be retained, even if expressed in a different, supply-side patois and given prescriptive expression within a radically altered institutional framework.

Radical stakeholderism was predicated on many things. Specifically, it assumed the existence of rivals to the Anglo-American capitalist model from which it could derive inspiration and which would exemplify the success of its conception of a "development" as against a "competition" state. These other models illustrated the economic as well as the moral virtues of constraining capitalism and making the market a servant not the master. But the Rhenish, Nordic and Japanese models have suffered setbacks. German and Japanese industrial capitalism have not proved as successful in the 1990s as they did for most of the rest of the post-war period. The difficulties experienced by the Nordic model in the late 1980s and early 1990s have raised doubts as to whether, given the greater internationalization of Scandinavian economies,[2] the percentage of GDP they had previously committed to social welfare expenditure

---

2. On this see, for example, A. Gould, "The End of the Middle Way? The Swedish Welfare State in Crisis", in C. Jones (ed.), *New Perspectives on the Welfare State in Europe* (London: Routledge, 1993), R. Meidner, "Why Did the Swedish Model Fail", in *Socialist Register, 1993* (London: Merlin, 1993), pp. 211–28 and Pontusson, *The Limits of Social Democracy*.

could be restored and maintained. And, in terms of economic performance, the Anglo-American model is now obviously in the ascendant, and that economic ascendancy has undermined a crucial part of the case for the expedients suggested by the proponents of radical stakeholderism. If in the post-war period British democratic socialism has indeed defined itself in relation to contemporary capitalism, the capitalism it now confronts, or in the case of New Labour seeks to accommodate, leaves little theoretical or prescriptive room for socialist advance or manoeuvre.

As importantly, radical stakeholderism was predicated upon the existence of a social democratic party that might be expected to subscribe to its agenda. Such a party may have existed when its proponents first took to the lists but, by the late 1990s, the Labour Party could no longer realistically be viewed as a potential agent of change. That party might seek to reconcile justice and efficiency, but justice was viewed increasingly in terms of the rewards that a competitive labour market bestowed and efficiency was seen as a function of a more flexible labour force rather than systemic or structural change. Rhenish and Japanese models have been overtly eschewed by New Labour and their erstwhile adherents vigorously lectured on the dangers of "Eurosclerosis" and the virtues of increasingly untrammelled and competitive markets. Given this trend, it is all too clear that radical stakeholders must look elsewhere for a political vehicle for their ideas and the implementation of their strategy. And, at the present juncture, no such a vehicle is apparent.

In the last three decades, the Left in Britain has formulated and reformulated political economies with an intellectual energy matched only by the speed with which history has rendered them defunct. The AES, Keynesian social democracy in its national and multilateral variants, new municipal socialism, decentralized producer co-operative socialism, market socialism, post-Fordist socialism and radical stakeholderism have all had their historical moments in the sun. But capitalism in Britain has assumed a form with which it has become increasingly difficult for democratic socialism to engage. The apotheosis of the Anglo-American model has produced a barren soil in which the seeds of democratic socialism cannot take root and it has, in effect, foreclosed on the socialist project. Despite the disparate and desperate attempts to infuse the Third Way with social democratic content, it now seems clear that the Left, in Britain, has entered an ideological wilderness from which there seems little prospect of return.[3]

---

3. For the views of those who see the centre-left as having a future if not always a political economy see N. Lawson & N. Sherlock (eds), *The Progressive Century: The Future of the Centre-Left in Britain* (London: Macmillan, 2001).

Bibliography

Aaronovitch, S. 1981. *The Road from Thatcherism: The Alternative Economic Strategy.* London: Lawrence & Wishart.

Aaronovitch, S. 1986. "The Alternative Economic Strategy: Goodbye to All That?" *Marxism Today,* February.

Abell, P. 1983. "The Viability of Industrial Producer Co-operatives", in *Organizational Democracy and Political Processes,* C. Crouch (ed.). New York: Wiley.

Abell, P. 1989. "An Equitarian Market Socialism", in *Market Socialism,* J. Le Grand & S. Estrin (eds). Oxford: Clarendon.

Abernathy, W., K. Clark, A. Kantrow 1983. *Industrial Renaissance: Producing a Competitive Edge for America.* New York: Basic Books.

Abrams, M. & C. Rose 1960. *Must Labour Lose?* Harmondsworth: Penguin.

Albert, M. 1993. *Capitalism Against Capitalism.* London: Whurr.

Albo, G. 1994. "Competitive Austerity and the Impasse of Capitalist Employment Policy", *Socialist Register, 1994.* London: Merlin.

Alchian, A. & H. Demsetz 1972. "Production Information Costs and Economic Organization", *American Economic Review* **62**, 77–95.

Anderson, P. & N. Mann 1997. *Safety First: The Making of New Labour.* London: Granta.

Aoki, M. 1986. "The Motivational Role of an External Agent in the Informationally-Participative Firm", in *Democracy and Capitalism: Property, Community and the Contradictions of Modern Social Thought,* S. Bowles & H. Gintis (eds). New York: Basic Books.

Arestis, P. & M. Sawyer 1999. "What Role for the Tobin Tax in World Economic Governance", in *Global Instability: The Political Economy of World Economic Governance,* J. Michie & J. Grieve Smith (eds). London: Routledge.

Arrow, K. 1974. *The Limits of Organization.* New York: Norton.

Artis, M. & D. Cobham (eds) 1991. *Labour's Economic Policies, 1974–79.* Manchester: Manchester University Press.

Atkinson, C. 1980. "Introduction", in *The Economics of Prosperity: Social Priorities in the Eighties,* D. Blake & P. Ormerod (eds). London: Grant & Macintyre.

289

Atkinson, J. & D. Gregory 1986. "A Flexible Future: Britain's Dual Labour Force", *Marxism Today*, April, 12–17.

Bailey, D. & J. Clancy 1997. "Stakeholder Capitalism via Venture Socialism", *Renewal* **5**, 49–60.

Baker, D., G. Epstein, R. Pollin 1998. "Introduction", in *Globalization and Progressive Economic Policy*, D. Baker, G. Epstein & R. Pollin (eds). Cambridge: Cambridge University Press.

Balls, E. 1992. *Euro-Monetarism: Why Britain was Ensnared and How it Should Escape it*. London: Fabian Society.

Bardhan, P. & J. Roemer 1992. "Market Socialism: A Case for Rejuvenation", *Journal of Economic Perspectives* **6**, 101–16.

Barkai, H. 1977. *Growth Patterns of the Kibbutz Economy*. New York: North-Holland.

Barnett, R. & V. Barooah 1995. "The Additionality (or Otherwise) of European Community Structural Funds", in *An Enlarged Europe: Regions in Competition?*, S. Hardy *et al.* (eds). London: Kingsley.

Bassett, K. 1984. "Labour, Socialism and Local Democracy", in *Local Socialism? Labour Councils and New Left Alternatives*, M. Boddy & C. Fudge (eds). London: Macmillan.

Batkin, A. 1987. "The Impact of Local Authorities on Labour Party Economic Policy", *Local Economy* **2**, 14–24.

Batstone, E. 1982. "France", in *The Performance of Labour-Managed Firms*, F. Stephen (ed.). London: Macmillan.

Batstone, E. 1983. "Organization and Orientation: A Life-Cycle Model of French Co-operatives", *Economic and Industrial Democracy* **4**, 139–61.

Beckerman, W. 1983. "A New Realism", *New Statesman*, 2 December.

Benington, J. 1986. "Local Economic Strategies: Paradigms for a Planned Economy", *Local Economy* **1**, 7–25.

Benn, T. 1980. "Granada Guildhall Lecture", *New Statesman*, 16 May.

Benn, T. 1981. *Arguments for Democracy*. Harmondsworth: Penguin.

Benn, T. 1983. "Trade Unionism in the Eighties", in *Fighting Back: Speaking for Socialism in the Eighties*, T. Benn (1988). London, Hutchinson.

Benn, T. 1983. "The Unemployment Tragedy", in *Fighting Back: Speaking for Socialism in the Eighties*, T. Benn (1988). London, Hutchinson.

Benn, T., F. Cripps, F. Morrell 1975. *A Ten Year Industrial Strategy for Britain*. Nottingham: IWC.

Ben-ner, A. 1984. "On the Stability of the Co-operative Form of Organization", *Journal of Comparative Economics* **8**, 247–60.

Ben-ner, A. 1987. "Producer Co-operatives: Why do they Exist in Capitalist Economies?", in *The Nonprofit Sector: A Research Handbook*, W. Powell (ed.). New Haven: Yale University Press.

Ben-ner, A. 1988. "Comparative Empirical Observations on Worker-Owned and Capitalist Firms", *International Journal of Industrial Organization* **6**, 1–31.

Berger, S. 1996. "Introduction", in *National Diversity and Global Capitalism*, S. Berger & R. Dore (eds). Ithaca: Cornell University Press.

Bergson, A. 1967. "Market Socialism Revisited", *Journal of Political Economy* **75**, 655–73.

Berman, M. 1977. "Short-Run Efficiency in the Labour-Managed Firm", *Journal of Comparative Economics* **1**, 309–14.

Best, M. 1986. "Strategic Planning and Industrial Policy", *Local Economy* **1**, 65–77.

Best, M. 1989. "Sector Strategies and Industrial Policy: The Furniture Industry and the Greater London Enterprise Board", in *Reversing Industrial Decline? Industrial Structure in Britain and Her Competitors*, P. Hirst & J. Zeitlin (eds). Oxford: Berg.

Betcherman, G. 1996. "Globalization and Labour Markets", in *States Against Markets: The Limits of Globalization*, R. Boyer & D. Drache (eds). London: Routledge.

Beuret, K. & D. Coole 1986. "Rethinking the Present", in *Market Socialism: Whose Choice?*, Fabian Tract 516, I. Forbes (ed.). London: Fabian Society.

de Beus, J., 1998. "Modernized Social Democracy and the Fundamental Democratization of Europe", in *European Social Democracy: Transformation in Progress*, R. Cuperus & J. Kandel (eds). Amsterdam: Wiardi Beckman Stichtig.

Beynon, H. & H. Wainwright 1979. *The Workers' Report on Vickers*. London: Pluto.

Bienefeld, M. 1996. "Is a Strong National Economy a Utopian Goal at the End of the Twentieth Century?", in *States Against Markets: The Limits of Globalization*, R. Boyer & D. Drache (eds). London: Routledge.

Blair, T. 1995. "Power for a Purpose", *Renewal* **3**, 11–16.

Blair, T. 1996. *New Britain: My Vision of a Young Country*. London: Fourth Estate.

Blair, T. 1996. "Switch on the Bright Ideas", *Guardian*, 27 May.

Blair, T. 1996. "My Vision for Britain", in *What Needs to Change: New Visions for Britain*, G. Radice (ed.). London: HarperCollins.

Blair, T. 1998. *The Third Way: A New Politics for the New Century*, Fabian Pamphlet 558. London: Fabian Society.

Blake, D. & P. Ormerod (eds) 1980. *The Economics of Prosperity: Social Priorities in the Eighties*. London: Grant & Macintyre.

Blazyca, G. 1983. *Planning is Good for You: The Case for Popular Control*. London: Pluto.

Blumberg, P. 1968. *Industrial Democracy: The Sociology of Participation*. New York: Schocken.

Blunkett, D. & K. Jackson 1987. *Democracy in Crisis: The Town Halls Respond*. London: Hogarth.

Boddy, M. 1984. "Local Economic Strategies", in *Local Socialism? Labour Councils and New Left Alternatives*, M. Boddy & C. Fudge (eds). London: Macmillan.

Boddy, M. & C. Fudge 1984. "Local Socialism? Labour Councils and New Left Alternatives", in *Local Socialism? Labour Councils and New Left Alternatives*, M. Boddy & C. Fudge (eds). London: Macmillan.

Bonin, J. and L. Putterman 1987. *The Economics of Cooperation and the Labor-Managed Economy*. London: Academic Press.

Bowles, S. and H. Gintis 1992. "A Political and Economic Case for the Democratic Firm", in *The Idea of Democracy*, D. Copp, J. Hampton & J. Roemer (eds). Cambridge: Cambridge University Press.

Bowles, S., H. Gintis, B. Gustaffson 1993. "Introduction", in *Markets and Democracy: Participation, Accountability and Efficiency*, S. Bowles, H. Gintis & B. Gustaffson (eds). Cambridge: Cambridge University Press.

Bradley, K. 1980. "A Comparative Analysis of Producer Co-operatives: Some Theoretical and Empirical Implications", *British Journal of Industrial Relations* **18**, 155–68.

Breitenbach, H. & D. Coates 1990. *Features of a Viable Socialism*. Hemel Hempstead: Wheatsheaf.

Britton, A. 1991. *Macroeconomic Policy in Britain, 1974–87*. Cambridge: Cambridge University Press.

Brown, G. 1994. *Fair is Efficient: A Socialist Agenda for Fairness*, Fabian Pamphlet 563. London: Fabian Society.

Brown, G. 1994. "The Politics of Potential: A New Agenda for Labour", in *Reinventing the Left*, D. Miliband (ed.). Cambridge: Polity.

Brown, G. 1999. "Enterprise and Fairness", in *Is New Labour Working?*, G. Kelly (ed.). London: Fabian Society.

Brown, M. B. 1972. *From Labourism to Socialism: A Political Economy for Labour in the 1970s*. Nottingham: Spokesman Books.

Brown, M. B. 1985. "Can European Workers Cope with Transnational Capital?", in *Joint Action for Jobs: A New Internationalism*, K. Coates (ed.). Nottingham: Spokesman Books.

Brown, M. B. 1991. *European Union: Fortress or Democracy?* Nottingham, Spokesman Books.

Brown, M. B. & K. Coates 1996. *The Blair Revolution: Deliverance for Whom?* Nottingham: Spokesman Books.

Brus, W. 1985. "Socialism – Feasible or Viable?", *New Left Review* **153**, 43–62.

Brus, W. & K. Laski 1989. *From Marx to the Market: Socialism in Search of an Economic System*. Oxford: Oxford University Press.

Brusco, S. 1982. "The Emilian Model: Productive Decentralisation and Social Integration", *Cambridge Journal of Economics* **6**, 167–84.

Brusco, S. & E. Righi 1989. "Industrial Policy and Social Consensus: The Case of Modena", *Economy and Society* **18**, 405–24.

Callaghan, J. 1997. "Stakeholding and the Scottish Parliament", *Renewal* **5**, 59–65.

Campaign for Labour Party Democracy 1986. *The Case for Public Ownership*. London: CLPD.

Campbell, M. 1987. "The Economics of Local Jobs Plans", *Local Economy* **2**, 167–84.

Carens, J. 1981. *Equality, Moral Incentives and the Market: An Essay in Utopian Politico-Economic Theory*. Chicago: University of Chicago Press.

Carrington, J. & Edwards, G. 1979. *Financial Industrial Investment*. London: Macmillan.

Caulkin, S. 2000. "Third Way Loses its Bearings", *Observer*, 6 February.

Cavestro, W. 1989. "Automation, New Technology and Work Content", in *The Transformation of Work*, S. Wood (ed.). London: Unwin Hyman.

Centre for Local Economic Strategies 1987. *Economic Sense: Local Jobs Plans, a National Perspective*. London: CLES.

Cerny, P. 1995. "Globalization and the Changing Logic of Collective Action", *International Organization* **49**, 595–625.

Chandler, J. & P. Lawless 1985. *Local Authorities and the Creation of Employment*. Aldershot: Gower.

Chang, H. 1998. "Globalization, Transnational Corporations and Economic Development", in *Globalization and Progressive Economic Policy*, D. Baker, G. Epstein & R. Pollin (eds). Cambridge: Cambridge University Press.

Child, J. 1984. "New Technology and Developments in Managerial Organisation", *Omega* **12**, 211–23.

Clarke, A. & A. Cochrane 1987. "Investing in the Private Sector: The Enterprise Board Experience", in *Developing Local Economic Strategies: Some Issues and Ideas*, A. Cochrane (ed.). Milton Keynes: Open University Press.

Clarke, S. 1990. "New Utopias for Old: Fordist Dreams and Post-Fordist Fantasies", *Capital and Class* **42**, 131–53.

Clarke, T. 1977. "Industrial Democracy: The Institutionalised Suppression of Industrial Conflict", in *Trade Unions Under Capitalism*, T. Clarke & L. Clements (eds). London: Fontana.

Clayre, A. (ed.) 1980. *The Political Economy of Co-operation and Participation*. Oxford: Oxford University Press.

Coakley, J. & L. Harris 1992. "Financial Globalisation and Deregulation", in *The Economic Legacy, 1979–1992*, J. Michie (ed.). London: Academic Press.

Coates, D. 1981. "Labourism and the Transition to Socialism", *New Left Review* **129**, 3–22.

Coates, D. 1989. *The Crisis of Labour*. London: Allan.

Coates, D. & D. Johnston (eds) 1983. *Socialist Strategies*. Oxford: Martin Robertson.

Coates, K. (ed.) 1976. *The New Worker Co-operatives*. Nottingham: Spokesman Books.

Coates, K. 1985. "Time for a New Internationalism?", in *Joint Action for Jobs: A New Internationalism*, K. Coates (ed.). Nottingham: Spokesman Books.

Coates, K. 1993. "The Dimensions of Recovery", in *A European Recovery Programme*, K. Coates & M. B. Brown (eds). Nottingham: Spokesman Books.

Coates, K. 1993. "The Spectre of Unemployment", in *A European Recovery Programme*, K. Coates & M. B. Brown (eds). Nottingham: Spokesman Books.

Coates, K. & T. Topham 1972. *The New Unionism: The Case for Workers' Control*. London: Owen.

Cochrane, A. 1983. "Local Economic Policies: Trying to Drain the Ocean with a Teaspoon", in *Redundant Space in Cities and Regions*, J. Anderson *et al*. London: Academic Press.

Cochrane, A. 1986. "What's in a Strategy? The London Industrial Strategy and Municipal Socialism", *Capital and Class* **28**, 187–93.

Cochrane, A. 1987. "The Future of Local Economic Strategies", in *Developing Local Economic Strategies*, A. Cochrane (ed.). Milton Keynes: Open University Press.

Cochrane, A. 1988. "In and Against the Market: the Development of Socialist Economic Strategies in Britain", *Policy and Politics* **16**, 159–68.

Cole, G. D. H. 1950. *Socialist Economics*. London: Gollancz.

Comisso, E. 1980. *Yugoslav Worker Self-Management Under Plan and Market*. New Haven: Yale University Press.

Commission on Social Justice 1994. *Social Justice: Strategies for a National Renewal*. London: Vintage.

Conference of Socialist Economists 1979. *Struggle Over the State*, State Group. London: CSE Books.

Conference of Socialist Economists 1980. *The Alternative Economic Strategy: A Labour Movement Response to the Economic Crisis*, London Working Group. London: CSE Books.

Conte, M. 1982. "Participation and Performance in US Labor-Managed Firms", in *Participatory and Self-Managed Firms*, D. Jones & J. Svejnar (eds). Lexington: Lexington Books.

Cooley, M. & H. Wainwright 1979. *The Workers' Report on Vickers*. London: Pluto.

Cooley, M. & H. Wainwright 1981. "The Lucas Plan: Its Lessons for Labour", *New Socialist* **2**, 13–16.

Coote, A. 1981. "The Alternative Economic Strategy: A New Starting Point", *New Socialist* **2**, Nov./Dec., 4–7.

Cornforth, C. 1983. "Some Factors Affecting the Success or Failure of Worker Co-operatives: A Review of Empirical Research in the United Kingdom", *Economic and Industrial Democracy* **4**, 163–90.

Cornforth, C. *et al.* 1988. *Developing Successful Workers' Co-operatives*. London: Sage.

Corrigan, P. 1979. "The Local State: The Struggle for Democracy", *Marxism Today*, July.

Corrigan, P. 1979. "Popular Consciousness and Social Democracy", *Marxism Today*, December.

Costello, N., J. Michie, S. Milne 1990. *Beyond the Casino Economy*. London: Verso.

Coventry Trades Council/Lucas Aerospace Shop Stewards Combine Committee 1981. *Popular Planning for Social Need*.

Cowe, R. 2000. "Stakeholder Rights", *Guardian*, 9 March.

Cowling, K. 1990. "The Strategic Approach to Economic and Industrial Policy", in *A New Economic Policy for Britain*, K. Cowling & R. Sugden (eds). Manchester: Manchester University Press.

Cowling, K. & M. Sawyer 1990 "Merger and Monopoly Policy", in *A New Economic Policy for Britain*, K. Cowling & R. Sugden (eds). Manchester: Manchester University Press.

Crewe, I. 1982. "The Labour Party and the Electorate", in *The Politics of the Labour Party*, P. Kavanagh (ed.). London: Allen & Unwin.

Cripps, F. 1981. "The British Crisis – Can the Left Win?", *New Left Review* **128**, 93–7.

Cripps, F. & W. Godley 1978. "Control of Imports as a Means of Full Employment and the Expansion of World Trade: The UK Case", *Cambridge Journal of Economics* **2**, 327–34.

Cripps, F. & F. Morrell 1979. "The Abandonment of Full Employment", in *What Went Wrong? Explaining the Fall of the Labour Government*, K. Coates (ed.). Nottingham: Spokesman Books.

Cripps, F. & T. Ward 1985. "Employment Creation", in *The Regulation of International Banking*, K. Coates & M. B. Brown (eds). Cambridge: Woodhead/Faulkner.

Cripps, F. *et al.* 1981. *Manifesto: A Radical Strategy for Britain's Future*. London: Pan.

Crosland, C. A. R. 1956. *The Future of Socialism*. London: Jonathan Cape.

Crossman, R. 1960. *Labour in an Affluent Society*, Fabian Tract 325. London: Fabian Society.

Crouch, C. 1990. "United Kingdom: The Rejection of Compromise", in *European Industrial Relations: The Challenge of Flexibility*, C. Crouch & G. Baglioni (eds). London: Sage.

Crouch, C. & D. Marquand (eds) 1995. *Reinventing Collective Action: From the Global to the Local*. Oxford: Blackwell.

Cumming-Bruce, N. & M. White 1996. "Blair Unveils Economic 'Big Idea'", *Guardian*, 8 January.

Cuperus, R. & J. Kandel 1998. "Introduction", in *European Social Democracy: Transformation in Progress*, R. Cuperus & J. Kandel (eds). Amsterdam: Wiardi Beckman Stichtig.

Currie, D., G. Holtham, A. Hallett 1989. "The Theory and Practice of International Monetary Co-ordination", in *Macroeconomic Policies in an Interdependent World*, R. Bryant *et al.* (eds). Washington: Brookings Institution, IMF and Center for Economic Policy Research.

Danson, M. 1995. "The Spatial Impact of the Social Chapter", in *An Enlarged Europe: Regions in Competition?*, S. Hardy *et al.* (eds). London: Kingsley.

Davies, G. 1996. "Tony Blair puts Meat on the Stakeholder Bones", *Independent*, 15 January.

Davies, J. 1988. "From Municipal Socialism to . . . Municipal Socialism", *Local Government Studies* **14**, 19–22.

Deakin, S. 1992. "Labour Law and Industrial Relations", in *The Economic Legacy, 1979–1992*, J. Michie (ed.). London: Academic Press.

Defourney, J., S. Estrin, D. Jones 1985. "The Effects of Worker Participation on Enterprise Performance: Empirical Evidence from French Co-operatives", *International Journal of Industrial Organization* **3**, 197–217.

Delors, J. 1989. "A New Frontier for Social Democracy", in *Europe Without Frontiers: Socialists on the Future of the European Community*, P. Dankert & A. Koopman (eds). London: Cassell.

Delors, J. 1993. "The Scope and Limits of Community Action", in *A European Recovery Programme*, K. Coates & M. B. Brown (eds). Nottingham: Spokesman Books.

Desai, M. 1981. *Testing Monetarism*. London: Pinter.

Devine, P. 1980. "The Labour Party – Why Decline?" *Marxism Today*, January.

Dickson, T. 2000. "A Model of Co-operation", *Financial Times*, 13 April.

Dixon, K. & D. Perraud 1985. "Le Fin: France Abandons Socialism", *Marxism Today*, January.

Domar, E. 1966. "The Soviet Collective Farm as a Producer Co-operative", *American Economic Review* **56**, 734–58.

Dorey, P. 1997. "The Blairite Betrayal: New Labour and the Trade Unions", in *Labour's Renewal: The Policy Review and Beyond*, G. Taylor (ed.). London: Macmillan.

Dow, G. 1993. "Democracy Versus Appropriability: Can Labour-Managed Firms Flourish in a Capitalist World?", in *Markets and Democracy: Participation, Accountability and Efficiency*, S. Bowles, H. Gintis & B. Gustaffson (eds). Cambridge: Cambridge University Press.

Doyle, P. 1996. "From the Top", *Guardian*, 19 October.

Drache, D. 1996. "From Keynes to K-mart: Competitiveness in a Corporate Age", in *States Against Markets: The Limits of Globalization*, R. Boyer & D. Drache (eds). London: Routledge.

Driver, S. & L. Martell 1998. *New Labour: Politics After Thatcherism*. Cambridge: Polity.

Dunning, J. 1993. *The Globalization of Business: The Challenge of the 1990s*. London: Routledge.

Earle, J. 1986. *The Italian Co-operative Movement: A Portrait of Lega natzionale delle co-operative e mutue*. London: Allen & Unwin.

Eaton, J., M. B. Brown, K. Coates 1975. *An Alternative Economic Strategy for the Labour Movement*. Nottingham: Spokesman Books.

Eatwell, J. 1983. *Whatever Happened to Britain? The Economics of Decline*. London: Duckworth.

Ebel, K. 1985. "Social and Labour Implications of Flexible Manufacturing Systems", *International Labour Review* **124**, 133–45.

The Economist 1990. "The Tale of Two Parties", *The Economist* 23 June.

Eijk, van der, C. & M. Franklin 1996. "The Problem: Representation and Democracy in the European Union", in *Choosing Europe,* C. van der Eijk & M. Franklin (eds). Ann Arbor: University of Michigan Press.

Eijk, van der, C., M. Franklin, M. Marsh 1996. "Conclusions: The Electoral Connection and the Democratic Deficit", in *Choosing Europe,* C. van der Eijk & M. Franklin (eds). Ann Arbor: University of Michigan Press.

Eisenschitz, A. & D. North 1986. "The London Industrial Strategy: Social Transformation and Modernising Capital", *International Journal of Urban and Regional Resources* **10**, 419–40.

Eisenschitz, A. & J. Gough 1993. *The Politics of Local Economic Policy*. London: Macmillan.

Elam, M. 1990. "Puzzling out the Fordist Debate: Technology, Markets and Institutions", *Economic and Industrial Democracy* **11**, 9–37.

Elliott, D. 1977. *The Lucas Aerospace Workers' Campaign*. London: Young Fabian pamphlet.

Elliott, D. & M. Marshall 1989. "Sector Strategy in the West Midlands", in *Reversing Industrial Decline? Industrial Structure in Britain and Her Competitors*, P. Hirst & J. Zeitlin (eds). Oxford: Berg.

Elliott, G. 1993. *Labourism and the English Genius*. London: Verso.

Elliott, L. 1996. "Better off as the 51st State", *Guardian*, 3 June.

Elliott, L. 1997. "In Place of Fear", *Guardian*, 13 January.

Elster, J. 1989. "From Here to There: Or, if Co-operative Ownership is Desirable, Why are there so Few Co-operatives?" *Social Philosophy and Policy* **6**, 93–111.

Elster, J. & K. Moene 1989. "Introduction", in *Alternatives to Capitalism*, J. Elster & K. Moene (eds). Cambridge: Cambridge University Press.

Epstein, G. 1996. "International Capital Mobility and the Scope for National Economic Management", in *States Against Markets: The Limits of Globalization*, R. Boyer & D. Drache (eds). London: Routledge.

Epstein, G. & H. Gintis 1992. "International Capital Markets and the Limits of National Economic Policy", in *Financial Openness and National Autonomy: Opportunities and Constraints*, T. Banuri & J. Schor (eds). Oxford: Clarendon.

Esping-Andersen, G. 1990. *The Three Worlds of Welfare Capitalism*. Cambridge: Polity.

Estrin, S. 1980. "Income Dispersion in a Self-Managed Economy", *Economica* **47**, 181–94.

Estrin, S. 1989. "Workers' Co-operatives: Their Merits and their Limitations", in *Market Socialism*, J. Le Grand & S. Estrin (eds). Oxford: Clarendon.

Estrin S. & W. Bartlett 1982. "The Effects of Enterprise Self-Management in Yugoslavia: An Empirical Survey", in *Participatory and Self-Managed Firms*, D. Jones & J. Svejnar (eds). Lexington: Lexington Books.

Estrin S. & J. Le Grand 1989. "Introduction", in *Market Socialism*, J. Le Grand & S. Estrin (eds). Oxford: Clarendon.

Estrin, S. & V. Perotin 1987. "Co-operatives and Participatory Firms in Great Britain", *International Review of Applied Economics* **1**, 152–76.

Estrin, S. & J. Svejnar 1987. "The Productivity Effects of Worker Participation: Producer Co-operatives in Western Economies", *Journal of Comparative Economics* **11**, 40–61.

Estrin S. & D. Winter 1989. "Planning in a Market Socialist Economy", in *Market Socialism*, J. Le Grand & S. Estrin(eds). Oxford: Clarendon.

Evans, P. 1997. "The Eclipse of the State? Reflections on Stateness in an Era of Globalization", *World Politics* **50**, 62–87.

Fairclough, M. 1986. "Conditional Degeneration and Producer Co-operatives: A Reappraisal of the Socialist Tradition", in *Proceedings of the National Conference on Research on Workers' Co-operatives*. Milton Keynes: Co-operatives Research Unit, Open University.

Fairclough, N. 2000. *New Labour, New Language*. London: Routledge.

Fanning, C. & T. McCarthy 1986. "A Survey of Economic Hypotheses Concerning the Non-Viability of Labor-Directed Firms in Capitalist Economies", in *Labor-Owned Firms and Workers' Co-operatives*, S. Jansson & A. Hellmark (eds). Aldershot: Gower.

Farnham, D. 1996. "New Labour, the New Unions and the New Labour Markets", *Parliamentary Affairs* **49**, 584–98.

Fernie, S. & D. Metcalf 1995. "Participation, Contingent Pay, Representation and Workplace Performances: Evidence from Great Britain", *Discussion Paper No. 232*. London: Centre for Economic Performance.

Fielding S. 1996. *Labour: Decline and Renewal*. Manchester: Baseline.

Fine, B. 1981. *Multinational Corporations, the British Economy and the Alternative Economic Strategy*. London: Birkbeck.

Fine, B. 1981. "The British Economic Disaster: Review Article", *Capital and Class* **13**, 139–53.

Fine, B. & L. O'Donnell 1981. "The Nationalised Industries", in *Socialist Economic Review*, D. Currie & R. Smith (eds). London: Merlin.

Fine, B. *et al.* 1985. *Class Politics: An Answer to its Critics*. London: Community Press.

Fitoussi, J.-P. 1985. "Comment", in *Economic Policy and Policy-Making under the Mitterrand Presidency, 1981–84*, H. Machin & V. Wright (eds). London: Pinter.

Forbes, I. (ed.) 1986. *Market Socialism: Whose Choice?*, Fabian Tract 516. London: Fabian Society.

Foster, J. 1988. "The Fetish of Fordism", *Monthly Review* **39**, 14–33.

Frankel, B. 1985. "The Historical Obsolescence of Market Socialism – A Reply to Alec Nove", *Radical Philosophy* **39**, 28–33.

Freeman, R. & W. Evans 1990. "Corporate Governance: A Stakeholder Interpretation", *Journal of Behavioural Sciences* **19**, 337–59.

Frieden, J. 1991. "Invested Interests: The Politics of National Economic Policies in a World of Global Finance", *International Organization* **45**, 425–52.

Friedman, M. & A. Schwartz 1982. *Monetary Trends in the United States and the United Kingdom*. Chicago: University of Chicago Press.

Fukuyama, F. 1995. *Trust: The Social Virtues and the Creation of Prosperity*. New York: Free Press.

Furbotn, E. & S. Pejovich 1974. *The Economics of Property Rights*. Cambridge, Mass.: Ballinger.

Galbraith, J. K. 1992. *The Culture of Contentment*. London: Sinclair-Stevenson.

Gamble, A. 1987. "Class Politics and Radical Democracy", *New Left Review* **164**, 113–22.

Gamble, A. 1994. *The Free Economy and the Strong State: The Politics of Thatcherism*, 2nd edn. Basingstoke: Macmillan.

Gamble, A. & G. Kelly 1996. "Stakeholder Capitalism and One Nation Socialism", *Renewal* **4**, 23–32.

Garrahan, P. & P. Stewart 1992. "Management Control and a New Regime of Subordination: Post-Fordism and the Local Economy", in *Fordism and Flexibility*, R. Burrows *et al.* (eds). London: Macmillan.

Garrett, G. & P. Lange 1989. "Government Partisanship and Economic Performance: When and How Does 'Who Governs' Matter?", *Journal of Politics* **51**, 676–93.

Garrett, G. & P. Lange 1991. "Political Responses to Interdependence: What's Left for the Left?", *International Organization* **45**, 539–64.

Geddes, M. 1988. "The Capitalist State and the Local Economy: 'Restructuring for Labour' and Beyond", *Capital and Class* **35**, 85–120.

Geddes, M. 1988. "Social Audits and Social Accounting in the UK: A Review", *Regional Studies* **22**, 60–5.

Gelb, A. & K. Bradley 1982. "The Mondragon Co-operatives: Guidelines for a Co-operative Economy? ", in *Participatory and Self-Managed Firms*, D. Jones & J. Svejnar (eds). Lexington: Lexington Books.

Ghilespy, D. *et al.* 1986. *Socialist Enterprise: Reclaiming the Economy*. Nottingham: Spokesman Books.

Gill, C. 1985. *Work, Unemployment and the New Technology*. Cambridge: Polity.

Gill, S. 1992. "The Emerging World Order and European Change: The Political Economy of the European Union", *Socialist Register, 1992*. London: Merlin.

Ginsburg, N. 1979. *Class, Capital and Social Policy*. London: Macmillan.

Glotz, P. 1985. "Europe – The Helpless and Silent Continent", *New Statesman*, 20/27 December.

Glyn, A. 1978. *Capitalist Crisis: Tribune's Alternative Economic Strategy or Socialist Plan*. London: Militant.

Glyn, A. 1998. "Internal and External Constraints on Egalitarian Policies", in *Globalization and Progressive Economic Policy*, D. Baker, G. Epstein & R. Pollin (eds). Cambridge: Cambridge University Press.

Glyn, A. & Sutcliffe, R. 1972. *British Capitalism, Workers and the Profit Squeeze*. Harmondsworth: Penguin.

Godley, W. 1993. "A Federal Government ?", in *A European Recovery Programme*, K. Coates & M. B. Brown (eds). Nottingham: Spokesman Books.

Gold, M. 1993. "Introduction", in *The Social Dimension: Employment Policy in the European Community*, M. Gold (ed.). London: Macmillan.

Goldthorpe, J. *et al.* 1968. *The Affluent Worker: Political Attitudes and Behaviour*. Cambridge: Cambridge University Press.

Goldthorpe, J. *et al.* 1980. *Social Mobility and Class Structure in Modern Britain*. Oxford: Clarendon.

Goodman, J. 1992. *Monetary Sovereignty: The Politics of Central Banking in Western Europe*. Ithaca: Cornell University Press.

Goodman, J & L. Pauly 1993. "The Obsolescence of Capital Controls? Economic Management in an Age of Global Markets", *World Politics* **46**, 50–82.

Goodwin, M. & S. Duncan 1986. "The Local State and Local Economic Policy: Political Mobilisation or Economic Regeneration", *Capital and Class* **27**, 14–36.

Gough, I. 1979. *Political Economy and the Welfare State*. London: Macmillan.

Gough, I. 1980. "Thatcherism and the Welfare State", *Marxism Today*, July.

Gough, J. 1986. "Industrial Policy and Socialist Strategy: Restructuring and the Unity of the Working Class", *Capital and Class* **29**, 58–82.

Gould, A. 1993. "The End of the Middle Way? The Swedish Welfare State in Crisis", in *New Perspectives on the Welfare State in Europe*, C. Jones (ed.). London: Routledge.

Gould, B., J. Mills, S. Stewart 1981. *Monetarism or Prosperity?* London: Macmillan.

Gould, B. 1989. *A Future for Socialism*. London: Cape.

Gray, J. 1996. *After Social Democracy*. London: Demos.

Greater London Council 1985. *London Industrial Strategy*. London: GLC.

Green, G. 1991. "The New Municipal Socialism", in *Politics or Welfare? The State of the Market in Contemporary Britain*, M. Loney et al. (eds). London: Sage.

Green, R. 1983. "Going Forward", *New Statesman*, 23 September.

Greenberg, E. 1981. "Industrial Democracy and the Democratic Citizen", *Journal of Politics* **43**, 964–81.

Greenberg, E. 1986. *Workplace Democracy: The Political Effects of Participation*. Ithaca: Cornell University Press.

Grice, A. 1996. "Has Stakeholding Shrunk to a Slogan?", *Sunday Times*, 21 January.

Gros, D. & N. Thygsen 1995. "The Relationship between Economic and Monetary Integration: EMU and National Fiscal Policy", in *Reinventing Collective Action: From the Global to the Local,* C. Crouch & D. Marquand (eds). Oxford: Blackwell.

Grunberg, G. 1998. "Socialism and Liberalism", in *European Social Democracy: Transformation in Progress*, R. Cuperus & J. Kandel (eds). Amsterdam: Wiardi Beckman Stichtig.

Gunn, C. 1984. *Workers' Self-Management in the United States*. Ithaca: Cornell University Press.

Gyford, J. 1985. *The Politics of Local Socialism*. London: Allen & Unwin.

Hackett, G. *et al.* 1987. "Socially Useful Production", in *A Taste of Power: The Politics of Local Economics*, M. Mackintosh & H. Wainwright (eds). London: Verso.

Hain, P. 1995. *Ayes to the Left*. London: Lawrence & Wishart.

Hall, P. 1987. "The Evolution of Economic Policy under Mitterrand", in *The Mitterrand Experiment: Continuity and Change in Modern France*, G. Ross, S. Hoffman & M. Malzacher (eds). Oxford: Polity.

Hall, S. 1980. "Questions of Theory", in *The Hard Road to Renewal: Thatcherism and the Crisis of the Left*, S. Hall (1988). London: Verso.

Hall, S. 1984. "The State: Socialism's Old Caretaker", *Marxism Today*, November.

Hall, S. 1984. "The Culture Gap", in *The Hard Road to Renewal: Thatcherism and the Crisis of the Left*, S. Hall (1988). London: Verso.

Hall, S. 1984. "On the Kinnock/Hattersley Labour Party", in *The Hard Road to Renewal: Thatcherism and the Crisis of the Left*, S. Hall (1988). London: Verso.

Hall, S. 1985. "Faith, Hope or Clarity", *Marxism Today*, January.

Hall, S. 1985. "Realignment", in *The Hard Road to Renewal: Thatcherism and the Crisis of the Left*, S. Hall (1988). London: Verso.

Hall, S. & M. Jacques 1983. "Introduction", in *The Politics of Thatcherism*, S. Hall & M. Jacques (eds). London: Lawrence & Wishart.

Hall, S. & M. Jacques 1990. "March without Vision", *Marxism Today*, December.

Ham Common Concordists 1843. *The New Age*, 6 May.

Hansman, H. 1990. "The Viability of Worker Ownership", in *The Firm as a Nexus of New Treaties*, M. Aoki, B. Gustaffson & O. Williamson (eds). New York: Sage.

Hanson, C. & P. Rathkey 1984. "Industrial Democracy: A Post-Bullock Shopfloor View", *British Journal of Industrial Relations* **22**, 154–68.

Harrington, M. 1986. *The Next Left: The History of a Future*. New York: Holt.

Harrington, M. 1993. *Socialism: Past and Future*. London: Pluto.

Harris, L. & B. Fine 1985. *The Peculiarities of the British Economy*. London: Lawrence & Wishart.

Harris, N. 1986. "What to do with London? The Strategies of the GLC, 1981–86", *International Socialism* **2**, 113–34.

Harrison, J. 1981. "The Politics of the Alternative Economic Strategy", *Marxism Today*, May.

Harrod, R. F. 1964. "Are Fiscal and Monetary Policy Enough?", *Economic Journal* **74**, 903–15.

Hatfield, M. 1978. *The House the Left Built: Inside Labour Policy-Making, 1970–75*. London: Gollancz.

Hattersley, R. 1983. *Labour's Choices*, Fabian Tract 489. London: Fabian Society.

Hattersley, R. 1985. "Exchange Control", *New Statesman*, 22 February.

Hattersley, R. 1985. "An Alternative to the Alternative: Labour's Economic Strategy", *Marxism Today*, October.

Hattersley, R. 1987. *Choose Freedom: The Future for Democratic Socialism*. Harmondsworth: Penguin.

Hay, C. 1996. "A State of Disarray: Huttonomics, New Labour and the Contemporary British Impasse", *Renewal* **4**, 40–50.

Hay, C. 2000. *The Political Economy of New Labour: Labouring Under False Pretences*. Manchester: Manchester University Press.

Hayes, R. & S. Wheelwright 1984. *Restoring our Competitive Edge: Competing Through Manufacturing*. New York: Wiley.

Hayter, T. 1987. "Industrial Democracy: The GLEB Experience", in *A Taste of Power: The Politics of Local Economics*, M. Mackintosh & H. Wainwright (eds). London: Verso.

Heffernan, R. 2000. *New Labour and Thatcherism: Political Change in Britain*. New York: St Martin's Press.

Held, D. 1988. "Farewell Nation State", *Marxism Today*, December.

Held, D. 1991. "Democracy, the Nation State and the Global System", *Economy and Society* **20**, 138–72.

Held, D. 1995. *Democracy and the Global Order: From the Modern State to Cosmopolitan Governance*. Cambridge: Polity.

Helleiner, E. 1994. *States and the Emergence of Global Finance: From Bretton Woods to the 1990s*. Ithaca: Cornell University Press.

Hendry, D. & N. Ericson 1983. *Monetary Trends in the UK*, Paper No. 22. London: Bank of England Panel of Academic Consultants.

Hettne, B. 1997. "The Double Movement, Global Market Versus Regionalism", in *The New Realism: Perspectives on Multilateralism and World Order*, R. Cox (ed.). London: Macmillan.

Hilton, A. 1987. *City Within a State: A Portrait of Britain's Financial World*. London: Tauris.

Hirsch, F. 1977. *The Social Limits to Growth*. London: Routledge.

Hirsch, J. 1997. "Globalization of Capital, Nation-States and Democracy", *Studies in Political Economy* **54**, 39–58.

Hirsch, J., W. Bonefield, J. Holloway 1991. *Post-Fordism and Social Form*. London: Macmillan.

Hirschorn, L. 1984. *Beyond Mechanization: Work and Technology in a Post-Industrial Age*. Boston: MIT Press.

Hirst, P. 1988. "Associational Socialism in a Pluralist State", *Journal of Law and Society* **15**, 139–50.

Hirst, P. 1994. *Associative Democracy: New Forms of Economic and Social Governance*. London: Polity.

Hirst, P. & G. Thompson 1996. *Globalization in Question: The International Economy and the Possibilities of Governance*. Cambridge: Polity.

Hirst, P. 1989. "The Politics of Industrial Policy", in *Reversing Industrial Decline? Industrial Structure in Britain and Her Competitors*, P. Hirst & J. Zeitlin (eds). Oxford: Berg.

Hirst, P. & J. Zeitlin (eds) 1989. *Reversing Industrial Decline? Industrial Structure in Britain and Her Competitors*. Oxford: Berg.

Hirst, P. & J. Zeitlin 1991. "Flexible Specialisation vs Post-Fordism: Theory, Evidence and Policy Implications", *Economy and Society* **20**, 1–56.

Hobsbawm, E. 1981. "The Forward March of Labour Halted?", in *The Forward March of Labour Halted?*, M. Jacques & F. Mulhern (eds). London: Verso.

Hobsbawm, E. 1986. "Labour's Prospects", *Marxism Today*, October.

Hobsbawm, E. 1987. "Out of the Wilderness", *Marxism Today*, October.

Hodgson, G. 1979. *Socialist Economic Strategy*, Labour Party Discussion Series, No. 2. Leeds: ILP.

Hodgson, G. 1981. *Labour at the Crossroads: The Political and Economic Challenge to the Labour Party in the 1980s*. London: Martin Robertson.

Hodgson, G. 1982. "On the Political Economy of the Socialist Transformation", *New Left Review* **133**, 52–66.

Holland, S. 1972. *The State as Entrepreneur*. London: Weidenfeld & Nicolson.

Holland, S. 1975. *The Socialist Challenge*. London: Quartet.

Holland, S. 1978. *Beyond Capitalist Planning*. Oxford: Blackwell.

Holland, S. 1980. *Uncommon Market: Capital, Class and Power in the European Community*. London: Macmillan.

Holland, S. 1983. *Out of Crisis: A Programme for European Recovery*. Nottingham: Spokesman Books.

Holland, S. 1984. "Out of Crisis – International Economic Recovery", in *The Future of the Left*, J. Curran (ed.). Cambridge: Polity.

Holland, S. 1985. "An Alternative Economic Strategy", in *Joint Action for Jobs: A New Internationalism*, K. Coates (ed.). Nottingham: Spokesman Books.

Holland, S. & K. Coates 1995. *Full Employment for Europe*. Nottingham: Spokesman Books.

Holmes, M. 1985. *The Labour Government, 1974–79*. London: Macmillan.

Holmes, P. 1980. "Economic Growth and Unemployment", in *Labour into the Eighties*, D. Bell (ed.). Beckenham: Croom Helm.

House of Commons 1981. *Report from the Treasury and Civil Service Commission*, House of Commons Paper 163-1. London: HMSO.

Hughes, J. 1985. "The Dole Economy: Can We Plan Our Way Out?", in *Joint Action for Jobs: A New Internationalism*, K. Coates (ed.). Nottingham: Spokesman Books.

Hughes, J. 1991. *The Social Charter and the Single European Market: Towards a Socially Responsible Community*. Nottingham: Spokesman Books.

Hutton, W. 1996. *The State We're In*. London: Vintage.

Hutton, W. 1996. "Raising the Stakes", *Observer*, 17 January.

Hutton, W. 1996. "Fool's Gold", *Observer*, 2 June.

Hutton, W. 1998. "It's Stakeholding not Sclerosis Stupid", *Observer*, 1 March.

Hutton, W. 1998. "Now Gordon", *Observer*, 8 October.

Hutton, W. 1999. *The Stakeholding Society: Writings on Economics and Politics*. Cambridge: Polity.

Hutton, W. & J. Kay 1996. "Only Working Together", *Observer*, 13 October.

Hyman, R. 1988. "Flexible Specialisation: Miracle or Myth?", in *New Technology and Industrial Relations*, R. Hyman & W. Streeck (eds). Oxford: Blackwell.

Ingham, G. 1984. *Capitalism Divided? The City and Industry in British Social Development*. London: Macmillan.

Ingham, G. 1988. "Commercial Capital and British Development", *New Left Review* **172**, 45–65.

Institute for Workers' Control Motor Group 1979. *A Workers' Inquiry into the Motor Industry*. London: CSE Books.

Ireland, N. J. & P. Law 1982. *The Economics of Labour Managed Enterprises*. Beckenham: Croom Helm.

Jefferis, K. & M. Robinson 1987. "Social Investment in Production" , in *Developing Local Economic Strategies: Some Issues and Ideas,* A. Cochrane (ed.). Milton Keynes: Open University Press.

Jenkins, R. 1980. *Tony Benn: A Political Portrait*. London: Writers and Readers Publishing Co-operative.

Jensen, M. & W. Meckling 1979. "Rights and Production Functions: An Application to Labor-Managed Firms and Co-determination", *Journal of Business* **52**, 469–506.

Jessop, B., K. Bonnett, S. Bromley, T. Long 1984. "Authoritarian Populism: Two Nations and Thatcherism", *New Left Review* **147**, 32–60.

Jones, B. 1989. "Flexible Automation and Factory Politics: The United Kingdom in Comparative Perspective", in *Reversing Industrial Decline? Industrial Structure in Britain and Her Competitors*, P. Hirst & J. Zeitlin (eds). Oxford: Berg.

Jones, D. 1975. "British Producer Co-operatives and the Views of the Webbs on Participation and the Ability to Survive", *Annals of Public and Co-operative Economy* **46**, 23–44.

Jones, D. 1982. "The United States of America: A Survey of Producer Co-operative Performance", in *The Performance of Labour-Managed Firms*, F. Stephen (ed.). London: Macmillan.

Jones, D. 1980. "Producer Co-operatives in Western Industrialised Economies", *British Journal of Industrial Relations* **18**, 342–56.

Jones, D. & J. Svejnar 1985. "Participation, Profit-Sharing, Worker Ownership and Efficiency in Italian Producer Co-operatives", *Economica* **52**, 449–65.

Jones, E. 1851. "The Co-operative Movement", in *Notes to the People*, vol. 1, pp. 470–6.

Jones, E. 1852. "Discussion at Halifax", in *Notes to the People*, vol. 2, pp. 793–806.

Jordan, J. 1986. "A System of Interdependent Firms as a Development Strategy", in *Labor-Owned Firms and Workers' Co-operatives*, S. Jansson & A. Hellmark (eds). Aldershot: Gower.

Julius, D. 1989. *Global Companies and Public Policies: The Challenge of the New Economic Linkages*. London: Chatham House.

Kagarlitsky, B. 1999. "The Challenge of the Left: Reclaiming the State", *Socialist Register, 1999*. London: Merlin.

Kaldor, N. 1976. "The New Monetarism", in *Monetarism and Keynesians*, C. Johnson (ed.) (1991). London: Pinter.

Kalma, P. & T. Meyer 1998. "Foreword", in *European Social Democracy: Transformation in Progress*, R. Cuperus & J. Kandel (eds). Amsterdam: Wiardi Beckman Stichtig.

Kampfner, J. 1995. "Politics of the Possible", *Financial Times*, 14 December.

Katz, H. & C. Sabel 1985. "Industrial Relations and Industrial Adjustments in the Car Industry", *Industrial Relations* **24**, 295–315.

Kaufman, G. (ed.) 1983. *Labour's Britain in the 1980s*. Harmondsworth: Penguin.

Kay, J. 1993. *The Foundations of Corporate Success*. Oxford: Oxford University Press.

Kay, J. 1996. *The Business of Economics*. Oxford: Oxford University Press.

Kellner, P. 1980. "The Economic Consequences of Jim", *New Statesman*, 17 October.

Kellner, P. 1981. "Plan for Growth", *New Statesman*, 6 February.

Kellner, P. 1981. "Monetarism: The Fight Starts Here", *New Statesman*, 6 March.

Kellner, P. 1981. "But What Exactly is Labour's Alternative?", *New Statesman*, 3 July.

Kellner, P. 1983. "Labour Pays the Price for Too Much Unity", *New Statesman*, 3 June.

Kellner, P. 1983. "Are there really 8.5 Million Socialists in Britain?", *New Statesman*, 24 June.

Kelly, G. 1982. "Useful Work and Useless Toil", *Marxism Today*, August.

Kelly, J. 1999. "An Era of Broader Interests", *Financial Times*, 19 March.

Keynes, J. M. 1972. "The Economic Consequences of Mr. Churchill", in *Essays in Persuasion*, D. Moggridge (ed.), *The Collected Writings of John Maynard Keynes*, vol. IX. London: Macmillan.

Kindleberger, C. 1969. *American Business Abroad: Six Lectures on Direct Investment*. Cambridge, Mass.: MIT Press.

Kinnock, N. 1984. "A New Deal for Europe", in *The Future of the Left*, J. Curran (ed.). Cambridge: Polity.

Kinnock, N. 1986. *Making Our Way*: Oxford: Blackwell.

Kitching, G. 1983. *Rethinking Socialism: A Theory for a Better Practice*. London: Methuen.

Kitching, G. 1987. "A Reply to Ellen Meiskens Wood", *New Left Review* **163**, 121–8.

Kochan, T. *et al.* 1986. *The Transformation of American Industrial Relations.* New York: Basic Books.

Kornai, J. 1990. *The Road to Freedom.* New York: Norton.

Kurdle, R. 1999. "Market Globalization and the Future Policies of the Industrial State", in *Globalization and Governance*, A. Prakash & J. Hart (eds). London: Routledge.

Labour Co-ordinating Committee n.d. *There is An Alternative: Politics for Prosperity in the Eighties.* London.

Labour Party 1979. *The Labour Way is the Better Way.* London: Labour Party.

Labour Party 1981. *Manifesto for the GLC.* London: Labour Party.

Labour Party 1982. *Economic Planning and Industrial Democracy.* London: Labour Party.

Labour Party 1982. *Labour's Programme 1982.* London: Labour Party.

Labour Party 1983. *The New Hope for Britain: Labour's Manifesto.* London: Labour Party.

Labour Party 1991. *Made in Britain: A New Economic Policy for the 1990s.* London: Labour Party.

Labour Party 1992. *It's Time to Get Britain Working Again.* London: Labour Party.

Labour Party 1993. *Labour's Economic Approach.* London: Labour Party.

Labour Party 1993. *Making Britain's Future.* London: Labour Party.

Labour Party 1994. *Winning for Britain: Labour's Strategy for Economic Success.* London: Labour Party.

Labour Party 1994. *Rebuilding the Economy.* London: Labour Party.

Labour Party 1995. *A New Economic Future for Britain.* London: Labour Party.

Labour Party 1997. *Labour in Government: Delivering Our Contract to the People*, NEC statement. London: Labour Party.

Labour Party 1997. *New Labour: Because Britain Deserves Better.* London: Labour Party.

Labour Party 1997. *New Labour: A Government for Entrepreneurs.* London: Labour Party.

Laclau, E. 1987. "Class War and After", *Marxism Today*, April.

Lane, T. 1987. "Fit for Active Service?", *Marxism Today*, February.

Lawson, N. & N. Sherlock (eds) 2001. *The Progressive Century: The Future of the Centre-Left in Britain.* London: Macmillan.

Leadbeater, C. 1987. "The Sid in Us All", *Marxism Today*, January.

Leadbeater, C. 1987. "In the Land of the Dispossessed", *Marxism Today*, April.

Leadbeater, C. 1998. "Who Will Own the Knowledge Economy?", *Political Quarterly* **69**, 375–85.

Leadbeater, C. 1987. *The Politics of Prosperity*, Fabian Tract 523. London: Fabian Society.

Leadbeater, C. 1988. "Clearing the Decks: Round Table Discussion", *Marxism Today*, October.

Leadbeater, C. 1996. "What's the Big Idea?", *Observer*, 4 August.

Leadbeater, C. & G. Mulgan 1996. "Stakeholding: Nice Idea, Shame about the Reality", *Observer* 6 October.

Leadbeater, C. & G. Mulgan 1996. "Labour's Forgotten Idea", *Financial Times*, 2 October.

Leadbeater, C. & G. Mulgan 1998. *Mistakeholding: Whatever Happened to Labour's Big Idea?* London: Demos.

Le Grand, J. 1981. *The Strategy of Equality.* London: Allen & Unwin.

Lemke, C. & G. Marks 1992. "Introduction", in *The Crisis of Socialism in Europe*, C. Lemke & G. Marks (eds). North Carolina: Duke University Press.

Leonard, P. 1979. "Restructuring the Welfare State", *Marxism Today*, December.

Leviatan, U. & M. Rosner 1980. *Work and Organization in Kibbutz Industry.* Philadelphia: Norwood.

Lewis, W. & D. Wighton 1996. "Labour Softens on Stakeholding", *Financial Times*, 26 June.

Leyshon, A. & N. Thrift 1995. "European Financial Integration: The Search for an 'Island of Monetary Stability' in the Seas of Global Financial Turbulence", in *An Enlarged Europe: Regions in Competition?*, S. Hardy *et al.* (eds). London: Kingsley.

Lightfoot, S. 1999. "Prospects of a Euro-socialism", *Renewal* **7**, 7–17.

Lindberg, E. 1985. "The Rise and Fall of the Swedish Model", *Journal of Economic Literature* **23**, 1–36.

Livingstone, K. 1985. "Planning on a European Scale?", in *Joint Action for Jobs: A New Internationalism*, K. Coates (ed.). Nottingham: Spokesman Books.

Lloyd, J. 1987. "Unions and Economic Management", in *Labour's First Hundred Days*, Fabian Tract 519, B. Pimlott (ed.). London: Fabian Society.

Lloyd, J. 1990. "Europeans by Default", *Marxism Today*, October.

London CSE Group 1979. "Crisis, the Labour Movement and the Alternative Economic Strategy", *Capital and Class* **8**, 68–93.

Lovering, J. 1988. "The Local Economy and Local Economic Strategies", *Policy and Politics* **16**, 145–57.

Lucas Aerospace Confederation Trade Union Committee 1979. *Lucas Aerospace: Turning Industrial Decline into Expansion – A Trade Union Initiative.* London: LACTUC.

Lucas Aerospace Shop Stewards' Combine Committee 1978. *Lucas: An Alternative Plan.* Nottingham: Spokesman Books.

Ludlam, S. & M. Smith (eds) 2001. *New Labour in Government.* London: Macmillan.

Lukes, S. 1984. "The Future of British Socialism", in *Fabian Essays in Socialist Thought*, B. Pimlott (ed.). London: Heinemann.

Lyons, M. 1983. "The 2p Rate and the Powers for Economic Development", *The Planner*, **69**(5), 163–4.

McCormick, J. 1985. "Apprenticeship for Governing: An Assessment of French Socialism in Power", in *Economic Policy and Policy-Making under the Mitterrand Presidency, 1981–84*, H. Machin & V. Wright (eds). London: Pinter.

McDonald, O. 1980. "Will Taxes go Up?", in *The Economics of Prosperity: Social Priorities in the Eighties*, D. Blake & P. Ormerod (eds). London: Grant & Macintyre.

Machin, H. & V. Wright 1985. "Introduction", in *Economic Policy and Policy-Making under the Mitterrand Presidency, 1981–84*, H. Machin & V. Wright (eds). London: Pinter.

Mackay, R. 1995. "European Integration and Public Finance: The Political Economy of Regional Support", in *An Enlarged Europe: Regions in Competition?*, S. Hardy *et al.* (eds). London: Kingsley.

McKenzie, R. & D. Lee 1991. *Quicksilver Capital: How the Rapid Movement of Wealth has Changed the World*. New York: Free Press.

Mackintosh, M. & H. Wainwright 1987. "Introduction", in *A Taste of Power: The Politics of Local Economics*, M. Mackintosh & H. Wainwright (eds). London: Verso.

MacShane, D. 1986. *French Lessons for Labour*, Fabian Tract 512. London: Fabian Society.

Maddison, A. 1995. *Monitoring the World Economy*. Paris: OECD Development Centre.

Majone, G. 1995. "The European Community: Between Social Policy and Social Regulation", in *Policy Issues in the European Union: A Reader in the Political Economy of European Integration*, M. Ugur (ed.). Dartford: Greenwich University Press.

Majone, G. 1996. "Introduction", in *Regulating Europe*, G. Majone (ed.). London: Routledge.

Mandelson, P. & R. Liddle 1996. *The Blair Revolution*. London: Faber.

Mandelson, P. & R. Liddle 1996. "Come the Revolution", *Guardian*, 27 March.

Mann, M. 1985. *Socialism Can Survive*, Fabian Tract 502. London: Fabian Society.

Marquand, D. 1990. "The Irresistible Tide of Europeanisation", in *New Times: The Changing Face of Politics in the 1990s*, M. Jacques & S. Hall (eds). London, Lawrence & Wishart.

Marquand, D. 1993. "After Socialism", *Political Studies* **41**, 43–56.

Marquand, D. 1996. "A Stake Through the Heart of Old Simplicities", *Independent*, 15 January.

Marquand, D. 1998. "The Blair Paradox", *Prospect*, 19/22 May.

Marquand, D. & C. Crouch 1990. "Introduction", in *The Politics of 1992: Beyond the Single European Market*, D. Marquand & C. Crouch (eds). Oxford: Blackwell.

Marquand, D. & T. Wright 1996. "Labour and the Intellectuals", *Political Quarterly* **67**, 1–3.

Marqusee, M. 1997. "New Labour and its Discontents", *New Left Review* **224**, 127–42.

Marshall, A. 1920. *Industry and Trade*. London.

Marvell, A. 1993. "Funding the Recovery Programme", in *A European Recovery Programme*, K. Coates & M. B. Brown (eds). Nottingham: Spokesman Books.

Mathews, J. 1989. *Age of Democracy: The Politics of Post-Fordism and Social Form*. Melbourne: Oxford University Press.

Mathews, J. 1989. *Tools of Change: New Technology and the Democratization of Work*. Sydney: Pluto.

Mawson, J. & J. Miller 1986. "Interventionist Approaches to Local Employment and Economic Development: The Experience of Labour Local Authorities", in *Critical Issues in Urban Economic Development*, vol. 1, V. Hausner (ed.). Oxford: Clarendon.

Meacher, M. 1981. "Models not Rhetoric", *New Statesman*, 14 August.

Meacher, M. 1982. *Socialism with a Human Face: The Political Economy of Britain in the 1980s*. London, Allen & Unwin.

Meade, J. 1972. "The Theory of Labour-Managed Firms and Profit Sharing", *Economic Journal* **82**, 402–28.

Meade, J. 1974. "Labour-Managed Firms in Conditions of Imperfect Competition", *Economic Journal* **84**, 817–24.

Meade, J. 1989. *Agathopia – The Economics of Partnership*. Aberdeen: Aberdeen University Press.

Meade, J., P. Pelikan, R. Kocanda 1967. "The Socialist Enterprise as a Participant in the Market", *Czechoslovak Economic Papers* **9**, 49–64.

Meidner, R. 1993. "Why did the Swedish Model Fail?", in *Socialist Register, 1993*. London: Merlin.

Merkle W. 1992. "After the Golden Age, is Social Democracy Doomed to Decline?", in *The Crisis of Socialism in Europe*, C. Lemke & G. Marks (eds). North Carolina: Duke University Press.

Metcalf, P. 1996. "Stakeholding Versus Competition", *Renewal* **4**, 75–8.

Meurs, M. 1986. "Agency Problems and Comparative Systems Theory", in *Markets and Democracy: Participation, Accountability and Efficiency*, S. Bowles, H. Gintis & B. Gustaffson (eds). Cambridge: Cambridge University Press.

Michie, J. (ed.) 1992. *The Economic Legacy, 1979–1992*. London: Academic Press.

Michie, J. 2000. "Introduction", in *Global Instability: The Political Economy of World Economic Governance*, J. Michie & J. Smith (eds). London: Routledge.

Milenkovitch, D. 1984. "Is Market Socialism Efficient?", in *Comparative Economic Systems*, A. Zimbalist (ed.). Boston: Kluwer.

Miliband, R., L. Panitch, J. Saville 1988. "Problems and Promise of Socialist Renewal", *Socialist Register, 1988*. London: Merlin.

Mill, J. S. 1848. *The Principles of Political Economy*. London.

Miller, D. 1981. "Market Neutrality and the Failure of Co-operatives", *British Journal of Political Science* **11**, 309–29.

Miller, D. 1989. "Why Markets?", in *Market Socialism*, J. Le Grand & S. Estrin (eds). Oxford: Clarendon.

Miller, D. 1989. *Market, State and Community: Theoretical Foundations of Market Socialism*. Oxford: Clarendon.

Miller, D. & S. Estrin 1986. "Market Socialism: A Policy for Socialists", in *Market Socialism: Whose Choice?*, Fabian Tract 516, I. Forbes (ed.). London: Fabian Society.

Minns, R. 1981. "Challenging the Bankers", *New Statesman*, 21 August.

Minns, R. 1982. *Taking Over the City: The Case for Public Ownership of Financial Institutions*. London: Pluto.

Mishra, R. 1996. "The Welfare of Nations", in *States Against Markets: The Limits of Globalization*, R. Boyer & D. Drache (eds). London: Routledge.

Mitchell, A. 1981. "Political Aspects of Unemployment: The Alternative Policy", in *Unemployment*, B. Crick (ed.). London: Methuen.

Mitchell, A. 1983. *The Case for Labour*. London: Longman.

Miyazaki, H. 1984. "On the Success and Dissolution of the Labor-Managed Firm in the Capitalist Economy", *Journal of Political Economy* **92**, 909–31.

Moses, J. 1994. "Abdication from National Policy Autonomy: What's Left to Leave?", *Politics and Society* **22**, 125–48.

Mulgan, G. 1996. "A High Stake Society", *Guardian*, 30 January.

Murray, F. 1987. "Flexible Specialisation in the Third Italy", *Capital and Class* **33**, 84–95.

Murray, F. 1993. "The Decentralisation of Production – The Decline of the Mass Production Worker?", *Capital and Class* **19**, 74–99.

Murray, R. 1977. *Multinational Companies and Nation States*. Nottingham: Spokesman Books.

Murray, R. 1984. "New Directions in Municipal Socialism", in *Fabian Essays in Socialist Thought*, B. Pimlott (ed.). London: Heinemann.

Murray, R. 1983. "Benetton Britain: The New Economic Order", in *The Politics of Thatcherism*, S. Hall & M. Jacques (eds). London: Lawrence & Wishart.

Murray, R. 1987. *Breaking with Bureaucracy: Ownership, Control and Nationalisation*. London: Centre for Local Economic Strategies.

Murray, R. 1987. "Ownership, Control and the Market", *New Left Review* **164**, 87–112.

Murray, R. 1990. "Fordism and Post-Fordism", in *New Times: The Changing Face of Politics in the 1990s*, S. Hall & M. Jacques (eds). London, Lawrence & Wishart.

Mygind, N. 1986. "From the Illyrian Firm to the Reality of Self-Management", in *Labor-Owned Firms and Workers' Co-operatives*, S. Jansson & A. Hellmark (eds). Aldershot: Gower.

Negrelli, S. & E. Santi 1990. "Industrial Relations in Italy", in *European Industrial Relations: The Challenge of Flexibility*, C. Crouch & G. Baglioni (eds). London: Sage.

Newman, I. 1986. "Greater London Enterprise Board: Vision and Reality", *Local Economy* **2**, 57–68.

Nicholl, W. 1994. "Maastricht Revisited: A Critical Analysis of the Treaty on European Community", in *The State of the European Union*, vol. 2, A. Cafruny & G. Rosenthal (eds), pp. 19–34. Boulder: Lynne Rienner Publishers.

Nolan, P. & L. O'Donnell 1987. "Taming the Market Economy: A Critical Assessment of the GLC's Experiment in Restructuring Labour", *Cambridge Journal of Economics* **11**, 251–63.

Nove, A. 1983. *The Economics of Feasible Socialism*. London: Allen & Unwin.

Nove, A. 1990. "The Role of Central Planning under Capitalism and Market Socialism", in *Alternatives to Capitalism*, J. Elster & K. Moene (eds). Cambridge: Cambridge University Press.

Oakeshott, R. 1978. *The Case for Workers' Co-operatives*. London: Routledge.

Observer 1996. "Trust Me Says Blair", *Observer*, 14 January.

O'Connor, R. & P. Kelly 1980. *A Study of Industrial Workers' Co-operatives*. Dublin: ESRI.

Ohmae, K. 1990. *The Borderless World: Power and Strategy in the Inter-Linked Economy*. London: HarperCollins.

Ohmae, K. 1995. *The End of the Nation State: The Rise of Regional Economies*. London: HarperCollins.

O'Mahoney, D. 1979. "Labour Management and the Market Economy", *Irish Journal of Business and Administrative Research* **1**, 16–41.

Palmer, J. 1985. "A Common Programme for Europe's Left?", in *Joint Action for Jobs: A New Internationalism*, K. Coates (ed.). Nottingham: Spokesman Books.

Palmer, J. 1986. "Municipal Enterprise and Popular Planning", *New Left Review* **159**, 117–24.

Palmer, J. & H. Wainwright 1983. "Plans, Co-operatives and the Struggle for Socialism", *Socialist Review*, October, 15–17.

Panitch, L. 1981. "Trade Unions and the Capitalist State", *New Left Review* **125**, 21–43.

Panitch, L. 1994. "The Impasse of Social Democratic Politics", *Socialist Register, 1994*. London: Merlin.

Panitch, L. & C. Leys 1997. *The End of Parliamentary Socialism: From New Left to New Labour*. London: Verso.

Pauly, W. & S. Reich 1997. "National Structures and Multinational Corporate Behaviour: Enduring Differences in the Age of Globalization", *International Organization* **51**, 1–30.

Pecchioli, R. 1983. *The Internationalization of Banking*. Paris: OECD.

Penn, R. 1992. "Flexibility in Britain During the 1980s: Recent Empirical Evidence", in *Fordism and Flexibility*, R. Burrows *et al.* (eds). London: Macmillan.

Perraton, J., D. Goldblatt, D. Held, A. McGrew 1997. "The Globalization of Economic Activity", *New Political Economy* **2**, 257–77.

Pfeffer, J. 1994. *Competitive Advantage Through People*. Boston, Mass.: Harvard Business School Press.

Pilling, G. 1986. *The Crisis of Keynesian Economics: A Marxist View*. Beckenham: Croom Helm.

Pimlott, B. 1987. "Introduction", in *Labour's First Hundred Days*, Fabian Tract 519, B. Pimlott (ed.). London: Fabian Society.

Piore, M. 1986. "The Decline of Mass Production and the Challenge to Union Survival", *Industrial Relations Journal* **19**, 207–13.

Pitt-Watson, D. 1991. *Economic Short-Termism: A Cause of the British Disease*, Fabian Pamphlet 547. London: Fabian Society.

Piven, F. 1993. "Comment on Economic Imperatives and Social Reform", in *Changing Classes*, G. Esping-Andersen (ed.). London: Sage.

Plender, J. 1997. *A Stake in the Future: The Stakeholding Solution*. London: Brealey.

Pollert, A. 1988. "Dismantling Flexibility", *Capital and Class* **34**, 42–75.

Pollin, R. 1998. "Can Domestic Expansionary Policy Succeed in a Globally Integrated Environment? An Examination of Alternatives", in *Globalization and Progressive Economic Policy*, D. Baker, G. Epstein & R. Pollin (eds). Cambridge: Cambridge University Press.

Pond, C. 1983. "Rediscovering Poverty", *Marxism Today*, May.

Pontusson, J. 1992. *The Limits of Social Democracy: Investment Politics in Sweden*. Ithaca: Cornell University Press.

Poole, M. 1986. *Towards a New Industrial Democracy: Workers' Participation in Industry*. London: Routledge.

Potter, B. 1891. *The Co-operative Movement in Great Britain*. London: Allen & Unwin.

Prabhakar, R. 1999. "Social Capital, Stakeholding Capitalism and the Third Way", *Renewal* **7**, 84–8.

Prais, S. 1976. *The Evolution of Giant Firms in Britain*. Cambridge: Cambridge University Press.

Prakash, A. and J. Hart 1999. "Globalization and Governance: An Introduction", in *Globalization and Governance*, A. Prakash & J. Hart (eds). London: Routledge.

Prezworski, A. and M. Wallerstein 1988. "Structural Dependence of the State on Capital", *American Political Science Review* **82**, 11–30.

Prior, M. & D. Purdy 1979. *Out of the Ghetto*. Nottingham: Spokesman Books.

Purdy, M. 1981. "The Social Contract and Social Policy", in *The Popular and the Political*, M. Prior (ed.). London, Routledge.

Putnam, R. 1995. "Bowling Alone: America's Declining Social Capital", *Journal of Democracy* **6**, 65–78.

Putterman, L. 1982. "Some Behavioural Perspectives on the Dominance of Hierarchical over Democratic Forms of Enterprise", *Journal of Economic Behaviour and Organization* **3**, 139–60.

Putterman, L. 1984. "On Some Recent Explanations of Why Capital Hires Labour", *Economic Inquiry* **22**, 171–87.

Putterman, L. 1986. "After the Employment Relation: Problems on the Road to Enterprise Democracy", in *Markets and Democracy: Participation, Accountability and Efficiency*, S. Bowles, H. Gintis & B. Gustaffson (eds). Cambridge: Cambridge University Press.

Rainnie, A. 1985. "Small Firms, Big Problems: The Political Economy of Small Business", *Capital and Class* **25**, 140–68.

Reich, R. 1993. *The Work of Nations*. New York: Simon & Schuster.

Robins, K. 1989. "Global Times", *Marxism Today*, December.

Rocard, M. 1994. "Social Solidarity in a Mixed Economy", in *Reinventing the Left*, D. Miliband (ed.). Cambridge: Polity.

Rodgers, J. & W. Streeck 1994. "Productive Solidarities: Economic Strategy and Left Politics", in *Reinventing the Left*, D. Miliband (ed.). Cambridge: Polity.

302

Roemer, J. 1992. "The Possibility of Market Socialism", in *The Idea of Democracy*, D. Copp, J. Hampton & J. Roemer (eds). Cambridge: Cambridge University Press.

Roemer, J. 1994. *A Future for Socialism*. London: Verso.

Rogaly, J. 1996. "Right Still Calls the Tune", *Financial Times*, 27 January.

Ross, G. 1987. "From One Left to Another", in *The Mitterrand Experiment: Continuity and Change in Modern France*, G. Ross, S. Hoffman & M. Malzacher (eds). Oxford: Polity.

Ross, G. 1993. "The European Community and Social Policy: Regional Blocs and a Humane Social Order", *Studies in Political Economy* **40**, 41–72.

Rowthorn, B. 1980. "The Alternative Economic Strategy", *International Socialism* **8**, 385–94.

Rowthorn, B. 1981. "The Politics of the Alternative Economic Strategy", *Marxism Today*, January.

Rowthorn, B. 1981. "An Interview with Wynne Godley", *Marxism Today*, July.

Rowthorn, B. 1982. "Britain and Western Europe", *Marxism Today*, May.

Roy, D. 1980. "The Problem of Rising Prices", in *The Economics of Prosperity: Social Priorities in the Eighties*, D. Blake & P. Ormerod (eds). London: Grant & Macintyre.

Rustin, M. 1986. "Lessons of the London Industrial Strategy", *New Left Review* **155**, 74–84.

Rustin, M. 1990. "The Trouble with 'New Times'", in *New Times: The Changing Face of Politics in the 1990s*, S. Hall & M. Jacques (eds). London, Lawrence & Wishart.

Sabel, C. 1982. *Work and Politics*. Cambridge: Cambridge University Press.

Sabel, C. 1989. "Flexible Specialisation and the Re-emergence of Regional Economies", in *Reversing Industrial Decline? Industrial Structure in Britain and Her Competitors*, P. Hirst & J. Zeitlin (eds). Oxford: Berg.

Sabel, C. & M. Piore 1984. *The Second Industrial Divide*. New York: Basic Books.

Saville, J. 1990. "*Marxism Today*: An Anatomy", *Socialist Register, 1990*. London: Merlin.

Sayer, A. 1989. "Post-Fordism in Question", *International Journal of Urban and Regional Research* **13**, 666–95.

Scharpf, F. 1991. *Crisis and Choice in European Social Democracy*. London: Sage.

Sedgemore, B. 1977. *The How and Why of Socialism*. Nottingham: Spokesman Books.

Sellgren, J. 1987. "Local Economic Development and Local Issues in the Mid-1980s", *Local Government Studies* **13**, 51–68.

Seyd, P. 1987. *The Rise and Fall of the Labour Left*. London: Macmillan.

Shaiken, H. 1984. *Work Transformed: Automation and Labor in the Computer Age*. New York: Holt, Rinehart and Winston.

Shaiken, H., S. Herzenberg, S. Kuhn 1986. "The Work Process under more Flexible Production", *Industrial Relations* **25**, 167–83.

Sharples, A. 1981. "The Politics of the Alternative Economic Strategy", *Marxism Today*, April.

Sheffield City Council 1986. *Steel Crisis*, Department of Employment and Economic Development. Sheffield: Sheffield City Council.

Sherman, B. 1984. "Trade Unions", in *Fabian Essays in Socialist Thought*, B. Pimlott (ed.). London: Heinemann.

Silvia, S. 1991. "The Social Charter of the European Community: A Defeat for European Labour", *Industrial and Labour Relations Review* **44**, 626–43.

Sirc, L. 1977. "Workers' Management under Public and Private Ownership", in *Can Workers Manage?*, B. Chiplin *et al.* (ed.). London: IEA.

Skapinker, M. 2000. "Governance Responds to Globalisation", *Financial Times*, 2 June.

Smith, D. 1987. *The Rise and Fall of Monetarism: The Theory and Politics of an Economic Experiment*. Harmondsworth: Penguin.

Smith, M. 1994. "Understanding the 'Politics of Catch-up': The Modernization of the Labour Party", *Political Studies* **42**, 708–15.

Smithers, R. 1996. "Blair Woos US", *Guardian*, 12 April.

Speke Joint Shop Stewards' Committee 1979. *Dunlop, Jobs for Merseyside: A Trade Union Report*, S.1. The Committee.

Stiglitz, J. 1994. *Whither Socialism? Perspectives from the Economics of Information*, Wicksell Lectures. Cambridge, Mass.: MIT Press.

Stopford, J. & S. Strange 1991. *Rival States, Rival Firms: Competition for World Market Shares*. Cambridge: Cambridge University Press.

Strange, S. 1986. *Casino Capitalism*. Oxford: Blackwell.

Strange, S. 1998. *The Retreat of the State: The Diffusion of Power in the World Economy*. Cambridge: Cambridge University Press.

Streeck, W. 1996. "Public Power, Beyond the Nation State: The Case of the European Community", in *States Against Markets: The Limits of Globalization*, R. Boyer & D. Drache (eds). London: Routledge.

Swartz, D. 1981. "The Eclipse of Politics: The Alternative Economic Strategy as Socialist Strategy", *Capital and Class* **13**, 102–13.

Taylor, R. 1996. "Change of Tack", *Financial Times*, 9 July.

Therborn, G. 1984. "The Prospects of Labour and the Transformation of Advanced Capitalism", *New Left Review* **145**, 5–38.

Thomas, H. 1982. "The Performance of the Mondragon Co-operatives", in *Participatory and Self-Managed Firms*, D. Jones & J. Svejnar (eds). Lexington: Lexington Books.

Thomas, H. & C. Logan 1982. *Mondragon: An Economic Analysis*. London: Allen & Unwin.

Thompson, G. 1987. "The American Industrial Policy Debate: Any Lessons for Britain?", *Economy and Society* **16**, 1–74.

Thompson, G. 1988. "Flexible Specialisation, Industrial Districts, Regional Economies: Strategies for Socialists?", *Economy and Society* **18**, 527–45.

Thompson, N. 1988. *The Market and its Critics: Socialist Political Economy in Nineteenth Century Britain*. London: Routledge.

Thompson, N. 1996. *Political Economy and the Labour Party: The Economics of Democratic Socialism, 1884–1995*. London: UCL Press.

Thompson, N. 1996. "Supply Side Socialism: The Political Economy of New Labour", *New Left Review* **216**, 37–54.

Thompson, N. 1996 "Economic Policy and the Development of Economic Opinion in the 1970s", in *The Troubled Economy: Britain in the 1970s*, R. Coopey & N. W. C. Woodward (eds), 55–80. London: UCL Press.

Thompson, N. 1998. *The Real Rights of Man: Political Economies for the Working Class, 1775–1850*. London: Pluto.

Thompson, N. 2001. "Social Opulence and Private Asceticism: Ideas of Consumption in Early Socialist Thought", in *The Politics of Consumption: Material Culture and Citizenship in Europe and America*, M. Daunton & M. Hilton (eds). Oxford: Berg.

Thornley, J. 1981. *Workers' Co-operatives: Jobs and Dreams*. London: Heinemann.

Thornley, J. 1983. "Workers' Co-operatives and Trade Unions: The Italian Experience", *Economic and Industrial Democracy* **4**, 321–44.

Thurow, L. 1985. *The Zero Sum Solution*. New York: Simon & Schuster.

Tolentino, P. 1999. "Transnational Rules for Transnational Corporations", in *Global Instability: The Political Economy of World Economic Governance*, J. Michie & J. Grieve Smith (eds). London: Routledge.

Tomaney, J. 1990. "The Reality of Workplace Flexibility", *Capital and Class* **40**, 29–60.

Tomlinson, J. 1981. "British Politics and Co-operatives", *Capital and Class* **12**, 58–65.

Totterdill, P. 1989. "Local Economic Strategies as Industrial Policy: A Critical Review of British Economic Developments in the 1980s", *Economy and Society* **18**, 478–526.

Townsend, P. 1981. "A Taste of Dr Owen's Medicine", *New Statesman*, 30 January.

Tsoukalis, L. 1991. *The New European Economy: The Politics and Economics of Integration*. Oxford: Oxford University Press.

TUC 1976. *Economic Review*. London: TUC.

TUC 1981. *Plan for Growth*. London: TUC.

TUC 1988. *Maximising the Benefits, Minimising the Costs: TUC Report on Europe 1992*. London: TUC.

Vandenbroucke, F. 1998. "Globalization, Inequality and Social Democracy", in *European Social Democracy: Transformation in Progress*, R. Cuperus & J. Kandel (eds). Amsterdam: Wiardi-Beckman Stichting.

Vanek, J. 1970. *The General Theory of Labor-Managed Market Economics*. Ithaca: Cornell University Press.

Vanek, J. 1975. "Decentralization under Workers' Management: A Theoretical Appraisal", in *Self-Management: The Economic Liberation of Man*, J. Vanek (ed.). Harmondsworth: Penguin.

Vanek. J. 1975. "The Basic Theory of Financing", in *Self-Management: The Economic Liberation of Man*, J. Vanek (ed.). Harmondsworth: Penguin.

Vanek. J. 1973. "Some Fundamental Considerations on Financing and the Form of Ownership under Labour Management", in *Economic Structure and Development*, H. Bos (ed.). Amsterdam: North-Holland.

Wachtel, H. 1986. *The Money Mandarins: The Making of a New Supranational Economic Order*. New York: Pantheon.

Wade, R. 1996. "Globalisation and its Limits: Reports of the Death of the National Economy are Greatly Exaggerated", in *National Diversity and Global Capitalism*, S. Berger & R. Dore (eds). Ithaca: Cornell University Press.

Wainwright, H. 1986. "Bye Bye GLC", *New Statesman*, 21 March.

Wainwright, H. & D. Elliott 1982. *The Lucas Plan: A New Trade Unionism in the Making*. London: Allison and Busby.

Ward, B. 1958. "The Firm in Illyria: Market Syndicalism", *American Economic Review* **48**, 566–89.

Ward, M. 1983. "Labour's Capital Gains; The GLC Experience", *Marxism Today*, December.

Webb, M. 1991. "International Economic Structures, Government Interests and International Co-ordination of Macroeconomic Adjustment Policies", *International Organization* **45**, 309–42.

Webb, S. & B. Webb 1914. "Co-operative Production and Profitsharing", *New Statesman*, special supplement, February, 1–31.

Webb, S. & B. Webb 1920. *A Constitution for the Socialist Commonwealth of Great Britain*. London: Fabian Society.

Webster, D. 1981. *Labour and the New Left*, Fabian Tract 477. London: Allen & Unwin.

Weiss, L. 1984. "The Italian State and Small Businesses", *Archive of European Sociology* **25**, 214–41.

Weiss, L. 1998. *The Myth of the Powerless State: Governing the Economy in a Global Era*. Cambridge: Polity.

Westergaard, J. 1984. "The Once and Future Class", in *The Future of the Left*, J. Curran (ed.). Cambridge: Polity.

White, S. 1998. "Interpreting the 'Third Way'", *Renewal* **6**, 17–33.

Whyte, W. & K. Whyte 1988. *Making Mondragon: The Growth and Dynamics of the Worker Co-operative Complex*. Ithaca: Cornell University Press.

Wickham-Jones, M. 1995. "Anticipating Social Democracy, Pre-empting Anticipations: Economic Policy-Making in the British Labour Party, 1987–1992", *Politics and Society* **23**, 465–94.

Wickham-Jones, M. 1996. *Economic Strategy and the Labour Party: Politics and Policy-Making, 1970–83*. London: Macmillan.

Wiles, P. 1977. *Economic Institutions Compared*. Oxford: Blackwell.

Willetts, D. 1996. *Blair's Gurus: An Examination of Labour Rhetoric*. London: Centre for Policy Studies.

Williams, K., T. Cutler, J. Williams, C. Haslam 1987. "The End of Mass Production?", *Economy and Society* **16**, 405–39.

Wilson, H. 1979. *Final Term: The Labour Government 1974–76*. London: Weidenfeld & Nicolson and Michael Joseph.

Winter, D. 1989. "Market Socialism and the Reform of Capitalism", in *Market Socialism*, J. Le Grand & S. Estrin (eds). Oxford: Clarendon.

Wintour, P. 1981. "Driving Under the Influence", *New Statesman*, 31 July.

Wintour, P. 1996. "Blair Insists", *Guardian*, 19 January.

Wise, M. & R. Gibb 1995. "A Social Charter for a European Social Market", in *Policy Issues in the European Union: A Reader in the Political Economy of European Integration*, M. Ugur (ed.). Dartford: Greenwich University Press.

Womack, J. & D. Jones 1996. *Lean Thinking: Banish Waste and Create Wealth in Your Corporation*. New York: Simon & Schuster.

Wood, E. 1986. *The Retreat from Class*. London: Verso.

Wood, S. 1989. "Introduction", in *The Transformation of Work*, S. Wood (ed.). London: Unwin Hyman.

Wood, S. 1988. "Between Fordism and Flexibility? The US Car Industry", in *New Technology and Industrial Relations*, R. Hyman & W. Streeck (eds). Oxford: Blackwell.

Zeitlin, J. 1989. "Local Economic Strategies: An Introduction", *Economy and Society* **18**, 367–73.

Zevi, A. 1982. "The Performance of Italian Producer Co-operatives", in *Participatory and Self-Managed Firms*, D. Jones & J. Svejnar (eds). Lexington: Lexington Books.

Zevin, R. 1992. "Are World Financial Markets More Open? If So, Why and with What Effects?", in *Financial Openness and National Autonomy: Opportunities and Constraints*, T. Banuri & J. Schor (eds). Oxford: Clarendon.

Zuboff, S. 1988. *In the Age of the Smart Machine: The Future of Work and Power*. New York: Basic Books.

Zysman, J. 1996. "The Myth of a 'Global' Economy: Enduring National Foundations and Emerging Regional Realities", *New Political Economy* **1**, 157–84.

Index